LUCID KNOWLEDGE
ON THE CURRENCY OF THE PHOTOGRAPHIC IMAGE

8th Triennial of Photography Hamburg 2022

TABLE OF CONTENTS

4 **Foreword**
Dirk Luckow

6 **Introduction**
Koyo Kouoh

10 Fields of Perception

10 **Fields of Perception**
Koyo Kouoh

12 **Keynote: "He Is My Ancestor," Lanier Argues, "Not a Museum Asset"**
Ariella Aïsha Azoulay

25 **Abolition**
Ariella Aïsha Azoulay in Conversation with Natalia Brizuela

32 **Lapsus Imaginis: The Image in Ruins**
Eduardo Cadava

53 **Overseas**
Akinbode Akinbiyi in Conversation with Bonaventure Soh Bejeng Ndikung, with a Response from Koyo Kouoh

64 Narrative Currents

64 **Narrative Currents**
Rasha Salti

66 **Wake**
Robin Coste Lewis

84 **The Body and the Tropics**
Antawan I. Byrd on Mimi Cherono Ng'ok and Miguel A. López on Victoria Cabezas, with a Response from Nicholas Tammens

101 **Tracing Constellations**
Maaza Mengiste in Conversation with Biljana Ciric, with a Response from Tala Hadid

118 **Aida, Save Me!**
Joana Hadjithomas and Khalil Jorelge

138 Image as Currency

138 **Image as Currency**
Oluremi C. Onabanjo

140 **Picturing Catastrophe: The Visual Politics of Racial Reckoning**
Rizvana Bradley

151 **Image as Currency**
Tina M. Campt in Conversation with Ariel Goldberg

162 **Instruments of Circulation and Resistance**
Frieda Ekotto in Conversation with Françoise Vergès, with a Response from Antawan I. Byrd

176 **The Photograph between Trace and Evidence**
Elias Sanbar in Conversation with Léopold Lambert

200 The Errant Photo Album

200 **The Errant Photo Album**
Gabriella Beckhurst Feijoo

202 **Sabri, 38th Street**
Tala Hadid

206 **The Chowkidar: Epistemic Markers and Transnational Flows**
Uzma Rizvi

210 **Scribal Subjectivities: Activating the Silent and the Speaking Parts of a Woman's Life**
Nancy Adajania

216 **Diana Solís: Intimacies in Resistance**
Ariel Goldberg

220 **Intangible**
Kapwani Kiwanga

224 **All the Family Photo Albums Show Me**
Andreas Schlaegel

234 **The Witness without a Camera**
Samaneh Moafi

238 **Is Apollo Gay? Herbert List's Reinterpretation of Male Bodies**
Esther Ruelfs

244 **Reiterating an Itinerary to Translucency**
Doreen Mende

251 **Looking for Lost Captions, or How I Found Ancestral Solidarity in Cyberspace**
Tuan Andrew Nguyen

258 **As You Go…**
Biljana Ciric

262 **The Camera Is Broken**
Natalia Brizuela

268 **Contributors**

275 **Bibliography**

279 **Colophon**

FOREWORD

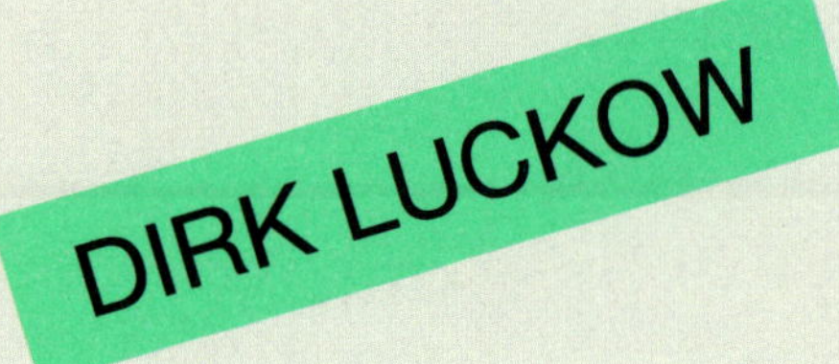

For more than two decades, every three years the Triennial of Photography Hamburg has brought together several of the city's major museums and cultural institutions to present an expansive range of concepts that engage with photography, its techniques, and its styles. This is realized across a multitude of programs that take place throughout the city alongside exhibitions and commissions that include symposia, lectures, portfolio reviews, and screenings.

For its 8th edition, the Triennial of Photography Hamburg explores the theme of *Currency* from various angles and in different interpretations via twelve exhibitions that launch starting May 19, 2022. Ranging from revisiting photo albums of the colonial era, dreams incarnated as images, experimental photography, and social documentary photography, the exhibitions engage the diverse ways in which photographs are produced, circulated, and interpreted.

We are honored to have Koyo Kouoh, the executive director and chief curator of the Zeitz Museum of Contemporary Art Africa (MOCAA) in Cape Town, South Africa, as Artistic Director of this edition of the Triennial. As an incisive thinker and a genuinely collaborative curator, Kouoh has appointed a courageous international team of curators to work with her—Rasha Salti, Gabriella Beckhurst Feijoo, and Oluremi C. Onabanjo. Their efforts are expertly coordinated by Cale Garrido.

Kouoh and her international team have designed the exhibition *Parcours* through Hamburg together with the curators of the ten participating museums and exhibition venues in Hamburg. Through its theme of *Currency*, the 8th Triennial considers the association of this economic term in relation to "cultural capital," and its manifestations in discourses on visual culture. Exploring processes of canon-making, classification, and circulation, the Triennial includes exhibitions at the Bucerius Kunst Forum; the Deichtorhallen Hamburg's House of Photography, Hall for Contemporary Art, and Falckenberg Collection; the Hamburger Kunsthalle; Jenisch Haus; the Kunsthaus Hamburg; the Kunstverein in Hamburg; the Museum am Rothenbaum—Kulturen und Künste der Welt; the Museum der Arbeit; the Museum für Hamburgische Geschichte; and the Museum für Kunst und Gewerbe Hamburg. These exhibitions will be accompanied by numerous events and the Triennale Expanded program, which is dedicated to Hamburg's independent art and photography scene and which takes place from June 2 through 6, 2022.

As a prelude to the 8th Triennial, an international, interdisciplinary group of more than thirty artists, curators, poets, scholars, and theorists was invited to Hamburg for Lucid Knowledge, a three-day symposium. Their presentations and contributions to the discussion, distilled here by Nicholas Davies and Andreas Schlaegel, respectively in English- and German-language volumes, form the basis of this critical reader. The results of the symposium, together with *Allegories of the Visible*, an online space for theoretical exchange and artistic reflection that launched in August 2021, and a guide to the Triennial events, provide the key publications of this year's Triennial.

Lucid Knowledge: On the Currency of the Photographic Image represents an intersection of approaches derived from the fields of cultural studies, fine arts, and visual studies to form a multidisciplinary discourse on the current relevance, value, and truth content of photography.

The preparation and execution of the Triennial of Photography has been conducted within the context of the COVID-19 pandemic, which has transformed all forms of relation across the globe and posed challenges to collective gatherings—which are so important to all our fields, and especially to the life of an event such as this. This publication, then, is also a testament to finding ways to come together and exchange ideas about the stakes of photography during this singular moment in time.

With that, we close with an expression of our deep gratitude to the German Federal Cultural Foundation and the Federal Government Commissioner for Culture and the Media for their generous support of the symposium and this publication. Furthermore, our warmest thanks go to the Hamburg Ministry of Culture and the Media for the major funding of the Triennial, namely Dr. Carsten Brosda, Minister of Culture and Media, as well as Nina Dreier, Head of the Department of Film and Photography. Finally, we are extremely grateful to BMW Niederlassung Hamburg, Otto Group, WhiteWall and the ZEIT-Stiftung Ebelin und Gerd Bucerius, Hamburg for their generous support of this edition of the Triennial. I extend personal thanks to the curatorial team of the Triennial, as well as to Bert Antonius Kaufmann, Commercial Director of the Deichtorhallen Hamburg and the Triennial; to Daniela Guhl, Project Manager of the Triennial, and Alicja Mazurkiewicz and Mareile Hanke who so ably assisted her; and to the teams at Studio Safar and PR-Netzwerk. Without their tireless work and dedication, this convening would not be possible.

Founded in 1999, the Triennial of Photography is an initiative of F. C. Gundlach, who passed away in the summer of 2021, having just turned 95. Gundlach, a seminal photographer, gallerist, collector, curator, philanthropist, and photographic visionary, was one of the first figures in Hamburg to campaign for the recognition of photography as an art form—before the medium had a permanent place in museums and a dominant position in the art market. With every edition of the Triennial, we are proud and honored to bring extensive programming inspired by Gundlach's initiative to a wide public audience, thereby keeping his life's work alive.

INTRODUCTION

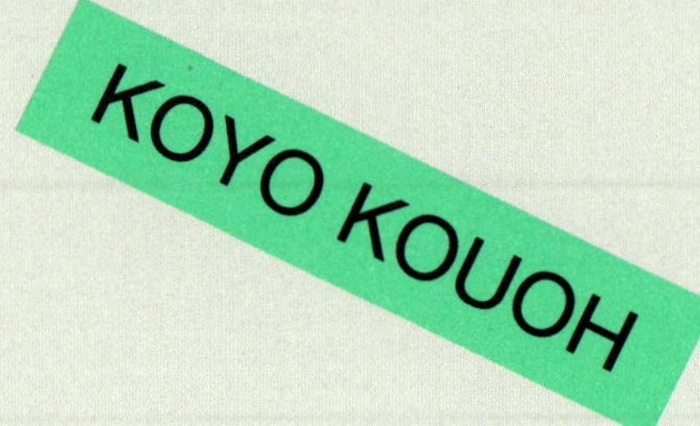

Lucid Knowledge: On the Currency of the Photographic Image is the editorial touchstone of the exhibitions, projects, and related activities staged on the occasion of the 8th Triennial of Photography Hamburg.

Collected in this critical reader are the transcripts of a symposium that took place in Hamburg in late 2021—a gathering that lit fire in our bellies and the flame to carry forward. To begin, it is necessary to share a note on origins. *Lucid Knowledge* explores the various ways in which forms of knowledge are derived from photographic images. Lucidity conveys the intelligibility of thought—a making clear, or an imperative around truth-telling. It anticipates that knowledge can be derived from this truth. To ask what photographs make lucid, in the most expansive sense of something being "written in light," is to investigate the claims that photographic images make on behalf of their makers and the depicted. It requires investigating what is conveyed—not just in demonstrable or figurative terms—but of the conditions of photographic production, how the photograph came to be, and how it continues to affect and have a value for those that receive it.

Currency is the guiding prompt for this edition of the triennial and is a provocation that hums in all the contributions contained in this volume. Whether naming photography as a tool of "cultural capital" or its use in incarnating a rationale or ideology, currency evokes photography's long relationship to capitalist and imperial structures of imaging and valuing. This instrumentation is as old as the history of the medium: "When we speak of 'shooting' with a camera, we are acknowledging the kinship of photography and violence," observes the photographer and author Teju Cole.[1] For this reason, the photographic image holds a great deal of tension and possibility as an object, staked in small and seismic freedoms, social justice and reparation, intergenerational connection and transnational solidarity: its poetics allow us to imagine and to dream. Extended through *Lucid Knowledge*, currency glimpses possible counternarratives by alternative ways of reading, sensing, listening to and engaging with photographic images. With methods deeply interdisciplinary—spanning artistic, curatorial, and resistance practices, literary critical fabulation, performance, and poetry—we are deeply moved and encouraged by the attention of our authors to historical and contemporary formations.

Four thematic chapters connect the contributions of our authors: **Fields of Perception**, **Narrative Currents**, **Image as Currency**, and **The Errant Photo Album**. Through their respective practices, each contributor brings conceptual, theoretical, and reflective rigor to the volume. Their perspectives are the multiple "fields" referred to in "Fields of Perception." Following this polyvocal echo, we traverse the visual politics of depiction and portrayal; the intersecting histories of photography, literary, and critical practices; and appraise the ethics of spectatorship, attribution, and the collection of photographic artifacts. This is all done with the aim of making space for different encounters with photography.

The question of *how* we look, and who has ownership over this act is at the heart of **Fields of Perception**. Ariella Aïsha Azoulay positions Tamara Lanier's pending case for her ancestor Renty's portrait as not only an example of familial lineage work, but also as a kind of institutional-critical "gift" to the academic institution of Harvard University. Azoulay offers a critical vocabulary through which to think about the fraught histories and epistemological stakes of the photographic encounter. The incendiary rally for decolonial justice we receive here shares resonance with the contributions that follow. "There can be no image that is not about destruction and survival," opens Eduardo Cadava's essay on the "image in ruins," a sentiment that underscores the kinesis between loss and life and the "impossibility of the image" to tell of or be faithful to events. A conversation between long-term interlocutors Akinbode Akinbiyi and Bonaventure Soh Bejeng Ndikung turns us to acts of making and its shaping by ethos, influence, and acknowledgement. It was an honour for me to chair this conversation, which fused the sociopolitical imperative of photography with the sensitivities of a photographic practice developed through connection and trust.

Narrative Currents introduces the acuity of vision and commitment to waiting as a wake-work sustained by Robin Coste Lewis over the last twenty-five years. Lewis's realization in sitting with a photographic archive of her grandmother's is that the affective powers of this inheritance test the boundaries of language and aesthetic interpretation, its lyricism poignant and piercing. In their stimulating conversation, Biljana Ciric, Tala Hadid, and Maaza Mengiste linger on the capacity of images in colonial albums to haunt us, and on the implicit challenge posed by the possibility of facing historical trauma frontally. Turning to the politics of the body in the work of Mimi Cherono Ng'ok and Victoria Cabezas, curators Antawan I. Byrd and Miguel A. López bring to the fore the political and personal significance of materiality and embodied form in artistic praxes that engage the photographic medium. Filmmakers and visual artists Joana Hadjithomas and Khalil Joreige close the chapter with their vision of *Aida, Save Me!*— a work formed through the interstitial space of recognition and fictional staging, and explorative of how "war shapes images." Their electric piece reveals the capacity of the document to license and circulate meaning, with humorous, absurd, and heartbreaking implications.

Image as Currency opens with Rizvana Bradley's essay "Picturing Catastrophe: The Visual Politics of Racial Reckoning." Indicting white supremacy for the violent and painful image economy of blackness it produces, Bradley's work draws on critical traditions of black thought and poesis to suggest a radical reinvention of *what it is to see*. This endeavor concerns interrogating this image consumption but goes beyond by laying the groundwork for dismantling this anticipated violence altogether. Seeds of this nature are scattered throughout the contributions that follow in conversations between Tina M. Campt and Ariel Goldberg, Elias Sanbar and Léopold Lambert, Françoise Vergès, Frieda Ekotto, and Antawan I. Byrd. The currency of the image is directed through practices of collective enunciation that refuse co-option; an astute sensing of the differences of photographing from within and at range; and the future of resistance practices when the future is under threat. As Vergès movingly notes in her piece, we have to be "careful in how we look at images." Such care abounds in the authors' insistence on rest and refusal as resistance.

The Errant Photo Album brings this volume to a close. The format invited contributors to respond to an image and their responses have been collected in a photo album with an errant spirit. This invitation takes us far and wide, from the political portraits and scribal subjectivities examined by Nancy Adajania; Tala Hadid's staggering meditation on New York City's 38th Street through a visual letter; and Tuan Andrew Nguyen's journey into lost captions and ancestral solidarity in cyberspace. Ariel Goldberg, Kapwani Kiwanga, and Esther Ruelfs each discern the affective spell of images and the intimate register of the photograph as a bodily index for subjective encounters. Uzma Rizvi, Andreas Schlaegel, and Natalia Brizuela use the prompt to think through that which is, or has been, unseen, or what Shawn Michelle Smith has referred to lying "at the edge of sight."[2] For Rizvi, through the figure of the chowkidar; for Schlaegel, by confronting the collapse between familial memories and the violence of political history; and, for Brizuela, by breaking the camera apparatus itself in favor of what line and sound offer through Indigenous Yanomami cosmologies.

My sincere thanks go to managing editors Nicholas Davies and Andreas Schlaegel, who respectively shepherded the English and German editions of *Lucid Knowledge* to publication, and to my colleagues Rasha Salti, Oluremi C. Onabanjo, Gabriella Beckhurst Feijoo, and Cale Garrido, who have been integral to composing this volume. Our weekly conversations over many months have built a cherished communal space from which the symposium and this publication emerged. The Lucid Knowledge symposium was generously supported by the German Federal Cultural Foundation and Federal Government Commissioner for Culture and the Media, as is this publication, and I thank Carsten Brosda and Nina Dreier, Daniela Guhl, Dirk Luckow, Bert Antonius Kaufmann, Mareile Hanke, Alicja Mazurkiewicz, Jürgen Carstensen, Martin Kahl, and the Aussenborder team for all their work in producing the event. Lastly, I linger on the gratitude I feel toward our authors. The questions you have raised, the "fields" you have opened, and the possibilities you have provided will allow us to grow in our respective practices.

1. Teju Cole, "When the Camera Was a Weapon of Imperialism. (And When It Still Is.)," *New York Times Magazine*, February 6, 2019, https://www.nytimes.com/2019/02/06/magazine/when-the-camera-was-a-weapon-of-imperialism-and-when-it-still-is.html.
2. Shawn Michelle Smith, *At the Edge of Sight: Photography and the Unseen* (Durham: Duke University Press, 2013).

FIELDS OF PERCEPTION

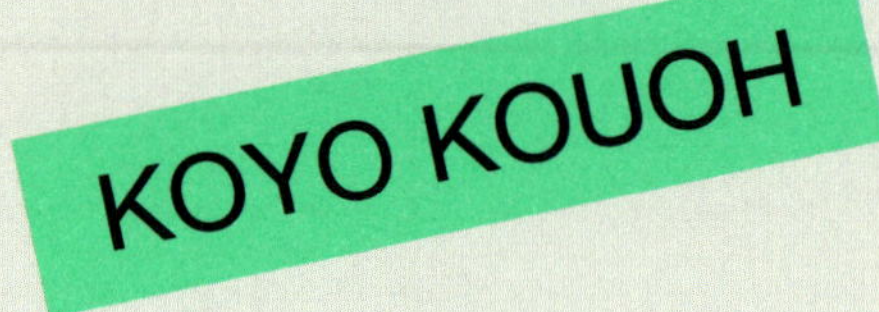

Since the early twentieth century, thinkers have attributed prosthetic qualities to the medium of photography for the ways it shapes and structures perception and experience. Walter Benjamin referred to this as an "optical unconscious," describing the psychic processes in which cognition is collectively shaped by instruments of communications media—including film, television, and photography. Social relations are molded and mediated through this prosthetic vision in both representational and emotional ways, constituting our sense of distance and proximity to an event or phenomena.

The opening chapter of this volume foregrounds a series of explorations into the photographic impetus, the critical ethics of photographic restitution, and repair work that anticipates the transformation of imperial histories of photography. Traversing image-making, collecting, and decolonial praxis, "Fields of Perception" engages alternative registers for understanding the dialectic between sight and image, and the logic of material possession. While the authors here discuss historical artifacts, they crucially remind readers that photography as a "social document" elicits an ongoing response. The persistent logic of photographs as property informs the critical injunction of Ariella Aïsha Azoulay's defining essay. For Azoulay, acknowledging photographs as social documents is central to holding institutions like Harvard University to account, as they have both the critical capacity and resources to end the perpetuation of violence caused by withholding photographs of subjugated and enslaved family members to their living ancestors.

In the proceeding dialogue between Azoulay and Natalia Brizuela, the care of photographic material culture is positioned as an act of caretaking that can neither be entrusted to institutional relations as they currently operate nor take place within the institution. For this, the work of restitution can be understood as the work of *abolition*—a term that Azoulay and Brizuela bring to bear on the spaces of the museum and cultural institution. These are vital conversations around the status of historical photographs that reside in the present; images which refer to a time or period. However, as Eduardo Cadava posits in his essay, time is also interrupted by the image's fragmented picturing of history, the image by nature being incomplete and partial.

Thinking through a series of entangled *fields*, instead of a singular unitary *field*, the contributions in this section are attuned to ongoing efforts to account for photography as a site of encounter, appearance, and exchange—one that requires careful consideration and contextualization of the photographic event. This lays the path for a different set of relations. As Akinbode Akinbiyi and Bonaventure Soh Bejeng Ndikung find in their conversation, shifting the question from what photography *is* to what it *does* or has the capacity to do, is to propose a radical shift in photographic imaginaries. "OK, image, where are you?" is how Akinbiyi describes his sense of waiting patiently for the image to emerge. Whether prioritizing slow and returning observations against the media flows of late capitalism or challenging positions of exteriority or scholarly objectivity when encountering the world in image form, the invited propositions are of thinking, feeling, and sensing photography beyond institutionalized logics of interpretation, temporality, and historicization.

"He Is My Ancestor," Lanier Argues, "Not a Museum Asset"

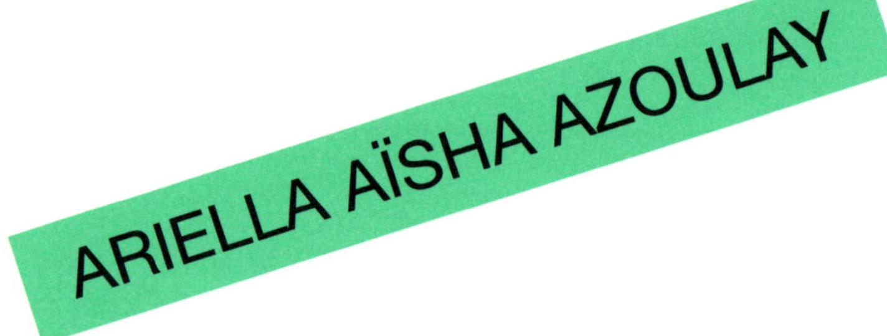

In March 2019, Tamara Lanier filed a lawsuit against Harvard University and the Peabody Museum for "wrongful seizure, possession and expropriation of photographic images" of her enslaved ancestors, Renty Taylor and his daughter, Delia. After Lanier's mother passed away in 2010, she had started researching information on Papa Renty. An acquaintance called her attention to the existence of daguerreotypes of her ancestors, which Elinor Reichlin, on staff at the Peabody, had found in 1976.

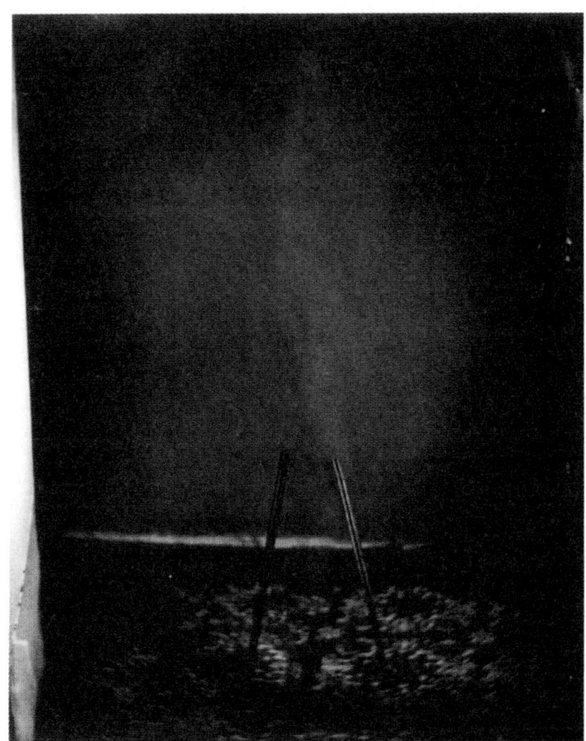

The scene of the crime: the studio of photographer Joseph Zealy. Alfred was here [the image was redacted by Ariella Aïsha Azoulay in collaboration with Yonatan Vinitsky].

Reichlin's preliminary research showed that in 1850, Louis Agassiz had commissioned these daguerreotypes under the mantle of authority provided by his position at Harvard. Since its very beginnings, photography offered itself as an efficient technology for imperial actors, and Agassiz's use of it is not surprising. He saw Africans as inferiors and commissioned a photographer to force them to pose for the camera to prove his polygenic theory: that different human races had evolved separately, and that white people were superior. Unlike other daguerreotypes commissioned by enslavers, who sought to portray slavery as a paternalistic and benevolent form of white rule, these images had a different purpose: to capture in silver plates the inherent "truth" of white superiority. Stripping Renty, Delia, Drana, Alfred, Jack, George Fassena, and

Jem bare in front of the camera satisfied Agassiz and his collaborators' plan: to let what they considered the naked truth of black inferiority *imprint* itself directly from the bodies onto the photographic plate, without the interference of clothing or other props that were frequently used in photographers' studios. "If it is a shock to see full frontal nudity in early American photography," writes Brian Wallis, "it is even more surprising to see it without the trappings of shame or sexual fantasy."[1]

Until Lanier stepped forward and claimed that these were her ancestors, the daguerreotypes had been assumed to be the private property of Harvard University. That Lanier's multiple attempts to communicate with representatives of the university institutions were rebuffed testifies to the gravity and endurance of the institutional afterlife of slavery. Years before Lanier reached out to Harvard, Harvard could have commissioned its scholars to track down the descendants of these relatively well-documented daguerreotypes. Even after she contacted the university and identified herself as the descendant, these same scholars have not been invited to engage with Lanier in order to help or collaborate with her on the research into the daguerreotypes. Instead, Harvard has done its best to foreclose the possibility that the status of the daguerreotypes, which the university holds as its private property, will come into question. Harvard's dismissal of Lanier brings to mind Walter Benjamin's observation that when history is written by the victorious at the expense of the victims and survivors, the spoils become "cultural treasures."[2] Only the victorious are permitted to claim as legally theirs that which was seized from others. These latter were deprived of their freedom and rights and continue to live under the institutional conditions that ensure their grievances go unheard. Should academic institutions base their ownership claims on victors' justice?

In March 2021, when Lanier's lawsuit was dismissed by a Massachusetts court—[an appeal is pending at the time of this printing]—the court affirmed not only Harvard's ownership of the daguerreotypes, but also the terms and the stake of the case. The court's decision hinged on the question of possession: To whom does Renty Taylor's daguerreotype belong? Yet Harvard came to "possess" these photographs through a cultural logic of wealth, property, and ownership that flows directly from slavery and preserves its lingering presence in our own era. Against this logic, I propose that we ask different questions. What if we insist on treating Renty as the person who was used against his will so that others might extract an image of his enslavement, rather than as the object that was seized from him? Then, we must ask: Where and with whom will Renty find peace and recognition of his rights?

The history of object restitution offers some guidance here as a form of historical accountability. It reminds us that the photograph is a social document, rather than an object to be possessed. I argue that, in their social contexts, both the taking of the daguerreotype and its continued ownership and display by Harvard University constitute crimes against humanity that need to be redressed. The daguerreotypes are not property that can be owned, but ancestors who need caretaking. This understanding is the only way forward if we wish to repair the harms of enslavement.

***

Imagine if Renty's relatives, who likely heard no word from him after he was kidnapped from the kingdom of Kongo and enslaved in the United States, could have had the opportunity to see his likeness alongside the millions of Americans celebrating the newly invented medium of the daguerreo-

Ariella Aïsha Azoulay

type. We must question the privileges accorded to both scholars and the general public as viewers of these daguerreotypes. Instead of privileging their gaze, we should prioritize Renty's relatives, in both Africa and the United States. Indeed, daguerreotypes were invented and perceived by millions to keep dear ones close to their hearts and in their homes.

In the 1850s, the American writer, scientist, and former dean of Harvard Medical School Oliver Wendell Holmes described the daguerreotype as a "mirror with a memory."[3] It is cruelly ironic that, during the same year that Agassiz revoked Renty and Delia's right to participate in the gifting of these "mirrors with memory" to their relatives, Holmes, known for his racist theories of eugenics, revoked the admission of the first three black students to Harvard Medical School. Not only does Harvard now keep these daguerreotypes from the relatives waiting to hold them but it also shaped the white supremacist principle through which photography was institutionalized and through which millions were enslaved. In holding these images as part of its archival and museal capital, Harvard extends the 1850 Fugitive Slave Act and requires millions to view Renty, Delia, and others not as ancestors or relatives, but as slaves.

We ought to draw clear lines between scholarship and the perpetuation of violence—the latter of which can be partially repaired by attending to the voices, grievances, and claims of those who were excluded from participating in public debates about the regimes that enslaved them. Furthermore, we need to attend to the way that practices such as photography have been shaped. We have the opportunity now—amid a wealth of scholarship and activism on the entanglement of photography, museums, and slavery, and based on increasing numbers of restitution cases—to redress what Renty and his relatives were deprived of in the 1850s. We have the opportunity for the unique imprint of Renty's presence on a silver plate to find at last its place where it belongs: with his family.

Restitution and Historical Accountability

When it comes to the question of the restitution of objects as part of an accountability process for institutional complicity with totalitarian regimes—of which enslavement of Africans is constitutive—one cannot ignore the commitment of the United States to restituting objects plundered from the Jews of Europe by the Nazis and other political regimes, notably Vichy France. The end of these disastrous regimes was marked by the embracing of a fundamental principle of restitution by postwar governments. Two early examples are the 1950s German Restitution Laws and the French ordinance of April 21, 1945, which enabled victims, survivors, and their heirs to claim confiscated and looted property. Dating from the years following World War II, these laws are still used to bring justice internationally.

One of the latest examples involves property held in the United States. In 2017, a French court ordered a US couple to return a Camille Pissarro painting they had purchased in 1995. Unbeknownst to the new owners, the painting had been plundered from its original Jewish owner, whose heirs were living in France.[4]

The importance the US government accorded restitution at the end of World War II is indicated by the special military corps of British and US historians, curators, art scholars, and museum directors called Monuments, Fine Arts and Archives. Known as the "Monuments Men," they are tasked with locating plundered art across Europe, tracking its provenance, and pursuing its just restitution to the original, primarily Jewish, owners.

Restitution was also mentioned in the Nuremberg Trials of the Nazi leadership led by the Allied powers, which sought to indict perpetrators for their crimes against humanity. The category *crimes against humanity* played a central role in the trials and was refined further in the years after. In her two books—*The Origins of Totalitarianism* and *Eichmann in Jerusalem* (both published in the United States, the author's chosen place of exile)—Hannah Arendt significantly impacted how the term is understood today. Arendt analyzed specific Nazi practices and explained what distinguished them as crimes against humanity but she also made it clear that the Jews were not the sole victims of this type of crime and neither did solely Nazis perpetrate it. Arendt argued that a polity whose laws were used in the process of committing crimes against humanity has an obligation to repair the social and political foundations of their laws. The only way to do this is to end definitively the lasting consequences of these crimes and change the law under which they could be committed.

As an Arab Jewish scholar myself, working in the tradition of Arendt, I feel a personal commitment to ensuring that redress, restitution, and repair are not solely the province of Jewish victims of crimes against humanity. Such an approach further exceptionalizes Jews at our own expense as well as that of other marginalized groups. We should hold Euro-American institutions to the same standard of reparation for all victims of violence.

The Status of Photographs

In today's scholarship and in the practice of archives and museums, it is widely acknowledged that photographs are not discrete items that can be "owned" or understood outside the context of their production—that is, the reasons they were taken, the power relations between the photographer and the

"He Is My Ancestor"

photographed, and the initial forms of use and display. Put differently, given the different lives and afterlives of photographs, one cannot assume that a photograph is just a photograph.

This is not just a contemporary assertion. Throughout the history of photography, and certainly in its first decades when Agassiz commissioned these daguerreotypes, questions about the nature of the daguerreotype—to whom it belongs, whether it can be owned, who can own it—and its proper usage were answered differently by diverse actors and institutions. It was never a given that the photograph belonged to the person who took it or the hands that happened to hold the plate or the print.

Photographs taken under circumstances of violence are not reducible to what is recorded in them, since the violence that enabled their creation does not disappear after the camera's shutter clicks. Photographs taken to support violent regimes or acts retain that original violence in the image; they continue to sustain the original act of violence well after the image is produced. Numerous artists, scholars, curators, museum directors, communities, activists, and statesmen have made this point, seeking to recover, bury, withdraw from circulation, or restitute objects, images, remains, and other items that have been plundered or seized by violent regimes and are now held as aesthetic commodities or generic historical documents in museums, archives, and public collections.

Photographs are the outcome of encounters between people—they are social objects—and their fate cannot be determined once and for all by the conditions of their original production. If photographs were produced through force and in service of a regime of violence, then their future should not be determined

Ariella Aïsha
Azoulay

without hearing the victims and offering reparative justice to them, their heirs, and/or survivors of that regime. Participants in the photographic encounter, or their heirs and communities, who were initially denied the right to refuse to have their images seized from them, should be heard and their views taken into account—regarding not only the individual images at stake but also the nature of the regime under which people could be forced to pose in front of a camera. What is recorded in photographs is not yet over; redress is possible, and justice can still be granted.

Crimes against Humanity

The daguerreotypes of Renty and Delia cannot be discussed with the legal terms usually reserved for photographs, as they could only have been produced as part of a regime that perpetrated crimes against humanity. Enslavement is recognized today by the United Nations and by International Law (Article 7, the Rome Statute of the International Criminal Court) as a crime against humanity. Slavery in the United States ended, however, without any kind of proceeding akin to the Nuremberg Trials, in which perpetrators were indicted and punished, and which were followed by reparations and restitution. Though some efforts were made to recompense formerly enslaved persons during the early Reconstruction era, this was an uneven and failed process that never involved the specific mandates around restitution and reparations that were put in place in the wake of World War II.

Although the punishment of individual perpetrators is no longer relevant in the case of slavery, the term *crime against humanity*—introduced in Nuremberg by the chief prosecutor in the trials, US Associate Supreme Court Justice Robert Jackson—is still relevant here to understand the urgency and reparative justice of bringing Harvard to release these daguerreotypes it seized from enslaved persons and restituting them to their family.

Since the end of World War II, scholars of political theory and law have attempted to parse the broader ethical, cultural, and legal aspects of this category of crime. In her discussion, Arendt quotes Telford Taylor, the Counsel for the Prosecution at the Nuremberg Trials, who emphasized that such crimes are "not committed only against the victim, but primarily against the community whose law is violated."[5] Arendt concluded that it is "the body politic itself that stands in need of being 'repaired.'"[6] In 2004, law professor David Luban clarified that these actions constitute crimes, not wrongs, because they "violate important community norms." Thus, Luban argues, the community has the need and right "to vindicate those norms independently of the victim."[7]

Arendt elucidates another major aspect of crimes against humanity: the creation of a racial order aiming to eliminate, physically and/or politically, groups of people from the shared world. This organized assault on human diversity is an attack, Arendt argues, "upon a characteristic of the 'human status' without which the very words 'mankind' or 'humanity' would be devoid of meaning."[8] As a regime, slavery created a world in which white people acted as the sole agents authorized to define, organize and lead the various spheres of life, while black people were eliminated as actors. But most white people did not perceive this as a crime. They did not view as crimes the kidnapping, sale, or purchase of black persons, neither the actions of forcing them to execute tasks, subjecting them to physical and psychological violence, nor of treating human beings as property. This was owing to the regime of white supremacy and the fabrication of the natural inferiority of black people as dogma, inflected with patriarchy and with the subjugation of black women in particular—a belief that Agassiz sought to uphold when he ordered the forcibly nude photographs of Renty, Delia, and others. In this way, even white people who did not themselves directly enslave black persons saw them as *potential* slaves or as fugitive slaves who had to be returned to those who authorized themselves, with the help of violence and the legal system they established, to be their "owners." A world in which only white people were allowed to determine who could be property and what constituted a crime—and where the harming of non-whites was imperceptible to the system of law they enacted—constitutes a sustained attack against human diversity.

That the victims' skin color is what made the crimes against them imperceptible in the eyes of the white inhabitants of Columbia, South Carolina, where the daguerreotypes were seized from Renty and Delia, is one of the indices of a crime against humanity. Making this crime recognizable and nameable—rather than unacknowledged and imperceptible according to laws legislated and enacted by enslavers—is at stake here. Agassiz did not act in a vacuum; he was not a lone scholar pursuing an unpopular project. He was inspired by his professor Georges Cuvier, who worked at the Muséum national d'Histoire naturelle in Paris and had access to the body of Sara Saartjie Baartman, an enslaved Khoekhoe woman, who was presented in public using the racist slur "Hottentot Venus." Cuvier used Baartman's body as "proof" of his theories of scientific racism. After her death, he conducted an autopsy of her body and "proved" that her remains were markedly different from European corpses. Agassiz was also likely in regular contact with Dr. Samuel Morton, with whom he could discuss how the new technology of the daguerreotype might be used to prove his theories. Morton himself had a vast collection of skulls ("the American Golgotha"), which he used for the racist science of phrenology, "proving" the evolutionary superiority of some races over others through studies of the skull.

"He Is My Ancestor"

Other scientists and enslavers gave Agassiz inspiration and guidance or were directly involved in the production of his daguerreotype images. Among them was Robert W. Gibbs, a local physician who used his plantation contacts and visits to select the "ideal type" for Agassiz's photographs from among enslaved people.

The Simple Truth

In the eyes of the white men who planned the photographic session, Renty, Delia, Drana, Alfred, Jack, George, and Jem were less than human—it was not their likenesses that Harvard scholars sought to produce. Rather, the aim was to generate visual proofs that could justify the enslavement of black people. This distinction is quite important: Agassiz, the photographer Joseph T. Zealy, and the others involved did not take photographs *of* slaves, but rather forced Renty, Delia, Drana, Alfred, Jack, George, and Jem to be photographed *as* slaves. Under the pretext that photographs carry an objective truth, these daguerreotypes were made to force black people to remain captives of slavery, and to serve as proof of their innate potential for enslavement. These white men could seize these images from these black people precisely because the latter were *enslaved*, thus the seized images were of their *enslavement*. The camera they encountered in the photographer's studio was part of what Hortense Spillers describes as the "tortures and instruments of captivity."[9]

For too long, the images seized from Renty and the others were presented and discussed as images *of* slaves, ignoring the power of photography to prolong the status of *slave* forced onto the photographed persons—the perpetuation, following Arendt's argument, of a crime against humanity. In all its publications and interpretations, Harvard denies the simple truth of the matter: as long as spectators possess the right to view the photographed persons in scenes of captivity—with the photographs handled as if they are the museum's property—black people will forever be presented as slaves. This is yet another example of the violent afterlives of slavery.

But Harvard skirts this truth, instead positioning itself as a universal spectator who can "free" the photographed persons from their captivity. The statements Harvard has offered on the photographs position the institution as a white savior with the right to "preserve" this horror "lest people forget"—ignoring entirely the descendants of enslaved persons and the fact that they have never forgotten their enslavement, as Lanier's demand examplifies. Restituting these daguerreotypes to descendants, who are also survivors of this regime of slavery, would accomplish far more than displaying them to white audiences ever will.

Harvard's position, argued in court, about how best to exhibit the images—"these images can be used, first of all, to give life to the individuals in the daguerreotypes"[10]—is outrageous. It refuses to bring to a close its possession of what Harvard extracted from Renty, and furthermore seeks to perpetuate this possession while denying the simple truth of Lanier's claim—in which, voiced as it is by an heir who claims Renty as her ancestor, the paradox collapses. Renty is not in need of any savior, and certainly not a savior that is the institution that seized his image in the first place; he just needs to go home. It is among his family that his presence will outlive the daguerreotype.

At home, the image could perhaps be kept as people keep images of their relatives: touched by hands, worn, forgotten, recalled, shown to others. Images get stained, placed in drawers, retrieved, lost, invoked in conversations, and used to spark longing, even as their

Ariella Aïsha
Azoulay

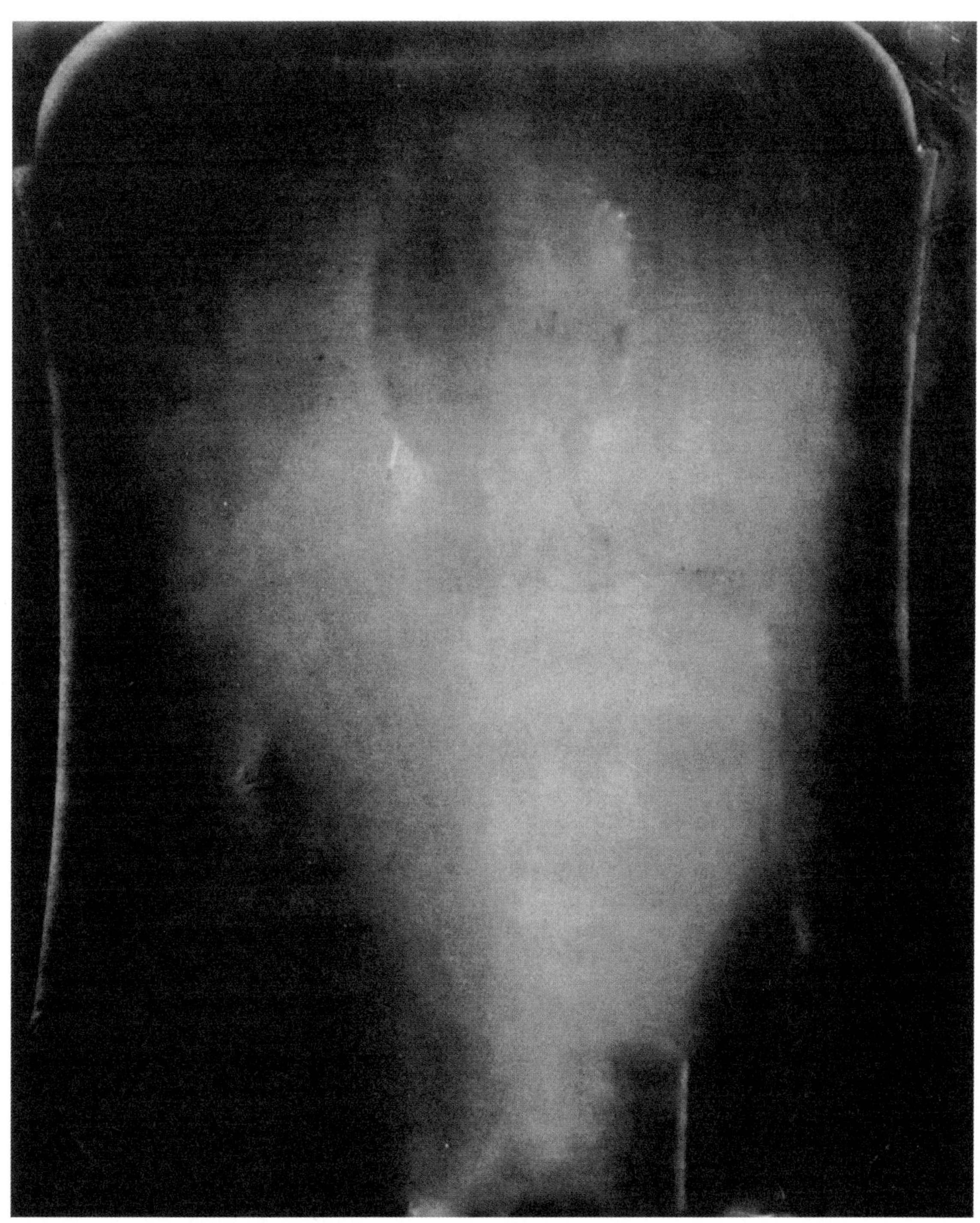

Renty was there [the image was redacted by Ariella Aïsha Azoulay in collaboration with Yonatan Vinitsky].

colors and contrasts fade away. But the proximity of the nakedness of enslavement might guide Lanier to touch this daguerreotype differently. The last thing Harvard's experts should do after the photograph's restitution is ask Lanier her plans for the daguerreotype. It is exactly the termination of this reminder of the right of enslavers to determine how descendants of slavery are allowed to mourn or celebrate their ancestors that the Taylors' reunification with Lanier could achieve.

A decision to allow Renty to go home should raise questions about how this might pertain to other objects held in Harvard's museums and archives, and in similar institutions in the West. But it will not create a precedent, since precedents have already been created. Objects, including those plundered by the circle of Agassiz, are continually being restituted. The University of Pennsylvania announced its plans to repatriate human skulls from Morton's collection, including those of several enslaved persons. The museum director, Christopher Woods, said: "An initial phase of rigorous evaluation was critical for ensuring an ethical and respectful process around repair."[11] At the request of Nelson Mandela during his first year as president of an apartheid-free country, Sara Baartman's body was restituted to South Africa and buried there. The French returned skulls of Algerian warriors they had seized in 1849. The Humboldt Forum in Berlin has recently announced its plans to restitute some of the Benin Bronzes, seized by British forces from West Africa in the nineteenth century. For more than seventy-five years, Jewish property has been restituted in the wake of Nazi expropriation and looting. And the list continues.

The whole idea behind the category *crimes against humanity,* as was made clear in Nuremberg and since, was to create a legal precedent—one not to be used to secure unjust gains but to prevent such crimes from being committed again. These objects were seized as part of a regime that perpetrated crimes against humanity. The day Tamara Lanier recognized in Renty not a *slave* but her great-great-great-grandfather, she invited us all to join her efforts to free her ancestors from captivity in a world in which their status as slaves was being prolonged, their freedom not fully recognized, and their rights not yet redressed.

Kinship, Property, and Rights

In photography's first decades, when these daguerreotypes were taken, photographers did not have exclusive property rights in the images they produced. Harvard's lawyers argue: "the rule is that a photograph is the property of the photographer, not the subject, and there are cases that we've cited in our brief that apply that rule even in cases when the subject of the images did not consent to the images being captured."[12] But this imposes one conception of photography retroactively on a complex history composed of competing claims about ownership, belonging, and rights.

Visitors to photographers' studios purchased the daguerreotypes produced by their presence in front of the camera—*their* daguerreotypes—and held them as property. Much less frequently, photographers produced additional plates from the same pose and kept them, but this was largely permissible since the answer to the question "Who owns the daguerreotype?" was not yet centralized nor standardized. That photographs taken of others, including photographs taken in their own studios, were automatically the property of the photographer was not guaranteed even when a case went to court.

For example, in 1860, Louis-Auguste Bisson, the official photographer of Napoléon III, was commissioned by the painter Adolphe Yvon to take the emperor's photograph

Ariella Aïsha Azoulay

for Yvon to use as a model for one of his paintings. When the painter realized Bisson had printed many copies of the commissioned photograph, he feared that these would devalue his painting, sued the photographer, and won. The court ruled that the photograph was Yvon's property, not the photographer's.[13]

I don't raise this as a precedent to determine legally who has property rights to photographs, but to remind us that the ownership of photographic images was undecided and in a state of flux at that time. This is still the case in our own time, as debates over image banks or archives of colonial violence in former empires exemplify today. Photographs transcend the idea of private property and cannot be dealt with in these limited terms.

As I have argued at length over the past decade-and-a-half in my work across different academic fields, photographs are the outcome of different people coming together under different circumstances.[14] These situations cannot be assessed using a single model since the "photographic event"—as I call this coming together of people—varies greatly, from relations of love, consent, and exchange, to exploitation, coercion, and violence. Photographs transcend the question of simple ownership because the objects themselves were produced, seized, circulated, and used in ways that violated the rights of others. We are not solely dealing with the right of one party to own a certain object, but the rights of the other parties involved in the photographic encounter.

After abolition, many individuals and institutions who acquired their wealth through slavery did not question that they had done so by turning black people into property, rendering black people propertyless, and expropriating the fruits of their labor. Those who profited from slavery were not challenged in the decades following abolition; thus, their heirs have assumed that the wealth they inherited is rightly theirs, or that their privileged access to it should be protected. Whenever this injustice enters the courtroom, it creates an opportunity to remedy it— first for the sake of its direct victims; second to free the heirs of perpetrators from structural and institutional complicity in perpetuating their ancestors' violence by not ending the continuing effects of the crimes against humanity carried out in their societies. In rejecting Lanier's genuine demand to let her ancestors exit the museum, Harvard not only rejects the grievance of a descendant of slavery but asks all of us to refuse to see slavery's crimes against humanity and their lingering presence.

These daguerreotypes of Renty and Delia are not property and are not Harvard's property. Even after they are restituted to Lanier, they will not be her property: they will be under her custody or guardianship. These daguerreotypes should not have been taken. But they were taken, and they do exist. So, we should think about them as we would think about a family member who needs the caretaking of close relatives.

The question of kinship here is primary. Tamara Lanier and Harvard University are not equal parties debating ownership of a piece of property. These daguerreotypes were seized from Renty and Delia in a world in which, as Spillers describes it, "flesh [was] for sale, flesh [was] summed up as a medium of exchange."[15] Tracing the transition from enslaved to free, Spillers counts "touch" as the first sense to be engaged after freedom:

Touch may be the first measure of what it means not to be enchained anymore. When I can declare my body as my own space and when you have to gain permission from me implicitly to put your hands on me, I think it makes a difference.[16]

We do not know and neither do we need to know the details

"He Is My Ancestor"

that led to the photographed persons posing for the camera naked or half-naked to conclude that they did not consent to appear in the photographs, appear to each other, appear to those whites who trafficked in their flesh, or appear to us stripped of their world. What we do know is that these daguerreotypes are the outcome of violence and cannot be approached as ordinary photographs.

Renty, Delia, Drana, Alfred, Jack, George, and Jem are slowly departing from those daguerreotypes. Harvard seeks to prevent them from freeing themselves from the frame by limiting the viewing time of each daguerreotype to ten hours a year. Preservation measures, elaborated in museums over centuries to continue to hold various ancestors as objects, could not stop this departure. This photograph [Fig. 1], from which I have deliberately removed the capture of Alfred, is a refusal of the gaze offered to us by white enslavers, which acknowledged their right to show us people they were holding as slaves, and a support of Lanier's claim to let her family care for their ancestors. The ubiquitous nature of the violence of slavery is such that the arena of this crime—Zealy's photography studio, which Renty, Delia, Drana, Alfred, Jack, George, and Jem were forced to enter—did not require additional torture devices.[17] As a result of the full nudity forced upon the photographed persons, Alfred's presence in front of the camera could conceal only the upper part of the headrest, commonly used in photography studios at the time to keep subjects still while their images were being captured. By repatriating these daguerreotypes to their families, Harvard should finally be compelled to reckon with the infrastructure that academic knowledge and museum practices provide for the perpetuation of

Ariella Aïsha
Azoulay

slavery, and invest in repairing its relationship with the communities this infrastructure continues to expropriate. Lanier claims Harvard has no right to continue to touch her great-great-great-grandfather, neither to force him to be half-nude in front of others, nor to breach the touch between kin and replace it with a public gaze. Under slavery, Spillers writes, "kinship loses meaning, since it can be invaded at any given and arbitrary moment by the property relations."[18] Denying Harvard the property rights to what was stolen from her great-great-great-grandfather and his kin is a way to repair kinship for Lanier, wounded by the long afterlife of slavery. "If 'kinship' were possible," Spillers continues, "the property relations would be undermined."[19] If not then—now.

Expanding the conversations about ethical approaches to collections formed under regimes of violence today pushes museums to "deal with claims for the restitution of artefacts and the repatriation of human remains,"[20] as German museum studies scholar Larissa Förster writes. This distinction is crucial in the case of Renty and Delia, as narrowing the question to focus solely on the restitution of museum items accepts the terms imposed by the museum, and the terms involved in their captivity. Lanier, in saying "this is my ancestor," not a museum asset, also demands repatriation. Renty and Delia were forced to enter a museum collection and Lanier demands they be repatriated to where they belong: among their relatives.

This demand finds justification in the fact that these daguerreotypes-become-museum-objects could not have been seized without Renty and others first being kidnapped into slavery. The light reflected from their naked bodies and captured in daguerreotype plates was also abducted. Any technical or scientific explanation of the procedure of the daguerreotype cannot ignore that these would not exist without the subjects having been forced to have a portion of their naked skin open to the light and reflected onto the sensitive surface of these plates. These daguerreotypes are, in a literal sense, the remains of their presence, forced enslavement, and unwilling nudity.

Given this history, Harvard should have immediately renounced any claims of ownership of ancestors. Lanier gifted the university with the opportunity to encourage black people to consult its archives and restore their connection to kin whom Harvard has in its holdings, as well as to work to ensure that all its faculty and students learn from Lanier—not only regarding matters of restitution but also of the release of ancestors held as property and the facilitation of the repair of kinship relations.

Restitution as Family Reunion

When Renty, Delia, and the others were forced to go to Zealy's studio, they did not encounter a photographer who wanted to interact with them to produce their likenesses. They encountered another enslaver, invested in the regime of slavery, for whom there was nothing more obvious than the fact that these black persons were slaves and must be made to surrender their bodies to perpetuate their plight. (Zealy himself held six black persons in captivity and counted them as his property.) The entire session at the photographer's studio, involving several white people, was devoted to producing visual proof that Renty, Delia, and the others were what the enslavers and profiteers forced them to be: *slaves*.

This was possible because the regime of slavery relied on creating a society of peers who recognized not only the right of whites to enslave blacks, but also the potential of any new technology to reaffirm the regime—a society of peers whose crimes against humanity are, for the perpetrators, rendered imperceptible, "natural." This

imperceptibility is materialized in these daguerreotypes: since their creation, viewers have been asked to recognize "the absolute power of masters over the bodies of their slaves,"[21] here obliged to pose naked.

And the imperceptibility of the crime to the eyes of perpetrators persists, exemplified by Harvard University and the Peabody Museum's expectation that Renty, Delia, and the others continue to provide scientific proofs with their bodies—now in the service of Harvard's "educational mission" and the institution's self-study.[22] As the black artist Carrie Mae Weems said, these daguerreotypes stand for the way "Anglo America—white America—saw itself in relationship to the black subject."[23] This is true not only in what could be seen in the daguerreotypes but also in the institution's obstinate refusal to recognize Lanier as the heir of Renty and his kin.

***

Restitution demands that we hear from different places and people, and that we attend to the provenance of items in our museums and question their status as "private property." Restitution asks that we consider these items in museums to be the ancestors of the communities from which they were taken, part of a life-world that was destroyed through the processes of colonization, enslavement, or plunder. This was the premise of the 1990 US Federal Law of the Native American Graves Protection and Repatriation Act (NAGPRA), and it is repeated all over the world. As two recent articles on the repatriation of the Benin Bronzes illustrate, art held in museums is not property to those from whom it was taken, but ancestors. Headlines read "'They're Not Property': The People Who Want Their Ancestors Back from British Museums" (*The Guardian*)[24]

"He Is My Ancestor"

and "In the West, the Looted Bronzes are Museum Pieces. In Nigeria, 'They Are Our Ancestors'" (*The New York Times*).[25]

Renty never owned the daguerreotype that was seized from him. Obviously, if he had ever been asked, he should not have been enslaved, and this daguerreotype should not have been brought into existence. What was seized from him is congealed in the photographic image itself—it is a remnant of his presence, an imprint of his flesh interacting with light, that Harvard continues to claim as a museum asset. "He is my ancestor," Lanier argues, not your "medium of exchange." Lanier claims the restitution of the object but expects the repatriation of her ancestor's remains.

1. Brian Willis, "Black Bodies, White Science: Louis Agassiz's Slave Daguerreotypes," *American Art* 9, no. 2 (Summer 1995): 40.

2. Walter Benjamin, "Theses on the Philosophy of History," in *Illuminations: Essays and Reflections*, ed. Hannah Arendt, trans. Harry Zohn (New York: Schocken Books, 2007), 256.

3. Quoted in Geoffrey Batchen, *Forget Me Not: Photography and Remembrance* (New York: Princeton Architectural Press, 2004), 8.

4. Ugo-Xavier Loiacono, "How a French Ordinance of 1945 Fostered the Restitution of a Pissaro's [sic] Painting Looted during World War II," *Nomos* (November 7, 2017), https://www.nomosparis.com/how-a-french-ordinance-of-1945-fostered-the-restitution-of-a-pissaros-painting-looted-during-world-war-ii/.

5. Quoted in Hannah Arendt, *Eichmann in Jerusalem: A Report on the Banality of Evil* (New York: Penguin Books, 2006), 261.

6. Arendt, *Eichmann in Jerusalem*, 261.

7. David Luban, "A Theory of Crimes against Humanity," *Yale Journal of International Law* 29, no. 1 (2004): 88.

8. Arendt, *Eichmann in Jerusalem*, 88.

9. Hortense J. Spillers, "Mama's Baby, Papa's Maybe: An American Grammar Book," *Diacritics* 17, no. 2 (Summer 1987): 67.

10. "The Peabody is a museum with an educational mission and these images are crucial for not only understanding the lives of—trying to understand the lives of the people that are—that were captured in the daguerreotypes, but trying to understand the institution of slavery itself" (Pretrial conference, October 20, 2020, 56).

11. Taylor Dafoe, "The University of Pennsylvania Will Restitute a Group of Human Skulls Once Used to Propagate White Supremacist Theories," *Artnet*, April 13, 2021, https://news.artnet.com/art-world/penn-museum-morton-collection-1958672.

12. Pretrial conference, October 20, 2020, 12.

13. See, for example, Gisèle Freund, *Photographie et sociéte* (Paris: Éditions du Seuil, 2017).

14. See, for example, Ariella Azoulay, *The Civil Contract of Photography* (New York: Zone Books, 2008) and *Civil Imagination—A Political Ontology of Photography* (New York: Verso Books, 2012).

15. Hortense J. Spillers, "Shades of Intimacy: What the Eighteenth Century Teaches Us," filmed March 18, 2016, at The Flesh of the Matter: A Hortense Spillers Symposium, Cornell University, Ithaca, NY, video, https://www.cornell.edu/video/hortense-spillers-shades-of-intimacy-eighteenth-century.

16. Spillers, "Shades of Intimacy."

17. Lanier contends: "Harvard is saying 'your enslavement, your victimization doesn't matter.' Harvard is saying, that 'any time a photographer takes a picture, that picture belongs to the photographer, irrespective of the violence associated with that.' And we know that not to be the case. We know that if I were to put a gun to someone's head, and forced them to take them off the street and to bring them to *this isolated place* and tell them 'take your clothes off and let me take pictures of you'—that is criminal. I would not only be committing a crime, but I wouldn't be [allowed] to keep the proceeds of the crime, and I wouldn't be able to go on and be enriched by the proceeds of the crime." (Emphasis mine), https://twitter.com/mikaelowunna/status/1417637355557642242?s=21.

18. Spillers, "Mama's Baby," 74.

19. Spillers, "Mama's Baby," 75.

20. Larissa Förster, "Plea for a More Systematic, Comparative, International, and Long-Term Approach to Restitution, Provenance Research, and the Historiography of Collections," *Museumskunde* 81, no. 1 (2016): 49.

21. Alan Trachtenberg, *Reading American Photographs: Images as History—Mathew Brady to Walker Evans* (New York: Farrar, Strauss and Giroux, 1990), 54.

22. Pretrial conference, October 20, 2020, 56.

23. Carrie Mae Weems, artist's note for her photograph *You Became a Scientific Profile*, https://www.moma.org/collection/works/91838.

24. David Shariatmadari, "'They're Not Property': The People Who Want Their Ancestors Back from British Museums," *The Guardian*, April 23, 2019, https://www.theguardian.com/culture/2019/apr/23/theyre-not-property-the-people-who-want-their-ancestors-back-from-british-museums.

25. Ruth Maclean and Alex Marshall, "In the West, the Looted Bronzes are Museum Pieces. In Nigeria, 'They Are Our Ancestors'," *The New York Times*, 23 June, 2021, https://www.nytimes.com/2021/06/23/world/africa/benin-bronzes-Nigeria-stolen.html.

Ariella Aïsha Azoulay

Abolition

ARIELLA AÏSHA AZOULAY

IN CONVERSATION WITH

NATALIA BRIZUELA

Natalia Brizuela: You show us in your work that the ways in which Harvard's continued possession of these images of people *as* slaves—not only *of* slaves—perpetuates the dispossession at the center of racial capitalism by retaining these persons as possession and as property, and that this is in fact a perpetuation of slavery through what is analogous to the imprisonment of the photographs. And we know all too well, in the case of the United States, the direct relationship between slavery and the mass incarceration of black people, and particularly black men. I wonder if you could help us think about the ways in which these institutions—by retaining and disallowing mobility—are participating in the problem of the prison industrial complex.

To continue that thought: can the crime of this slavery, which you classify as a crime against humanity, be redressed through the restitution of photographs that were taken without consent? We could certainly argue that slavery and its inherent dispossession and dehumanization cannot be rectified through the return of a photographic image. But the temporality of photography reinscribes and reactualizes past slavery in the present. Returning the daguerreotypes of Renty and Delia to Tamara is not only about the return of an object taken without consent—an object that should, as you argue, be treated as human remains—but also about disrupting the temporal and political order of the photographic object. The restitution of the photographs would disrupt the constant reinscription of Renty and Delia *as* slaves, because the stolen images would be removed from their context of production—which is extractive and violent—and they would enter another ecology, one in which Renty and Delia would return home and leave the logic of slavery behind. Upon this return home, the images might have another life, one structured around the humanity of the people they depict. This return would break the bond that is implied in the question of property and allow the repair of the unfathomable damage of slavery to begin.

Do you have thoughts about such a radical shift in temporality, which would allow the photograph to be transformed in ways that, to date, it has not been—ways that are not represented when it is claimed as property by Harvard?

The demand for the restitution of plundered objects—objects currently housed in museums throughout the world—to their places of origin, to their homes, has a lengthy history that has intensified over the last three years. Here, the contested site is that of wrongful or illegal seizure, of expropriation, of the theft of objects from people from Africa, Latin America, and elsewhere through colonial violence. But that debate has also given rise to questions around how the return of plundered objects will give a sense of what some scholars and activists have called "spiritual reconstruction" to those who will regain what was taken from them generations ago. This will give the Indigenous peoples of Africa, the Americas, and elsewhere, opportunities to learn from objects that are part of their heritage and patrimony. They have been deprived of the right to understand these objects, which contain knowledge that, even in altered ways, has a place in their contemporary cultures. The wounds of the plunder remain but a sense of belonging and understanding merge in this notion of spiritual reconstruction.

In that context, there has been a further argument around the fact that specific typologies are important, that not all objects are the same, that each such object has its own history. And you are offering us—and building—a new typology, one that is specific to the photographic image. And there is a difference between plundered objects that were once

Ariella Aïsha
Azoulay
Natalia Brizuela

devotional or everyday objects in their context of origin and these photographs that are of persons as slaves. And now, you bring in this fundamental idea that such images should be treated as human remains. I wonder if you have thought of this particular project in relationship to the development of a typology for this question of restitution?

My final comment has to do with the question of debt. Your work raises the question of who owes what to whom? This is a crucial question of our times—immediately because of the forms of debt culture that drive capitalism and its current neoliberal moment but also because there are scholars like Denise Ferreira da Silva and Frances Négron-Muntaner, who argue there is an unpayable debt at the heart of the development of global racial capitalism. So, in that construction, institutions like Harvard are holding on to the objects that are aligned with that form of capitalism—and the configuration that has given to the world is no surprise, in that if it did not hold on to things such as these objects, Harvard and other institutions in similar positions would be open to being transformed, to becoming undone. And in doing so, such institutions would become debtors, owing almost everything they hold in material and symbolic terms to other individuals and to larger communities. This question of debt could help us continue your thinking through what you presented.

Ariella Azoulay: There have been prior projects engaging with these images, notably one by the artist Carrie Mae Weems. Something different happens when, based on tracking down kinship relations, Tamara Lanier steps forward and claims these objects as her ancestors. When Weems used these images without asking for permission, she challenged Harvard and provoked them: "Sue me. No problem, I have a moral case." As is well known, Harvard didn't sue Weems—but rather purchased her work and enriched its collection with a work criticizing their regime. In 2019 Lanier rejected the authority of that regime and sued them. What is the meaning of this act? The question of debt that you mentioned is important; I would like, however, to introduce a different term and raise the idea of *gift* in this context. From the very first moment Lanier knocked on Harvard's door—including through the complaint—she is actually offering Harvard a gift. The gift of liberating them from being forever captives of their crimes. That until today Harvard refuses to even talk with Lanier, exemplifies why descendants of the violence of slavery are also survivors of this regime. There is a moment of grace in Lanier's engagement with Harvard: she invites Harvard to stop relating to Renty as property that they will have to extract—or to subtract—from their collection; rather, she invites Harvard to do the right thing at last and right part of the wrong. While it is not surprising that Harvard ignores the gift, we have to ask seriously if institutions such as Harvard can do the right thing and stop being what they used to be.

Aboliton

It's already a decade since Lanier offered Harvard this gift; Harvard's students were supportive and organized a campaign endorsing Lanier's call to #Free Renty. I don't recall hearing any of Harvard's faculty members stating "we endorse Tamara Lanier." Hannah Arendt's interpretation of the concept of crimes against humanity is relevant here, since she speaks about the command to change the laws under which such crimes could takes place, laws under which we continue to live. In this sense, Lanier's gift is also offered to us—scholars, and scholars of photography in particular—a gift that compels us to ask what photography *is* and to abolish the laws under which it was institutionalized.

So, in relation to your second question, my answer is: *abolition*. The museum is part of the carceral system, and we have to question that separation between people and objects and recognize the continuity where colonialism disrupted it. This is exemplified in the fact that, when slavery was abolished, those people who were kidnapped from Africa were not allowed to reunite with their objects, which were also forcibly displaced from Africa and held captive in museums. Imperialism is a regime that separates people from their objects and turns objects into private property owned by institutions dedicated to art and education. That Harvard can continue until today—almost a decade after it was contacted by Lanier—to detain Renty and Delia, and that it withdraws from accountability and reparations, is a direct outcome of this separation. So, yes, I agree with your conception of the museum as prison.

We have to think about museums within the broader vision of abolition. In this context, not only the question of temporality but also that of the body politic is crucial. Imperial temporality is indexed on the invention of the past in a way that creates the assumption that what was achieved through violence is over and can no longer be changed. This is how photography was institutionalized and its history had been written - by the victors. Hence it is not surprising that Harvard adheres to victors' justice. Here we see how the question of temporality and that of the body politic intersect. Renty and Delia were not recognized as part of the body politic and were unable to oppose the seizure of the images from them, and under victors' justice that should be considered irreversible. And along comes Tamara Lanier, who insists on her right to inhabit the position of her ancestors and say *No*. This, in my eyes, is the call we must respond to and support. We must reverse the imperial temporality that tells us on the one hand that slavery is over and, on the other, that what was imposed under its regime cannot be transformed or abolished.

Ariella Aïsha
Azoulay
Natalia Brizuela

NB: I brought up the idea of unpayable debt, and you noted we should also think about this beautiful gift that Lanier offers Harvard. The notion of gift is so central to the development of a modern anthropological theory. Some scholars working on the question of restitution in the field of anthropology are also thinking that if we have built one strand of modern anthropology around the notion of the gift, we should also have a theory for it. It is also our responsibility to develop a theory of dispossession. I think that in a way, that's what you're doing: you're developing a theory of dispossession through the photograph.

AA: You also mentioned—and it's very important—typology and taxonomy around the theory of gift—but not, perhaps, in the way it was elaborated in anthropology. We see it in different colonial contexts, when the colonized, or the former enslaved, or the survivors who were dispossessed, make an offering of a gift that, outrageously, is not responded to. We have to break away from this single meaning of *photograph*, as if a photograph is a photograph is a photograph. We must insist on the ontological differences between different types of photographs and for that we have to speak about the political ontology of photography, as I have suggested elsewhere. This includes, as one example, an incredible manifesto[1] written by Cases Rebelles, in which they asked to remove images of their ancestors from circulation under circumstances of violence and particularly sexual violence.

Bonaventure Soh Bejeng Ndikung: To the point on the question of photography and restitution—how do we restitute a photograph, especially when what is at stake is often dehumanization? Such restitution has to do with the restitution of dignity. How do we do that?

AA: I think Tamara Lanier has her answer. She claims that when Renty is back home, he will regain his dignity among his relatives. When the lawsuit was published two or three years ago, several curators of photography claimed that Lanier would be unable to protect the daguerreotype at her home, that the image would disappear completely. I think nobody has the right to ask Lanier what she will do with this image when it is resituated. The likeness of Renty may disappear. The image may die. The image may be forgotten in her attic, but this is something that belongs to her family, and they will find a way to help Renty regain his dignity. It's not for Harvard to make it part of the negotiation. What we see with the restitution of other objects—very few, as we have not seen many cases—is that museums try to define the terms under which objects will be restituted. I believe that an essential element of the dignity involved here is that nobody can intervene in the way Renty will go back home—not any expert, and certainly not an expert from Harvard.

Aboliton

Ariella Aïsha
Azoulay
Natalia Brizuela

Stefan Köhler: Last year in Hamburg, we started an artistic residence called Reverse Exploration. We invite artists from the Global South to explore Hamburg and the collections in the Museum am Rothenbaum Kulturen und Künste der Welt [MARKK]. This spring, we arranged a collaboration between the Algerian artist Amina Zoubir and the museum. MARKK gave her access to the photo collection, and she created a project called *Archaeology of the Colonized Body*. Zoubir was permitted to make copies of photographs in the collection to make collages to restore dignity to women who were photographed nude by European explorers. There are thousands of such photographs stored here in Hamburg, and it's difficult to contact the descendants in many African countries. Do you think it is legitimate to conduct this process of the spiritual reconstruction of dignity through artists working with photo collections in museums?

NB: I think that's a wonderful project for several reasons. We need to open the doors to these collections to artists, more than scholars or scientists, so they can reinvent them. You're taking that a step further by inviting artists from the Global South who are most probably the subjects—in that their ancestors were the subjects—of this kind of plunder. In the context of Latin America, there's usually very little interest when, say, a Latin American author writes about their exploration of a European country. Europe is not interested in what others think of them—but there are always these bestsellers about, you know, Frenchmen traveling to the Andes and seeing whatever. So, yours is a gesture that invites *looking at* because those artists are not only looking at the collection but they're also looking at the history that brought those collections into being, and inevitably that is an engagement in reverse exploration or reverse ethnography.

AA: I will complicate things a bit—let me give an example from the Union of Congolese Artists [Cercle d'Art des Travailleurs de Plantation Congolaise—CATPC], who, in collaboration with Renzo Martens, are aiming to "reverse gentrification," to use their own term. Museums cannot just invite artists to work with the collection and allow them to make copies. "Allowing" them to make copies suggests that these photos are not theirs and they are being given permission. What does it mean that the museum continues to give permission to make copies? Nobody has proposed anything yet to Lanier but why would she agree to leave a copy of the daguerreotype with Harvard? We cannot accept that photography equals photographs, that photographs equal representations to which artists can apply new interpretations. It's not only about interpretations; it's not only about representations, it's about the infrastructure of racial capitalism that runs through these museums, that accompanies the persona of *artist*, that runs through the reproduction of a distribution of wealth that was achieved through the extreme violence of colonialism, slavery and indentured labor, forced migration and land theft. While I share the intuition that what artists may do is much better than what is in the museums, nevertheless, we cannot allow museums to stop there. Museums should relinquish their holdings.

NB: I think the question here is also how, in the case of these photographic collections, the project is in part to invite artists to come to Hamburg, where they might engage with this specific museum and its photographic collections. If one does not know the provenance of the images—we cannot track down all the Tamara Laniers out there—then what do we do? I agree with you—I brought up the idea of abolition earlier—but in the context of museums and similar institutions, what does one do with all those collections?

AA: In the case of Lanier, it was relatively easy to track the ancestry because the daguerreotypes have names that link them to known plantations. You're right, there are huge collections whose individual descendants we don't know how to identify—but we know how to track communities. Hence the example of Cases Rebelles, who wrote the manifesto I mentioned earlier, is fascinating. They don't say, "these particular women are our ancestors" but rather: "*All* these women are our ancestors. Don't touch them." This is part of this reversed temporality. Members of Cases Rebelles are saying, "they are ours *now* as they were *then*. They were unable to stop you from seizing these images *then*, so we are stopping you *now*." As long as this infrastructure is not transformed or abolished, archive-based projects such as the one you mention cannot be brilliant. But this is not the question. It's not about spectators engaging with a brilliant work. It's about radical change of the infrastructure, and I believe we are compelled to deal with it that way.

Lapsus Imaginis: The Image in Ruins*[1]

* This essay first appeared in *October* 96 (Spring 2001), 35–60.

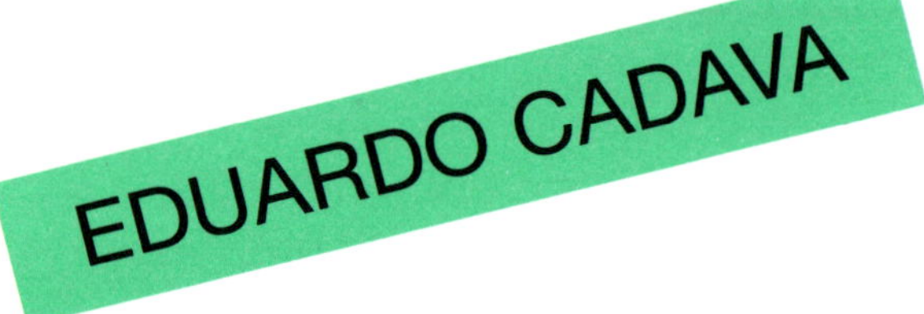

The disaster ruins everything, all the while leaving everything intact. It does not touch anyone in particular; "I" am not threatened by it, but spared, left aside. It is in this way that I am threatened; it is in this way that the disaster threatens in me what is exterior to me— an other than I who passively become other. There is no reaching the disaster. Out of reach is he whom it threatens, whether from afar or close up, it is impossible to say: the infinitude of the threat has in some way broken every limit.

—— Maurice Blanchot, *The Writing of the Disaster*[2]

There can be no image that is not about destruction and survival, and this is especially the case in the image of ruin. We might even say that the image of ruin tells us what is true of every image: that it bears witness to the enigmatic relation between death and survival, loss and life, destruction and preservation, mourning and memory. It also tells us, if it can tell us anything at all, that what dies, is lost, and mourned within the image—even as it survives, lives on, and struggles to exist—is the image itself. This is why the image of ruin—again, speaking for all images—so often speaks of the death, if not the impossibility of the image. It announces the inability of the image to tell a story: the story of ruin, for example. It is because of this silence in the face of loss and catastrophe—even when ruin remains undeclared—that the image is always at the same time an image of ruin, an image about the ruin of the image, about the ruin of the image's capacity to show, to represent, to address and evoke the persons, events, things, truths, histories, lives, and deaths to which it would refer.

This is why, we might say, the entire logic of the world can be read here, and it can be read as the logic of the image. Like the world, the image allows itself to be experienced only as what withdraws from experience. Its experience—and if it were different it would not be an experience at all—is an experience of the impossibility of experience. The image tells us that it is with loss and ruin that we have to live. Nevertheless, what makes the image an image is its capacity to bear the traces of what it cannot show, to go on, in the face of this loss and ruin, to suggest and gesture toward its potential for speaking. In other words, the fact of the image's existence—and here I refer only to an image worthy of the name "image," to an image that would remain faithful to the ruinous silences that make it what it is—ruins the ruin about which all images speak—or at least seek to speak.

The image, then: this means "of ruin"—composed of ruin, belonging to ruin, taking its point of departure from ruin, seeking to speak of ruin, and not only its own—but also "the ruin of ruin," the emergence and survival of an image that, telling us it can no longer show anything, nevertheless shows and bears witness to what history has silenced, to what, no longer here, and arising from the darkest nights of memory, haunts us, and encourages us to remember the deaths and losses for which we remain, still today, responsible.

I.

What does it mean to assume responsibility for an image or a history—for an image of history, or for the history sealed within an image? How can we respond, for example, to the image and history inscribed within this strange photograph—especially when, before our eyes, it ruins the distinctions it proposes. It bequeaths to us a space—the space of the photograph as well as the photographed space—in which we can no longer know what space is. It offers us a time—the time of the photograph and the photographed time—in which we no longer know what time is. We know neither what remains inside or outside the violated space, inside or outside the interrupted time, nor what space and time can be when they are ruined in this way. The limits, the borders, and the distinctions that would guarantee our understanding of the image have been shattered by an explosion from which no determination can be sheltered.

How can we begin to read this image, then? In exhibiting and archivizing the remains of its implosion, the image remains bound to the survival of the traces of a past and to our ability to read these traces as traces, to read, that is, what Walter Benjamin would call the image's "historic index." As he explains in a note from "Konvolut N" of his *Passagen-Werk*, to say that images are marked historically does not mean that they "belong to a specific time"—the time of the camera's click, for example—but that they only "enter into legibility [*Lesbarkeit*] at a specific time." "This 'entering into legibility,'" he goes on to say:

> constitutes a specific critical point of the movement inside them. Every present is determined by those images that are synchronic with it: every Now is the Now of a specific recognizability [Erkennbarkeit]. In it, truth is loaded to the bursting point with time. (This point of explosion, and nothing else, is the death of the intentio, which accordingly coincides with the birth of authentic historical time, the time of truth.) It is not that the past casts its light on the present or that the present casts its light on the past; rather, an image is that in which the Then [das Gewesene] and the Now [das Jetzt] come together into a constellation like a flash of lightning. In other words, an image is dialectics at a standstill. For while the relation of the present to the past is a purely temporal, continuous one, the relation of the Then to the Now is dialectical: not temporal in nature but imagistic. Only dialectical images are genuinely historical—that is, not archaic—images. The image that is read—which is to say, the image in the Now of its recognizability— bears to the highest degree the imprint of the perilous critical moment on which all reading is founded.[3]

For an image to be read (for it to "enter into legibility" in the "Now of its recognizability"), it must encounter a constellation of dangers, not the least of which is its own dissolution. The possibility of this dissolution, however, belongs to what makes an image an image, and, in particular, to what makes an image a genuinely historical image. It names, among so many other things (including the dissolution of the subjectivity that might wish to read the image), the movement at the image's interior, the dialectical transfer between the Then and the Now that, simultaneously composing and fissuring the image, occurs with what we might call "the flash of history." If the historical index of an image—"the imprint of the perilous critical moment on which all reading is founded"—therefore signals the relation between an image and the time in which it can be read, it tells this time (the time that dates it, but a time that is not only the time in which it was produced) that it can be read "Now." But this "Now," composed, like the present, of all the images that are synchronic with it, is never simply "Now." It is never separable from the Then that, coming together with it in a "constellation like a flash of lightning," is before or beyond the time from which the image seems to emerge. This means that Benjamin's "Now" does not name a present, just as his "Then" cannot be reduced to the past. Moreover, since the present is constituted in relation to all the images that "Now" give it its signature—that come to it from elsewhere but also from other historical moments—it, too, can never be present.

This is why the historical index of an image always claims the image for another time[4]—for another historical moment (itself plural, and composed of several other moments) and for something other than linear, chronometric time (which would be, for Benjamin, "purely temporal" and "continuous"). This is also why Benjamin's understanding of the image's historical index cannot be understood as either indexical or referential: it can never index or refer to a single historical moment or event.[5] As he puts it elsewhere, "in order for a part of the past to be touched by the present instant [*Aktualität*], there must be no continuity between them."[6] Confirming that the relationship between a past and a present is dialectical, in the strongest historical and imagistic sense, the index interrupts the presence of the image. It indicates that the image only exists in relation to a time that, signaling the explosion that marks both its birth and destruction, prevents it from ever being simply itself. Every effort to read the image therefore must expose it there where the image does not exist. It must displace it (make it standstill elsewhere), and this because, in the "Now" of the image's legibility, the truth of the image is, in the wording of Benjamin, "loaded to the bursting point with time." It is because

Eduardo
Cadava

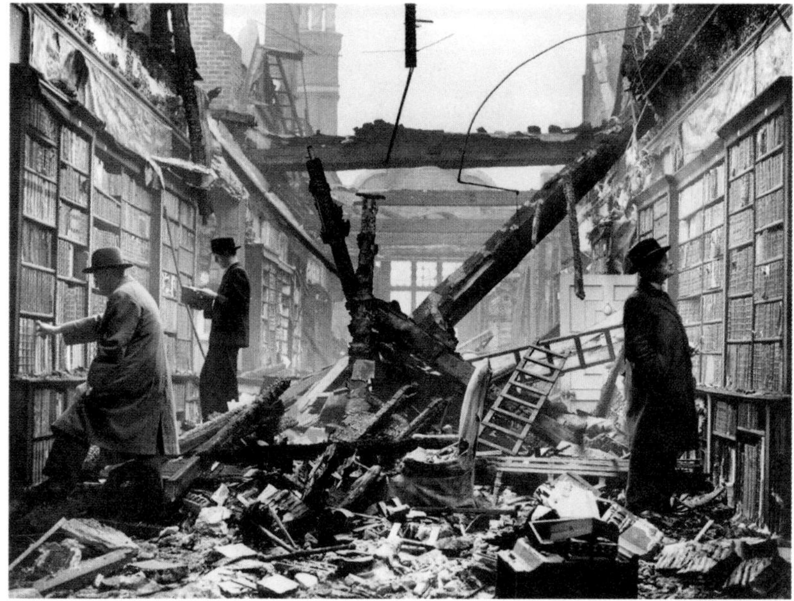

Holland House, Kensington, London, October 23, 1940. An interior view of the bombed library at Holland House with readers apparently choosing books regardless of the damage. Source: Historic England Archive (BB83_04456).

the traces carried by the image include reference to the past, the present, and the future, and in such a way that none of these can be isolated from the other, that the image cannot present the traces of the explosion it recalls—without at the same time exploding, or bursting, its capacity to (be) present. It is in this interruption and explosion of historical presentation that we engage the conditions of "authentic" historical understanding, an understanding that, offering us the truth of time, tells us that history is something to which we can never be present.

II.

How are we to interpret this image? How are we to develop or imagine it—within the space of this essay, within the assemblage of words that occupy the space of these few pages? What would responding mean here? Each detail of the photograph has its force, its logic, its singular place—among so many others, the three standing men looking at books (with each one demonstrating a different relation to the books—one holding and reading a book, the other about to touch one, and the last merely looking at them), the splintered wreckage behind them, the walls made of books, the collapsed ceiling, the shattered glass, the door and window, only partially visible behind the debris. A condensation of history and texts, this photograph remains linked to an absolutely singular event, and therefore also to a date, to a historical inscription. It opens a space for time itself, dispersing it from its continuous present. Looking both backward and forward, it asks us to think about "context" in general in a different way. Its context would include not only the date and circumstances of the photograph itself—this photograph of the bombed-out Holland House Library in London was taken on October 23, 1940, nearly three and a half weeks after the air raid that led to the library's destruction[7]—but also those of the initial air raid on September 27 and of the German Luftwaffe's Blitz on London that had begun on September 7. Moreover, it refers, in however encrypted a manner, to the legendary book burnings of 1933 that confirmed what Denis Hollier has called "a kind of Nazi bibliophobia,"[8] to the antifascist insistence, in response to the book burnings, on the survival of books, to the existence of wartime censorship, to our own passivity toward disaster, and to the disaster that names our passivity toward what we so often call "our time." It suggests as well our capacity to turn our backs on the disaster all around us by staring into books.

Given the several histories and contexts sealed within the photograph—it is, as Benjamin would suggest, full of history and time—what could responding mean here? How can we respond to the experiences commemorated, displaced, and ciphered by this image? How can we give an account of the circumstances in which it was produced, or better, of those it names, codes, disguises, or dates on its surface? What can memory be when it seeks to remember the trauma of violence and loss? How can we respond to what is not presently visible, to what can never be seen within the image? To what extent does what is not seen traverse the image as the experience of the interruption of its surface? If the structure of the image is defined as what remains inaccessible to visualization, this withholding and withdrawing structure prevents us from experiencing the image in its entirety or, to be more precise, encourages us to recognize that the image, bearing as it always does several memories at once, is never closed.

If the photograph evokes a moment of crisis and destruction, then, part of what is placed in crisis is the finitude of the context within which we might read it. This is why, when we respond to a photograph by trying to establish only the historical contexts in which it was produced, we risk forgetting the disappearance of context—the essential decontextualization—that is staged by every photograph. The moment in the image appears suspended and torn from any particular historical moment—past, present, or future. As Benjamin explains in his early essay on the *Trauerspiel* and tragedy, the

> time of history is infinite in every direction and unfulfilled at every moment. This means we cannot conceive of a single empirical event that bears a necessary relation to the time of its occurrence. For empirical events, time is nothing but a form, but, what is more important, as a form it is unfulfilled. This means that no single empirical event is conceivable that would have a necessary connection to the temporal situation in which it occurs.[9]

Time tells us that the event can never be entirely circumscribed or delimited. This is why the effort to determine and impose a meaning on the event recorded in this photograph, to stabilize the determination of its context—an act that involves reading what is not visible within the photograph—involves both violence and repression. This is also why whatever violence there is in the attempt to establish the context of this image remains linked, because of this repression, to an essential nonviolence.

It is in this highly unstable and dangerous relationship between violence and nonviolence that responsibilities form, responsibilities that have everything to do with how we read this image. As we have seen, Benjamin refers to the violence or nonviolence of reading when he claims that "the image that is read—which is to say, the image in the Now of its recognizability—bears to the highest degree the imprint of the perilous critical moment on which all reading is founded."[10] Suggesting that there can be no reading of an image that does not expose us to a danger—because such a reading would only demonstrate, if it could demonstrate anything, the noncontemporaneity of the present, the absence of linearity in the representation of historical time, and

Eduardo Cadava

therefore the fugacity of the past and the present—he warns us of the danger of believing that we have seen or understood an image. For Benjamin—who committed suicide on September 26, 1940, just one day before the Holland House bombing—the activity of reading is charged with an explosive power that blasts the image to be read from its context. This tearing or breaking force is not an accidental predicate of reading; it belongs to its very structure. In a passage from "Konvolut N" that associates the "critical, dangerous impulse" of truth with the work of "materialist history writing" (which he also describes as a kind of "blasting"), Benjamin suggests that the historical object emerges from out of a destructive explosion: "The destructive or critical momentum of materialist historiography," he writes, "is registered in the blasting of historical continuity with which the historical object first constitutes itself."[11] This is why history involves the capacity to arrest or immobilize historical movement, to blast the details of an event from the continuum of history, or, as Benjamin puts it, to spring them loose "from the order of succession."[12] It is because history breaks down into images that there can be no photographic image, no force of arrestment, which does not tell us of the relation between images and history, photography and memory, and space and violence.

III.

To read means being exposed to time and images. But if the reading of images draws us to the necessity of the disappearance into which they withdraw and from which they emerge—as Benjamin tells us elsewhere, "what we know we will soon no longer have before us—this is what becomes an image"[13]—it is because images themselves refer to time. Roland Barthes reinforces this point when, in his *Camera Lucida*, he suggests that, if "the photograph possesses an evidential force," its testimony "bears not on the object but on time."[14] But what we call time is precisely the image's inability to coincide with itself.

It demands that every image be an image of its own interruption—an image of the explosion of space and the erasure of time. Exposing the image to the movement of its disappearance or dissolution, it exposes it to ruin, to damage, to annihilation. A movement of alteration, it conveys the exposure—the interruption and breakdown—of the image and thereby prevents it from being merely this image or merely an image. This is why an image is never already constituted but is always in the process of its constitution. This is also why, simultaneously constructed and effaced, every image is a ruin, a *lapsus imaginis*. The space of ruin is itself exposed to the movement of ruin. The ruin stands in the image that stands in ruin: a *mise en abyme*, for which there are only ever further ruins of ruins. The ruin, the image of ruin, is therefore *without image*. It can never be presented.

The ruin in the image is in fact the law that forbids its own presentation. The image presents an interruption of history and does so only by interrupting the principle of presentation. Or, to put it another way, the disintegration of presentation exposes a caesura, a ruin in the presentation of historical experience. As Benjamin explains in his book on the German *Trauerspiel*, "In the ruin, history has materially distorted itself into the scene. And, figured in this manner, history does not assume the form of the promise of an eternal life so much as that of irresistible decay."[15] If ruin is at work in every image, this is because the ruin is not simply before the image, is not simply what makes the image an image; it is also what, in and with the image, is not the image and, in not being the image, allows the image to be what it is: an image in ruins. This ruin means that the image does not mean, does not designate anything—especially because it refers to time, to a time whose history is always a history of ruins. In the wording of Jacques Derrida,

Lapsus Imaginis

37

the ruin does not supervene like an accident upon a monument that was intact only yesterday. In the beginning there is ruin. Ruin is that which happens to the image from the moment of the first gaze…. [It] is not in front of us…. It is experience itself: neither the abandoned yet still monumental fragment of a totality, nor, as Benjamin thought, simply a theme of baroque culture. It is precisely not a theme, for it ruins the time, the position, the presentation or representation of anything and everything.[16]

This is to say that, if time ruins the image, this ruined image also interrupts the movement of time, in a manner that has, not the form of time, but rather the form of time's interruption, the form of a pause, of an explosion. This ruined image wounds the form of time. It suspends and deranges time. But since time—and all time—can be deranged in this way, time itself is perhaps a kind of madness.[17]

Like the image, it is never identical to itself. It can only be what it is by leaving itself, by abandoning itself. It is unrepresentable. Never something, never one thing, never this or that, it is what is never present. Nevertheless, as Immanuel Kant reminds us, everything passes in time but time itself. Time repeats itself endlessly. It begins in repetition. But what is repeated in time is a movement of differentiation and dispersion—and what is differentiated and dispersed is time itself. There can be no passing moment that is not already both the past and the future: the moment must be simultaneously past, present, and future in order for it to pass at all. This is why what is repeated in time is what is never simply itself, what is incessantly vanishing. If time is a matter of repetition, it is a repetition only of its unrepeatability.

This aporetic exposition of time and the image no longer allows for a linear, unbroken presentation of history.

Eduardo Cadava

It presents itself as a repetition of the prohibition against images, a repetition that tells us that history can only emerge in the interruption of the continuum of presentation. The sign of this prohibition is legible in the photograph in the "X" formed by the collapsed wooden beams at its center. It is as if the prohibition that this "X" should express, however, intervenes in its sign and makes it into a ruin of the sign that would correspond to the prohibition. By remaining faithful to the prohibition, the very sign in which it could present itself is interrupted or ruined. This suggests that, without interrupting the historical continuum, without blasting the techniques of representation, there can be no historical time. No history without the interruption of history. No time without the interruption of time. No image without the interruption of the image. If, however, this interrupted image is still an image, then "image" means: the disaster of the image. It means that every image is an image of disaster—that the only image that could really be an image would be the one that shows its impossibility, its disappearance and destruction, its ruin.[18] The image is only an image, in other words, when it is not one, when it says "*there is no image.*"[19] The image therefore does not demonstrate. No assertion about the image (and this means no "image of the image") can show us the truth of the image. The image is rather a monster of time—in which time does not properly tell time. It is, in the wording of Werner Hamacher, a "*monstruum* without *monstration.*"[20]

IV.

Let us return to this strange photograph. Taken on October 23, 1940, it stages a scene of reading that asks to be read in relation to the ruin and violence within which it takes place. This ruin and violence includes not only the ruin and violence given in the photograph, but also that effected by the German Luftwaffe air raids on London. One year after it invaded Poland, Germany began its Blitz on London in early September. It turned to night bombing in early October, and continued its barrage of bombs and incendiaries until November 13. Over six hundred bombers were directed against London in the initial Blitz. Until November 13, with only ten days excepted, between 150 and 300 Luftwaffe bombers dropped at least one hundred tons of explosives on London each and every night. Thirteen hundred tons of high explosives and almost one million incendiary bombs were dropped, killing more than thirteen thousand people and injuring twenty thousand more. First blasting the densely populated dockland streets of terraced houses, warehouses, and factories, these bombs and explosives eventually brought fires and the spread of burning embers across the city of London, in the process transforming it. Roads were blocked with debris, bus and rail services were dislocated, communication links were interrupted and even engulfed by fire. Churches, schools, hospitals, public houses, shops, and houses were ruined. Pavements and streets were covered with wreckage and the fine, frosty glitter of powdered glass left behind by shattered windows and collapsed roofs everywhere. Thousands of people were left homeless. Reading itself declined due to sheltering in ill-lit spaces. Moreover, by October 9, more than one hundred thousand books had been destroyed or severely damaged in the bombing of University College Library. The attacks were so intense, that the Blitz eventually became routine. Air-raid sirens were even at times ignored unless the noise of gunfire or bombs was dangerously close.[21]

During the two months of sustained bombing, the space called "London"—a space with an immense and stratified history, with its walls, its buildings, and its streets—became a space that could no longer be inhabited in the same way, that could no longer be recognized as itself: the German Blitz in fact attacked space more than it did people. During World War II, England lost about 365,000 people—only half the number killed in World War I. The destruction of property, however, included damage to four million houses, and the total destruction of nearly half a million.[22] This destruction also included the destruction of revered and talismanic buildings such as Holland House. The last of the great country estates in London and one of Europe's last international salons, this seventeenth-century Tudor house was completely destroyed except for its east wing when, on the night of September 27, incendiary bombs dropped on its west wing. From the mid-eighteenth century until the 1840s, Holland House had been a political, social, and literary center for the Whig aristocracy. It was frequented by the most eminent patricians and intellectuals of the day: associates of the *Edinburgh Review*, members of the diplomatic corps in London, ambassadors and ministers of European courts, and literati such as Byron. A transmission center for patronage, political discussion, and gossip, Holland House was once referred to by Charles Greville as "the house of Old Europe."[23]

Taken one day after the one-hundredth anniversary of Lord Holland's death, this strange photograph therefore figures, among so many other things, the ruin and memory of "Old Europe": the explosion and collapse of a certain idea of Europe—with its traditions, hierarchies, social orders and institutions—and the traces of its survival in the still-standing archive. It evokes a violence that wished to reduce "Europe" to rubble, that hoped to destroy an "older" Europe in the name of a younger one attempting to establish its hegemony across the Continent and beyond. Responding to this violence in the name of another Europe, England and its allies stalled this European "unification" by combating Nazism.

This war over the identity of Europe, over its spaces and borders, is no doubt indissociable from a Europe whose spaces and borders are today again not given. This

Lapsus
Imaginis

Europe that has never been and will never be identical to itself, this Europe is again, as Derrida has noted, the uncertain space of racism, anti-Semitism, and nationalist fanaticism—and this despite and even because of recent events in Eastern Europe and the former Soviet Union: what we call "perestroïka," the fall of the Berlin Wall, the different movements of "democratization," and the various calls for "new" national identities.[24] This Europe was already written into both the space of Holland House and the space of this ruined image, this image of ruins. It is this space—a space that ruins the distinction between the private and the public—that will be translated in 1955–57 into a people's park that includes a youth hostel, teashops, and a series of lawns. The postwar effort that works to transform this once aristocratic enclave into a more democratic public space will repeat the explosive work of the violence sealed within this ruined image.

V.

War not only names the central experience of modernity; it also plays an essential role in our understanding of technological reproduction in general and of photography in particular. As Ernst Jünger noted in 1930, evoking the relation that for him exists between war and photography:

> A war that is distinguished by the high level of technical precision required to wage it is bound to leave behind documents which are different from and more numerous than those of earlier times. It is the same intelligence, whose weapons of annihilation can locate the enemy to the exact second and meter, that labors to preserve the great historical event in fine detail. . . . Included among the documents of particular precision, which have only recently been at the disposal of human intelligence, are photographs, of which a large supply accumulated during the war. Day in and day out, optical lenses were pointed at the combat zones alongside the mouths of rifles and cannons. As instruments of technological consciousness, they preserved the image of these devastated landscapes.[25]

For Jünger, there can be no war without photography. This is why the entirety of his writings on photography suggest the ways in which the German war of light and disaster illuminated the links between photographic technology and the techniques of modern warfare. While the English began equipping their bombers with photographic apparatuses, the German Blitz flashed its death across the skies and landscape of Europe. Dividing night into night and day, it illumined the space of war. "What had taken place in the darkroom of Niépce and Daguerre," Paul Virilio explains, "was now happening in the skies of England."[26] Indeed, we could even say that the blackout that was enforced during the Blitz— the event that, according to historian Philip Ziegler, "impinged most forcibly on the life of the average Londoner"[27]—transformed the entirety of London into a kind of gigantic darkroom, into a massively photographic space.

Like the camera flash that enables the emergence of an image, the Luftwaffe bombers dropped incendiaries both to trace the bombing area in London and to light up nocturnal targets. London became subject to the glare of explosives and the blinding light of the searchlights whose skyward beams traced a kind of luminous cat's cradle in the night. To say that there could be no Blitz without the production of images is to say that there could be no lightning war without the flash of the camera.[28] No Blitz without photography—and in part because both are a matter of speed. Like the rapidity of the Blitz, the technology of the camera also resides in its speed. Like the instantaneity of a lightning flash, the camera, in the split-second temporality of the shutter's blink, seizes an image, an image that Benjamin likens to the activity of lightning. "The dialectical image," he tells us, "flashes (*aufblitzendes*)."[29]

Eduardo Cadava

Linked to the flashes of memory, the suddenness of the perception of similarity, and the irruption of events and images, Benjamin's vocabulary of lightning helps register what comes to pass in the opening and closing of vision. Lightning signals the force and experience of an interruption that enables a sudden moment of clarification or illumination. What is illumined or lighted by the punctual intensity of this or that strike of lightning, however—the emergence of an image, for example—can at the same time be burned, incinerated, consumed in flames. This is why, Benjamin notes in his discussion of the German mourning play, the

content of truth does not emerge in an unveiling, rather it manifests itself in a process that one might call, in a simile, the flaming up of the veil that enters the circle of ideas, the burning of the work, in which its form reaches the high point of its luminosity.[30]

A luminosity that blinds as much as it enlightens, the flame tells us that truth springs forth in the burning of the work—the work that burns, that is being consumed by the flames, but also the work that burns its contents. We could even say that truth means the making of ashes. That there can be neither truth nor photography without ashes means that, like Benjaminian allegory, both take place in a state of ruin, in a state that moves away from itself in order to be what it is. Like the photograph that tells us what is no longer before us, truth can only be read, if it can be read at all, in the traces of what is no longer present. That history is to be read in its transience means that its truth comes in the form of ruins. There is no photograph that does not turn its "subjects" to ruins. This is why this image of ruins tells us that, in every image, in every trace, and consequently in every experience, there is this explosion and incineration, this experience of explosion and incineration, which is experience itself.[31] Effacing what it inscribes, the image bears witness to the impossibility of testimony. It remains as a testament to loss.

VI.

In Benjamin's etiology, shock is what characterizes our experience. In his essay on Baudelaire, he links this shock to the work of the camera, claiming that the camera gives the moment "a posthumous shock."[32] In linking the experience of shock to the structure of delay built into the photographic event, he suggests what for him is the latency of experience; namely, the distance between an event and our experience or understanding of it. This distance tells us that we experience an event indirectly, through our mediated and defensive reaction to it. For Benjamin, what characterizes experience in general—experience understood in its strict sense as the traversal of a danger, the passage through a peril—is that it retains no trace of itself: experience experiences itself as the vertigo of memory, as an experience whereby what is experienced is not experienced.

It is here that we can begin to register the possibility of a history which is no longer founded on traditional models of experience and reference. The suggestion that we cannot experience experience directly requires that history emerge where understanding or experience cannot.[33] In Benjamin's words:

The greater the shock factor in particular impressions, the more vigilant consciousness has to be in screening stimuli; the more efficiently it does so, the less these impressions enter long experience [*Erfahrung*] and the more they correspond to the concept of isolated experience [*Erlebnis*]. Perhaps the special achievement of shock defense is the way it assigns an incident a precise point in time in consciousness, at the cost of the integrity of the incident's contents.[34]

Following Proust, he tells us that "only what has not been experienced explicitly and consciously, what has not

Lapsus
Imaginis

happened to the subject as an isolated experience [*Erlebnis*], can become a component of *mémoire involontaire*."[35] It is what is not experienced in an event that paradoxically accounts for the belated and posthumous shock of historical experience. If history is to be a history of this "posthumous shock," it can only be referential to the extent that, in its occurrence, it is neither perceived nor experienced directly. For Benjamin, history can be grasped only in its disappearance.

This helps explain why these three men, looking at the books in this photograph, remain passive to the disaster behind them: it is as though what has happened has not happened. If we wish to situate the photograph within a discussion of the relation between shock and photography, we should note that, in its depiction of the men's seeming indifference to the disaster around them, the photograph also exhibits its relation to what was perhaps the most pervasive rhetoric of British propaganda during the war and, in particular, during the Blitz: the sense that—despite the fear, apprehension, confusion, and demoralization that so often attends war—the British were models of courage and fortitude. The speeches of Winston Churchill, the broadcasts of J. B. Priestley, and the daily and weekly reports of the BBC Radio News helped perpetuate the sense that civilian morale not only survived exposure to the violence and trauma of war but also guaranteed, in the wording of Angus Calder, "that the British people, as a whole, deserved to save Europe and defeat Hitler."[36] Exhibiting calmness, indifference to the danger around them, resolution in the face of loss and death, Londoners worked to manufacture an image of themselves as exemplary survivors. The photograph of the bombed-out Holland House Library is only one of the innumerable photographs and representations that were circulated to confirm

Eduardo Cadava

this image of English endurance.[37] The effects of this propagandistic work were legible everywhere, and led Anna Freud—who with several of her colleagues had set up a network of psychiatric clinics to deal with the neuroses caused by the bombing—to say that she had never seen anything like the calm exhibited by the Londoners. As Ziegler notes, she expressed her surprise that "not one case of shell-shock had been reported and that she had not heard of a single breakdown that could be directly attributed to the bombing."[38]

If, however, this photograph conjures what Calder has called "The Myth of the Blitz"—the myth that the entirety of the British population exhibited courage and strength in the midst of violence and death—it also suggests another model for reading the presumed distance from disaster, a model offered to us by Anna Freud's father. In *Beyond the Pleasure Principle*, for example—and here he anticipates Benjamin's reflections on shock—Sigmund Freud insists on the distance between a traumatic event and our experience of it. Confronted by an event that paralyzes us by the magnitude of its demand, an event that we recognize as a danger, we fend off the danger through the process of repression: the danger is in some way inhibited, and its precipitating cause—in this instance, the Blitz itself—is forgotten.

The forgetting that attends the experience of shock, "the fact of latency," as Cathy Caruth has argued in regard to Freud, "would seem to consist, not in the forgetting of a reality that can hence never be fully known, but in an inherent latency within the experience itself." The historical power of shock, she goes on to explain, "is not just that the experience is repeated after its forgetting, but that it is only in and through its inherent forgetting that it is first experienced at all."[39] The force of trauma is so terrible and pervasive that it leads us to believe that we have not been touched. This is why, Blanchot explains, "we are not contemporaries of the disaster"[40];

it remains "unexperienced. It is what escapes the very possibility of experience."[41] In the long run, he goes on to suggest, the disaster is perhaps our own passivity to the disaster: we experience what we experience in the mode of forgetting. This is why there can be no reading that is not under the threat of disaster, that is not under its surveillance. Disaster is perhaps what gives us our right to read. Reading under the light of disaster—what Blanchot calls "the passivity of reading"[42] or "passivity's reading"—lets us know why ruin and disaster belong to the banal. As Benjamin would have it, "That things just go on," and have gone on this way, "this is the catastrophe. . . . Catastrophe is not what threatens to occur at any given moment; it is what is given at any given moment."[43]

Staging the relation between traumatic experience and the photographic effect—both perform their work by arresting time and experience, by disordering memory and the work of representation—this remarkable photograph evokes a devastation that destroys our ability to refer to it. It exhibits, in the wording of Rosalind Krauss, a "trauma of signification."[44]

VII.

What is our world? What can our world be if it can be revealed only by technology in general and photography in particular? If technology is a mode of unveiling, in what way can our world—a world that is always touched by technicity and therefore no longer simply a world— reveal the essence of technology? If modernity is another name for the globalization of the world, can our world be said to globalize the meaning of history? These are the questions that motivate Benjamin's efforts to represent history and modernity in the language of photography. In his "Theses on the Concept of History," assembled shortly before his suicide in 1940 while fleeing from Nazi Germany, Benjamin persistently conceives of history in the language of photography, as though he wished to offer us a series of snapshots of his latest reflections on history. Written from the perspective of disaster and catastrophe, the theses are a historico-biographical time-lapse camera that flashes across Benjamin's concern, especially in his writings of the 1930s, over the question of what remains of what passes into history—a question he explores in terms of the photograph.

Within the photograph—as I have suggested, a condensation of past, present, and future—time is no longer to be understood as continuous and linear, but rather as spatial, an imagistic space that Benjamin calls a "constellation" or a "monad." Where thinking suddenly stops in a constellation pregnant with tensions," he writes, "it gives that constellation a shock, by which it crystallizes into a monad. A historical materialist approaches a historical object only where it confronts him as a monad."[45] If this break from the present signals the taking over of a past, the arrest of present thought in a constellation or monad "blasts" this past open. It "shatters the continuum of history" and calls forth the history hidden in any given image. It discloses the breaks, within history, from which history emerges. Focusing on what is sealed or hidden within an image, on the transitoriness of events, on the relation between any given moment and all of history, Benjamin's historical materialist seeks to delineate the contours of a history whose chance depends on overcoming the idea of history as the mere reproduction of a past.

This history emerges in a moment of disaster, in the time of the disaster that structures the danger of history. In the almost-no-time of this breakdown, thinking comes to a standstill. It experiences itself as an interruption. As Benjamin explains, historical thinking involves "not only the movements of thoughts, but

Lapsus
Imaginis

their arrest as well."[46] As he explains elsewhere—citing a remark by Ernst Bloch—history happens when it "flashes its Scotland badge,"[47] when it enacts this force of arrest. This is why he associates the radical temporality of the photograph with what he elsewhere calls the "caesura in the movement of thought."[48] Announcing a point when the "past and the present moment flash into a constellation," the photographic image—like the image in general—interrupts history and thereby facilitates another history, another possibility for history. It translates an aspect of time into something like a certain *space*, a certain interval, and, in so doing, it works dialectically to spatialize time and temporalize space—without ever stopping time or preventing time from being "itself," since time can never be thought away from this spatialization. Within the photograph, time presents itself to us *as* this "spacing." What is spaced here—within what Benjamin elsewhere calls "the space of history [*Geschichtsraum*]"[49]—are the always becoming and disappearing moments of time itself. It is precisely this continual process of becoming and disappearing that, for Benjamin, characterizes the movement of time. Effecting a certain spacing of time, the photograph gives way to an occurrence: the emergence of history as an image.

This is why, from the very moment of the photographic event, the image that telescopes history into a moment—an abbreviation or miniaturization that tells us that history can end or break off—suggests that what inaugurates history is written into a context that history itself may never completely comprehend. This context exceeds the limits of its representation. This is why what is at stake in reading any image is the possibility of registering what withdraws from the image—its semantic and referential dimension—and what remains of the image after meaning has withdrawn

from it. To read what exceeds the permeable borders of an image therefore demands that we respond to what remains of the image, to what is not exhausted in our effort to understand these remains, beyond or before the temporalization of the image—a temporalization that renders signification and reference possible, even as it remains irreducible to them.

To write history—to read an image—is therefore not to re-present some past or present presence. "To articulate the past historically," Benjamin writes, "does not mean to recognize it 'the way it really was.' It means appropriating a memory as it flashes up in a moment of danger."[50] History therefore begins where memory is endangered, during the flash that marks its emergence and disappearance. It begins where representation ends. As Jean-Luc Nancy tells us,

> The historian's work—which is never a work of memory—is a work of representation in many senses, but it is representation with respect to something that is not representable, and that is history itself.[51]

This means that history and memory can only occur to the extent that they ceaselessly move away from us. If it were not for the disappearing trace of their own transience, history and memory would in fact never happen.

VIII.

This is why the movement of history corresponds to the photographic event: both ask us to think about what happens when an image comes to pass. In the fifth of his "Theses on the Concept of History," Benjamin addresses the possibility of seizing the image of the past for and in the present, suggesting that the "true picture" of history intends the present:

> The true image of the past flits by. The past can be seized only as an image that flashes up [*aufblitzt*] at the moment of its recognizability, and is never seen again . . . . For it is an irretrievable image of the past which threatens to disappear in any present that does not recognize itself as intended in that image"[52]

Eduardo
Cadava

What "threatens to disappear" here is not the past, but an "irretrievable image of the past." While we might say that we can recognize ourselves in this image of the past only insofar as we are destined by it, the temporality of this picture of history coincides with an interruption of both recognition and intention: it is irretrievable, it can neither be recognized nor intentionally realized in the present. This is why what the image intends is the irretrievability of the present itself.

This image of the past—and of the irretrievable present it intends—may be "fleeting" and "flashing" but it is also susceptible to being held fast—even if what is seized is only the image in its disappearance. In other words, if "the true picture of the past flits by," it is not so much that we are unable to grasp the truth of the past, but rather that the *true* picture of the past *flits by*, the *true* picture of the past is the one that is always in a state of passing away. If Benjamin suggests that a "true picture of the past" does not give us history—or rather, is the only thing of history we get—he still suggests that it can be viewed as true. This is why to understand history as an image is neither to assert that history is a myth nor to suggest that a certain "historical reality" remains hidden, behind our images. Rather, in Benjamin, it is always as if we were suspended between both: either something happens that we are unable to represent (in which case all we have are images that substitute for reality), or nothing happens but the production of historically marked fictional images. In either case, the image is a principle of articulation between language and history. This principle is indissociable from what, within the image, inaugurates history according to the laws of photography, the laws that determine—even as they are determined by—the involuntary emergence of an image. As Benjamin suggests in his notes to the "Theses," "History in the strict sense is an image from involuntary memory, an image which suddenly occurs to the subject of history in the moment of danger."[53]

For Benjamin, these laws not only account for the force of images on whatever we might call the "reality" of history, but also for the essential imagism at work within the movement and constitution of history. Images are essentially involved in the historical acts of the production of meaning. Their links with knowledge give them their force, and hence their consequence within the domains of history and politics. This is why the materialism of Benjamin's theory of history can be allegorized in the photographic image. To the extent that the function of the camera is to make images, the historiography produced by the camera involves the construction of photographic structures that both produce and reconfigure historical significance and understanding. Benjamin makes this point in his drafts to the "Theses," in a passage that not only understands history as imagistic, as textual, but also links it to the citational structure of photography itself:

> If one wants to consider history as a text, then what a recent author says of literary texts would apply to it. The past has deposited in it images, which one could compare to those captured by a light-sensitive plate. 'Only the future has developers at its disposal which are strong enough to allow the image to come to light in all its details. . . .' The historical method is a philological one, whose foundation is the book of life. 'To read what was never written,' says Hofmannsthal. The reader, to be thought of here, is the true historian.[54]

For Benjamin, the image can only "enter into legibility" at a particular time: when possible pasts emerge, like an image from a photographic negative, to meet us from future possibilities. This is why every image is an image from the future—an image of possible, future pasts. An image of the future, the image can never be said to exist.

IX.

Writing of the Emperor Shih Huang Ti, who "ordered the erection of the almost infinite wall of China" and "who also

Lapsus
Imaginis

decreed that all books prior to him be burned," Jorge Luis Borges suggests, in his 1950 essay, "The Wall and the Books," that "the burning of the libraries and the erection of the wall are operations which in some secret way cancel each other." He goes on to explain that "the wall in space and the fire in time were magic barriers designed to halt death," since "all things long to persist in their being." Nevertheless, if Shih Huang Ti walled in his empire because he knew that it was perishable and destroyed the books because he understood that they were sacred, this little parable about the preservation and abolition of history tells us that there can be no burning of books without the erecting of walls and no creating of walls without the burning of books—and this even if these acts are "not simultaneous."[55]

But what if the walls are walls of books that remain standing, while buildings are burned? What is space when it is linked to both texts and violence? What is it when it belongs to memory? This photograph—only one small piece of the mass of archival photographic material given to us by the war—this photograph belongs to the questions of artificial memory and of the modern modalities of archivation.[56] Affecting the entirety of our relation to the world, these questions not only touch on the relation between technology and memory, on the consequences of new techniques of archivation on our conception of history, but also on the question of whether or not there is an outside of the archive. In what way does the archive presume the possibility of memorization, of repetition, or of reproduction, and thereby a certain exteriority—the exteriority of what is to be remembered, repeated, or reproduced? To what extent does the logic of repetition that defines the archive belong to what Freud understands as the death drive, to destruction in general? To say that the archive begins with the breakdown of memory is to say that it begins with forgetfulness, with an amnesia that ruins its commemorative principle. This is why, as Derrida argues in *Archive Fever*, the question of the archive is never simply a question of the past but also a question of the future.[57] To the extent that the archive depends on both the preservation and destruction of inscriptions, its structure would seem to imply reference to things beyond its limits. But this strange image of shattered archival space is itself destined to the archive, is even archivized, fleetingly, in the pages of this essay. If the violence that exposes the archive to its radical precariousness, to its fragility, allows us to glimpse its finitude, this violence also enables its survival. We need only recall the history of the burning of libraries—from Alexandria to Strasbourg to Louvain—and all innumerable written accounts and literatures these conflagrations have occasioned.[58]

If the archive names a body of texts whose existence is threatened by war, the war also assures its continued existence. In *The Myth of the Blitz*, Calder notes that

> The Blitz (the bombing of 1940–41) exists . . . in an uncountable proliferation of published accounts and published and unpublished documents as well as in the tape-recorded or filmed memories of 'talking head' survivors.

"No archive of such abundance," he goes on to say, "exists for any other 'major event' in British history."[59] In linking the destructive violence of the Blitz—a violence often directed at the archive, as evidenced in the German bombing of the library at Louvain in May of 1940 or in the various book burnings ordered by the Nazi regime—to the proliferation of texts, Calder here suggests that the Blitz strangely helped preserve the archive, that the very destruction that exposed the archive to ruin also permitted and conditioned it. Not only is violence the very condition of this preservation, but, in turn, we might say that there could be no war, no destruction, without the archive: the archive ensures

**Eduardo
Cadava**

that violence will persist. This fact is all the more legible today when the militarization of technology corresponds to the textualization of its weaponry. Today missiles and warheads can be understood more and more as missives, as dispatches in writing, guided as they are by information and codes, inscriptions and traces.[60] To say that today's missiles are indissociably linked to language, to texts and writing, is not to reduce them to the inefficacy that some would rush to see in books. Rather, it signals—exposes and explodes—what in writing corresponds to the power of destruction: no destruction without texts, and no texts without destruction. As Derrida puts it, locating the Freudian death drive within the archive itself, what makes archivization possible is also what

> exposes to destruction, and in truth menaces with destruction, introducing *a priori* forgetfulness and the archiviolithic at the heart of the monument . . . . The archive always works, and *a priori*, against itself.[61]

The "silent vocation" of the death drive, he adds, is "to burn the archive and to incite amnesia."[62]

If texts survive the death they bring, however, it is because they come as what exceeds the categories of life and death. The archive has always been a name for both what passes away and what remains. The Blitz and its effects announce the paradoxes of the archive: as what always refers elsewhere, the archive exceeds its borders, enacting the "anarchivization" without which it would not be what it is. As Blanchot explains, citing and responding to a sentence from Mallarmé:

> '*There is no explosion except a book.*' A book: a book among others, or a reference to the unique, the last and essential Liber, or, more exactly, the great Book which is always one among others, any book at all, already without importance or beyond important things. 'Explosion,' a book: this means that the book is not the laborious assemblage of a totality finally attained, but has for its being the noisy, silent shattering which without the book would not take place (would not affirm itself). But it also means that since the

> book itself belongs to shattered being—to being violently exceeded and thrust out of itself—the book gives no sign of itself save its own explosive violence, the violence with which it excludes itself, the thunderous refusal of the plausible: the outside in its becoming, which is that of shattering.[63]

Pointing to the "dying of a book" that is "in all books,"[64] he evokes Mallarmé's insistence on the abolition and effacement of the book. As Mallarmé puts it in *Variations sur un sujet*, it is "a question of disaster in the library" ("*il s'agissait de désastre dans la librairie*").[65] For both Blanchot and Mallarmé, this disaster—the dispersion and explosion without which a book would not be a book—is what brings us to reading.[66] But this is why reading books and images means: reading the ruins left behind by a shattering explosion, reading the traces of what is no longer present. This is also why, we might say, ruins and traces always await us.

X.

There can be no image that does not emerge from the wounds of time and history, that is not ruined by the loss and finitude within which it takes place, without ever taking place. This means that the image testifies not only to its own impossibility but also to the disappearance and destruction of testimony and memory. This is why, if the history and events sealed within this photograph of the bombed-out Holland House Library call out for memory—and for a memory of the violence and trauma it evokes—this memory could never be a memory that aims to restore or commemorate. If the past is experienced in terms of loss and ruin, it is because it cannot be recovered. Nevertheless, that this violence and trauma, this loss and ruin, live on in the various historical, political, religious, or literary forms that today inherit their legacy

Lapsus

Imaginis

means that the experiences to which they would refer are not behind us. There is no historical "after" to the trauma of loss and violence.[67] If we can no longer believe that memory and commemoration will help us prevent disaster in the future, however, we are still obliged to imagine a means of remembering what remains without remaining, what, destroying and consuming itself, still demands to be preserved, even if within a history that can never enter into history. If nothing can replace what has been lost to history, is it possible to interrupt the course of history and its catastrophes, or are we endlessly condemned to reiterate and enact this condition of loss and displacement? This question tells us not only why we must learn to read the past—to read, that is, the irretrievable images of the past—in a way that knows how these images threaten to disappear to us as long as we do not recognize ourselves in them, but ourselves as the ones who, touched by the ruins of time and history, are no longer simply ourselves. This is why, as the Italian artist, Salvatore Puglia, has suggested, what remains for us is

> to collect the fleeting images of what has disappeared, to recollect the floating fragments of this history of disappearance. What remains is the possibility of a gesture: to hand, to hold out, in the scattered memories to which we are condemned, some vestigia, some expressions of a multiple anamnesis.[68]

What remains are the fragments, the ruins of an image or photograph—perhaps one like this.

Eduardo
Cadava

1. This essay began several years ago in response to Mark Wigley's invitation to contribute to a special issue of *Assemblage* devoted to the relation between space and violence. It is partially drawn from this shorter early version, published under the title *"Leseblitz*: On the Threshold of Violence" in *Assemblage* 20, from two longer and different versions I delivered at the Tate Gallery in London in the spring of 1997 and at the Department of Art and Art History at Stanford University in the spring of 2000, and from a brief meditation on the relation between images and history entitled "Vanishing Remains," published in *Via Dalle Immagini: Verso un'arte della storia*, ed. Salvatore Puglia (Salerno: Edizioni Menabo, 1999). I am grateful to the National Monuments Record in London for permitting me to reproduce this image of the bombed-out Holland House Library and to the many friends and colleagues who have discussed the essay with me in all its manifestations. I am especially grateful to Hal Foster and Benjamin Buchloh for encouraging me to gather, recontextualize, and expand these ruins and fragments into the present essay.

2. Maurice Blanchot, *The Writing of the Disaster*, trans. Ann Smock (Lincoln: University of Nebraska Press, 1986), 1.

3. Walter Benjamin, *The Arcades Project*, trans. Howard Eiland and Kevin McLaughlin (Cambridge: Belknap Press of Harvard University Press, 1999), 462-463. For the German text, see the *Passagen-Werk*, in *Gesammelte Schriften*, 7 vols., eds. Rolf Tiedemann and Hermann Schweppenhaüser (Frankfurt am Main: Suhrkamp Verlag, 1972), vol. 5, 577-578.

4. I am indebted on this point—and in my discussion of Benjamin's notion of the image's "historic index" in general—to Christopher Fynsk's "The Claim of History," in his *Language & Relation* (Stanford: Stanford University Press, 1996), especially pages 212–223. Associating Benjamin's discussion of the historic index of the image with what, in the second thesis of "Theses on the Concept of History," is referred to as the image's "secret index," Fynsk describes the relation it signifies in terms of what Benjamin calls a "secret agreement between generations" (see "Theses on the Concept of Philosophy," in *Illuminations*, ed. Hannah Arendt, trans. Hary Zohn [New York: Schocken Books, 1968], 254. See also *Gesammelte Schriften*, vol. 1, 693–694: "The past 'carries with it' a temporal index, the date of its emergence and of its expiration." This expiration date, he argues, means that the image "must be read by" and "will not be readable before" this date. Moreover, "if the present does not read the past (and itself as *implicated* in the past)—if it fails to read and write itself—the constellation of past and present will simply flit by" (see *Language and Relation*, 220–21). This is why the moment of reading is critical and dangerous: the past and the present are both at stake.

5. Benjamin's conception of the index should be read in its difference from Charles S. Peirce's distinction between the "index," which bears a physical relation to the object it represents, and the "icon," which resembles the object without having any necessary physical relation to it. See Peirce's "Logic as Semiotic: The Theory of Signs," in *The Philosophy of Peirce: Selected Writings*, ed. Justus Buchler (New York: Harcourt, Brace, 1950), 98–119. For an elaboration of the pertinence of Peirce's meditations to an understanding of photography in general, see Rosalind Krauss's "Notes on the Index," in *The Originality of the Avant-Garde and Other Modernist Myths* (Cambridge: MIT Press, 1985), 196–219.

6. Benjamin, *Arcades Project*, 470; *Gesammelte Schriften*, 5:587.

7. The photograph was taken by a photographer named Harrison, who worked for Fox Photos. We know nothing of its early circulation—Fox Photos itself was bombed during the Blitz and lost many of its documents and negatives—although it does appear that the censor of the Press and Censorship Bureau released the image for publication immediately after it was taken. What we know is that, in 1926, the financier Richard Fox, the photographer Reginald Salmon, and the journalist Ernest Beaver joined together to purchase a company called Special Press, and renamed it Fox Photos. In a letter from November 20, 2000, Sarah McDonald, a curator at the Hulton Getty (which bought the Fox Photo collection in 1989), writes that: "the agency soon established an international reputation, providing a service of press and industrial photography at a time when the new photo-led magazines and newspapers were clamouring for picture stories." The agency included the photographers Reggie Speller, Ernst Hess (who was one of the first to use color film for reportage), and William Vanderson. As McDonald notes, "Fox was one of the first agencies to use color extensively in outside presswork, with excellent coverage of personalities and royals. During the war years, the agency purchased Kodachrome 1 color film, virtually unused in the United Kingdom in 1939, in the United States and shipped it across the Atlantic on convoys. The exposed film was convoyed back to the States for processing and sale. Transparencies were later shipped back to England, forming a now rare collection of color World War II material." She also includes one interesting anecdote from the bombing of the library itself, a little story about the survival of ruins and, in particular, the circulation of books in ruin: "the damage was extensive and many volumes were destroyed. A librarian from the Augustin Rischgitz Picture Collection, with the help of a couple of GI's and some wheelbarrows, salvaged several sets of books from the wreckage which were otherwise to be disposed of, including a valuable seventeenth-century encyclopaedia. Hulton subsequently bought the Rischgitz Collection and we still have these volumes in our possession today. On the inner covers are the original Holland library plates."

8. Denis Hollier, "The Death of Paper: A Radio Play," *October* 78 (fall 1996): 4.

9. Benjamin, *Gesammelte Schriften*, vol. 2, 134.

10. Benjamin, *Arcades Project*, 463; *Gesammelte Schriften*, vol. 5, 578.

11. Benjamin, *Arcades Project*, 475; *Gesammelte Schriften*, vol. 5, 594.

12. Benjamin, *Arcades Project*, 475; *Gesammelte Schriften*, vol. 5, 594.

13. Walter Benjamin, *Charles Baudelaire: A Lyric Poet in the Era of High Capitalism*, trans. Harry Zohn (London: New Left Books, 1973), 87. See also Benjamin, *Gesammelte Schriften*, vol. 1, 590.

14. Roland Barthes, *Camera Lucida: Reflections on Photography*, trans. Richard Howard (New York: Farrar, Straus, and Giroux, 1981), 88–89.

15. Walter Benjamin, *The Origin of German Tragic Drama*, trans. John Osborne (London: New Left Books, 1977), 177. See also Benjamin, *Gesammelte Schriften*, 1:353–4.

16. See Jacques Derrida, *Memoirs of the Blind: The Self-Portrait and Other Ruins*, trans. Pascale-Anne Brault and Michael Naas (Chicago: University of Chicago Press, 1993), 68–69. There are, of course, several indications that Benjamin did not restrict his discussion of ruins to a theme of the baroque culture. In the "Berlin Chronicle," for example—in a passage that, suggesting that memory is a medium in which debris and buried ruins are reinterred in the act of recollection, presents the image as a ruin—he writes: "memory is not an instrument for exploring the past but its theater. It is the medium of past experience, just as the earth is the medium in which dead cities lie buried . . . . For the 'matter itself' is merely a deposit, a stratum, which yields only to the most meticulous investigation what constitutes the real treasure hidden within the earth: the images, severed from all earlier associations, that stand—like precious fragments or torsos in a collector's gallery—in the sober rooms of our later insights." See "Berlin Chronicle," trans. Edmund Jephcott, in *Walter Benjamin: Selected Writings, Volume 2, Part 2, 1931–1934*, ed. Michael W. Jennings et al. (Cambridge: Harvard University Press, 2005), 611. See also Benjamin, *Gesammelte Schriften*, 6:486–7.

17. I am indebted here to Werner Hamacher's discussion of the derangement of time in his essay, "Des Contrées des temps," in *Zeit-Zeichen: Aufschübe und Interferenzen zwischen Endzeit und Echtzeit*, eds. Georg Christoph Tholen and Michael O. Scholl (Weinheim: VCH, Acta Humaniora, 1990), 30–31. See also Blanchot's similar discussion in *The Writing of the Disaster*, especially pages 78–80.

18. Taking our point of departure from this image of disaster and ruin, we could even say that the truth of photography lies in the relation it stages between light and ashes. As Man Ray wrote in 1934, in an essay entitled

Lapsus
Imaginis

49

"The Age of Light," images are always only the residues of an experience. This is why what we "see" in an image is what has "survived an experience tragically, [what recalls] the event more or less clearly, like the undisturbed ashes of an object consumed by flames." See "The Age of Light," in *Photography in the Modern Era: European Documents and Critical Writings, 1913–1940*, ed. Christopher Phillips (New York: Metropolitan Museum of Art/Aperture, 1989), 53.

19. On this point, see Bernard Stiegler's "L'image discréte," in Jacques Derrida and Bernard Stiegler, *Échographies: de la télévision* (Paris: Éditions Galilée, 1996), 165.

20. See Werner Hamacher, "The Gesture in the Name: On Benjamin and Kafka," in *Premises: Essays on Philosophy and Literature from Kant to Celan*, trans. Peter Fenves (Cambridge: Harvard University Press, 1996), 316. Hamacher uses the phrase not to describe the image, but as a "name" for the name.

21. I have drawn here on Angus Calder's *The Myth of the Blitz* (London: Jonathan Cape, 1991), especially chapters 2 and 6, and Philip Ziegler's *London at War: 1939–1945* (New York: Alfred A. Knopf, 1995).

22. Calder, *Myth of the Blitz*, 41–42.

23. Cited in Leslie Mitchell's *Holland House* (London: Gerald

Duckworth & Co. Ltd., 1980), 306.

24. See Jacques Derrida, *The Other Heading: Reflections on Today's Europe*, trans. Pascale-Anne Brault and Michael B. Naas (Bloomington: Indiana University Press, 1992), 37–38.

25. See Ernst Jünger, "War and Photography," trans. Anthony Nassar, in *New German Critique* 59 (Spring/Summer 1993): 24.

26. Paul Virilio, *War and Cinema: The Logistics of Perception*, trans. Patrick Camiller (New York: Verso, 1989), 75. In the experience of the German light wars, the technology of warfare comes together with the techniques of perception. As Ernst Jünger writes in his essay "On Pain," "photography is a weapon employed by the modern type. For him, seeing is an act of aggression . . . . Today we already have guns equipped with optical cells, and even aerial and aquatic war machines with optical control systems" (Jünger, "Photography and the 'Second Consciousness': An Excerpt from 'On Pain'," trans. Joel Agee, in *Photography in the Modern Era: European Documents and Critical Writings, 1913–1940*, ed. Christopher Phillips [New York: Metropolitan Museum of Art/Aperture, 1989], 208–209). Capturing space and capturing images prove to be similar activities. This helps explain why, today more than ever, the camera is on the side of destruction. We need only recall the tragedy of what we now refer to as the "War in the Gulf." If this war taught us anything, it taught us what the Blitz already had suggested was true of all wars—that there can be no war that does not

depend on technologies of representation. This was a war whose entire operation depended on the technologies of sight: satellite aerial photography, light-enhancing television cameras, infrared flashes and sighting devices, thermographic images, and even cameras on warheads. This was a war in which the war machine was in every way a photographic machine. Linking war to photography and weapons to images, Jünger would go on to argue that modern technological warfare gives birth to a specifically modern form of perception organized around the experience of danger and shock. This is why, in his essay "On Danger"—written as an introduction to a 1931 collection of photographs and accounts of catastrophes and accidents titled *Der gefährliche Augenblick* [*The Dangerous Moment*]—he notes that the moment of danger can no longer be restricted to the realm of war. Identifying the contemporary zone of danger with the realm of technology in general, he claims that a modern type is arising in response to the "increased incursion of danger into daily life," whose aim is to develop an anaesthetized relation to danger (Jünger, "On Danger," trans. Donald Reneau, in *New German Critique* 59 (Spring/Summer 1993): 27). The effects of this anaesthetization can be read, in the image of the bombed-out Holland House Library, in the calm and leisure exhibited by the three men, and this despite the fact that they are standing amid several signs of war and danger.

27. See Ziegler, *London at War*, 67.

28. As Calder explains, the word "Blitz" was taken from *Blitzkrieg*, "lightning-war," and "applied by the world's press to the swift German conquest of Poland in September 1939, and then to the swift German advance in France and the Low Countries from May 10, 1940. As heavy bombing of London began in the late summer, the word 'Blitz' became 'almost overnight a British colloquialism for an air raid'" (*Myth of the Blitz*, 2).

29. Benjamin, *Arcades Project*, 473; *Gesammelte Schriften*, vol. 5, 592.

30. See Benjamin, *Origin of German Tragic Drama*, 31. See also *Gesammelte Schriften*, vol. 1, 211.

31. This sentence is drawn in part from a statement that Derrida made in a 1986 interview, published under the title "'There Is No One Narcissism' (Autobiophotographies)." See *Points… Interviews, 1974–1994*, ed. Elisabeth Weber, trans. Peggy Kamuf et. al. (Stanford: Stanford University Press, 1995), 209.

32. See Walter Benjamin, *The Writer of Modern Life: Essays on Charles Baudelaire*, ed. Michael W. Jennings (Cambridge: Harvard University Press, 2006), 191; *Gesammelte Schriften*, vol. 1, 630.

33. Cathy Caruth makes this point in her now canonical book, *Unclaimed Experience: Trauma, Narrative, and History* (Baltimore: The Johns Hopkins University Press, 1996), especially in Chapter 1.

34. See "On Some Motifs in Baudelaire," in *Walter Benjamin: Selected Writings, Volume 4, 1938–1940*, 319; *Gesammelte Schriften*, vol. 1, 615.

Eduardo Cadava

35. Benjamin, "On Some Motifs," 317; *Gesammelte Schriften*, vol. 1, 613.

36. See Calder, *Myth of the Blitz*, 142.

37. That the image is most probably staged can be confirmed by comparing it to the image of the bombed-out library that appeared only one day earlier in the *London Times*. In the photograph of the destroyed library that was reproduced in the October 22, 1940 issue of the *Times*, the books along the walls are much more disheveled, there is more debris scattered across the ground, there are no people inhabiting the space, and the atmosphere of the scene is strikingly more dark and ominous. In addition, the bombing of the library was not announced in the *Times* until over three weeks after the event. While this delay could be attributed to the disarray and chaos resulting from the Blitz, it is also most certainly an effect of censorship: the British Ministry of Information was reluctant to announce the destruction of some of the city's most revered and historically significant buildings. Both of these incidents—the reproduction of the image in the *Times* and the delay with which it appeared— suggest that the image before us was, among other things, staged to combat the psychological effects of the Blitz: the Germans may have tried to destroy our books, our buildings—the symbols of our civilization—but we are still reading. For an excellent discussion of the way in which the rhetoric of the survival of books—in the face of their incineration or threatened destruction—circulated within the several antifascist discourses of the Popular Front, see Hollier's "The Death of Paper." "Books may burn," he writes, "but the idea of the book, that is, the presence in itself of the idea of the Book, could never fall prey to the flames . . . book burning is destined to remain a symbolic act" (p.5). Hollier briefly discusses the image of the Holland House Library ruins, suggesting that it "fits perfectly into the line of antifascist iconography" (p.9).

38. Cited in Ziegler, *London at War*, 170–71.

39. Caruth, *Unclaimed Experience*, 17.

40. Blanchot, *Writing of the Disaster*, 6.

41. Blanchot, *Writing of the Disaster*, 7.

42. Blanchot, *Writing of the Disaster*, 101.

43. Walter Benjamin, "Central Park," trans. Lloyd Spencer, in *New German Critique* 34 (winter 1985): 50. See also *Gesammelte Schriften*, vol. 1, 683. Benjamin repeats this point in "Konvolut N." There, he writes: "The concept of progress should be grounded on the idea of catastrophe. That things 'just keep going on' is the catastrophe. Not an ever-present possibility, but what in each case is always given. Thus, Strindberg—in 'To Damascus'?—: Hell is not something that awaits us, but this very life, here and now." See *Arcades Project*, 473; *Gesammelte Schriften*, vol. 5, 592.

44. Krauss uses this phrase in reference to Marcel Duchamp's "With My Tongue in My Cheek." See "Notes on the Index," 206.

45. Benjamin, "Concept of History," 396; *Gesammelte Schriften*, vol. 1, 702–703.

46. Benjamin, "Concept of History," 396; *Gesammelte Schriften*, vol. 1, 702.

47. Benjamin, *Arcades Project*, 463; *Gesammelte Schriften*, vol. 5, 578.

48. Benjamin, *Arcades Project*, 475; *Gesammelte Schriften*, vol. 5, 595.

49. Benjamin, *Arcades Project*, 458; *Gesammelte Schriften*, vol. 5, 571.

50. Benjamin, "Concept of History," 391; *Gesammelte Schriften*, vol. 1, 695.

51. Jean-Luc Nancy, "Finite History," in *The States of Theory*, ed. David Carroll (New York: Columbia University Press, 1990), 166.

52. Benjamin, "Concept of History," 391; *Gesammelte Schriften*, vol. 1, 695.

53. Benjamin, *Gesammelte Schriften*, vol. 1, 1243.

54. Benjamin, *Gesammelte Schriften*, vol. 1, 1238.

55. See Jorge Luis Borges, "The Wall and the Books," trans. Eliot Weinberger, in *Jorge Luis Borges: Selected Non-Fictions*, ed. Eliot Weinberger (New York: Penguin Books, 1999), 344–346. Borges returns to the figure of the burning library in his 1977 collection of poems, *The History of the Night*. There, in a poem titled "Alexandria, A.D. 641," he writes: "Since the first Adam who beheld the night / And the day and the shape of his own hand, / Men have made up stories and have fixed / In stone, in metal, or on parchment / Whatever the world includes or dreams create. / Here is the fruit of their labor: the Library. / … The faithless say that if it were to burn, / History would burn with it. They are wrong. / Unceasing human work gave birth to this / Infinity of books. If of them all / Not even one remained, man would again / Beget each page and every line, / Each work and every love of Hercules, / And every teaching of every manuscript. / In the first century of the Muslim era, / I, that Omar who subdued the Persians / And who imposes Islam on the Earth, / Order my soldiers to destroy / By fire the abundant Library, / Which will not perish." See *Jorge Luis Borges: Selected Poems*, ed. Alexander Coleman (New York: Penguin Books, 1999), 393.

56. Charles Baudelaire was perhaps the first writer to define photography as an archive of memory. In his "Salon of 1859," in the section titled "The Modern Public and Photography," he uses this definition to distinguish photography from art. He notes, writing of photography: "If she saves from oblivion the crumbling ruins, books, engravings, and manuscript that time devours, the precious things whose form will disappear and which demand a place in the archives of our memory, she will deserve our thanks and applause." See "Salon of 1859," trans. P. E. Charvet, in *Selected Writings on Art and Literature* (London: Penguin Books, 1992), 297.

57. "The question of the archive is not," Derrida writes, "a question of the past. It is not the question of a concept dealing with the

Lapsus
Imaginis

past that might already be at our disposal or not at our disposal, an archivable concept of the archive. It is a question of the future, the question of the future itself, the question of a response, of a promise and of a responsibility for tomorrow. The archive: if we want to know what that will have meant, we will only know in times to come." See Jacques Derrida, *Archive Fever: A Freudian Impression*, trans. Eric Prenowitz (Chicago: University of Chicago Press, 1996), 36.

58. On the burning of the Louvain library, see Wolfgang Schivelbusch's *Die Bibliothek von Löwen: Eine Episode aus der Zeit der Weltkriege* (Munich: Carl Hanser Verlag, 1988).

59. Calder, *Myth of the Blitz*, 119.

60. On this point, see Virilio's *The Information Bomb*, trans. Chris Turner (New York: Verso, 2000). See also Derrida's "No Apocalypse, Not Now (Full Speed Ahead, Seven Missiles, Seven Missives," in *Diacritics* 14, no. 2 (Summer 1984): 29–30.

61. Derrida, *Archive Fever*, 12.

62. Derrida reinforces this point later when he suggests that "the archive is made possible by the death, aggression, and destruction drive, that is to say also by originary finitude and expropriation. But beyond finitude as limit, there is . . . . this properly in-finite movement of radical destruction without which no archive desire or fever would happen . . . [Freud's texts explain] why there is archivization and why anarchiving destruction belongs to the process of anarchivization and produces the very thing it reduces, on occasion to ashes, and beyond." *Archive Fever*, 94.

63. Blanchot, *Writing of the Disaster*, 124.

64. Blanchot, *Writing of the Disaster*, 124.

65. See "Étalages" in *Variations sur un sujet*, in *Oeuvres complètes*, eds. Henri Mondor and G. Jean-Aubry (Paris: Éditions Gallimard, 1945), 373.

66. In the wording of Blanchot, "Literature is only a domain of coherence and a common region so long as it does not exist, as long as it does not exist for itself and conceals itself. As soon as it appears in the distant presentiment of what it seems to be, it flies into pieces, it enters into the path of dispersion in which it refuses to be recognized by precise, identifiable signs." See "La Recherche du point zéro," in *Le livre à venir* (Paris: Gallimard, 1959), 277.

67. Evoking Theodor Adorno's famous claim about the impossibility of writing poetry after Auschwitz, Hamacher makes a similar point in relation to the possibility of writing history after an "absolute trauma." See his "Journal, Politics," trans. Peter Burgard et. al., in *Responses: On Paul de Man's Wartime Journalism,* eds. Werner Hamacher, Neil Hertz, and Thomas Keenan (Lincoln: University of Nebraska Press, 1988), 459.

68. This passage is from an unpublished manuscript titled "Abstracts of 'Abstracts (of Anamnesis).'" The text was delivered at the Alexander S. Onassis Center at New York University in conjunction with Puglia's exhibition, "Abstracts (of Anamnesis)" in the spring of 1995. On the necessity of interrupting or ruining the image, see Puglia's comments in an interview titled "An Art of the Possible" and included in Christopher Fynsk's *Infant Figures: The Death of the "Infans" and Other Scenes of Origin* (Stanford: Stanford University Press, 2000), 147–49.

Eduardo Cadava

Overseas

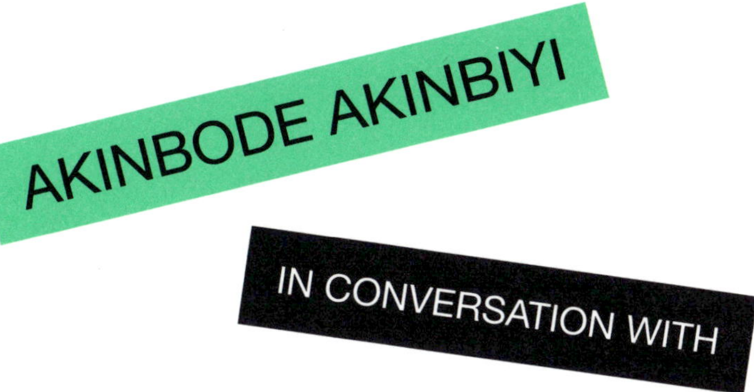

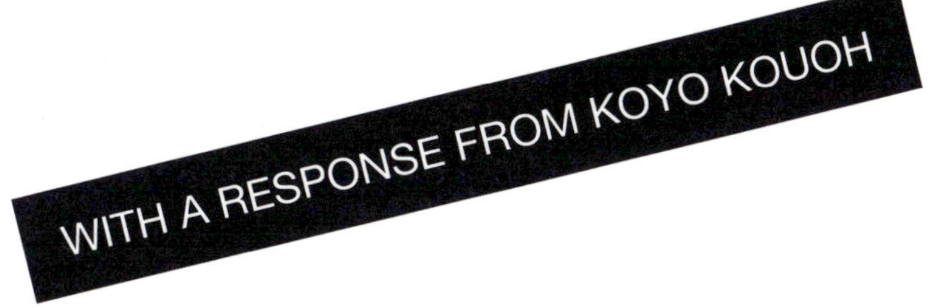

Akinbode Akinbiyi: In thinking about currency, something I always like to stress is that life is very much about giving and receiving, through conversation, all the time.

I'd like to read you something I wrote two or three years ago when Bonaventure invited me to be one of the co-curators of the Bamako Encounters in 2019. Over the course of that encounter, we produced a reader titled *Streams of Consciousness*, which I certainly recommend. I submitted my texts quite late, unfortunately, so they are at the very end.

Akinbode Akinbiyi
Bonaventure Soh
Bejeng Ndikung
Koyo Kouoh

Personal ruminations, born out of days and nights wandering, and endlessly up and down city sidewalks, meandering, forest paths, walking quietly along seafronts, the surf glistening in the night air.

I must say it's about wandering. I consider myself very much to be a wanderer, even more than a photographer or, actually, a being, a sentient being.

Where one stands, moves, where one's feet are firmly placed where it allows for the ability to look out, to look ahead and see what is out there. The landscape, the play of the afternoon light on city buildings, watching traffic shudder and stop, start up again, flow, speed by. The slower the wandering, the more taken in, perceived. Like some kind of silent griot, moving gracefully, purposefully in the afternoon cacophony of the inner city, feet reaching out carefully, deliberately, acutely aware of the ground, the pavement, of the vibrations quelling upwards through the limbs, the torso, beating and pulsating in constant regularity up to the heart, and further, deeper, into the intuition. The skin too sensually active, aware of the heat, the cloying fumes, the proximity of others, wending and forging their paths. The eyes flitter and scan fleetingly, striving simultaneously to focus on the immediacy of straight ahead and on the vagueness of the periphery. It is the ears, though, that are the most acute, most attuned to the constantly enveloping vibrations. They listen in, listen to, and, more often than not, see/hear more than the eyes. They strive to understand the sonority of the constant vibrations, decipher the various chords of the all-encompassing cacophony, the screeching brakes, the loud horn blasts of the articulated lorries, the fragmented sound bites of fleeting conversations. Like a dance, this firm-footed placement in the swirling movement of bodies and vehicles, amid the stoic silence of surrounding buildings. The standpoint becomes the vantage point, the look out and location of taking in, absorbing. Slowly, the gradual wish to fix the moment, to take, make, an image resonating with what is heard, what is so powerfully, momentarily embracing. This is the beginning of the photographic nitty gritty, the will, the urge, to make, to take, to bring into visual form. What to include, what to exclude within the frame, clearly demarcated in the viewfinder, on the screen. What should be the dominant motive. How to merge the foreground into the middle ground and to converge both into the background, all three planes stretching out further into an indeterminate distance, the infinity of the gaze. The inclusion or not of passersby, serendipitous players within the framed scene. No sooner than these parameters burst forth, they are quickly answered by eye-finger coordination and the almost instantaneous pressing down on the shutter button. Or more prescient, the touch-screen virtual tab. In another time, the wait to see the resultant image, chemical development in the home darkroom or giving the film in to be processed by a commercial lab. Now, in these present times of increasingly accelerating instant gratification, the photographer, the image maker, looks almost instantaneously at the screen to acknowledge what has been taken, made, or to use the militaristic term, captured. Today, an unimaginable overload of images generated, looked at, saved. Posted on social media platforms, disseminated in innumerable ways. They are often altered, enhanced, manipulated, to fit a particular algorithmic format. The original innocent standpoint gradually morphing in a sea swell of never-ending, constantly generated new images, flooding sensibilities and drowning everything in a swirl of disorientation. The onlooker adrift in a world of endless impressions, desperate for a foothold, longing for the assurance of the indisputable standpoint.[1]

Bonaventure Soh Bejeng Ndikung: Bode and I talk a lot about *listening* to photography. I think that's why, when I was invited to propose something for the last Bamako Biennial,

I derived the title of the exhibition from the title track on Max Roach and Abdullah Ibrahim's album *Streams of Consciousness*, which is lucid knowledge par excellence.

One of the things I was concerned with was not so much what photography *is*, which is a question each generation has been concerned with—but what it does. What can photography actually *do*? The excerpt I want to read is an effort to answer this question. What does photography do? What can it do? What might it do? This is from "Of a Photographic State of Being: Delivering the Photographic from Photography," which I dedicated to Bisi Silva and Okwui Enwezor.

I'll start with a short excerpt from Simon Njami's "Image, Where Are You?" This is the answer Djibril Diop Mambéty gave to that question:

> The image doesn't have a role, it takes orders. In film, an image by itself doesn't exist until you tell it what to do. But you have to follow up on your instructions. You have to say: "OK, image, where are you?" And it answers: "Here I am." And you say: "Go and do this." And it does it if you asked nicely and politely. The only divine act of creation accessible to [humankind] is the act of creating the wind. Have you ever asked yourself where the wind blows? I've never stopped asking myself this question. The fate of the image, the fate of the wind, [the] fate [of humankind], the fate of a breath, a feeling, a cause, is where the wind blows. To show the course of [humankind] is a solemn act, and you can't get it wrong.[2]

In my text, I tried to tackle perhaps ten notions of what I think photography can do—this is one of them:

What can photography do?

An argument that has to be made, though with large brushstrokes . . . is the role photographic expressions have played and still play in the construction, definition, and imagination of identities (sexual, gender, racial, political) through imagery. Maybe one of the best ways of expatiating on this would be to look at the work of three collectives (or collective practices) that work predominantly through and with the photographic medium of expression: MFON, Kamoinge, and Invisible Borders. I have chosen to highlight collectives here because the mere fact of being part of a collective seems to me a political gesture. Most of us know the tendency: when the going is good, we tend to be individuals; when the tides are high and we are in dire straits, then we are obliged to think and act collectively to survive. The work in general, and publications in particular, put together by MFON: Women Photographers of the African Diaspora[3] are revelatory in terms of geo-, gender, and race politics. Women, and especially black women, have always played an important role in the history of photography but, as in every other field, their voices, their experiences, and their accomplishments have been systematically overshadowed by men in the industry. By centering the work of black women and especially those in the diaspora, MFON's photography becomes a tool for gender, racial and geopolitical strides, avowal, and empowerment. This becomes even more evident as their stated objective is to "promote an international representative voice of women photographers of African descent," "fill a void while creating a space for intellectual discourse around issues represented by women photographers of African descent," and "create a powerful collective of women photographers, journalists, and scholars to build their practices through solid representation of their voices within the field of photography."[4] In their inaugural publication, MFON put together the photographic works of one hundred women photographers across the diaspora as well as essays by women scholars and other practitioners. MFON derives its name from and is a commemoration of the life and work of the Nigerian photographer Mmekutmfon "Mfon" Essien (1967–2001). At a time when publishing as a black photographer in the United States was anything but easy, at a time when black photographers were expected to serve a certain purpose and touch on a few clichéd topics, at a time when photo commissions and other jobs were distributed within a circle of white photographers, at a time when photography schools were not easily accessible to all, Kamoinge was born. It was 1963 and some African American photographers, in an effort to empower, challenge, and critique each other's practices and attain artistic equality, decided to form a collective. Kamoinge Workshop, whose creative and active directors included Anthony Barboza, Roy DeCarava, Louis Draper, and Beuford Smith, was birthed out of the fusion of two groups of African American photographers: Group 35, which included James Ray Francis, Louis Draper, Herman Howard, Earl James, and Calvin Mercer, and another group including Herb Randall, Albert Fennar, Shawn Walker and James Mannas. In the name of the group lies its mission and political agenda, as Kamoinge's etymology in Gikuyu means "a group of people acting together."

[…]

So what can photography do?

The photographic can capture the essence of a human's being. That is what we see in most of the works of people like Gordon Parks or Akinbode Akinbiyi, in how they capture not only the humans in their photographs, but also what holds, situates, and enables their being, how they capture the deepest vulnerabilities—which is to say strengths—of human existence, when the camera ceases to be an optical device and becomes as a seismographic tool. The photographic has especially framed and played an important role in the elastification of our understanding of what sexuality is or can be in the African world. Suffice it to look at the seminal work of Rotimi Fani-Kayode, whose practice flirted with queer sexuality and African and European liminal identities, reflected especially on the black male body and its long history of being imagined as the ultimate sexual "object" in the mind of the Other. The photographic permitted Fani-Kayode to portray queer sexuality not as an opposite of but as part and parcel of African traditions at large and Yoruba traditions in particular. Such is the case too with the ongoing series *Faces and Phases* by artist Zanele Muholi, who since 2006 has been portraying hundreds of black lesbians, trans people, and gender-nonconforming people, thereby creating a photographic archive of queerness that complicates the notions of sexual and gender identity in peoples of African origins. These two aforementioned artists, among many others, who chose photography as their primary medium of expression have done an enormous service to the understanding of black LGBTQIA+ cultures in Africa and its diasporas.

But in all these cases, what photography also does, beyond just reflecting realities, is perform a kind of refraction; a bending of light and waves as they pass an interface of mediums. There is a change in direction, as the angle of incidence is not equal to the angle of refraction. What you see is not what

Akinbode Akinbiyi
Bonaventure Soh
Bejeng Ndikung
Koyo Kouoh

you get, for the image one sees might be a distortion of the reality intended for representation. If we take, for example, the history of "anthropological" photography in Africa, [we get] an impression of what that refraction of/in photography has entailed. In the early images of the portrayal of African peoples, cultures, and spaces captured by European ethnographers and other pseudoscientists in the early phases of photography in the mid-nineteenth century, refraction entailed a stereotypical depiction which suited the image in the mind of the European beholder of that which was designed to be African within the imagination of the colonial enterprise, rather than what actually was. In the large archive put together by photographer and photo-historian Ben Krewinkel of peoples of African origins in photo books,[5] one sees an impressive presentation of what some places in Africa would have looked like at the end of the nineteenth and beginning of the twentieth centuries, yet at the same time a large variety of such incredibly refracted imagery.

I'll just mention one of the books in that archive:

In *The Red Book of West Africa: Historical and Descriptive, Commercial and Industrial Facts, Figures, and Resources* (1920),[6] a handful of photographers are on a mission to explain West Africa to anyone who wishes to know how Egba women carry their twins, or how half-naked men pose with their game after a hippopotamus hunt, or how the breasts of girls of Zaria fall, or how pagan men and women of Jos look like when stripped of their dignity.

A review of the images made of Africans during the nineteenth century by European photographers, such as those in Southern and East Africa, shows most emphatically this approach. The images show the extent to which the exotic quality of the African was part of the meaning being communicated through the photographic apparatus. And to that extent the photographs produced a type of knowledge of Africa and Africans. Some of these images, though formally interesting and even beautiful, were paternalistic and focused more on the erotic and ethnographic . . . . In this instance, photography was no longer the mimetic, evidentiary technique of drawing reality into visibility but constructed images as much as for their effect on the receiver as for their realistic representation."[7]

This statement by Okwui Enwezor in his seminal essay "Life and Afterlife in Benin: Photography in the Service of Ethnographic Realism" is an epitome of what I mean by the refraction of the photographic. While I do not, as it were, have a dog in the fight of nineteenth-century photography, I am deeply interested in how the three big Es: Exotic, Erotic, and Ethnographic, and the even bigger P: Paternalistic, have succeeded in creeping through time into the twenty-first century and are still fundamental in meaning making and knowledge dissemination through the photographic apparatus of Africa and Africans. It is still very common to see Western photographers present naked exotic, erotic, and ethnographic Maasai men or some other peoples in a very paternalistic way. But, again, I do not necessarily have a bone to pick with Western photographers, for the mere fact that the genealogy that leads them to this point is too obvious, and for the other fact that my center of gravity lies with the photography of Africans and peoples of African origins.

There is a tendency for people who have been subjected to certain conditions to sometimes internalize them. In the aforementioned statement by Enwezor, he points out the fact that some of the denigrating images produced by European photographers on Africans are sometimes "formally interesting and even beautiful." Photography produced by African artists today, especially of Africa and Africans, seems to be at its crest when it comes to aesthetic expressions, command over the medium, sociopolitical consciousness, and even its position in the market. Despite that, one notices a strand of artists who have internalized that sense of form and beauty that echoes those big Es prevalent in and so characteristic of the Western gaze toward Africa. Which is to say, one notices the self-ethnographization and self-anthropologization in what has become a particular and even celebrated form of refractive photography.[8]

AA: This has been an ongoing conversation between us. And I very much agree that the Western gaze still denigrates and dehumanizes us—black people, people of Africa, people of African descent. There's this continuing willingness, on the part of many photographers, somehow to see the Other in us. The opposite. Many of us have these racial, these gender and sexual hierarchies in our heads all the time. Over the years, Bon and I have often wondered how we can move away from this kind of thinking.

BSBN: These past years, I have been fascinated by the idea of circumventing that. How does one free oneself from this baggage? In looking at your photographs for several years now, I've tried to determine how you navigate and negotiate space. You don't strip people of their dignity in the images you take. Whenever you take a picture of somebody, it's as if you are communicating and have asked the person for permission. The image tells you that. How does that work?

AA: As a way of answering—yesterday, I was asked about my favorite photo books. There's one I didn't mention: Roy deCarava. I grew up in Nigeria and in Britain, so I was receiving all kinds of crazy messages—Charles Dickens, Walter Scott, H. Rider Haggard. And I couldn't see myself represented in any of that—just as many black people are saying nowadays. Then I heard Ray Charles—he blew my mind. Then, much later, I saw Roy deCarava's work, and Gordon Parks's, and some other black photographers. They didn't have that othering gaze.

As I wrote in the text—you look out and you take in. But please don't denigrate me in that exchange, just as I'm trying not to denigrate you. That always seems to be the way, especially on the African continent—all these white tourists come. They want to see animals, they want to see landscapes, they want to see us locals in our villages. It's a kind of fight. This is what we try to push back against. When I'm making images, I don't think about these issues consciously—but I try not to replicate the positioning of the subject in those kinds of images. Sometimes you have to be careful not to start down that path. You don't need to throw away the camera or the images; instead, you try to find your own way of dealing with these things.

Akinbode Akinbiyi
Bonaventure Soh
Bejeng Ndikung
Koyo Kouoh

BSBN: In the last curatorial team meeting we had for the Bamako Biennale, we were talking about portraiture. It was a heated debate. Who is *seen* in a portrait? Bode, you say it is actually the photographer you see when you look at a portrait. The portrait as mirror. I find that idea intriguing. The next edition of the Bamako Biennale is about the multiplicity of beings within one being. A strong photographer digs deep, captures some of the beings inside us that we don't otherwise dare express. So, I'm drawn by this concept of digging, of removing the surface, of getting to the undercurrent of the photographic.

AA: I think that touches on a notion with a lot of depth. To engage in a conversation with somebody outside oneself means one has to listen and try to understand. At the same time, you're carrying your own baggage. You're having your own masquerade or carrying your own placards. When somebody comes and says to me, *diversity* or *inclusivity*—some years ago, there was *hybridity*—I listen. I'm listening. And I'm trying to understand. I like that conversation because, in taking or making a portrait, what am I actually trying to say? What am I trying to see?

It's me looking out. That's for sure. But at the same time, I'm seeing my opposite— the person outside, the Other—and trying to represent them. How? You don't necessarily need the face—it could be the back of the head or the hands, which contain a lot of power. The feet, the body—so many other things immediately come into the conversation, especially around representation. If, for example, as a man, I'm taking photographs of a woman, perhaps the woman is clothed. But what if she is naked? Then, of course, conceptions of class are part of the conversation as well. If I'm wandering the city and see somebody who's homeless, what do I do? Do I walk past, do I perhaps give them something—or do I in fact take something? If I take a photograph—what is its purpose? For what reason? All this questioning is constant, so it's an ongoing conversation and there is not just one way to look at it.

A good friend of ours is now dealing with the archives of Leni Riefenstahl's work. Riefenstahl started off as an actor, then became a film director and, later on, a photographer. She photographed the Nuba people, in such a way that her work became popular worldwide. In Japan, Europe, in the States—thousands and thousands of copies of her book were sold, which is unusual for a photo book. And then you ask yourself: Why was it so popular? Even some African artists started working with her images—like the late sculptor Ousmane Sow. What was Riefenstahl's purpose? What's she trying to say? What is she trying to do? The archives are amazing. There are over seven hundred boxes of her diaries and letters, photographs, all kinds of stuff.

Akinbode Akinbiyi
Bonaventure Soh
Bejeng Ndikung
Koyo Kouoh

BSBN: You say you're a wanderer. You walk around, you feel space, you have your ear to the ground. Another thing we've been talking about is proximity. The necessity of maintaining distance or of coming very close to find the right depth of field. To find the right distance, alongside the need to work with intention and with dignity. This is a huge concern I have with a lot of photographs I see, especially when this has to do with African peoples—that the appropriate depth is not found. How do you find the proper distance?

AA: You have to dance. It's in the foreground, the middle ground, the background— you keep moving forward and back. This is why I don't like zoom lenses. I think you have to use your feet. You move in close, sometimes up really tight. Or you go back. There's no one answer. You mentioned the need for dignity—I think, even more than dignity, I prefer the idea of respect. You have to respect your surroundings, the environment. I like what you said: *ear to the ground*. You have to listen in. Sometimes, I want to make a photograph, but I know the people who will appear in it don't want me to. So, I don't—unless perhaps there's something unusual to see. But who determines what this unusualness is? Many people want to be photographed, though. There's the selfie now. The other day, in Berlin, I saw that somebody had indicated a location as a "selfie spot." Fascinating. Ariella [Azoulay] asked what the meaning of a photograph is. What is its currency, its weight? I think these are very important conversations. Perhaps we will not find one single answer and keep moving forward. But respect, I think is important. And we must consider who is defining what that respect consists of.

Koyo Kouoh: I would like to come back to a few points that are in the texts you read. The primary question you pose is, What can photography *do*?—and this in an active sense. You also develop a line of thought about liberating the photograph from the photographic. For me, this coalesces the recess between the photograph-as-object, and the qualifiers of the photographic, such that the photographic artifact gains independence from the photographer, the author, the subject, and places itself at the disposal—or the mercy—of the viewer, and especially of the particular context in which it is presented.

You also touch on the idea of the fetishization of black bodies and how that fetishization has become a frame of perception: this frame of seeing has defined and continues to define the construction of the imaginary. I want to refer to Ariella from her wonderfully enlightened writing about photography. In terms of what photography can do, she says the event of photography is never complete; it can only be suspended.[9] This links to our thinking around currency, which is the theme we consider in the upcoming Triennial of Photography Hamburg: the idea that the photograph is imbued with the currency of seeing, of showing, projecting, perceiving; a currency of currents, of narratives of all sorts—which can lead to the photograph becoming crystallized in stereotypes.

When it comes to questions of identity, representation, and the whole spectrum of what I would refer to as *recounting ourselves*, I would say that from time immemorial, humanity has related to images and objects—and that we will continue to do so. Along with language, these are the fundamental currencies and tools of interaction we use.

Bode, I find your texts read like the preparation of a meal. You remind me of a chef— you wander around, you seek, relate; you navigate spaces, cities, places, in search of something without knowing what you're searching for. Then you find—or, perhaps, you stumble—upon things, upon people who inspire you in a way that leads you to make a selection. This meandering is a bit like a chef going to market, choosing today's combination of ingredients. To me, your parallel version of this selection is in finding the moment and taking the shot; then, of course, the presentation of the image is like the consumption of the meal. I'm very much into food in many ways!

Your approach and your practice are very poetic in their softness and sensitivity. It's captivating. The series of works you have produced on cities like Dakar, Johannesburg, and Bamako demonstrate the gentleness you breathe into your work—I think it is this that signals the difference between your work and the work of others who don't practice that same gentleness. The position of the photographer—not only their physical position, but their intellectual, cultural, political, emotional position, their disposition—is of great significance because it has a profound influence on what is photographed, how things are photographed, how people are photographed.

AA: I like this suggestion of the gentle soul—thank you. Sometimes I come across photos—on the pavement, on the road—that people have dropped or thrown away. So, I pick them up. I collect them. Many years ago, on a rainy day in Johannesburg, I found a whole bunch of images, perhaps fifty or sixty, of a wedding. I had a look at them and found them fascinating. I picked them all up and dried them when I got home—I was staying at Maboneng at the time. I still have them up. I've also been taking pictures of photo booths for some time. Occasionally, people forget their strips of photos, so I take them. I have twenty or thirty of those and I'm still collecting them. And then, recently I found a large photograph of a young boy in the departure queue at the airport in Johannesburg; I found another, smaller photograph of a child, maybe two or three years old. So, I have all these images. This connects to Ariella's thinking: Whose are these images? Are they mine? Because now, I've taken them. Not in the sense that I myself have photographed them, but that I have taken them into my possession. Photographs can have so many meanings. People put photos on an altar in their homes to remember loved ones who have passed on. It's a kind of evocation but it represents so many things. I'm working out ideas around found images. In Graz, I went so far as to have my own photo booth installed—you put in a few coins and you get one of your images in among some of mine. Ownership, conversation: I'm questioning these kinds of things all the time. What is a photograph? What is it telling us? What are we trying to say with it?

BSBN: Rather than you finding the images, the images find you. Or, perhaps, you don't take the images—they take you. Maybe the image is on the floor waiting for you, so it's not the artist who creates the work. It's the work that chooses the artist and it's for the artist to deliver the work.

AA: Yes, that's right.

Stefan Köhler: To add to your conversation—I wanted to point out Georges Adéagbo's use of photographs in his installations. In any city where he has a show, he finds, buys, and collects photographs found in the street; sometimes he buys vintage photographs at flea markets. It's an interesting aspect, this blending and sharing of narratives, and how they overlap, I think these ideas complement what you are speaking about. A second thing: we learned something significant from Zanele Muholi a couple of years ago. We invited her to lead a workshop for teenagers in Benin, in Cotonou, about violence against women. The first thing she did was give every participant a notebook and say, "Whenever you take pictures of people, take down their name and how to contact them. Taking anonymous pictures, like of 'women pounding millet in their village,' is a colonial act. People have names." That's the first thing she taught the participants: never publish pictures of anonymous people. Name and identity are part of the process.

BSBN: Just to add something to that, especially in relation to the work that Georges does with the images he finds at flea markets: I've always thought of those as references—like citations in a text. He goes to a city and looks at its citations—kind of getting his bearings. What are the things within this space? Things I can lean on but also things I can build on. Georges integrates them into his installations. As I say, I see them as references, as citations of spaces and the beings that are in these spaces.

Frieda Ekotto: Bode, you spoke about respect and I thought about what Ariella talks about, this idea of the gift given to an institution [*see page 27*]. I wonder if this connects to what you are speaking about—about acknowledging one's own humanity,

Akinbode Akinbiyi
Bonaventure Soh
Bejeng Ndikung
Koyo Kouoh

about acknowledging the Other, saying, "I see you; I know you are there"? I'm thinking about Trinh T. Minh-ha's work when she talks about the impossibility of translating the Other. She talks about how she's always trying to listen to people, to get close to them, near to them. She has all these words to try to come to terms with this impossibility of even starting to say, "I see you."

AA: You said it, actually. It's very much about acknowledging, respecting, and then listening in. And, with time, understanding—or Bona and I sometimes say "overstanding." I've also learned to relax. Sometimes it takes time. Many years ago, I took a taxi from Cotonou to Grand Popo. And we drove through regions with different peoples—you see different body shapes, different types of people. I don't like the word *tribes*. And it's no big deal. We're all like one big family. So, when I'm coming to a new family, OK, I just chill. And then, with time, I understand what's going down, what's happening. This is something I talk about a lot because, eventually, you have to respect everybody.

Everybody also means those whose ideologies you may not agree with. You have to say, "OK, I'm among you, I'll eat and drink with you, listen to what you're trying to say." Perhaps you don't agree with them. And of course it can become conflictual. I spent decades in the belly of the beast—the beast being Western Europe. People there still don't respect us. But I'm trying to come to them with respect. To be frank and very fair, I have some very close European friends whom I grew up with. Recently, I was speaking with a woman in Berlin—she arrived there in her teens—and she has never made very close friends with Europeans, although she grew up in Germany. I ask myself why. There's no one solution. Everybody tries to find their own particular way of being.

BSBN: This might lead to a longer conversation but maybe one has to start by respecting oneself. I don't see how you can respect anybody if you can't respect yourself. As they say, to be able to dehumanize the Other, you have to dehumanize yourself first. Or you dehumanize yourself in the process of dehumanizing the Other. Perhaps that respect has to start from here.

1. Akinbode Akinbiyi, "Photographic Wanderings," in *Streams of Consciousness: A Concatenation of Dividuals*, ed. Bonaventure Soh Bejeng Ndikung (Dakar: Archive Books, 2019), 331–333.

2. Simon Njami, "Image, Where Are You?," quoted in Bonaventure Soh Bejeng Ndikung, "Of a Photographic State of Being: Delivering the Photographic from Photography," in *Streams of Consciousness*, 15.

3. MFON: Women Photographers of the African Diaspora was founded by Laylah Amutullah Barrayn and Adama Delphine Fawundu.

4. See http://mfonfoto.org/about/.

5. See "Africa in the Photobook," an internet archive initiated by Ben Krewinkel, https://africainthephotobook.com.

6. José Augusto da Cunha Moraes and Luciano Cordeiro, *Africa Occidental—Album Photográphico e Descriptivo. Primeira parte* (Lisbon: David Corazzi, 1887).

7. Okwui Enwezor, "Life and Afterlife in Benin: Photography in the Service of Ethnographic Realism," in *Life and Afterlife in Benin*, ed. Alex Van Gelder (New York: Phaidon, 2005).

8. "Of a Photographic State of Being," Delivering the Photographic from Photography," in *Streams of Consciousness*, 22–29.

9. See, for example, Azoulay's essay in this volume.

NARRATIVE CURRENTS

RASHA SALTI

Photographs outlive their photographers, as well as the subjects, landscapes, and objects they picture. As such, we who collect and classify photographs are mere passersby in their existence. We gaze, look away, and come back to look time and time again. We scrutinize, imprint images in the mind's eye, and lock them away in our mental archives, whether conscious or subconscious.

Photographs invite words. As captures of fleeting appearances, as evidence of events, traces of lives, documentary and imaginary imprints of the Real, photographs allow us to tell stories about ourselves and about others, to resurrect worlds and lives lapsed or deliberately driven into obsolescence, silence, or erasure. We use them to extract meaning and to project subjectivities onto the past and into the future.

Photographs can anchor the relationship that connects the Real we live, the Real we witness, the Real we aspire to, and the Real we imagine or interiorize. In his recent book *L'imagement*, Jean-Christophe Bailly writes: "Every photograph is a haunted house."[1] I have come to understand this as an invitation to dance with ghosts.

Narrative Currents—the thread that draws together this constellation of texts, conversations, and moments of poesis—is not ghost-dancing—or not exclusively that. It is an invitation to explore the interstices between a photograph and its caption, to overwrite or debunk captions, to plumb the myriad emancipating possibilities that lie in the slippage between the visual signifier and the lexical signified. The narrative currents, then, that flow from, around, about, against, and through photographs.

The Lucid Knowledge symposium deliberately sought the stories, reflections, speculations, reveries, and provocations of cultural theorists, writers, art historians, curators, artists, filmmakers, academics, social scientists with proclivities for archeology, botany, and literature, and of poets, with the intention of giving voice to the relevance of photography in these various disciplines and métiers. I acknowledge here the joy of gathering this assembly and my gratitude to all the contributors who accepted the invitation, who indulged our prompts, and who gave so generously of their time and creative energies.

1. Jean-Christophe Bailly, *L'imagement* (Roubaix: Les Éditions du Seuil, 2019), 12. Translation mine.

Wake

ROBIN COSTE LEWIS

Twenty-five years ago, in 1998, I discovered—accidentally—a small private archive comprised primarily of vernacular family photographs, all located within the history of Louisiana Gulf culture and the eventual phenomenon that has come to be known as the Great Migration. When I found the photographs, my grandmother had died. Her house was slated to be demolished. The church next door had bought her home in order to clear the land and construct a parking lot for its Sunday parishioners. I'd flown home to say goodbye—to everything. To her. The entire house—an old South Central Spanish bungalow, the backyard filled with dahlias, anthuriums, roses, her small greenhouse, and one avocado tree—had been emptied by our relatives in the days before I arrived.

My grandmother had died from Alzheimer's in an assisted living facility. She had not lived in her house for many years. It had been half a decade since she recognized anyone. Maybe longer since she had spoken. Once, a few years earlier, I'd gone to visit her. Her eyes were glazed over. I was certain she had no idea who I was. Because I had once heard that people with Alzheimer's benefit greatly from massage, after an hour, I asked her nurse for some lotion. I began with her hands—those vast, crooked, thick-veined hands I knew and adored, and which are now my crooked, thick-veined hands. After massaging her whole body, just as I had reached her feet, she looked down into my face, surprised, and exclaimed, "Hey Rob! When did you get here!"

Those were the last words she ever spoke to me. It remains the question of my life: When did I get here?

Now I sat—inconsolable—on top of her stripped bed inside her empty house, fully aware that a few days later the church would begin to raze the whole property—the bed that I had played on and around for every decade of my life as she worked at her sewing machine. I just sat there. In her room. Trying to eat the air. Forever. Looking at her mirror. Feeling all the years of our lives. And then, just then, this voice inside—quiet, warm, persistent—spoke up. It said, *Look under the bed.*

I have heard this voice all my life, but I don't like admitting it. It has saved my life on a few occasions, telling me, *Don't walk that way* or *Cancel that flight* or *Don't take these stairs*, or the saddest of all: *Leave her.* We aren't supposed to talk this way, so I keep all this to myself. And besides, I want no one's contrarian opinion upon what I know to be real in my life. But it was this same steady voice telling me, now, to get down on my hands and knees and look underneath my grandmother's bed.

Because I am stubborn about Grace, I knelt to the ground reluctantly, angry that, even at such a tender moment, this mysterious presence would choose to test me. But when I got down onto my grandmother's floor, that perfumed floor, and turned my head under her bed: there it was, this suitcase. I pulled it out, in complete disbelief, opened it, and there it was, a large pile of countless, brimming photographs. In fact, the suitcase contained photographic examples of the entire history of photography, beginning with a few daguerreotypes and tintypes, most of which were taken in New Orleans and Chicago, and then ending, during the 1970s, with a vivid array of black-and-white and color Polaroids, most of which were shot in the south basin of Los Angeles, well known sites of the Great Migration—Compton, South Central, Long Beach—as well as Hawaii, the Mojave Desert, Las Vegas. In total, what is now the Dorothy Mary Coste Thomas Brooks Collection (the DMCTB Collection) contained roughly 350 photographs.

Dorothy Mary Coste Thomas was born in 1908 on the West Bank, in Algiers, in New Orleans, Louisiana. During the 1940s, she, her sister Hildreth, and their sister Eunice (known as "Sis") all headed west, alone, after the war. Three sisters. Their brothers chose Chicago instead—fleeing the racist terror of the South, a few uncles, aunts, and grandparents had already moved there a decade before the war had begun. I don't know if it is true, but it was rumored that one uncle was a part of a group under investigation by the great Star and Crescent (also known as the New Orleans Police Department) for his possible involvement in the murder of a police officer—a police officer who was known to be a very sincere and active member of the Ku Klux Klan. Two sisters by marriage went alone to San Francisco.

For those of us who are part of what I call the Louisiana Diaspora, these three migrational sites—New Orleans, Chicago, Los Angeles, and, curiously, no other cities—form a sacred and well-traveled triangle. We knew the trains and, later, each and every highway needed to take back and forth to each other better than we knew our own new cities. It is for this reason, then, that later, when I was born in Compton in the autumn of 1964, one out of every third black person you might meet on any street corner in Los Angeles was descended from Louisiana.

:

Because it is easy, too easy perhaps, whenever a woman says the words *photograph and grandmother* in the same sentence— because our minds slide immediately into all kinds of nostalgic resonance (chenille bedspreads, pastel mints, toast-and-cheese sandwiches, the feel of her skin) instead of imagining the complex histories human beings endure, and the roles black women have played within that endurance, particularly with regard to the history of photography and collecting—I hope you can hear that one-word, fear-filled but courageous telegraph of the migrant traveling across white supremacist borders worldwide: *Arrived!* Or the four-word ones: *Mother's better* –(STOP)– *We made it* –(STOP)– Or: *Uncle safe* –(STOP)– *Will write soon* –(STOP)– Or: *Brother didn't make it* –(STOP)– *Don't tell father* –(STOP)–.

Robin
Coste Lewis

I also hope when I said "New Orleans—Chicago—Los Angeles" that the Black and Asian and Latino labor history of the railroad rose up immediately between my sentences. I hope you could see men of every color laying down the tracks all over a vast country for very little pay. I hope you could smell the iron and the new segregated train cars, train cars in which every one of the train fabricators were forbidden to ride, except in positions of subservience—cleaners, porters, waiters. I hope you can smell the ink of the Chinese Exclusion Act of 1882 haunting all these lines. I hope you can see each and every Chinese man who was strung up and hung by his braid or queue—lynched in numbers as high as their Black neighbors in the great warm sunshine-filled state of California, on the great rim of a mighty ocean—named for peace—called the Pacific. All of them together swinging outside history. I hope, too, that you heard the people imprisoned in Japanese internment camps. I hope you can hear all of the various Indigenous nations, five million, ten million, fifteen million, twenty million voices—upon whose land we were all born, upon whose land so many have died. And lived. Without ever asking permission.

When I look at my grandmother's photographs, this is what I hear: all the people of color fleeing their homes because of white supremacy, zigzagging across the false borders of a stolen country. I hear the colonial surveyors setting up their theodolites, inventing the straight lines, inventing a country, all of it to be classified under a young and clever word only a few centuries old, known as *property*. The poppy-filled air. The national collective hypnotism. The real land beneath the fake land. The almost-extinct sage-brush seeds lingering beneath the imported palm trees. The desert. The desert. Pretending not to be a sacred desert. And as Derek Walcott once said, "At the end of this sentence, rain will begin."

What I hope you hear most of all is that for decades my grandmother, a seamstress and a domestic from Louisiana, was also a voracious and aesthetically sensitive collector of vernacular photography. She may have also been an amateur photographer. And what is both tragic and glorious is that we will never know.

Wake

Over the past twenty-five years, I have sat with the DMCTB Collection, understanding completely that I was too naïve, intellectually and aesthetically, to know what should be done with the archive I inherited. I knew I was too young to deliver what my mind was asking of me. It didn't want me to pretend that a human being can be so easily comprehended, even though I had grown up with many of the people in every photograph. The photographs didn't want me to cue a choir and over-enunciate some hymn about bootstraps. Labor and survival were always a given. We were born into hard work, and into hard work they all died. Who didn't know that stupid fact? Besides, we were all Catholic. What my mind wanted, and what the photographs seemed to ask of me, was something less predictable than narrative, something I could not articulate then and still struggle to articulate now.

About one of her own difficult book projects, Hannah Arendt says, "This book has been written against a background of both reckless optimism and reckless despair. It holds that Progress and Doom are two sides of the same medal; that both are articles of superstition, not of faith."[1] That is one way to express my aesthetic reservation. Another way, sitting quietly behind that one, is this: Can any human being ever really be known? And then surrounding all that grew another additional iron question, a wall I'd constructed inside my psyche to protect my grandmother's pictures—and me, the quiet She-Wolf who sat guarding them. That is, I felt—and still feel—deeply that not every image can be touched, handled, known. Not every story is for you. On other days I ask, even myself, *How dare you look at them?*

I am fifty-six now. I returned to academia and did two more graduate degrees in order to begin to try to grasp what I actually inherited when I opened that suitcase in my grandmother's bedroom twenty-five years ago. I returned to school because I wanted to learn about the history of the camera. Which cameras did my grandmother and other relatives use, which paper, which studio? I wanted to think about their figurative hands; their clothes, the colonial history of textiles sleeping in the collars of

Robin
Coste Lewis

their shirts; and the type of dahlias or chestnut trees growing in the background on the land in Algiers and Los Angeles—all of which is now gone. Which street—and why? Why this corner and not that one? But more than anything—more than everything—I wanted to create a language that could recontextualize my family and my people within a historical idea that superseded a pitiful few American centuries, a lyric that exalted them both backward and forward simultaneously into a vaster honorific station in human history—and not because our time in the United States was not sufficient, but merely because we are far older and grander and more historically significant than America can ever hope to be.

:

I was in my early thirties when I knelt down and looked under my grandmother's bed in that empty house. Now I am middle-aged. What happens to a woman's life between those years changes her eyes entirely. What I saw then in the images and what I see now are completely different observations. Sometimes an entire picture has changed completely. What I see one day and understand tomorrow is always changing too.

:

I can't remember the first dead body I ever saw as a child. The dead were always there. Always. Alive. Present. Palpable. Standing nearby—listening. Relatives would often call to us children by the names of those who had recently passed within the last few generations. Every newborn face or finger or eyebrow shape—the color of an eye, someone's hairline, their widow's peak—was an ancestral artifact, a signal of an ancestor's return, their reentry, or perhaps their final farewell. Our childhood bodies were their telegrams—messages the dead sent the living to let everyone know they had *arrived*, which is to say, returned safely. Our new bodies were the dead's evidence.

:

For decades I believed the best thing that ever happened to me was that I was born into a family from Louisiana, a family that followed the wave of the Great Migration west, not—blah—north.

Wake

That was the best thing, I thought. Years later, I capitulated and thought, *No, it's that I know how to make real filé gumbo, the kind that takes three days, and uses six stocks—that's living, real Diasporic history.* Later still, I wept with gratitude that I was born on Central Avenue, in the exquisitely beautiful City of Compton, a neighborhood lush with Gulf culture, Gulf history, and Gulf sounds. But I don't believe any of that now. I've changed. Most of the people in these photographs are now dead. Now I believe that the very best thing that has ever happened to me, quite simply, is: them. Their faces. Their voices. Their failures. Their glee. Their transparency. To be a child of migration—to be born midflight—that was the greatest honor.

:

And so: when I was child, whenever a person died, everything stopped—the whole neighborhood ceased to move—the banter, the gossip, the rushing, the Man—none of that mattered any longer. All of it was put back into its insignificant position. People arrived at the door. Relatives, friends, their hands filled with food, money, clothes, endless flowers. Somebody's aunt who was a lawyer. The cousin who worked at the cemetery. The seamstress. The grandchildren. The uncle who drove two days and two nights without stopping. The étouffée. The bottles of liquor. Mahalia Jackson.

What mattered was there was a life. There had been a life. And now there was a body. The older generation called this final funerary ritual a *Wake*.

:

It was an honor to be asked to wash the body—perhaps the highest honor. And it was usually done alone, or with a very few people in the room. They washed and moisturized and groomed that body. Afterward, the body was dressed. The body was kissed. The body was perfumed. The hair was combed. Nylons or stylish socks were pulled over the quieted feet. Whispers were spoken into the ear of the body. The hands were held. Eyebrows were stroked. The face was made holy by the most beloved of all tears. Later still, for days and nights,

Robin
Coste Lewis

everyone who arrived sat quietly together with the body laid out in the living room. The body was kissed some more; the brows stroked again, more whispers into the body's ear; more promises; more hands holding the body's hands. More stories told on the porch.

:

The body was kept at home. The body was warm.

:

I think about this all the time now—how we loved our dead midflight. How we sat with them. And waited until they were ready—and until we were ready—too.

1. Hannah Arendt, *The Origins of Totalitarianism* (New York: Harcourt Brace Jovanovich, 1973), vii.

Illustrations on following pages:

P. 75: Ritchie Michael Lewis. Photographer unknown.

P. 77: Ritchie Michael Lewis and Steven Harry Lewis. Photographer unknown.

P. 79: Candy Theresa (née Lewis) Watkins. Photographer unknown.

P. 81: Photographer unknown.

P. 83: Robin Kelly Coste Lewis. Photographer unknown.

Wake

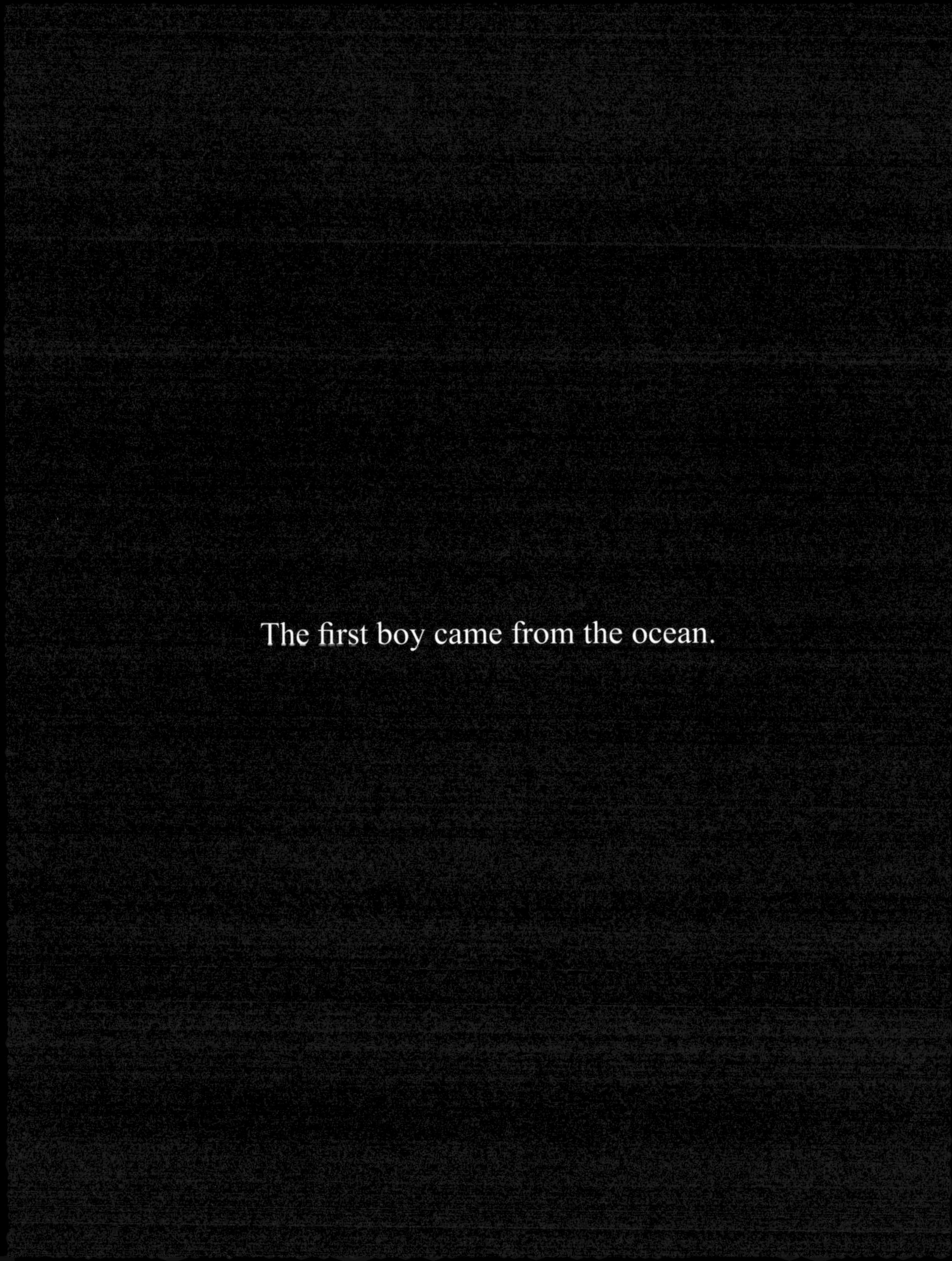

The first boy came from the ocean.

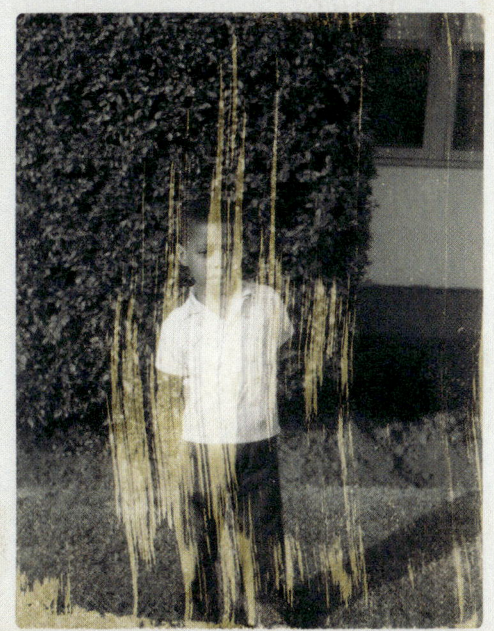

Son two crawled through the o
in her signature.

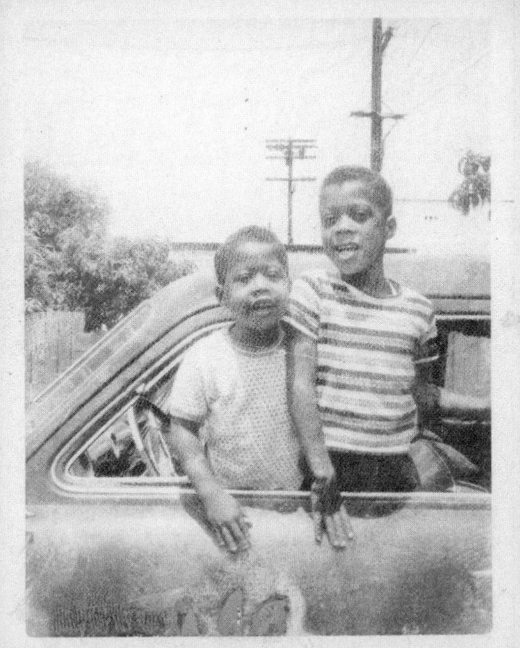

My sister arrived just after him
looking like she'd been pelted by a storm.

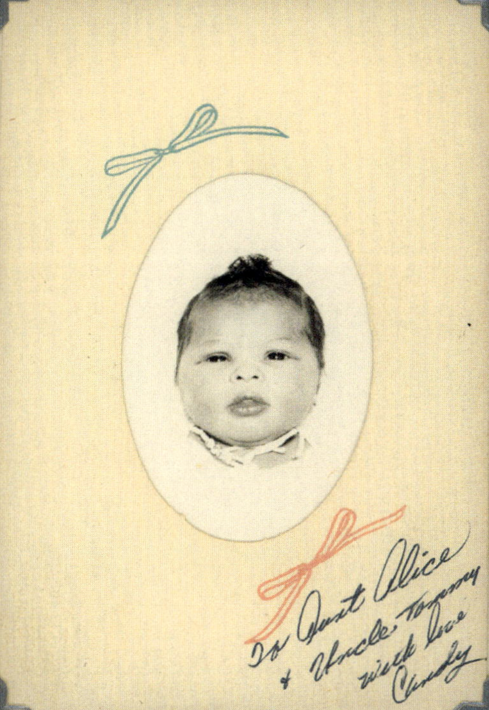
To Aunt Alice
& Uncle Tommy
with love
Cindy

Then another sister both came
and didn't come. The body arrived
but she went elsewhere—*where?*

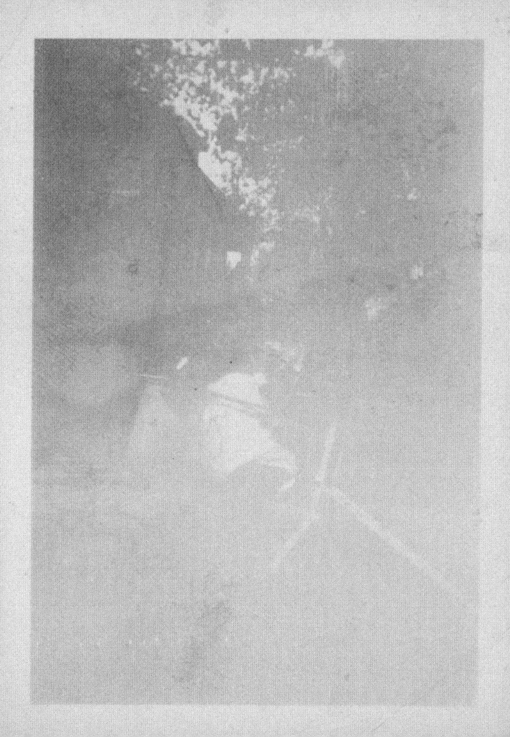

I snuck in next, taking up home
inside her salty red grave,
and here I became alive and suspicious.

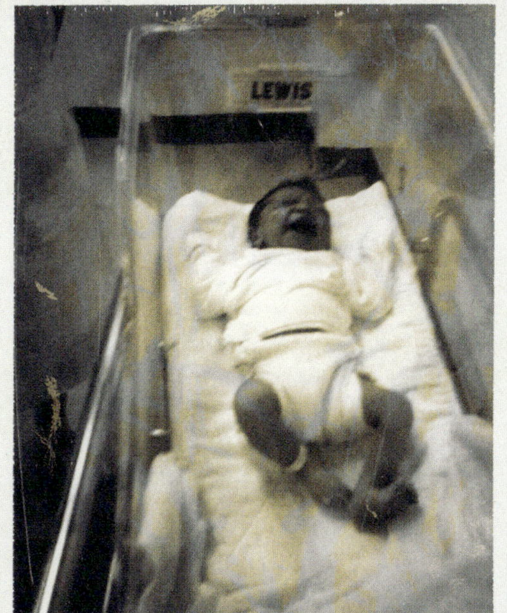
LEWIS

The Body and the Tropics

ANTAWAN I. BYRD

ON MIMI CHERONO NG'OK

AND MIGUEL A. LÓPEZ

ON VICTORIA CABEZAS

WITH A RESPONSE FROM NICHOLAS TAMMENS

Antawan I. Byrd: In thinking about today's theme of narrative currents, specifically the ways that photographs—through the images they carry, their material form, their methods of presentation—generate a range of narrative possibilities, the artist who came to my mind was Mimi Cherono Ng'ok. I've been thinking about her practice steadily for the past two years as I worked with her on a solo exhibition that I curated at the Art Institute of Chicago.

I'd like to give an overview of this exhibition and speak about how ideas of storytelling register, both through the show itself and through a set of working procedures that have been commonplace in Mimi's practice over the last five years. If you were to ask her what her work is about, Mimi would likely respond by saying it's about her—about her emotions, memories, and encounters. It's often about feelings of vulnerability and isolation; sometimes about experiences of grief, about tenderness. And it's about tracking these feelings and experiences as they develop and morph during her travels across the tropical regions of the Global South. African cities such as her hometown of Nairobi, or Dakar, Cape Town, Bamako, or Accra; or further afield in places like La Romana on the east coast of the Dominican Republic, or São Paulo, or Rio de Janeiro—these are the cities in which her practice unfurls.

Movement across geographies and the experience of cities is crucial to Mimi's work—it's partly a reflection of the influence of artists like Akinbode Akinbiyi, whose work is conducted across cities and who has been among her mentors. Mimi works largely by intuition. She makes images with an analog camera. Her subject matter is vast and her images cross genres of still life, landscape, and portraiture.

In the process of developing the Chicago show, Mimi examined the entirety of her output over the past decade and developed a narrative that revolves around links that are suggested here—links between the human and natural world. The title of the show, *Closer to the Earth, Closer to My Own Body*, is derived from a passage in Haitian American writer Edwidge Danticat's 1998 book *The Farming of Bones*—an evocation of the proximity of the human and natural worlds, particularly the ways in which we cohabitate with plants and how they console us and aid us in the process of healing. The show takes place in a 1,600 square-foot gallery and consists of just twelve objects—eleven photographs and a 16 mm film that was transferred to 4K video. It combines new work and pieces that were produced over the last eight years.

In this exterior view of the exhibition [Fig. 1], Mimi presents a composite work of five images of bougainvillea photographed in La Romana. Bougainvillea appears often in Mimi's work and signals her interest in histories of botanical migration. For

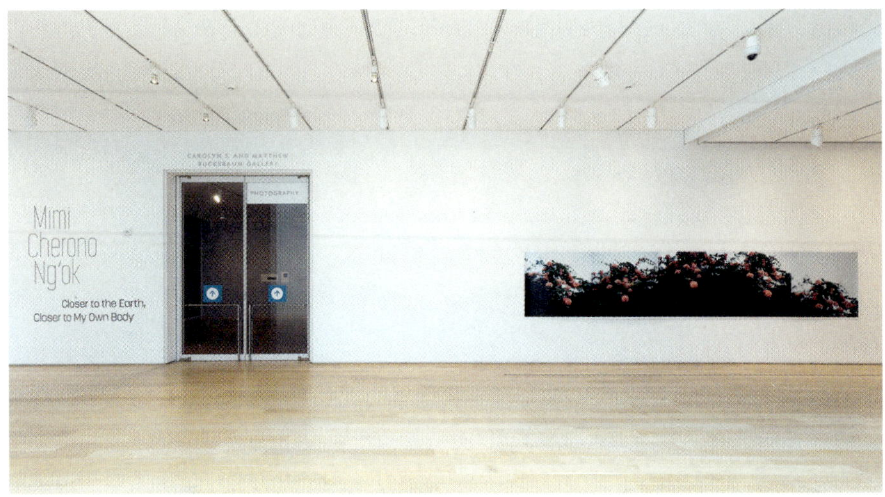

1. Installation view of Mimi Cherono Ng'ok: *Closer to the Earth, Closer to My Own Body*, the Art Institute of Chicago, June 18, 2021–February 7, 2022. Courtesy of the Art Institute of Chicago.

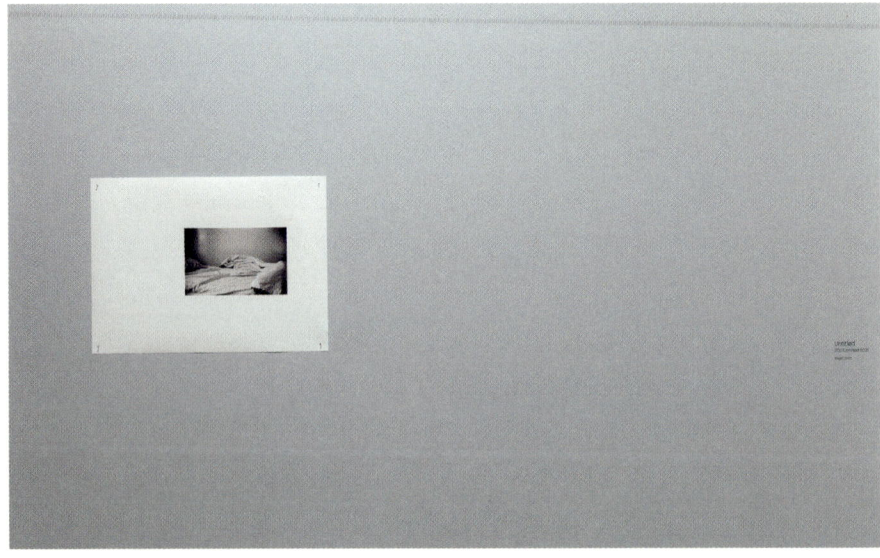

2. Installation view of Mimi Cherono Ng'ok: *Closer to the Earth, Closer to My Own Body*, the Art Institute of Chicago, June 18, 2021–February 7, 2022. Courtesy of the Art Institute of Chicago.

example, specimens of bougainvillea were collected in Brazil, the plant's indigenous region, by French naturalists during the eighteenth century, then exported to Europe, where it was cultivated and traded. Eventually, it found its way to the Botanical Society of Britain and Ireland and was subsequently exported during the nineteenth century to Britain's colonies—including Kenya, where, a century later, a young Mimi grew up enchanted with the vine. As is often the case with Mimi's work, the photographs in the show are untitled and offer little or no didactic detail. The botanical history I shared is secondary to the viewer's experience of the picture—but the format of the photograph alludes to that narrative possibility. The wide form of the work and its composite structure encourages reading the pictures sequentially from one image to the next. The bodily or optical experience of movement across the panorama here symbolizes for Mimi the plant's migration to Kenya from Brazil as well as the artist's own physical movement and encounters with the vine across tropical climates.

Closeness, intimacy—in Mimi's work, these feelings register not only on the level of content, but also in terms of presentation, material form, and spectator experience. All the prints in the exhibition are exposed—they're naked, so to speak—unframed, unmounted, and pinned directly to the wall. Some are reproduced in large scale while others are quite small. These formal choices are meant to encourage the spectator to consider their own body and proximity to the objects—and to step back, get up close, and move across the images. The first photograph shown here [Fig. 2] is from 2007 and is one of the earliest works in the exhibition. It serves as an invitation to the viewer to question their own experience with the imagery. It's a bed—but who slept there? How many people slept there? What kinds of intimacy or intimate experiences took place there?

The exhibition is, notably, very spare. It has a lightness to it, which Mimi cultivated so that the experience of the show would be one of tranquility. This sense is provoked by the concrete gray of the walls, as well as by the way the images are placed—they are nested on the paper, as if within a structure or landscape. Bodies don't often appear in Mimi's work; when they do, if they are not the bodies of family members, they don't appear in straightforward ways, as is suggested by this photograph [Fig. 3]. The body is cropped closely, which for Mimi is a way of introducing associations of tenderness with the black body. She once remarked:

> People don't often associate tenderness with Africans or African life, you know? And I guess those are the emotions and perceptions that I find myself thinking about at times—wanting to have a tenderness of heart, a tenderness in how we regard the lives of others. I was thinking about ways to convey ideas of tenderness through form and composition, wanting to bring the same reverence I have for plants and nature to my portrayal of human beings.[1]

The Body and
the Tropics

87

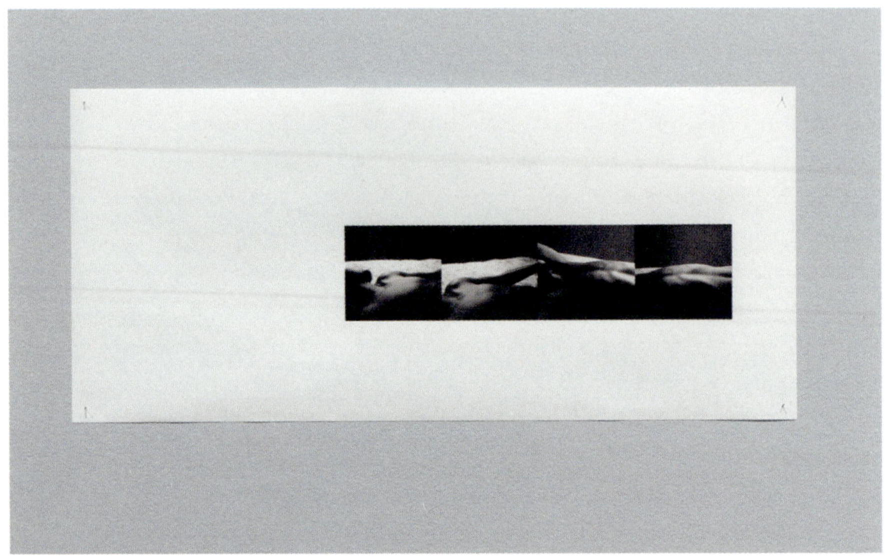

3. Installation view of Mimi Cherono Ng'ok: *Closer to the Earth, Closer to My Own Body*, the Art Institute of Chicago, June 18, 2021–February 7, 2022. Courtesy of the Art Institute of Chicago.

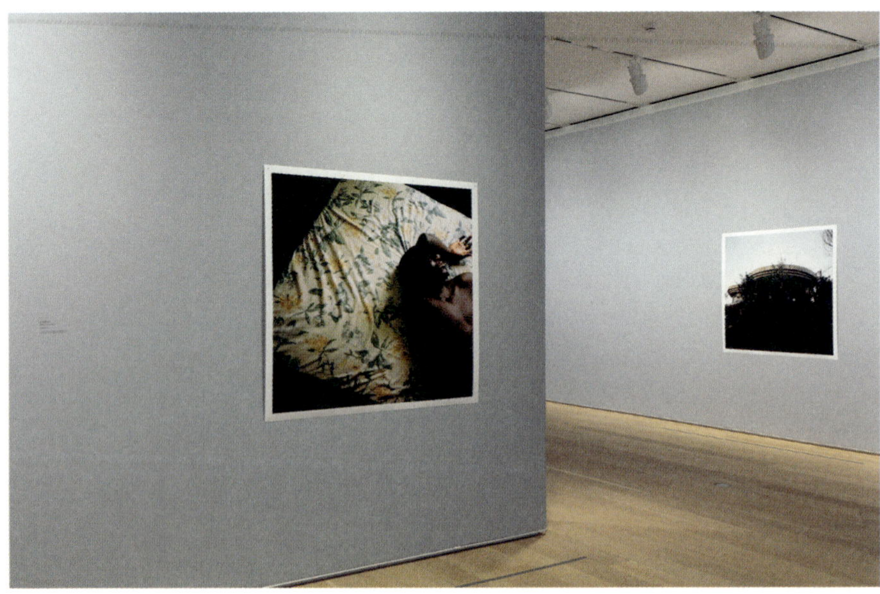

4. Installation view of Mimi Cherono Ng'ok: *Closer to the Earth, Closer to My Own Body*, the Art Institute of Chicago, June 18, 2021–February 7, 2022. Courtesy of the Art Institute of Chicago.

This print is justified to the right. Most of the photographs that have a formal relationship within the show are justified in a similar way, so the spacing of the prints in the exhibition, coupled with this justification, guides the viewer through the presentation space, as if moving from right to left to right. This pairing of photographs [Fig. 4] implies a relationship between plants and the human body, as well as domestic space, in that the domestic architecture is enshrouded by foliage. Throughout the exhibition, there is a ping-pong between architecture, the human body, and vegetal life—one overtaking the other, their proximity always merging in different ways.

I'd like to consider for a moment the materiality of these photographs. Most of them are presented on very delicate rice paper, which meant we had to be very careful during the process of installing them. A team of wonderful conservators developed various strategies for presenting the photographs—for example, by driving nails through them without disrupting the integrity of the prints. Despite this care, in some cases the photographs began to misbehave. In this same installation view, the paper of the photograph of a subject recumbent on a floral pattern bedspread has begun to come away from the wall. Similarly, the photograph to its right has begun to undulate—a pucker is developing in the image. This is something Mimi embraces. She reminded me that this is how paper behaves. Initially, I found this difficult to resolve—I wanted the images to replicate the experience of seeing photographs that are contained by their framing. Mimi's ability to exploit photography's ontological promise of freezing a moment and rendering it "permanent," while at the same time allowing for flux, contingency, and movement through the print's material form, ultimately encouraged me to adjust my expectations in ways that felt liberating. And this also enabled me to appreciate movement in another way: when the photographic prints are allowed to behave in an organic manner, there behavior becomes analogous to the way plants wilt and change form over time.

 I am in Cusco, Peru, and I want to start by acknowledging the land I am on today and paying respect to the people of Quechua, as well as the Machiguenga, Yine, Asháninka, Aymara, and other Indigenous communities who are present in this territory and who continue to face discriminatory practices and colonial Western violence against Indigenous traditions and knowledge.

I'd like to share a few ideas about the early work of Victoria Cabezas, a Costa Rican photographer with whom I've been working since 2015. I curated a historical overview of her photographic projects in dialogue with feminist artist Priscilla Monge in 2018 at TEOR/ética, a visual arts organization in Costa Rica that is dedicated to

The Body and
the Tropics

contemporary art from Central America and the Caribbean, and where I was Co-Curator and Chief Curator until last year. The exhibition traveled to the galleries of the Americas Society in New York in 2019 under the title *Victoria Cabezas and Priscilla Monge: Give Me What You Ask For.*

Between 1973 and 1974, Victoria produced a powerful series around the iconography of the banana and the exoticization of Central American countries, and addressed sexual identity and stereotypes in a critical way and in relation to tropical landscapes. The project was not well received in Costa Rica—experimental uses of photography were not at all common at the time—and most of that work remained generally absent from public discussion. Returning these images to public view after forty years revealed the ability of photography and humor to reflect disputes around power, economics, and gender politics, and invite us to return to recent history from a new perspective.

For the last century, the banana has been a key factor in the environmental, social, and political problems of Central America. In the 1950s and 1960s, the region was an empire of banana plantations run by the US-owned United Fruit Company. Those years also saw large-scale advertising campaigns for Chiquita bananas in North American magazines. The ads employed a romanticized representation of the tropics—one that erased the economic and political realities of the plantations. As we will see, Victoria's photographs are a bold and intelligent response to the so-called paradisaical constructions of the plantation worker—beginning with this 1973 polyptych of hand-colored gelatin prints [Fig. 5].

The series was produced in the early 1970s, after she had left Costa Rica to study at Florida State University, and is part of her "Banana Thesis"—a critique of the political situation in the so-called banana republics. In her photos, the fruit is depicted as a prosthetic, as in this image [Fig. 6]; in other images, these prosthetics are linked specifically to masculinity in photos in which bananas seem to grow unnaturally from the hands, feet, mouth, and sex of a white man. Behind the photos at the sides, Victoria glued reflective material, so the spectator could see their own face in relation to the photo. This work was destroyed, unfortunately.

Victoria portrays men in absurd compositions that "resonate with the myths of exotic lands," as scholar Antonella Pellizari recently wrote.[2] In Latin America in the 1970s, it was unusual to see women artists employing male models in their projects. Victoria used them not only to poke fun at normative masculinity but also to stress the links between patriarchal structures and the history of Western extraction.

Antawan I. Byrd
Miguel A. López
Nicholas Tammens

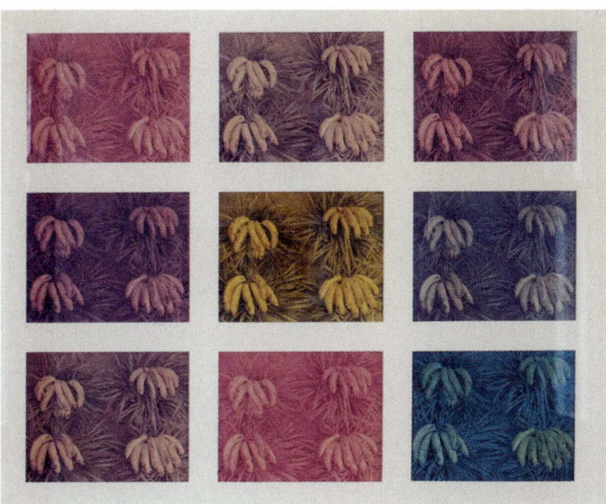

5. Victoria Cabezas, *Untitled*, 1973. Polyptych, hand-colored gelatin silver prints, 80 x 95 cm overall. By permission of the artist.

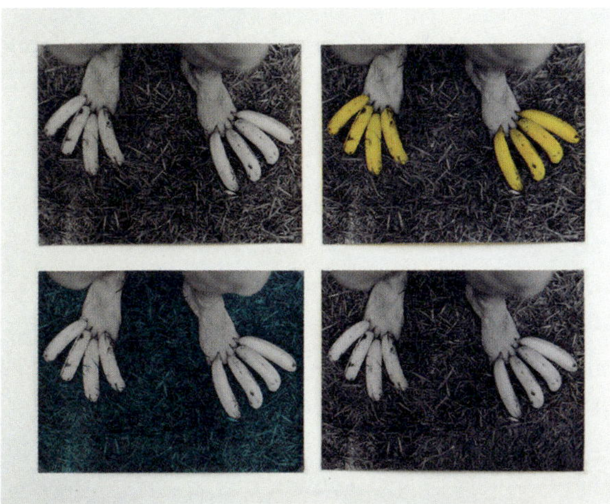

6. Victoria Cabezas, *Untitled*, 1973. Polyptych, hand-colored gelatin silver prints, 65 x 80 cm overall. By permission of the artist.

To quote Victoria regarding the origins of the project:

> I noticed that the supermarket carried Chiquita stickers, showing that [the bananas] were from Costa Rica. . . . What intrigued me the most was that when I mentioned Costa Rica to the Floridians, it was frequently referred to as a "banana republic" . . . . I went to the library and had my eyes opened. A lot of what I read was offensive, ridiculous, and misguided. I decided to make use of irony to refer to how I perceived that we, the inhabitants of the so-called banana republics, were being viewed by "the Other"—somewhat of a parody of "life in the luscious, sensuous tropics."[3]

Victoria moved ironically between the registers of documentary and the performative—dramatizing descriptions she found in books and magazines that describe the local workers—and the deeply exploitative working practices—and overlaying them with heroic and erotic connotations. A picture of a half-naked man lying on the grass, covered with bananas, suggests on the one hand a sort of ritual and, on the other, overproduction and monoculture. A Pop Art aesthetic, achieved by adjusting the balance of cyan, magenta, and yellow, introduces a strange element into the descriptive photographic representation. The 1960s and 1970s were years of war. US military interventions in Central America and the Caribbean, in countries such as Panama, Honduras, Nicaragua, Haiti, and the Dominican Republic, were driven by the protection of US commercial interests. The effects of the rise in consumption of bananas in the United States on Central America included changes to labor practices, as well as pesticide use on the environment and people. By presenting the banana plant in an alien context, Victoria interrupts and opposes the idea of an exotic paradise garden where the fruit flourishes.

These are two of my favorite photographs from the series [Figs. 7, 8]. In one, a man in formal attire tenderly hugs a large inflatable banana in the woods. Here, Victoria plays more explicitly with the fruit's sexual connotations, invoking a homoeroticism that confronts macho stereotypes. It is revealing that a white-collar worker is pictured—a person who probably performs managerial or administrative work; this creates tension with the representation of the "savage"—the half-naked man who has been parasitized by bananas or is part of a ritual ceremony. Perhaps this serves as a comment on the gender politics of international diplomacy at a moment when companies sought to gain total control over the banana trade, from production through distribution. This guy in a suit seems lost, out of place—but still he clings to the big, fake banana.

Antawan I. Byrd
Miguel A. López
Nicholas Tammens

Some of these toy bananas were also transformed into sculptural pieces, such as *El Banano emplumado*—the feathered banana, a sculpture in which the banana's peel is rendered in lace and glitter, alluding to superficial luxury or glamor, and which today can be read

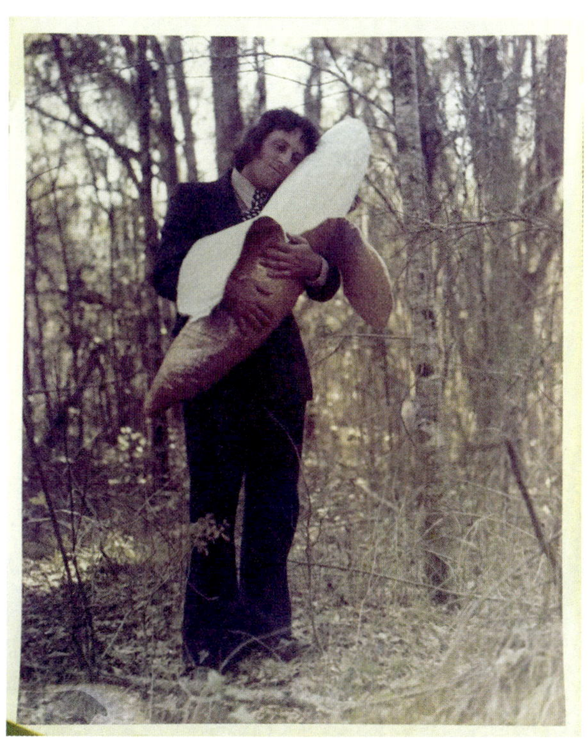

7. Victoria Cabezas, *En el bosque 1* (*In the Forest 1*), 1973. Chromogenic print, 25.3 x 20.3 cm. By permission of the artist.

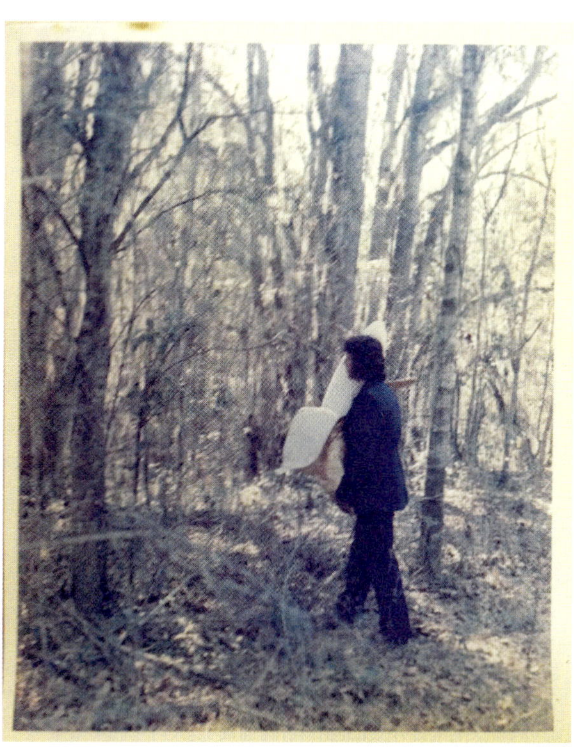

8. Victoria Cabezas, *En el bosque 2* (*In the Forest 2*), 1973. Chromogenic print, 25.3 x 20.3 cm. By permission of the artist.

as a process of queering. Victoria dresses the banana in a burlesque style reminiscent of cabaret shows, converting a sign of phallic authority into theatrical pantomime.

Victoria's practice also included engraving, always in an exploration of the visual economy of gender. From a series produced in the form of a deck of cards, most of them lost or destroyed, the works *King of Bananas* and *Queen of Bananas* make a mockery of the United Fruit Company's business of empire and corporate domination that undermined progress and sovereignty in Central American nations. In a playful way, Victoria also points out the struggles and power dynamics in gender relations.

Victoria uses photography to play with fantasy. Her images respond with irony to massive advertising campaigns and the promise of the perfectly shaped, always accessible banana, as well as to masculine tropes of colonial power and Western extractive practices. In her photos, the body is a place to negotiate new political meanings; from today's perspective, her feminist critique of imperialism and patriarchy is sharper and more urgent than ever.

Nicholas Tammens: Diving into the idea of narrative currents, which is driving our conversation today, here we are very much considering the currency of affect. Koyo [Kouoh] has spoken about currency being an open, elusive term—one we can use to consider notions of economics and value, and of affect and emotion. To draw this into our discussion, I wonder how we might read the images you have shown us within this frame of currency?

AB: To link Mimi's work to currency in the context of emotion and affect, when we began our conversation about the show, it became clear that she has an emotional attachment to a lot of her images and that she produces them as a way of processing her own emotions as she moves through spaces. Oftentimes, this arises from her experiences of traveling alone or of moving to a city that reminds her of home or a place she'd been before. Many times, she suggested that the process of making images was a consoling experience.

Mimi's display of her images for public consumption in an exhibition space is, I would suggest, a way of encouraging viewers to come to terms with their own feelings, their sense of alienation. This comes across largely because she refuses didacticism. All the objects are untitled. In the gallery, I would often overhear people saying, "Oh, this reminds me of Florida," for example. And that's something Mimi welcomes—if a film or an image reminds you of a place you've been or love, then it's imbued with affect. That is where the currency lies.

Antawan I. Byrd
Miguel A. López
Nicholas Tammens

NT: Mimi's photographs strike me as tender and elusive and—exactly as you say— they can be very associative. They don't expressly try to tell you something, which, significantly, is counter to current dominant representations of elements such as the body. We don't see these forms of elusive representation of the body in popular media and it's really in the space of art and photography that we can provide a counter-representation. This is also where I see a blurring of documentary and a sort of travel journal occurring, a diaristic sense that is not about establishing hard truths and facts but rather something we as viewers can project onto and so relate to in a different way.

AB: Thinking back to the various photographs of bodies we've seen over the past two days—those bodies are whole, they appear to be intact. Even though, in some cases, we can't name the subjects that appear, we recognize them as bodies situated in physical space. With the image I showed of a radically cropped body [Fig. 6], ideas of death come to mind, since the body is recumbent. Mimi is careful not to provide too much detail about her relationships to her subjects because she worries that will overdetermine the way they are read. At her exhibitions, people often ask her, "Is that your lover?" There is an assumption that any time a body is framed in such a way, there must be a kind of intimate connection. There's also a risk in such extreme cropping because it reminds you of the objectifying power of the camera. I think Mimi would say it's actually a bit liberating. It forces us to think differently about how bodies exist in space and the ideas and emotions we attach to them.

NT: Miguel, with Victoria's images, the camera acts as a kind of staging device through which the body performs in an entirely different way, providing a form of currency through ironic sociopolitical critique. Perhaps you could say something about how the camera functions for Victoria—or, perhaps, how the body functions with her camera.

ML: Her work offers several ways to enter a discussion about currency, which I would point to as a driving issue for her in the early 1970s, when her intention was to counter racist connotations of the notion of the "banana republic" and to generate public discussion about it. Unfortunately, the work did not generate the conversation she expected. Of course, the concept of the "banana republic" itself refers to economic colonization, so Victoria was interrogating the role of the representation of a commodity in that process, how such representations are celebrated and how they promoted the banana export. In that sense, perhaps we could read into her work the idea of the banana as currency, as a medium of exchange that allows her to foreground the violence and fragile democratic structures that underpin currency. Bananas become a sort of barometer of the political situation.

The Body and
the Tropics

Closely related to the notion of currency is the idea of value—in the case of Victoria's work, cultural value. Few people appreciate the way she approaches photography and her use of photography in relation to performativity. In the 1970s, these works were ignored. Then, in 1983, she presented a powerful series called *Mujeres, Gatos y Televisores*—women, cats, and television—which included self-portraits taken in her small apartment. They exploded the narrative that was shaping sociocultural needs and women's everyday lives and, in a way, they reclaim a female viewership by blurring the boundaries between fiction and reality.

I think it's very revealing that an art critic in Costa Rica—a man—described this work as an example of the "impoverishment of photography." This was not only because Victoria was expressing an affirmative representation of female sexuality but also a reaction to the way she approached the photography itself, which was from a position opposite to that of a purist—she was experimenting with printing techniques. It's telling that it was her approach itself that created the conditions for the material not to be appreciated. She was trying to move toward alternative techniques because she felt a more traditional documentary approach could end up aestheticizing violence.

The way Victoria uses photography as a performative device is related to this—she was reclaiming fiction as a way to respond to a political reality. She described herself in the 1980s as a manipulator, as trying to raise questions about the perceived objectivity of the photograph. She plays with photography, with performativity, with the body, understanding them as political vehicles for the creation of fictions that also function as responses to a political situation.

NT: We've been speaking about the photograph as something taken by photographers but there is this shift, especially in the art world, to photography being a tool in the artist's toolbox—particularly for conceptual and performance artists. Photography in this context becomes integral to the artist's form of communication in various ways. With Victoria, we get a good example of how photography can be used to conceive a political message. This also taps into what you've said about a materiality that is directly related to different kinds of printing techniques. Mimi's work is very different. I think this is significant in terms of the artist's relationship to how a photograph is presented or represented, as well as how we as viewers or collectors— or museums—deal with them.

AB: This resonates with an exchange that emerged when Mimi and I began to have conversations about acquiring some of her photographs for the collection of the Art

Antawan I. Byrd
Miguel A. López
Nicholas Tammens

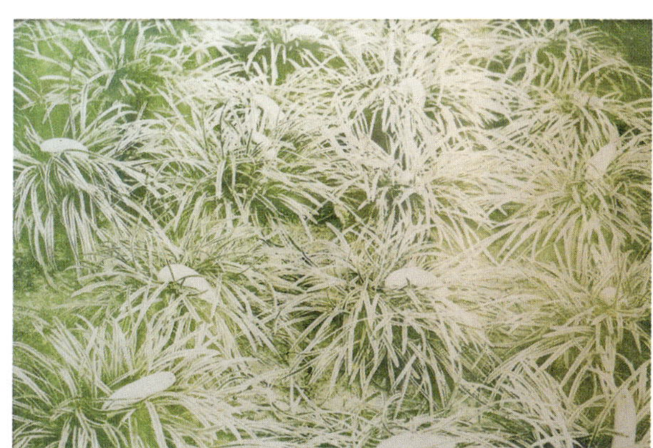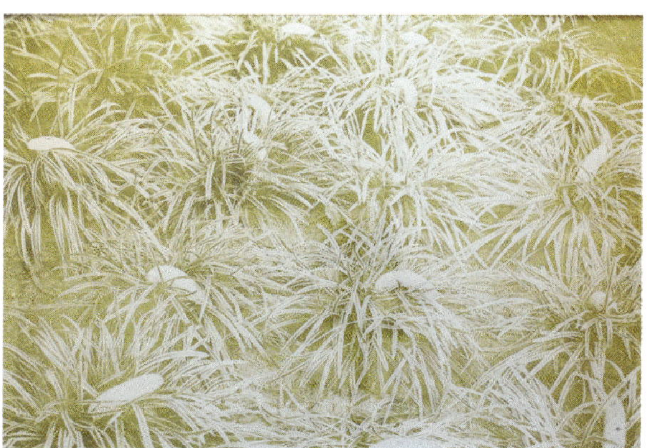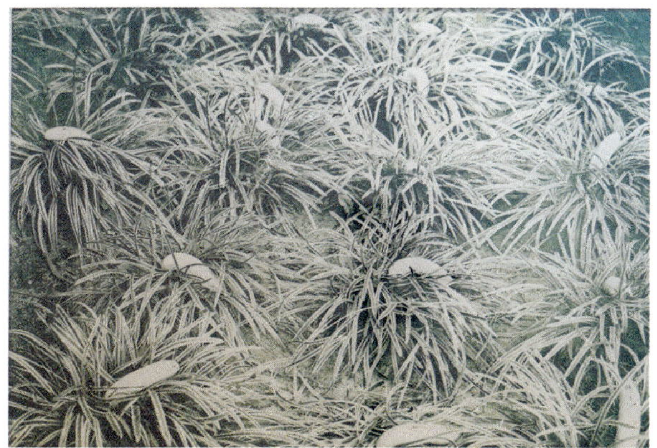

9. Victoria Cabezas, *Untitled*, 1973. Triptych, ink print on aluminium, 37 × 54 cm each. By permission of the artist.

Institute of Chicago. She has a very clear sense of division between how photographs are exhibited and how they're acquired. She regards most of her photographs—I mean the prints themselves—as ephemeral. They're often destroyed after they have been exhibited. That allows her greater freedom, whether to pierce them with nails or to adhere them directly to walls. But once they enter the collection, they become the property of an institution and come under the care of conservators. The Art Institute acquired a set of Mimi's photographs, some of which were in this exhibition, and those prints now reside in the collection. In the future, they may be mounted or framed, and Mimi is fine with this. Such conservation work would enable the prints to be displayed, for example, as part of a rotation of the museum's permanent collection. This experience of the images is very different from observing them in a solo exhibition.

NT: Miguel, could you say something further about the printing techniques Victoria used? Her use of color, for instance, and hand-tinting. We'd love to hear more about those playing cards as well.

ML: She was conducting these experiments, creating colored copies. In the 1970s, she also used reflective materials to create connections between the viewer and the photographs, as I mentioned, and she used solarization a lot. She invented a technique—from working with gum bichromate, she moved into a process she called selective silverplating, for which she obtained a US patent. It includes introducing layers of silver into photographs—she used the technique most notably in nude self-portraits in the early 1980s. Those were among a number of works that she has never had the chance to exhibit.

When I curated the exhibition of her work at TEOR/ética in 2018, it was like encountering a totally different Victoria Cabezas than the one the local art community knew. We were working very closely and I insisted on showing work that she thought wasn't important or relevant for various reasons. I started working with her in 2015 and, on one of my first visits to her home, in early 2016 probably, I learned that she had just thrown out some etchings on metal she had made in 1973 because they had minor creases. As with some of her photographs, these beautiful metal plates were ironic depictions of bananas growing oddly in the middle of nowhere [Fig. 9]. They were in a dumpster, covered with dirt, waiting for the garbage truck. So, that morning, we rescued the plates from the trash and washed them in her kitchen.

Antawan I. Byrd
Miguel A. López
Nicholas Tammens

She had created these amazing works forty-five years earlier, exhibited them just once, then put them away. It was not a big deal for her to discard this work that no one had ever studied or cared for—these etchings were effectively ignored since 1973. This brings me to considering what we, as curators, can do in a situation like this—how curatorial research and practice should help to preserve bodies of work and counter the circumstances that consign them to oblivion. We should also be conscious of creating and acknowledging cultural value around women artists, artists of color—value that comes naturally to white male artists. This also means creating value that opposes racism, the patriarchy, homophobia, and normative notions of quality that organize and determine what is seen and what is not—which is not a question of being aware or not aware of one specific artist, but about the structure of valorization that is in place to reinforce Western white male privilege.

Natalia Brizuela: I would like to hear both of you share thoughts on the differences between art praxis by women in the 1970s and the contemporary period. Cabezas is very much of her time, in her performative use of the photograph, which also speaks to a moment of female artmaking in the 1970s. I don't know Mimi's work but from what I see, it seems like the possibility of a woman artist presenting work that has a delicacy to it speaks to the present—and that it probably would not have been possible in the 1970s. This leads me to wonder—and I ask this with all respect—what does it mean for male curators to produce value out of the work of women artists?

AB: I think it's a great question. Gender has come up in my conversations with Mimi, largely in relation to content. She has a very particular approach to the male body, as I mentioned, and to ideas of tenderness. Her sisters often appear in her work, and they're very much present, their faces are visible, they are visible. In terms of my own experience of interacting with her, I think I've absorbed a sensitivity, but also a fierceness, a toughness. I think there is a fragility, a vulnerability to a lot of her photographs, which she courts in terms of presentation; but thinking of her mural-sized installations, I see boldness. We're perhaps inclined to think about sensitivity or boldness in gendered terms and I think in some ways her practice confounds those stereotypes.

Collaborating with Mimi has been incredible—and challenging for both of us, in part because we respect each other a great deal. But we also have very strong opinions and ideas. We've done numerous interviews over the course of working on the show, tracking our thinking as it evolves, which has been really illuminating. Even now, whenever I go back to the show, I'll send her a message saying, "I just thought about *this*. Were you thinking about *this*?" There's always this never-ending experience of learning. This resonates with Ariella [Azoulay]'s comment about the duration of photography—it's something I experience both as a curator and as a spectator of Mimi's work.

The Body and
the Tropics

Antawan I. Byrd
Miguel A. López
Nicholas Tammens

ML: I describe my work as a curator as building cultural infrastructure and, of course, creating value is a key aspect of that. I'm interested in how representations become spaces of grief, loss, rage, of a public fight against violence—homophobic violence, racist violence, gender violence. I grew up in Peru, in the middle of armed conflict that was organized as a violent value structure. I think constantly about how images can help us to push political discussions in different directions. In that sense, I'm very much committed to the idea of creating value that stands against patriarchy and against racism.

I also think a lot about how we as curators can take responsibility for class privilege and cultural capital and do the work of creating public discussions that counter the dominant male culture, social inequality, and discrimination. This is not necessarily an intellectual approach; it's more an intimate, personal issue. I have never felt that I fit into a normative masculine model, so I'm always trying to move away from that, trying to find answers to my feelings and emotions through work that opens up new possibilities and new worlds that help us imagine other architectures for social organization, other choreographies.

What I love about working with Victoria and reclaiming her works for our time is that I have come to recognize the political power of humor and irony. I'm not sure it is as present today as it has been in the past. I am energized to see how artists—especially younger artists and feminist artists—experience very intimate connections to Victoria's work. I could compare it to discovering a long-lost relative—her work addressed questions of feminism in the 1970s, and very few people took notice. Now, through a lens of contemporary feminism, it's clear that Victoria's work is urgent and relevant. Relevance and political and cultural meaning change over time, and I think this relates to the frameworks we create as curators, which can reclaim this power and urgency and encourage new conversations that can reactivate and reanimate the struggles we are facing now.

1. Antawan I. Byrd and Mimi Cherono Ng'ok, "A Tenderness of Heart: Mimi Cherono Ng'ok on Connection and Image Making," The Art Institute of Chicago, June 29, 2021, https://www. artic.edu/articles/925/a-tenderness-of-heart-mimi-cherono-ngok-on-connection-and-image-making.

2. Antonella Pelizzari, "Slipping on the Banana Peel of Life," in *Victoria Cabezas and Priscilla Monge: Give Me What You Ask For* (New York: Americas Society, 2019), 32.

3. Quoted in Pelizzari, "Slipping on the Banana Peel," 31–32.

Tracing Constellations

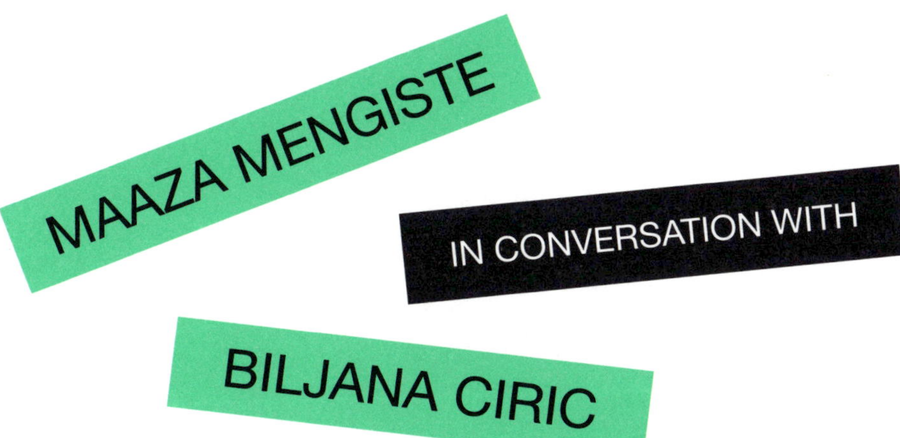

Maaza Mengiste: I own an old black-and-white photograph of two men standing side by side, inches apart [Fig. 1]. One is East African, the other, Italian. The East African—either Ethiopian or Eritrean—wears frayed trousers so old and worn that large patches of his skin show through gaping holes. The bottoms are ripped unevenly, narrowing raggedly and stopping at his calves. An overgrown jacket sags against his slender frame, the open flaps exposing his bare chest. He has crossed his arms almost protectively, and one hand rests against the bend of his opposite elbow. He is barefoot. While it is difficult to tell his age, it is clear that his once-dark hair is now sprinkled generously with white. He squints at the camera with a lowered chin, his mouth a grim line.

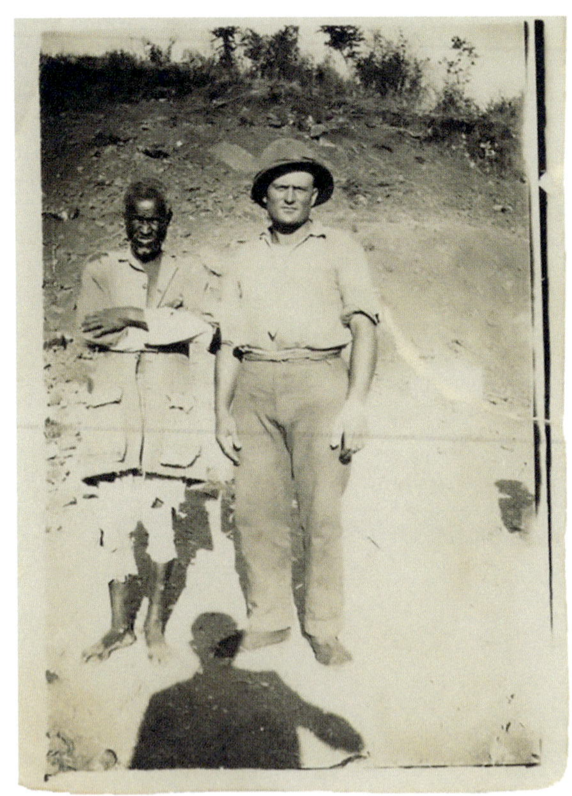

1. Private collection of the author.

The Italian beside him is fully clothed, a hat perched at an angle on his head. It shields his face from the worst of the sun, so he is able to gaze forward, undisturbed. He is taller than the man next to him, more powerfully built. His arms rest easily at his side and his sleeves are rolled up. His shirt is neatly tucked into his trousers and the waistband has been folded over, as if to make do in the absence of a belt. He wears shoes. His left thumb is bandaged. He sports an undershirt beneath his button-down. As he stares into the camera, his chin up, his expression is relaxed—perhaps even satisfied. Though there are two men here, it is he the photographer has placed squarely in the middle of the frame. He is the central figure, the one that cuts the vertical photograph in half. On the other side of this Italian is empty space. It is human-sized, large enough to accommodate one more. It is as if a hollow has been carved out, as though someone else has been scraped away to leave behind a bleached patch of earth.

I no longer recall where I found this photograph. What I remember instead is the moment of encounter with it—that first jolt of recognition that I was looking at *something*, even though I could not yet comprehend what it was. I kept staring at the man with his hands folded across his chest. Why was he standing like that? Was he defiant? Frightened? In pain? What happened to his shirt? Are those scars on his legs recent? Did the Italian standing next to him cause them? I took the photo home and continued to stare, noting the white hair, the beard, the sturdy bones of his visible hand. His feet are dusty. He stands firm, on the ground, upright. That he is barefoot was typical of that time.

But what was this photo, this picture, telling me? What was I *not* seeing, even after staring at it for so long?

In 1935, Benito Mussolini invaded Ethiopia to colonize the country. It was not fair that Britain, France, Germany, Belgium, and other countries had staked their claims on the African continent while Italy had not. It was, Mussolini stated, right to have a place in the sun. Fascism would establish a second Roman Empire on African soil, and it would do so by conquering Ethiopia. One of the first steps toward invasion and war involved photography, the generation of a visual narrative to establish a definition of Ethiopians as uncivilized, backward in every sense, and lacking in all imaginative capabilities. Soldiers brought their cameras to war. Photos sent back to Italy illustrated the stark difference between East Africans and Italians, highlighting the exotic and the unusual, seemingly unbridgeable gaps that existed between two vastly dissimilar groups of people.

I knew all of this when I first encountered this photo. Though I couldn't be certain of the date, I made an educated and informed guess that this image was made after the

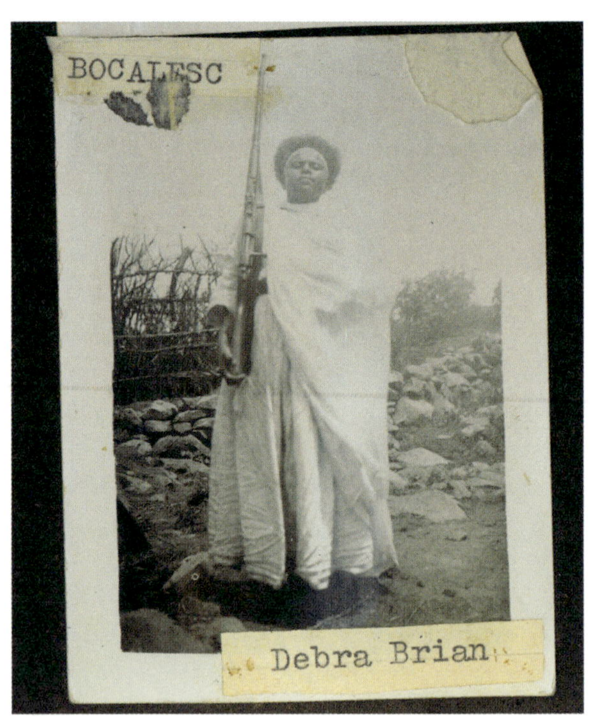

2. Private collection of the author.

October 1935 invasion. War had likely already started, and though Mussolini declared victory in May 1936, I knew this had proven to be premature. The war simply shifted from traditional confrontation to guerrilla warfare. Perhaps this photograph was made in that chaotic period between the declaration of victory and the start of guerrilla war. Perhaps what I was looking at was an image of instability and uncertainty. The Italians. Perhaps the ground that rises sharply behind the two men hides armies of Ethiopians waiting for dark to cover their ambush. Maybe the man squinting into the sun is a prisoner. Perhaps he has been injured and the arms folded in front of him cradle an awful wound. Maybe when the light fades and he is back in the place where he is being held, he will hear a soft whistle and understand that help has come and that he will soon be free.

While the urge is strong, I cannot will a narrative that probably did not exist onto this picture. And, while I might be able to excuse myself by pointing to the brutalities of war, I have to refuse the instinct to protect and even save this man. It is too easy to place myself in the photograph, to reach into the past to settle the pieces into some reassuring order. But it eases my confusion. It leaves me satisfied. It stops the recursive, nagging contemplation that might lead me to other discoveries.

I have in my possession a certain photo album. The picture on its first page depicts a young Ethiopian woman reclining on a rock, propped up on her elbow, squinting into the sun. A valley unfolds in wide, easy sweeps above her bare shoulders. That she is naked from the waist up is an uncomfortable detail but not unusual. This is Ethiopia and it is 1937. By now, we know the larger history of war that frames this photograph. Slivers of paper pasted onto the photo offer an Italianized spelling of her name—Belaynesh—and a town—Shano. At the bottom, in florid handwriting, is the date: 1937. Belaynesh is the first photo in an album once owned by an Italian soldier. It was taken a year into the Italian occupation of Ethiopia. On its own, it carries no real weight. It's exploitative but relatively benign—not as bad as some.

When I first found this album, I opened it, stared at the photo of Belaynesh, and felt immediate anger and revulsion. Then I turned the page, and the next. And the next. And the next. What stared back was a series of women and girls, most of them Ethiopian, all of them equally exploited, indecently revealed. I was taken aback by the precise arrangement of the album. Almost all the photos include a label, typed by hand, specifying the woman's name or the girl's name. The cities noted at the bottom of each photograph indicate a zigzag across Ethiopia. Most of them are dated 1936 or 1937. At times, as if it were unacceptable to leave a picture unmarked, a label simply announces the subject as *donna abissina*—an Abyssinian woman. The album was carefully curated. The photos are organized, meticulously labeled, guided by a patient eye. This is a detailed, crafted story of one man's time in Ethiopia, a way to speak of his "great African adventure." It was difficult to look through this album. It made me so uncomfortable that I closed it and shut it up in a drawer for some time—indeed, for a number of years.

Eventually, prodded very insistently by a friend, I retrieved the album. I looked through it again. This time, I looked at it all the way to the end. And there is one photo that stands out. It is different from the others. Toward the end of the album is the picture of a woman named Bogalech, from Debre Birhan [Fig. 2]. Unlike the others, she is fully clothed in traditional Ethiopian dress. She has a shawl draped over one shoulder and stands with her chin raised, a rifle in her hand. Bogalech is not afraid, unlike some of the other women in this album, nor is she demure. She looks determined and resilient. Strong. She is a startling vision in an album such as this, and for a while, eager to strip away the awful residue of those other photos, I told myself this is a positive portrayal.

Considered on its own, it might point to the photographer's leanings toward a more complex understanding of women. In an album otherwise full of exploitative images of women, however, a photograph of a woman with a gun becomes not a sign of female strength, but a mockery of it. The implication that she is weak is exposed by all the other pictures that came before her. This woman is bound by the fate of the others. They are ghosts, hovering behind her outside the frame. When I looked at Bogalech, I needed to see them. I needed to see the album. I needed to see the hands that made the album, that pasted the labels, that propped the camera in front of his eye, and clicked the shutter to photograph not a woman, but power and manhood.

When I look at her, I need to see him—because what her picture is, in essence, is a self-portrait of this photographer.

Look at him. Do you see him? Do you see him now, the man standing between these two in that space where an entirely new landscape rests? That shadow of a man who has insisted that he, too, appear in the photo—this photographer who makes himself both visible and invisible, rendering this image of two men a self-portrait. It was impossible for me to see him without those women, without Bogalech, without the discomfort that brought me back again and again, to this first sighting—this first disruption. There he is: not the answer to a question but a path toward another kind of journey, one that considers what is *there*, even with all the unknowns, and what we can learn from it—from him—about power, about ways of seeing, about the uncomfortable terrain that lies between confusion and the sort of transformation that

Maaza Mengiste
Biljana Ciric
Tala Hadid

provides new questions. Perhaps, too, about all the ways power repeatedly remakes itself in the image of the Other, in desperate acts of failed resurrections.

Biljana Ciric: There is a pop song from Yugoslav times—I knew the words when I was a child. In fact, I know them even today. The song is about Haile Selassie—roughly translated, it includes lyrics that go something like this: "Haile Selassie, Prince of Africa and Asia." As a kid, I knew the song but I didn't know who Haile Selassie was. Three years ago, before my first trip to Ethiopia, this song reappeared in my head. It is a testament to non-aligned legacies, interrupted histories, geopolitics, and how these shape our lives. But it is also a reminder that we need more songs to be written differently.

Sara Ahmed says it is always important to articulate how you arrive at the work you do.[1] Here is my attempt to situate myself: I appear as white. I'm half-Serb, half-Macedonian. I was born in Germany, but I grew up in Yugoslavia with my grandparents. My place of birth indicates that my parents sought a better future in the West as *Gastarbeiter*—"guest workers"—who were trying to become part of privileged white European society, at the same time trying to bridge the gap between failed socialism and Western modernity. I went the opposite direction—to the East—not really understanding what that would mean or where it would lead me. In 2000, I went to China, and China gave me so much. Thanks to the rise of Chinese contemporary art, I learned about curating; thanks to the international exposure of that art, my work was exposed internationally. Through this passage, I made friendships and working relationships, and navigated to my own position, from where I speak, practice, and listen. In the meantime, the self-organized culture and relationality of the Chinese art system disappeared. These working conditions make me question constantly what kind of international I want to produce, and how that international is produced. Where do I start? What tools do I use? These questions have become all the more sensitive and more difficult to face since the start of the pandemic.

Can you imagine the blue horse? [Fig. 3]

In her book *No Document,* Anwen Crawford suggests if a person could imagine a blue horse, that signaled a kind of freedom. Not just whimsy—the freedom to imagine remaking the world.[2] The Indigenous thinker Bruce Pascoe has taught us that when Indigenous people look at the sky, they look not at the points of bright light but at the darkness between them.[3] If you look at the spaces between the stars, you will be able to find the Dark Emu.

Can you see the Dark Emu?

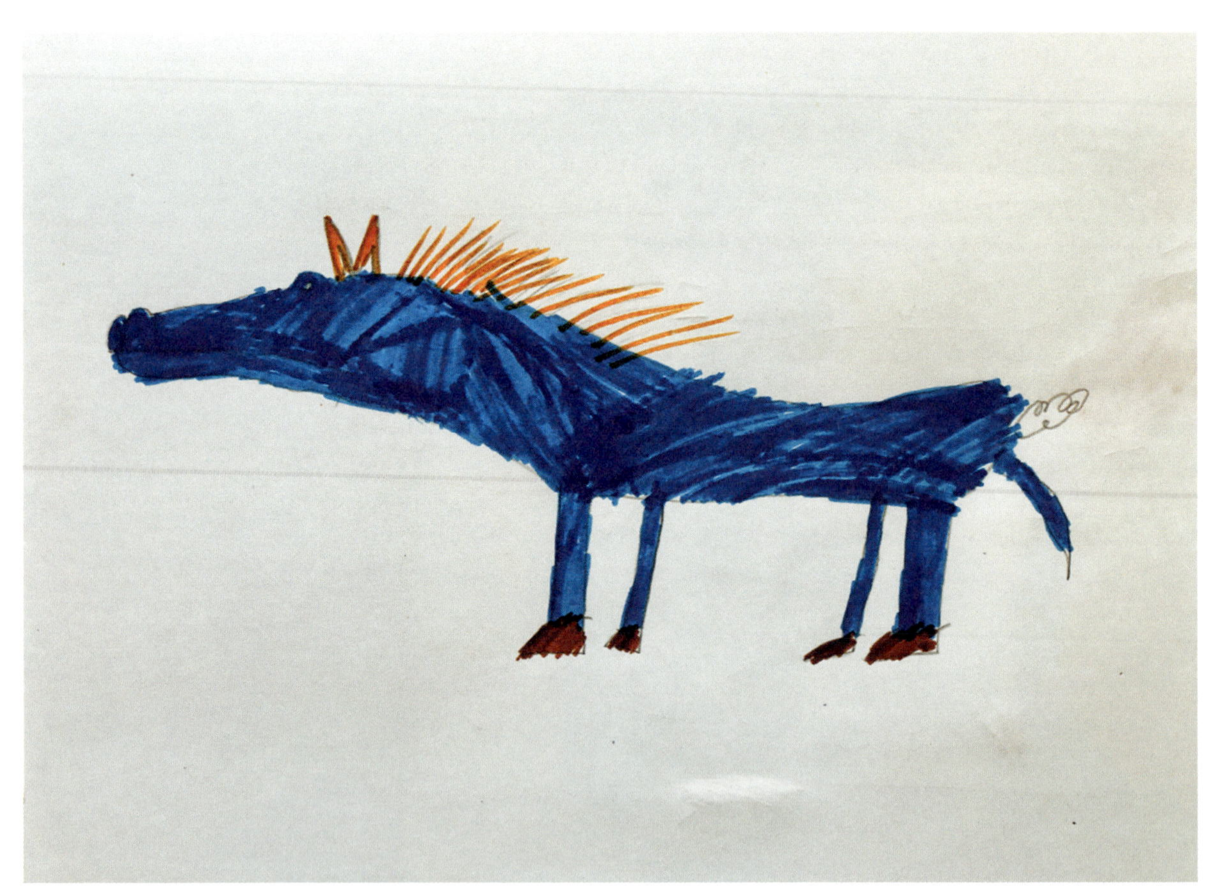

3. *Blue Horse* by Teodor Hu. Courtesy the artist.

When, in 1966, anthropologists John Adair and Sol Worth gave Navajo people cameras to film their own community members, they filmed them from behind, not wanting to capture and imprison their souls. When filming animals, they would ask permission to borrow the images from their owners.

We ask for too few permissions.

I've been working on an inquiry called As You Go… Roads under Your Feet, towards the "New Future" for almost two years. And I would like to share with you the kind of space it creates. The project reflects on the Belt and Road Initiative [BRI] and how it will alter the aesthetics and practice of everyday life in various local contexts. I conceived and initiated the project in 2019, after conducting curatorial research in East Africa, Central Asia, and a number of Balkan countries, where the project is situated. Our work questions whether the new cold war that is slowly unfolding in front of us, caused by the pandemic, can engender connections that no state can control—that are truly ours and that we need.

Early maps of the BRI show its overland and maritime routes. A more recent map shows that it is a very dynamic project, which includes a military base in Djibouti. Details of forts, pipelines, and several other infrastructure projects are apparent. When the pandemic started, it's something that began as a Health Silk Road with the support of vaccines, CPR equipment, and PPE equipment, among many other things.

The importance of the bodily knowledge I acquired, by walking through and listening within these places, shaped both the project and my understanding of my own limitations, leading to an urgency to expand what curating can do. As You Go… is structured as long-term research over three years, with partner cells, individuals, and institutions. They are: What Could/Should Curating Do? in Belgrade; the Times Museum in Guangzhou, the Rockbund Art Museum in Shanghai; Robel Temesgen and Sinkneh Eshetu, respectively an artist and a writer based in Addis Ababa; Zdenka Badovinac from Ljubljana; the Public Library in Bor, a small town in the east of Serbia; and Artcom, a civic association in Astana, Kazakhstan.

This configuration of cells and partners did not come together through mutual friendship or shared values. I am friends with some of them, while some of them are collaborators or people whose work I know and respect. These cells came together via my invitation, which was extended knowing they would recognize the potential lying in such a relationship and the possibility of gaining something from it. That "something" is different for individual cells, each of which comes to the table with its own intention to learn, to unlearn, to become visible or invisible, and to relate to the international community. What they all share is a discomfort with regard to how the international has been performed through contemporary art practice, and a desire to create pathways for working and imagining otherwise.[4]

In his seminal text "Our Sea of Islands," Epeli Hau'ofa proposes thinking about oceans with islands as points of connection, rather than separation.[5] The curatorial for me is that point of connection or interdependence; this is how I envision my curatorial role in this project.

The natural position of the cells of the body and our "pleasing instability"[6] redefines notions of authority. It also opens up the possibility of collaborative reflection and authorship, as well as the bliss of ignorance that, in the presence of another mind, is not always easy to achieve. The proposition opens up a number of not easily answered questions. How might we maintain horizontality within the project among partners? How might we go beyond economic means within a project? Is it possible to speak about solidarity across different contexts? On what terms? How might we go about it? Is it possible to slow down the process of production, affording artists and researchers the time and space to develop projects that may have a real impact on their local context? And how do we imagine and develop different working rituals with each other through this process?

Those members of cells who have stable internet connections meet every two weeks. It took time to acknowledge that such basic functionality is not the same for everyone, and to negotiate the creation of a space within the project to embrace this unevenness, rather than register it as a deficit. Creating and nurturing that relational space for almost two years brought the partner cells to respect the knowledge to which they may not have access, to recognize this lack of access, and to build trust in other cells—at the same time acknowledging their own urgencies as well as knowledge situated within other cells that is not yet part of their own. This is the point where the spatial conditions of multiplicity slowly emerge.

My own role as a mediator and translator of these relationships within the nurturing space we have created brings a new challenge to the curatorial. Mediating objects, people, things, and thoughts gives priority to certain ideas. Prioritized ideas are distributed and that very act of distribution gives them power. Such distribution moves in two directions: things and ideas both go out and come in. This operation of multiple directions actively formulates this nurturing space.

Maaza Mengiste
Biljana Ciric
Tala Hadid

To practice intimacy between cells, opacity is needed rather than visibility. That intimacy defines how ideas are shared, and to what extent. Visibility is defined and controlled by the way the Western economy of discourse works hand in glove with the global economy.[8] Many of these localities, situated as they are at the margins of the global economy, regained a momentum of visibility through geopolitical conflict when the BRI entered the sphere of interest of other global powers. Will this new visibility and geopolitics create alternatives to our existence, or will it uphold the extractive, capitalist logic of Western European modernity, which has been in place for so many years? Following the BRI, As You Go… enters a space of ambiguity, similar to what the Southern Conceptualism Network addresses: "exposing practices to visibility, they gain more attraction that could be used and consumed in different ways."[9]

Édouard Glissant discusses the "right to opacity" as the right to resist being transparent to the gaze that "constructs the Other as an object."[10] For Glissant, the right to opacity is not being available to be understood according to Western logic. His *opaque* is not obscure; "it is that which cannot be reduced."[11] An opaque position for most of the partner cells seems an important position to take, especially within this present moment. We do not seek the visibility the infrastructural projects of the BRI provide. They are there, stable and visible with their bridges, roads, and railways, while we try to maintain our right to opacity through proximity, working together in the hope this process can open up new spaces through imagining differently.

In June of last year in Ethiopia, Oromo singer Hachalu Hundessa was murdered. After that, there was significant unrest and more than eighty people were killed. During that time, the state shut down the internet and telecommunication systems for three weeks, and we were unable to reach our collaborators. I asked Sarah Bushra, an Addis Ababa-based curator, to write about was happening at that time:

> I finally found a friend to accompany me to the telecom, still unaware that it was in fact the government who had shut down the internet. We walked up the streets and suddenly came face to face with the stampede of wide-eyed young men, holding heavy-duty sticks, unmistakably handled as weapons. In a traditional dance of the Oromo people, the men sport a sturdy stick, much in the same way as the men in front of us did. I remembered the dancer standing next to me: as he once struggled to learn this dance, teeth clenched, sweat beads trickling, launching the stick up and down to the rhythm of a heavy staccato breathing.[12]

Sarah refuses to expose her fear to us when facing the threatening young man. She refuses to victimize herself in an English text for an international project but reminds us of the dance ritual, its beauty, and the difficulty of performing. She knows she's expected to describe brutality, but she does not.

What I have learned through researching different forms of coming together is that moments of visibility are fragile and that they corrupt relationships. They are the moments when the public image is captured, created, and reproduced.

Using slow modes of working as a core for a curatorial methodology, remaining within the process, and taking time, being together, caring with each other, allows us to delay the fragile moment until we are ready to come together in our visibility and learn collectively how to perform it.

That public moment could be an exhibition, but it could also be a protest, shelter, or a continuation of walking with. Not naming it an exhibition delays the definition of what it could be or become, allowing relationships to transform the need for going public into one of being situated in that need rather than in the pre-determined formats we are accustomed to in relation to exhibitions and events. It gives us time to imagine what that moment could become by listening dynamically to the times we are in. Proposed as such, a public moment is not conceived of as an ultimate goal or final destination but, rather, part of the journey toward co-immunity.

If you would like to imagine the image of this inquiry, it is an image of walking—not as a way of getting somewhere but as sharing time and creating space for unevenness to coexist. The image you see is fragmented. You can't see things in full. It might appear illogical to you at times. You will see the bed of the Akaki, Kebena, and Bantyiketu Rivers but also fish in the bathroom of a Chinese chef in a small town in eastern Serbia. Perhaps you can see us from moment to moment but our connection cuts and there is a blackout. You will see the Dark Emu and the Blue Horse in that dark space.

Tala Hadid: Maaza, in an interview in which you spoke about your wonderful book, *The Shadow King,* you said you felt you were surrounded by ghosts and that sometimes you could feel them rise up and demand their right to speak—to be, in your words, "remembered and ushered into the rooms of the honored."[13] Perhaps you could speak about the summoning of ghosts, or of finding a way to see them—how you look at these gaps, these hidden landscapes and uncomfortable terrains or, as in the image you showed us, at shadows that are present in the image. And Biljana, you mentioned that one of your goals is to unlearn how we work together. I wonder if that was made possible through working in the way you described, which takes

Maaza Mengiste
Biljana Ciric
Tala Hadid

place on indiscernible lines, in the gaps—or as Bruce Pascoe, whom you quote, says: "looking at the dark shapes between the stars?"[14]

Perhaps you could both speak about how you unlearned how to look in a certain manner or, rather, how to awaken the eye to look at what is hidden and in-between—or, as André Bazin wrote, to strip away "those piled-up preconceptions, that spiritual dust and grime with which" the eye is covered, so as to be able to offer things up to attention and love.[15] Perhaps we could talk about this way of looking, and a possible journey forward.

MM: When I was writing *The Shadow King*, I felt I was surrounded by ghosts. Part of that feeling was the result of having collected photographs taken by Italian soldiers of their time in East Africa, as well as in Libya. I have been collecting these images for about twenty years now, which is much longer than I have been writing. I didn't know what I was doing in collecting them. The photographs somehow seemed to call to me. It was only much later that I started writing the novel. While I was writing, I felt the same way I felt when I am looking at those photos—a sense of looking at landscapes of the disappeared. All along, in looking at that terrain, I had been taught there was nothing there—that their absence meant they had never existed.

I began to think about the difference between the *disappeared* and the *absent*, and the gaps left by people who are disappeared. The way that, when you're dealing with the disappeared, grief never fully forms nor meets its end in healing. I think this is why, when regimes come to power, one of the first things they do, in addition to quieting the poets, is start to disappear people. I wanted to think about how I might learn to see into that space, where supposedly there is nothing. I think the album of naked women and girls I spoke about was my first true lesson in how to see for myself. When I was buying that album, I got into a bidding war with somebody. I wondered, "Who are you? Why do you want these images?" But I got them. I felt as though they were mine, that these were my sisters—but I couldn't look at them. Then—and this comes back to the ghosts—at the urging of a friend, I finally opened the album. It had been calling to me, but I didn't yet have a vocabulary to begin to understand the photographs it contained—and it felt exploitative to look without understanding. Finally, I pulled the images out. As I mentioned, each photograph had its location noted, so I got out a map of Ethiopia and put it on my wall and started marking each of the locations with pins.

I realized I was looking at a cartography of the disappeared. What I saw was a line that led, depending on which way you wanted to trace it, from Addis Ababa to the Northern

Highlands, where the war was raging, or from the Northern Highlands to Ethiopia, which is the path the Italians took during their conquest of the country. Completely by chance—or perhaps not—I had been reading testimonials of Ethiopians who survived the concentration camps the Italians had built across Ethiopia, and into Somalia and parts of Eritrea. At that point, I just happened to have been reading a statement by a young child who had survived an execution camp. And this person was recounting something in Shano, which is where that first picture I mentioned, of Belaynesh naked on a rock, was taken. She was posed as if she were an odalisque. I realized then that right behind her shoulder was a landscape of atrocity. It was a black site. An execution site. Then I looked up more of these testimonials, and there was a camp in Debre Birhan, there was a camp in Dessie. Everywhere this album named—every name of a town that was attached to a naked woman or girl—had been an execution site. I realized that this photographer was using the women and girls as a coded language to begin to speak of the other violences of war; that whoever this was had been at all of these execution sites but could not photograph that—but could use these women as an alternate vocabulary. The ghosts I speak of were in those images. I didn't quite understand that until I could put everything together.

So Bogalech might have been holding the rifle of a soldier from an execution site. The mockery resounds through so many layers. This album is something I'm still trying to figure out. But when I speak of writing this book with the ghosts, it's because I think—as Ariella [Azoulay] mentioned—that the event of photography is never over. It can only be suspended. These are events that are not finished yet. I feel still the weight of that. I think there's more to discover, but the ghosts were very, very present for me in the writing of this book.

BC: Over these last many months, I've been thinking a lot about what has been happening to us and whether there is the possibility we are working toward being a different kind of human—in relation to what Maaza just mentioned. Where are these referents of being different types of humans? I think what we learn through education creates only a specific kind of human—one that is very individualistic and can survive competition. The idea of *success* is always there. That is a lot to think about, as a mother, a curator, and educator. Where do we go from today? For me, the pandemic presented an important opportunity—maybe we have missed a chance to rethink and try doing things differently. Maybe not.

How can we practice the interdependence the pandemic has reminded us of? In the context of contemporary art, our relationships are always linked to temporal events. I wanted to try to expand this relationship in time and see what can come out of that.

Maaza Mengiste
Biljana Ciric
Tala Hadid

For me, what is important is to learn to listen, and my role within the whole inquiry is very much that of a mediator—constantly nurturing this in-between space and making it elastic. So, to learn to listen—and to listen to the silence, which became a very important element within the inquiry, one we all read very differently because we translate only what we understand, and our points of understanding are always different. This listening is something I've been trying to practice, and I think, especially within this specific project, it is an exercise of unlearning and learning to work together.

TH: Biljana, you mentioned the right to opacity in relation to visibility, and work that's done in the margins in a way that might allow us to chart a map—which links to this topography Maaza mentioned, which is initially drawn with invisible ink. It is the summoning up of those ghosts that needs protection—for lack of a better term—or a sacred space. I wonder about that—not an invisibility but an opacity or opaqueness.

BC: As we are moving toward intimacy, I think opacity is needed. The partners of this project didn't know each other before we began this practice, so we needed a space of intimacy to come to know each other and where we are speaking from. At the same time, there is an interesting element of opacity—as I said, we can only translate what we understand. We learned to embrace that and to create a space where that can play out. Living through this uncertain time over the last two years, so many things have happened around this inquiry—colleagues have caught COVID, their family members have died, colleagues have lost positions, their budgets have been cut, and there is extreme control over the public realm. I think we also need that opacity to try to think about how we are going to go forward from this moment, outside the local contexts we work in, because we are struggling under very difficult conditions.

Natalia Brizuela: Maaza, could you speak about your beautiful and very detailed description of the first image you showed and its relationship to this conjuring of or living with ghosts?

MM: I described the photograph according to the progression of seeing that happened for me. That first encounter was just what I described to you—the first instance of what I could and might see—and what I was guessing. It was only in being able to set that image next to others that I was able to come back to it and notice the photographer's shadow. That photograph was an inspiration for the title of *The Shadow King*. I describe that image in a scene in the novel. My character's shadow is in the book. But I haven't yet figured out the imbalance in that image. The Italian man is in the center of the image but there's space for someone else. I noted that space—perhaps it is where the ghosts are. It's there. It feels like a deliberate choice because everything else is so composed. That is a deliberate space and the photographer has placed his shadow there. It's just not in balance. That's another look that I have to take into this but it's a process. Like the waiting Robin [Coste Lewis] spoke about today. There is waiting in all of these photographs. One leads to another and to the next. I'm still waiting for the story to unfold.

Antawan I. Byrd: Maaza, I'm interested that you've been collecting photo albums for twenty years. Could you tell us more about the criteria of the objects you collect? You mentioned that you find it difficult sometimes to find the vocabulary to describe some of the images you confront. I wonder if, in acquiring albums, you think about your ability to explain them as you go about selecting images?

MM: My collecting of the photographs preceded my ability to understand what I have. I still don't fully comprehend everything. I realized there are aspects to this history and to the interconnectedness among nations and peoples and geographies that I haven't quite come to understand yet. As I mentioned, I've been collecting these images for about twenty years. I have come by them in often unpredictable ways. Every time I'm in Italy, I go to flea markets and antique shops. Sometimes I go online, and I'm sure with certain images I'm competing against the same people, especially for the photographs of women. The images I have and the images I want to have in my possession have changed over the years. Initially, I didn't know what to look for—I was collecting portraiture or images taken by photojournalists.

Later, I realized the real history of war lay in personal images made by soldiers, soldiers who took the camera to war and didn't have to worry about censorship by the fascists. That's when I feel my collecting really took off. Sometimes, I still don't understand what I'm looking at. I don't know enough.

I have no interest in collecting any kind of Nazi paraphernalia but an album made, I think, by a quite young Nazi soldier, stationed in Naples, came into my possession. I think it is from 1943. Among the relatively casual images of soldiers, most of them fourteen, fifteen, sixteen years old, there is one image I fought to obtain. It's a picture of two black soldiers wearing what I think are Nazi uniforms. Beneath them is written "Abyssinian soldiers." I'm still trying to understand that.

There's a reason I own that—this is what I mean when I speak of ghosts. There's a reason these photographs drag me back to them, time and again, and that reason may not become apparent for years yet. There's something there and I don't know what that is yet. I don't understand yet. I have found my own face in a museum in Oxford,

Maaza Mengiste
Biljana Ciric
Tala Hadid

in photographs of my uncles. Images find you in ways that are unexpected. So, I wait and try to remain open to everything that might come.

1. See Sara Ahmed, "Sara Ahmed: Dresher Conversations." Interview by Jessica Berman, Dresher Center Director. UMBCTube, YouTube video, March 20, 2019, https://www.youtube.com/watch?v=zadqi8Pn0O0.

2. Anwen Crawford, *No Document* (Artarmon: Giramondo Publishing, 2021).

3. Bruce Pascoe speaking to children about his book *Young Dark Emu* at the Ian Potter Center for Performing Arts, Monash University, Melbourne, 2021.

4. Elisabeth Povinelli, "After the Last Man: Images and Ethics of Becoming Otherwise," *e-flux journal* 35 (2012), https://www.e-flux.com/journal/35/68380/after-the-last-man-images-and-ethics-of-becoming-otherwise/.

5. Epeli Hau'ofa, "Our Sea of Islands," *The Contemporary Pacific* 6, no. 1 (Spring 1994): 147–161.

6. Merve Emre, "Critical Love Studies," *LA Review of Books*, May 3, 2020, https://lareviewofbooks.org/article/critical-love-studies/.

7. Stephen Muecke, "The Great Tradition: Translating Durrudiya's Songs," in *The Mother's Day Protest and Other Fictocritical Essays* (Lanham: Rowman & Littlefield International, 2016), 27–38.

8. Stephen Muecke, *Textual Spaces: Aboriginality and Cultural Studies* (Sydney: New South Wales University Press, 1992), 15.

9. Alvano de Benito Fernandez, "Latin American Conceptualism Bursts into the Institutional Arena Bringing New Management Models," interview with Jesus Carrillo, *Artealdia,* year unknown, http://www.artealdia.com/International/Contents/Profiles/Latin_American_Conceptualism_Bursts_into_the_Institutional_Arena_Bringing_New_Management_Models.

10. Édouard Glissant, *Poetics of Relation* (Ann Arbor: Michigan University Press, 1997), 189.

11. Glissant, *Poetics of Relation*, 189.

12. Sarah Bushra, *Treading a Line, As You Go...* online journal, August 2020, http://wcscd.com/index.php/wcscd-curatorial-inquiries/as-you-go-journal/treading-a-line/.

13. Maaza Mengiste, from Maaza Mengiste Q&A, The Booker Prizes 2020, https://thebookerprizes.com/maaza-mengiste-the-shadow-king-interview.

14. Bruce Pascoe, *Dark Emu, Aboriginal Australia and the Birth of Agriculture* (London: Scribe UK, 2018), 1.

15. André Bazin, "The Ontology of the Photographic Image," in *What Is Cinema? Volume I*, ed. and trans. Hugh Gray (Berkeley: University of California Press, 1967), 15.

Tracing
Constellations

Aida, Save Me!

JOANA HADJITHOMAS AND KHALIL JOREIGE

Here we are, standing in the dark, waiting. We've checked the focus and the frame. The sound is good. The image is fine. As the film starts, we throw one more glance at all the heads in the darkness. The audience seems focused. It's the Lebanese premiere of our feature film, *A Perfect Day*. The evening goes well. We are relieved. But the next day, the distributor of the film phones us. He sounds panicked. A woman named Aida has just called him. She is outraged and claims that our film uses images of her husband without her consent.

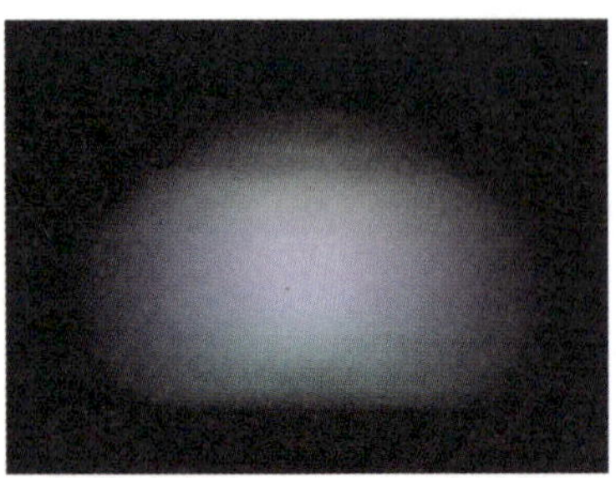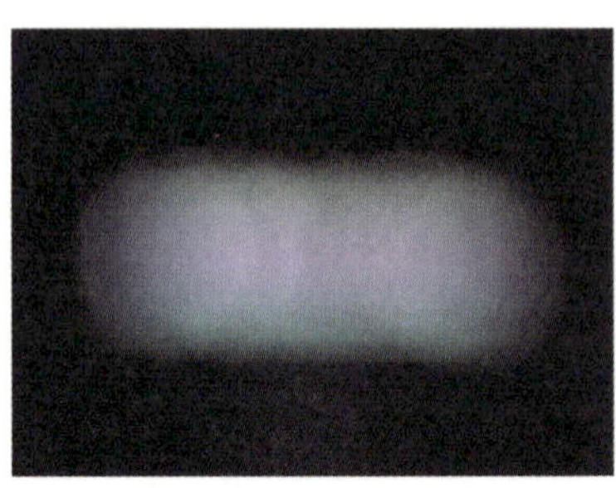

1. The search for focus in the opening of *A Perfect Day* (Joana Hadjithomas and Khalil Joreige, 2005).

A Perfect Day was produced on a microscopic budget. We had to take finance-related decisions that translated into radical aesthetic choices. The film hardly ever recreates reality; on the contrary, we insert ourselves into reality by filming in public spaces and using more of a documentary style. Some shots were taken on the fly or provoked, according to a method by which situations are created that capture the energy of the place and allow the story to unfold. For a number of scenes in nightclubs, for example, we filmed without extras, simply asking the people who were there if they agreed to be filmed. We thus inserted the action of the film into the reality at hand, into the energy of Beirut nights.

Following the same principle, we also filmed in the streets of Beirut. Our assistants asked everyone we filmed for their consent but chances were that a few permissions were missing. We had no idea exactly which sequence in the film Aida took issue with, nor who her husband was. But soon, she phoned us sounding very upset. She accused us of having used the image of her husband in the notice of the disappearance of the protagonist's father, who was kidnapped during the Lebanese Civil War—just like Khalil's maternal uncle, whose story inspired *A Perfect Day*.

During the war, kidnapping was common practice in Lebanon. In choosing their victims, kidnappers mostly relied on ID cards, which state the holder's religious confession. Seventeen thousand people have been reported missing in Lebanon since the war—which officially ended in 1990. We might expect that the vast majority of those missing have been killed. But how is it that their bodies have never been found? Beirut is a highly urbanized city, a huge building site, a city in full reconstruction. There is constant drilling and digging, yet nothing is ever found—no mass graves, no traces. How shall we mourn the dead in the absence of corpses, in the absence of evidence? The missing bodies come back to haunt us. The disappearance doesn't dissipate: it's an abyss that opens up fields of possibilities.

The status of missing persons is regulated by a national law that states that missing persons may be declared deceased four years after their disappearance. In part, *A Perfect Day* tells the story of a young man named Malek and his mother Claudia, who go through the process of declaring the legal death of Claudia's missing husband—and Malek's father—who disappeared more than fifteen years ago. We chose to use newspapers in which the notice of his disappearance would have been published at the time of kidnapping. To effect this, we essentially forged news clippings to fulfill the needs of fiction.

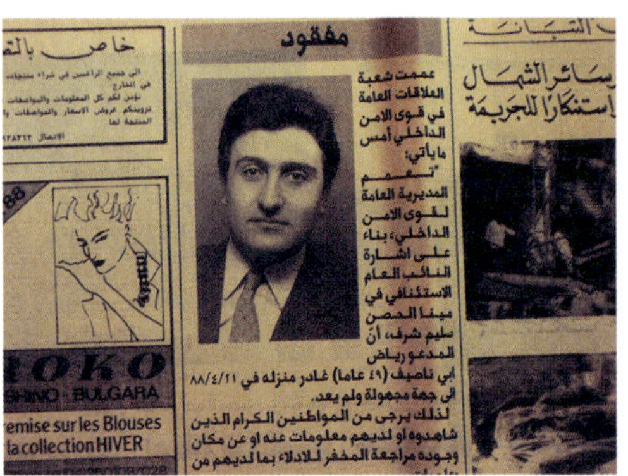 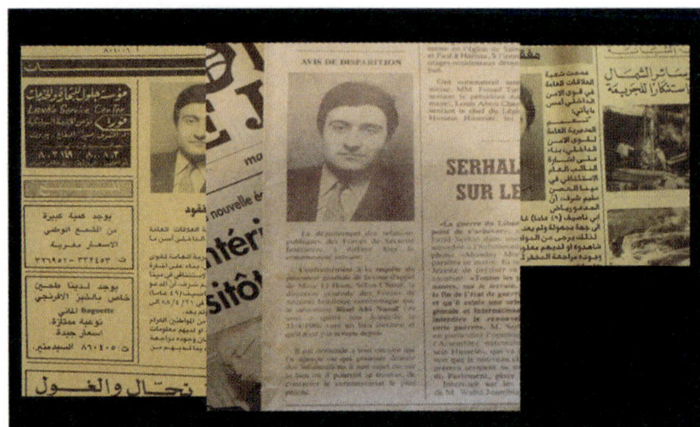

2. The fictional notices of disappearance in *A Perfect Day* (Joana Hadjithomas and Khalil Joreige, 2005).

Let us briefly consider the notion of forging false documentation for the purposes of a fictional film. We obtained permission from the three major Lebanese dailies at that time to produce facsimile editions of their newspapers dated two days after the fictional disappearance of Malek's father. After some research, we settled on April 25, 1988. On that day, there had been a massive car bombing in Tripoli, in North Lebanon, which had the potential to have triggered a wave of abductions. This allowed us to establish a parallel between a fictional, personal event within the film, and a real-life, collective event that took place during the war. Next, we had to find a picture showing the face of Malek's father, which is all that remains of this absent, missing father whose fate remains unknown. This face of the missing father is also the face of a man who lends his appearance to a missing person whose death is reported in the film.

While shooting our short film *Ashes*, we discovered that a substantial part of Lebanese society is very superstitious about death. *Ashes* tells the story of Nabil, a young man who returns to Lebanon with the cremated remains of his father, who died abroad. In Lebanon, however, a country ruled by religious laws, cremation is forbidden.

Nabil is confronted by the rest of his family, who insist that his father's body—a body that no longer exists—be buried according to local rites and customs.

In preparing *Ashes*, we were faced with a quite disturbing problem: most people refused to act or appear in the film because it dealt with mourning. Some refused to play the role of a relative of the deceased for fear their participation would bring about the death of someone in their own family. In one sequence, a character is asked to lie in a coffin and act dead. It proved extremely difficult to find an actor willing to play this role—so difficult, in fact, that we turned the problem into a research project: a short film about asking numerous people on the set if they would play dead.

As we tried to come to grips with this problem, we started to have our own serious doubts. What if something happened to the actor who agreed to lie in the coffin? Or to the family who lived in the house in which we were shooting? And what if someone died in the building in which the coffin stood? Little by little, we let ourselves be overwhelmed by superstition, and all this concern eventually affected the screenplay. We finally found an actor who agreed to play the role. The character he plays—the one who acts dead—dies later in the film. While that character is in the coffin, Nabil imagines the doomed character's body stiffening, his breath ceasing, his hands slowly turning blue—as though pretending to be dead were like actually dying.

When looking for a picture of the missing father in *A Perfect Day*, we faced the same problem. We were stuck until one of our assistants came up with a solution. Antoine, her maternal aunt's husband, had died several years earlier. Her aunt and their two adult daughters agreed to allow us to use Antoine's image in the film and provided the pictures we needed. They were glad to do so because they saw this as a way to help the cause of the missing. Armed with his family's unrestricted consent, we used pictures of Antoine in the facsimile newspapers.

Our assistant had not informed us, however, that, before his death, Antoine had divorced her aunt and married Aida. Nor did she tell us that Aida had not been notified of the making of the film. Upon

Aida,
Save Me!

asking her about the situation, we came to understand that there were persisting tensions between Antoine's first and second wives.

Aida told us she had bought a ticket to see *A Perfect Day*, not knowing exactly what it was about. Sitting snugly in her seat, she suddenly saw Antoine appear on the screen. She yelled at us on the phone: "I was watching the film when I suddenly saw Antoine before me—Antoine looking at me and saying: 'Aida, save me. I don't know what I'm doing in this film, save me!'" The image of Antoine had thus spoken to Aida, who was now asking us to cut it out of the film, or at least to obscure it. We tried to explain; we tried to convince her we had acted in good faith; we told her we didn't know of her relationship to Antoine, that we had the consent of his daughters; but Aida wouldn't let Antoine stay in the film.

The lawyer we spoke to assured us that Aida had no case against us. Everyone we turned to for advice told us we shouldn't bow to pressure, invoking the legal situation (we were certain to win a court case), private cause (the two women's conflict was none of our concern), psychological reasons (it would be a way for Aida to reconnect with her late husband), or a potential publicity and commercial boost (our distributor figured that our film, which wasn't commercial enough for his taste, would benefit from a minor scandal). But what if all these reasons were invalid? What if Aida's shock was real and we had provoked that shock? What if she was right, that Antoine shouldn't appear in this film and would not have wanted to do so? Should we remove the scenes with Antoine?

The story dragged on. When we left Beirut for New York, where the film was screening at a festival, we were still haunted by doubts. We had barely arrived when we received an alarming call from Beirut: the police had visited our flat seeking to interrogate us. They had also raided the chain of theaters that had scheduled *A Perfect Day* and tried to confiscate the reels. We had to fly home straight away. The whole affair was no longer a matter of image rights but a penal issue. In real life, Antoine had not died from natural causes but had been killed. The investigation was still underway, and whoever had killed him was still on the loose. The judge in charge of the case wished to understand why we had

Joana
Hadjithomas
and Khalil
Joreige

used the image of a man killed under mysterious circumstances. She wanted to question us and was considering adding the film to the file as evidence. This left us speechless. We were devastated. The picture of Antoine—one of the few images in the film we had staged—was no longer a fiction. The image was now invested with legal potency and had become a piece of evidence. Extracted from a fabricated work, it had become documentation. And we had become suspect, echoing the irrationality that governs much of Lebanon and its judicial system. (This same irrationality explains why, in all these years, our country has not been functioning according to the principle of cause and effect: you kill someone but you don't necessarily go to prison; former militia chiefs are now state ministers or Members of Parliament.)

This lack of a cause-and-effect relationship provides the primary momentum of *A Perfect Day*, a film about states of being and feeling rather than a linear narrative with resolved conflicts. Many of our works ask this question: How can one write a story—in the traditional sense of that word—when the very thread of history has been disrupted by a still-unresolved civil conflict?

A further element only served to enhance the unbelievable-but-true aspect of this story: Aida told us she and Antoine were married on April 25, 1988—the very date we had chosen for the notice of Malek's father's disappearance. How was this possible? Aida wondered if we had not been instrumentalized by Antoine's first wife. Were the two women using us and the film to fight a private war? Aida said: "By making him disappear on the day of our marriage, by dating the notice of disappearance in the newspaper to April 25, 1988, you killed him before I married him. You negated our marriage." By using Antoine's picture to announce the father's disappearance in the film, we had annulled his marriage to Aida ex post facto. How could such a collision of timeframes occur? How could this picture acquire such power?

Aida never considered the image of Antoine to be an element of fiction. In her mind, it was Antoine himself whom we caused to disappear. Presumably, this was also the opinion of the judge who, like Aida, took for granted the principle of fiction for the film as a whole but not for the specific sequences involving Antoine, which thus became moments of reality. Oddly, this story echoes our research as filmmakers and visual artists. In our artistic practice, we often rely on fiction—not to pretend to question or approach some kind of truth but rather to use existing documents and thus question images and representations and the writing of Lebanese history or histories.

Our project *Wonder Beirut*, for instance, is based on a series of postcards from the 1960s and 1970s that are still sold in Lebanese bookshops, despite the fact that most of the locations they depict were destroyed during the war. For this project, we invented the character of Abdallah Farah, a photographer from the 1960s whom we proposed had taken these pictures, which show the city center or the Lebanese Riviera—images that convey an "ideal" of pre-war Lebanon. During the war, Abdallah burned his photographs to reflect the pattern of ongoing bombings and street battles, as though trying to make images of the past conform to the present. To do this, he followed a precise recording of destructive events, destroyed his images and rephotographed in the present the sites they had captured. These new images thus document events as they unfolded and can be likened to an attempt to chronicle certain episodes of the Lebanese Civil War. As he frequently lacked chemicals and paper during the war, Abdallah took to shooting film without developing it. Film rolls thus kept accumulating. This project, titled *Latent Images*, presents hundreds of exposed but undeveloped film rolls, each one dated, listed, and stored in a drawer. The content of each photograph is described in precise detail. Presented in the form of contact sheets in which text appears in the place of developed images, they form a diary of Abdallah's family life, his photographic research, and the tormented story of contemporary Lebanon.

We have never developed a single roll. They remain in their latent state: invisible images of an exposed surface. There remains a fundamental question, which has been asked by the writer and artist Jalal Toufic, concerning the conditions of appearance—or, rather, revelation—of latent images. At which moment, and for what reason, might the photographer Abdallah Farah decide to develop his film, to expose his images to the light? And what would then have changed around him, in him and beyond him?[1] Several years ago, we initiated a reflection on the notion of latency[2] as the state of *that which exists in a non-apparent*

Joana
Hadjithomas
and Khalil
Joreige

manner, yet which can at any moment manifest itself—like something sleeping that might perhaps wake up. *A Perfect Day* addresses this very condition. Malek, who suffers from narcolepsy, falls asleep as soon as he stops moving. Beirut itself was filmed to convey the feeling we experienced at that time: that of being surrounded by latent images, stuck in a continuous and hysterical present. Latency also has connotations linked to notions of the repressed, the hidden, the inscrutable, the invisible. We tried to convey this latency in the film as an obscure, disquieting form; a vague and incontrollable, covert state—as though everything could resurface, as though everything were still there.

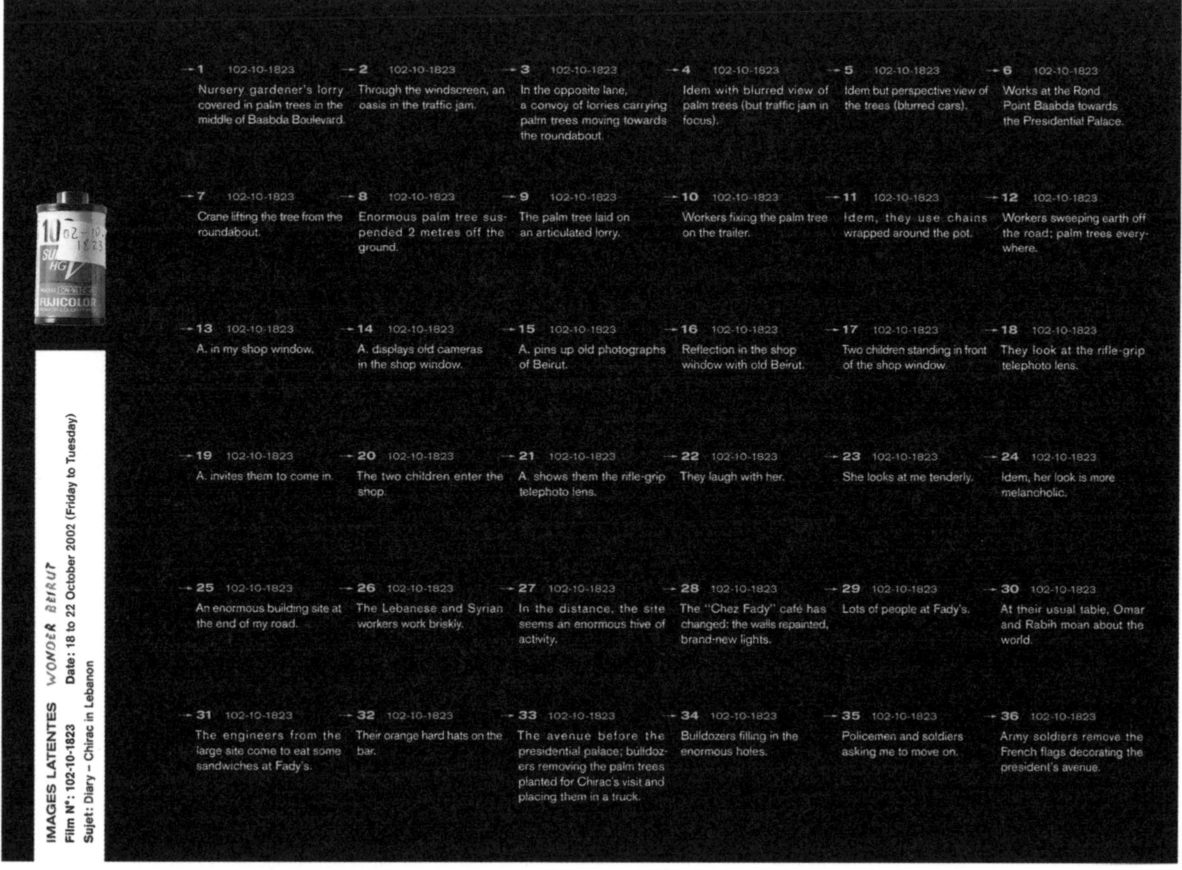

3. Contact sheet of a latent film from *Wonder Beirut* (Joana Hadjithomas and Khalil Joreige, 1997–2006).

Latency can furthermore be a political attitude against dominant representations—both those of the authoritarian powers in place and those of Orientalist imagery—that consist of emphasizing the notion that *we are there even if you don't see us* and of telling our personal stories, our secret histories, our lasting images—lasting because, despite their latency, images often refuse to disappear and can come back to haunt us. This also links Aida's experience to our work: the image of Antoine suddenly reappeared in the film before her eyes, like a lasting image that came back to haunt her. Sometime before, we produced an installation based on an 8 mm film we had found among the personal belongings of Khalil's maternal uncle, Junior Kettaneh, who had been kidnapped on August 19, 1985, and whose body was never found. He is still listed as missing, and the circumstances of his abduction remain mysterious. Evidence that would allow us to ascertain what really happened is scarce.

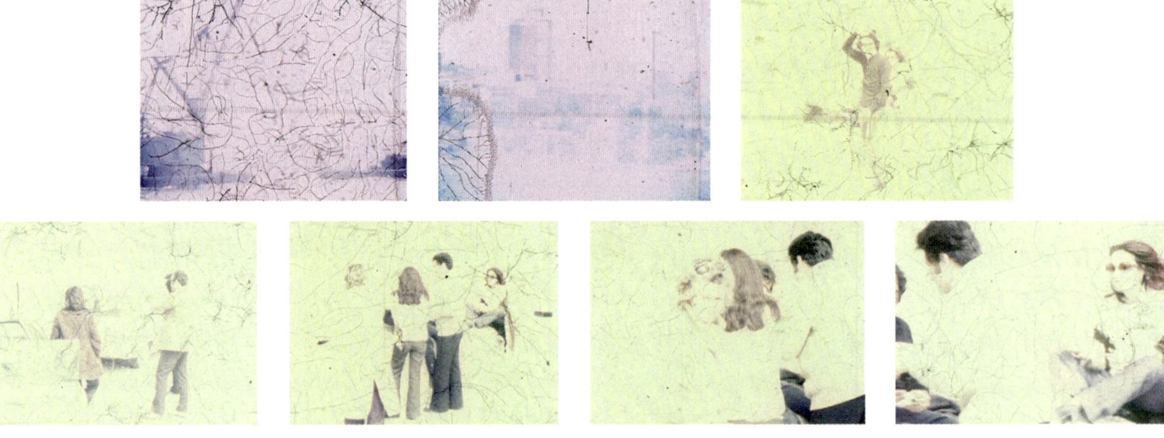

4. Stills from *Lasting Images*, a Super 8 film by Alfred Kettaneh Jr. (born 1937; kidnapped 1985 during the Lebanese Civil War. Considered missing).

Junior Kettaneh is one of the seventeen thousand individuals listed as missing up to this day. *A Perfect Day* was inspired by his personal story and his family's suffering. While writing the script, we found a latent film among Junior's archives. He must have filmed it shortly before his abduction and not had time to have it developed. It had thus remained in its yellow foil wrapper for fifteen years and had survived the turmoil of war, during which the house had burned down. This film possibly contained the last images Junior ever shot, maybe even some frames showing himself. The technicians we asked for advice discouraged us from developing the film. According to them, the latent image wouldn't show up after all this time. And indeed, despite all our precautions and research, the film came out showing nothing but a long sequence of white images. We decided to scan the forty-five hundred frames of this three-minute-long film one by one and find out what they still contained. Working on color correction and contrast, we eventually noticed slight variations, subtle shifts in the images. Piercing through the whiteness of the film, a ghostly image resurfaced, as though it could not be completely erased. All you need to do is look at it for it to appear and reveal itself. Can ghosts, can the missing return?

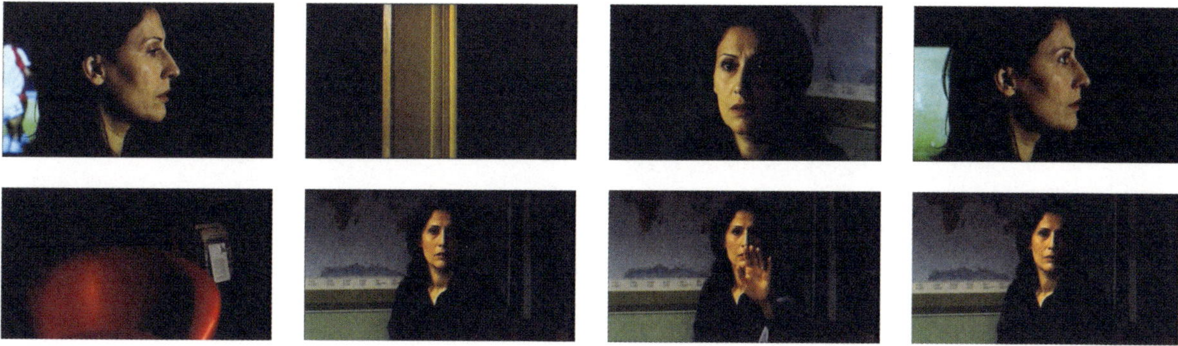

5. Claudia sees the "ghost" of her husband in *A Perfect Day* (Joana Hadjithomas and Khalil Joreige, 2005).

Over the course of *A Perfect Day*, Claudia learns to control her fear. In one of the final sequences of the film, she takes refuge in her son's room, listening to the sounds in the house, hearing choppy breathing approaching. As she had hoped, she sees what she perceives as a presence, as the ghost of her husband. She comes to terms with this idea, accepts living with it, accepts remaining haunted by the man she loves—a ghost who refuses to die and whom she in turn refuses to "kill" symbolically. This idea echoes another notion outlined by Jalal Toufic:

Toufic continues by drawing a parallel with Hamlet, who sees and hears the ghost of his father whereas his mother does not—as though all her senses were atrophied, as though she had become a zombie. This also characterizes what distinguishes Malek from his mother, who senses the father's presence and clearly tells Malek so: "Sometimes, I see him, I sense him—you don't."

Aida saw Antoine again. He appeared before her: she saw him; she heard him. Unwittingly, in this film, we had awoken the image of Antoine. We had to find a solution to Aida's quandary. It was Monday; the judge in chambers was to sit on Tuesday; our film was to be launched on Thursday. Everyone pleaded with us to make a gesture to get Aida to drop the case, to avoid having the matter go to court, and to dodge the penal issue. Meanwhile, the judge had acknowledged that we had acted in good faith; still, she didn't understand why we were reluctant to alter the image of Antoine, for instance by blurring it, a common practice on TV. Joana's father came to see us, proposing that we use pictures of him instead of those of Antoine. We explained to him that this simply wasn't possible. The judge then proposed we add a moustache to the picture of Antoine to make him unrecognizable. We tried to convince her this was essentially impossible, explaining that this was a 35 mm print and that cinema runs at twenty-four frames per second, meaning we would have to rework thousands upon thousands of individual frames. But what if we added a beauty spot on Antoine's left cheek (a dot being easier to add to thousands of frames than a moustache)? In that case, would Antoine still be Antoine? Would he become someone else? The images we used for the film were not recent, not Aida's, and showed the Antoine Aida never knew. Our proposals were rejected. Yet, a question remains: At which point are we still the same? This question is at the heart of our artistic reflection. The image is there, it reappears, it is lasting. But which image returns? Does it live up to our expectations?

Joana
Hadjithomas
and Khalil
Joreige

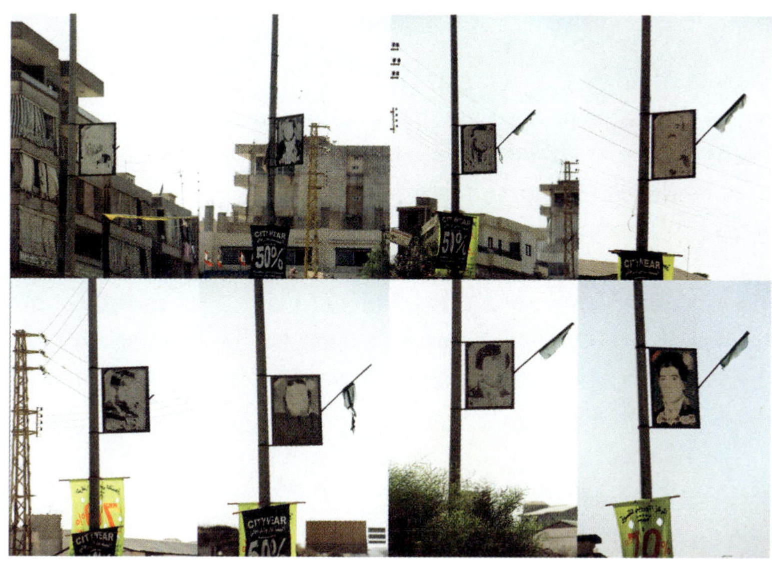

6. Hydro poles with photos of martyrs, Beirut.

We have thought a lot about images of *martyrs*. In Lebanon, we call martyrs those who die tragically during attacks, in combat or in suicide operations. They are from different political backgrounds, various creeds and religions, different regions of the country. We live surrounded by their images, which are posted throughout the city: images of the dead looking at us. In 2001, we illustrated a text[4] with photographs taken by graphic designer Ahmad Gharbieh. His pictures show thirty-four electrical posts lining a large avenue in the southern suburbs of Beirut. These posts are covered with framed pictures of young men, all of them "martyrs." What struck us most, however, were the numerous empty posts, as though they were waiting for pictures to come. The same posts were photographed again in 2007. In the interim, the posts had been repainted and the avenue refurbished. But the pictures of martyrs had vanished, bleached by the weather. Does the image ever live up to its promise?

In our project *Faces*, we extended this research to other locations in Lebanon. We photographed martyrs from all confessions and political backgrounds, choosing posters that had been substantially altered by the weather. These posters remain in place, while the features and names of the individuals they represent disappear. All that remains is an outline of the face, a mostly unrecognizable shadow.

We photographed these images at different stages of their vanishing process, then tried to recreate certain facial features and highlight others in an attempt to recover, by means of drawing, a trace, a lasting image. But how are these images to be read? As disappearances or appearances? Below the images of martyrs, one often reads the Arabic expression *hay fyna*, meaning "alive in us." We thus live or coexist with the dead, but they are the living dead inside us, whom we can never quite bury. What if these martyrs, by vanishing into blankness, have tried to escape from their images, from their frames, from us? Since we cannot mourn them, can the dead themselves decide to retreat?

By inserting the image of Antoine in *A Perfect Day,* we brought Aida face to face with the impossibility of mourning. For Aida—as for all the wives and mothers of the missing—there can be no peace of mind until she knows what really happened to Antoine, until she knows who killed him. Unwittingly, and by sheer coincidence, we had drawn a parallel between Aida's situation and that of the many women who are still waiting to learn what has happened to their missing sons, husbands, or fathers. We also brought Aida face to face with the Antoine from before their first encounter, Antoine with a wife and children—the Antoine whom she did not know, yet recognized.

The question of recognizing, or recognition, has preoccupied us for some time. *"Recognition is the action by which one recovers in one's memory the idea or image of an object or a person when faced with them again."* Does recognizing, establishing an identity, perceiving oneself as the same, resist the temporal confusion in which we are sometimes embedded, the discontinuity of our history, and the violence of certain events we experience?

In certain contexts, reality evanesces, and an excerpt from reality can lead to confusion. In the 1990s, in the devastated center of Beirut, we no longer recognized anything. We were looking at buildings, places where the architecture was chaotic and upside down, places whose architectural substance or everyday features were no longer recognizable. The impact of destruction shifts the gaze and transforms our relationship to what we see. This brings to mind a line from one of Mahmoud Darwish's poems: "the form of a form which has no form."

Joana
Hadjithomas
and Khalil
Joreige

Several years ago, one of our friends lapsed into a weird state of mind marked by great confusion. We no longer recognized him. We tried, unsuccessfully, to bring him back toward us. We went to see a psychotherapist for advice. She gave us only one tip: "Tell him you recognize him. Say: 'I recognize you.'" We tried but somehow failed to pretend recognition; can it actually be feigned? We often think about this. If we had told him with sufficient conviction that we recognized him, would he have returned? Do we have this sort of power? The power to recognize and identify? Could we have brought him back? This thought haunts us.

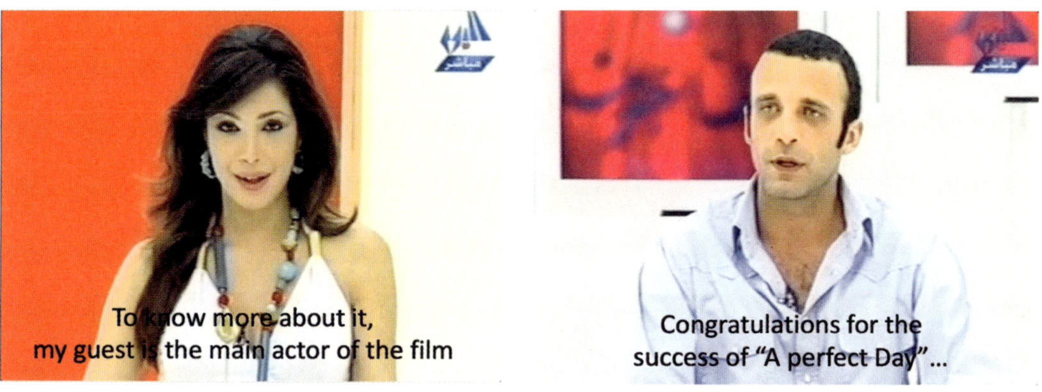

7. Extract from television interview, *Ayoun Beirut* (Ziad Saad, 2008).

Another strange episode took place when *A Perfect Day* was being promoted. Ziad Saad, the actor who plays Malek, is a musician. He wasn't keen on doing promotional work but, several days before the film hit Lebanese screens (at the same time we were negotiating with Aida), he was invited to appear on a popular live local TV show. He decided to ask one of his friends to go in his stead. So, here was his friend on the set, and the program started. Everything went well at first; then the presenter showed a clip from the film. Obviously, there was a mismatch between Ziad's face in the film and his friend's face on TV. After the excerpt was broadcast, however, things went on undisturbed. The presenter resumed the talk as though nothing was remiss. Next came another excerpt, this one with a lot of close-up shots of Ziad. Surely, this time around, the presenter would spot the fraud? But no, they continued as though everything was normal and started speaking about music. It wasn't until the third excerpt that the presenter told Ziad's friend that she thought he had changed quite a bit since the film had been shot—but again, she let herself be convinced by the answers offered by the false Malek, and the show continued.

Over the course of the broadcast, four excerpts from *A Perfect Day* were shown, focusing on Malek, often showing his face in close-up. It must have appeared to viewers that the guest on the program was not the actor in the film, yet no one seemed to notice. Of course, we could say that this episode—which Saad subsequently turned into an artwork—demonstrates how the machinery of television crushes people and feeds off the flow of images without being aware of what it ingests, or that it proves that a man can pass himself off as someone else without anyone noticing or caring. But beyond that—as in the case of Antoine and Aida—we have to ask ourselves: At which moment are we ourselves? Are the things around us, around this film, in this time and age, imbued with non-recognition? Here lies some kind of mystery that eludes us.

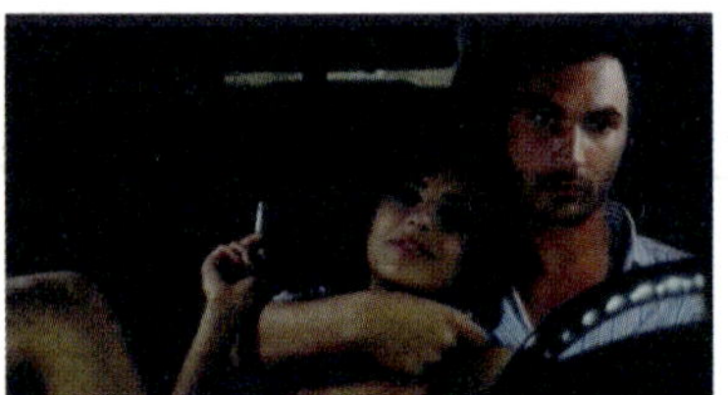
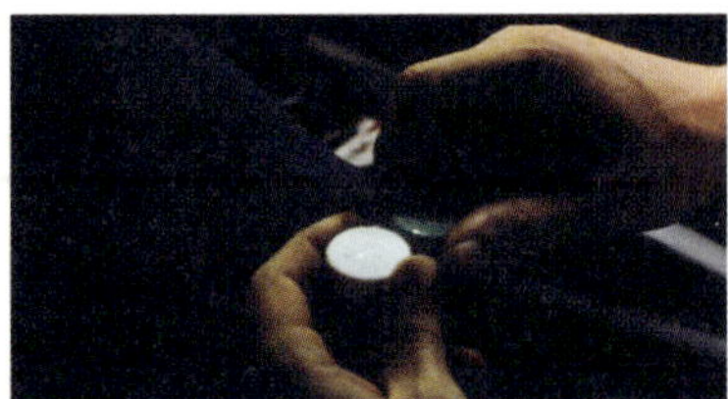
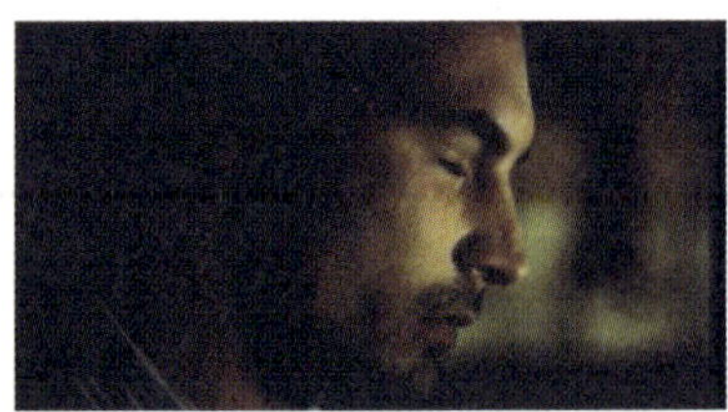
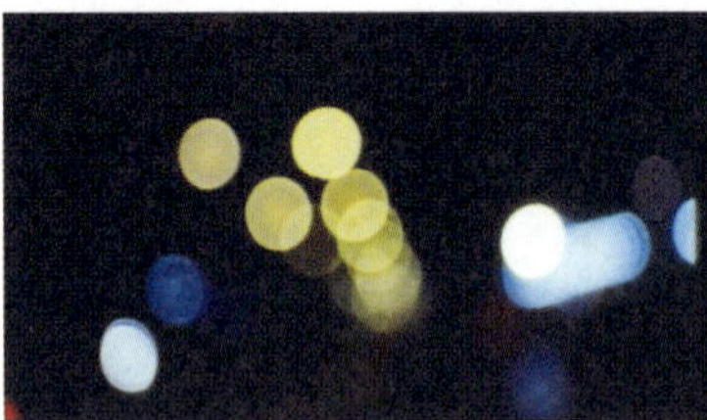
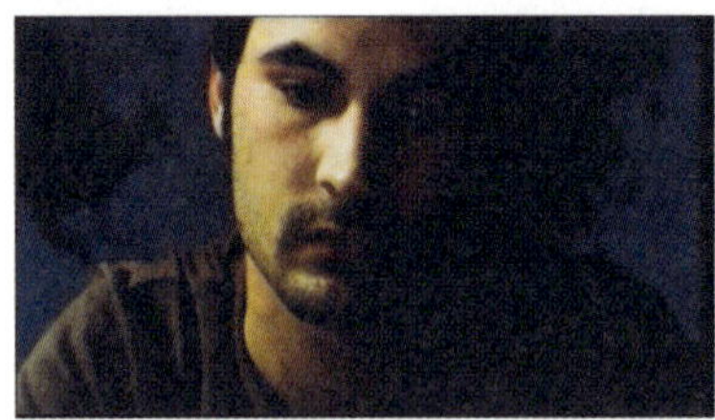

8. Ziad looks through his girlfriend's contact lenses in *A Perfect Day* (Joana Hadjithomas and Khalil Joreige, 2005).

In one scene in *A Perfect Day*, Malek is seen freewheeling through Beirut with Zeina, with whom he is very much in love. She has removed her contact lenses and looks at the city lights, which appear skewed because of her short-sightedness. When she leaves, she forgets her lenses in the car. Malek puts them in his own eyes, to adopt the viewpoint of his beloved, to try to look at the world through the eyes of another. Since he is not short-sighted, the optical correction effect allows him to experience an impression of what Zeina saw. In other words, the inverse correction provokes a similar effect.

Seeing through the eyes of the other—albeit in a skewed way—conveying, invoking the other when we feel blinded: This is the subject of our film *I Want to See*, which simultaneously references a personality from the history of cinema, Catherine Deneuve, and a personality from our artistic territory, Rabih Mroué, in an attempt to recover another perspective after the war in Lebanon in 2006. The film questions the way we look at wars, according to the premise that a perspective on war can be displaced at the risk of confronting the void, even at the risk of not seeing anything. How can we show or represent violence and war in the wake of the terrible, unbearable images shown on TV? How can we recover a different emotion? How can we refuse to become inured to, or to tolerate such images, which provoke compassion in parallel with confusion and distantiation? Seeing, identifying, recognizing, but also undermining dominant representations: these actions are necessary to re-engage a common reflection on the political and to inscribe our history within a more global history, be it the history of cinema or otherwise.

I Want to See references Alain Resnais's *Hiroshima mon amour*, echoing its noted dialogue exchange:

"I saw everything in Hiroshima."
"You saw nothing in Hiroshima."

The film tries to unravel the phantasm by which today's representations of war are covered up or disguised. It is a deliberate attempt to undermine the scopic impulse, voyeurism, the notion of "wanting to see the war." The film furthermore questions the return of fiction in a devastated reality.

How can we film when the weight of reality is too heavy, too imposing? What distance should our camera adopt in its approach to things or events to avoid instrumentalizing the real, to allow us to create images we can believe in? Where do we position ourselves?

Aida,
Save Me!

What can we do? What can cinema do? *I Want to See* works with the very matter of the image, of fiction, of cinema, trying to provoke a kind of chemical reaction between an icon of cinema—a fictional figure embodied by Deneuve—and places in which the weight of reality is excessively present, excessively heavy. Will the clash between the two allow us to see, to show, and, as Jacques Rancière puts it, to "shift the gaze," to change "the representation of Lebanese as eternal victims of wars" so as to reflect not "on the images of war but on what war does to images," and to the representations of ourselves? Rancière wrote that "from this violence to images, Joana Hadjithomas and Khalil Joreige have derived the principle of a new art of resistance . . . . The politics of art do not serve the cause of the oppressed. They subvert the positions of victor and victim by subverting the relationships between reality and fiction."[5] *I Want to See* recounts and films an "encounter"—that of Rabih and Catherine, which took place in front of our camera at the very beginning of the film, and which we then followed. In telling the story of this specific encounter, the film addresses the issue of our faces, our history, our singularity, and the way in which, in the West, we have progressively lost these to adopt the status of victims—victims who stir compassion but with whom one does not identify; whom one pities without actually seeing.

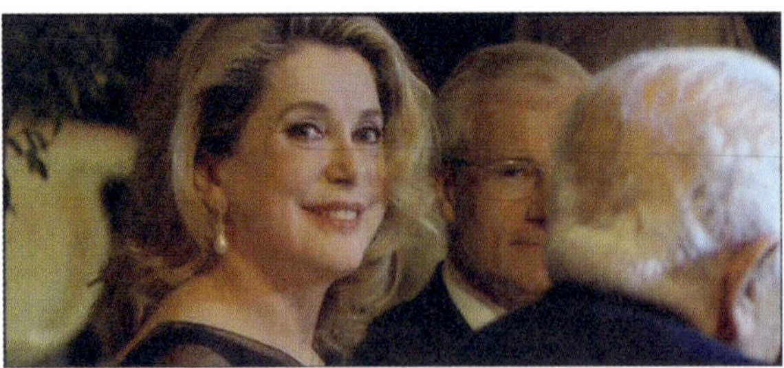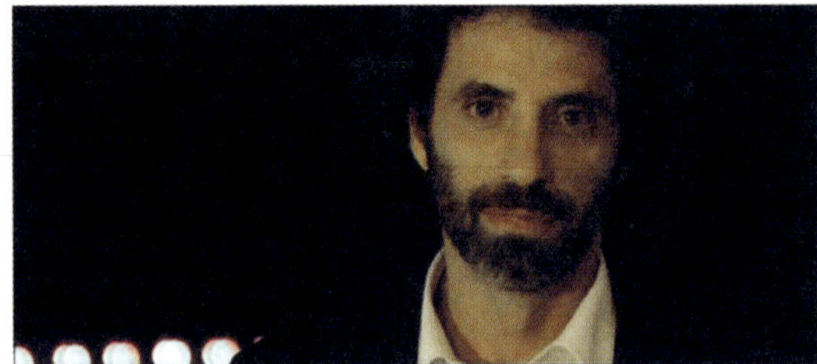

9. The first shot/countershot construction in *I Want to See* (Joana Hadjithomas and Khalil Joreige, 2008).

To this effect, the film uses one of the central devices of classic narrative cinema: the shot/counter-shot. At the outset, Catherine and Rabih look at each other, together but separated by the framing. At the end of the film, they are reunited in a shot/counter-shot, the first use of the device in the film. Catherine is looking for Rabih; when she eventually sees him, instantly her eyes light up. The shot/ counter-shot inscribes their points of view as they look at each other. They recognize each other. It is a moment of mutual recognition, the recognition of the face and history of the other—and the affirmation of life after disaster, the return to fictional possibility.

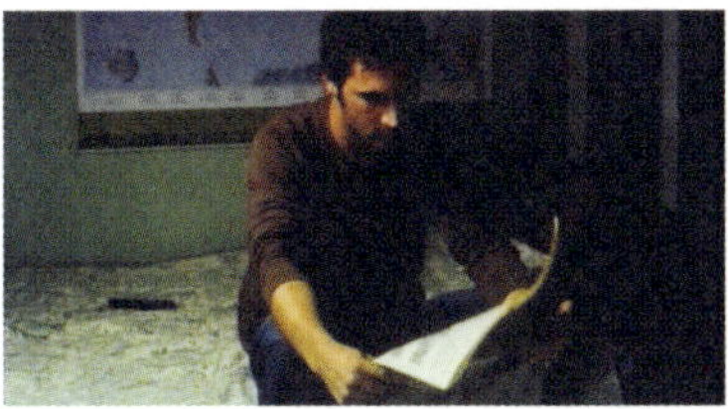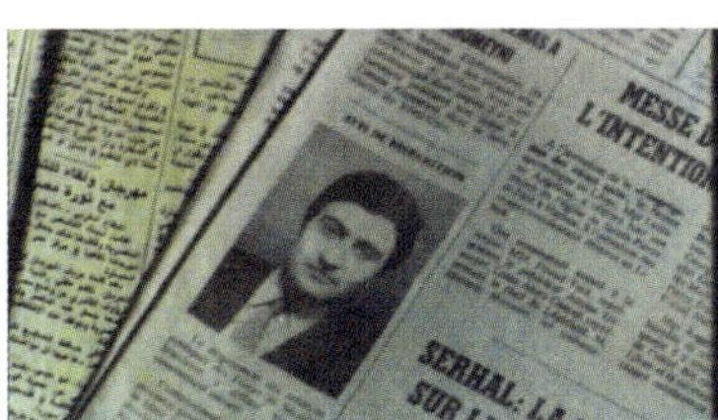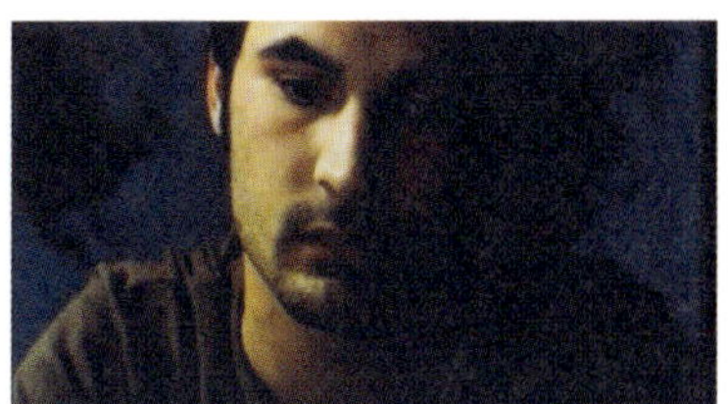

10. Malek reads the newspaper notices of his father's death in a shot/countershot construction in *A Perfect Day* (Joana Hadjithomas and Khalil Joreige, 2005).

The question of slippage between documentary and fiction lies at the heart of Aida's adventure. The image of Antoine has become a document; reality has caught up with the film's fiction. The shot/counter-shot is an equally important conceit in *A Perfect Day*, although in a different sense. At one moment in the film, Malek is looking at images of his father and seems profoundly disturbed—as though the images were looking back at him. How could we erase Antoine from such a sequence and make up for the absence that would result? This elision would only emphasize the disappearance of the father in the film. By deleting the image of Antoine, we would change the meaning of the film; this shot/ counter-shot would become an impossibility. Malek could never look at his father, whose image would thus elude him entirely. In keeping with Toufic's statement, Malek would become even more of a zombie: he would neither sense, nor hear, nor see. Sometimes, images elude us. There is nothing we can do about this except observe them eluding us.

Eventually, we reached an agreement with Aida. At no point did she try to take financial advantage of the situation; her request was sincere, dictated by the love she felt for Antoine and the respect with which she wished to encompass his death. We listened to her request and we learned a lot from this adventure. Together with her, we took the decision to remove the image of Antoine from the film for any screenings in Beirut, while it would remain in the film elsewhere. There was only one territory—her own—where Aida took issue with seeing Antoine pictured like this, beyond which she was able to put up with the fiction. But in her neighborhood, her town, the place where she and Antoine had lived together, where he could be recognized by family, friends, and neighbors, he could only be Antoine and so could not embody someone else after his death. Images, documents, and fiction can also be issues of geography. Recognition can be an issue of context. This left us thoughtful as to the way in which our films and images are perceived at any given time, and in a given place, country, or territory. Aida asked us to phone her up from time to time. We now had something in common: we shared Antoine. We spent two nights erasing images of Antoine from the film.

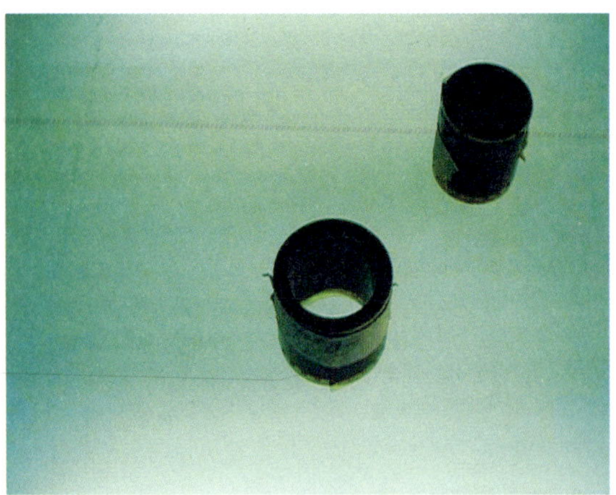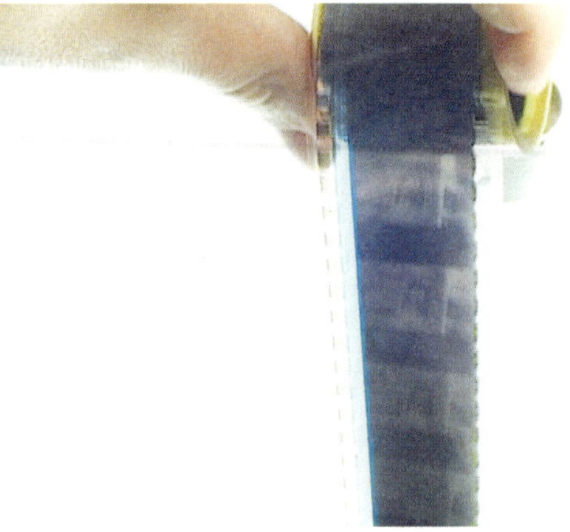

11. Segments of film removed from *A Perfect Day* (Joana Hadjithomas and Khalil Joreige, 2005).

Those images are still in our home in Beirut, on cut-out and rolled-up film, hidden away in a large metal box. A friend told us something had struck him. He had attended a private screening of *A Perfect Day* before Aida had seen it and launched the whole affair, about which our friend knew nothing. He had seen the images of the father, which had caught his attention. When he saw the film again, but in its altered version, he felt as though some images were missing. He was puzzled and wondered whether his memory hadn't added images—those of the father—thus compensating for Antoine's absence through imagination. We still hesitate whether to tell him the whole story. Because one day, the images will return to the film.

This text led to a performance titled Aida, Save Me*, given in December 2009 at the Halles de Schaerbeek in Brussels. A co-production of the Halles de Schaerbeek, Chantier TEMPS D'IMAGES 2009. Translation from the original French: Boris Kremer.* Aida, Save Me *was previously published in a longer format (Beirut: Tamyras Éditions, 2010) and has been edited for this volume. © 2010 by Joana Hadjithomas and Khalil Joreige.*

1. Jalal Toufic, *Distracted*, 2nd edition (Berkeley: Tuumba Press, 2003).

2. See Joana Hadjithomas and Khalil Joreige, "Latency," in *Homeworks* (Beirut: Ashkal Alwan, 2002).

3. Jalal Toufic, *(Vampires): An Uneasy Essay on the Undead in Film*, 2nd edition (Sausalito: The Post-Apollo Press, 2003).

4. See Joana Hadjithomas and Khalil Joreige, "A State of Latency," in *Iconoclash: Beyond the Image Wars in Science, Religion and Art* (Cambridge: MIT Press, 2002).

5. Jacques Rancière, "Hommage à Joana Hadjithomas & Khalil Joreige," in cat. Paris Cinéma, Paris, 2007.

IMAGE AS CURRENCY

OLUREMI C. ONABANJO

It is widely recognized that the profusion of images that undergird subjectivity and globalized imaginaries are tethered to late capitalist relations—a thesis that serves as the foundation for a collection of diverging critical positions in Kevin Coleman and Daniel James's significant volume, *Capitalism and the Camera*. While acknowledging the camera's position in the production of particular publics, this current "retinal era" can be understood as an extension of systemic processes of commodification. After more than a century of lens-based production and consumption, circulation and exchange, it has become commonplace to comprehend the world "photographically," that is, through a lens that shapes and organizes the social lives of not just things but also images future and past. While images are dense, relational conceptual formations, these mental repositories inscribe a set of visual prostheses that structure our perception of the world around us.

Even prior to the rapid pace of digital image-making to which many have become acclimatized, in her seminal text *On Photography*, Susan Sontag observed, "a capitalist society requires a culture based on images. It needs to furnish vast amounts of entertainment in order to stimulate buying and anesthetize the injuries of class, race, and sex."[1] These structures are mutually reinforcing, Sontag continues:

> The camera's twin capacities, to subjectivize reality and to objectify it, ideally serve these needs and strengthen them. Cameras define reality in the two ways essential to the workings of an advanced industrial society: as a spectacle (for masses) and as an object of surveillance (for rulers). The production of images also furnishes a ruling ideology. Social change is replaced by a change in images.[2]

Here, *currency* becomes useful as a term via which to plumb the contemporary relations of photography through pivotal terms of inscription and value-making, classification, and circulation. In its most prevalent usage, currency is an economic indicator deemed fundamental to quantifying the health of a national or regional economy, of which the cardinal coordinates are value and distribution. By extending the term to visual culture, we invite a critical engagement with photography and its relationship to canon-making, flow, trade, exchange, regulation, dominance, subjugation, conformism, dissent, and resistance—themes that are discussed at length in the contributions that follow. In apprehending these terms, we query their operations as anything but commonplace, while calling attention to their diffuse nature.

The notion of currency also highlights how new meanings are made and re-encoded by incepting the structures of instrumentation. The results that follow expose a set of circulations resistant to and defiant of conventional approaches. For example, Tina M. Campt engages the term while remaining attuned to the individuated visual "frequencies" of photographs, in conversation with the thorough, precise writer Ariel Goldberg, who themself is perceptive to the discursive role of the caption in relation to the image. Elias Sanbar and Léopold Lambert take up the photograph as an entity that oscillates between discourses of evidence while maintaining a diaphanous presence, as a trace. Thinking through absence and presence, whether as gesture or across expanses of land, the two offer rich entry points, provocations, and coaxing possibilities for understanding the politics and histories of image circulation. Powerhouse feminist thinkers Frieda Ekotto and Françoise Vergès think together about the position of photographic images as instruments of circulation and resistance—at stages of production, strategic dissemination, consumption, and the various iterations of circulation embedded in these processes.

Collectively, these contributions reflect on visual production, circulation, and consumption through the lenses of art and film, as well as literary and cultural theorizations guided by feminist, queer, trans, ecological, decolonial, and Indigenous epistemologies.

1. Susan Sontag, *On Photography* (New York: Picador, 2001), 178.

2. Sontag, *On Photography*, 194.

Picturing Catastrophe: The Visual Politics of Racial Reckoning*

* This essay first appeared in *The Yale Review* 109, no. 2 (Summer 2021), 158–177.

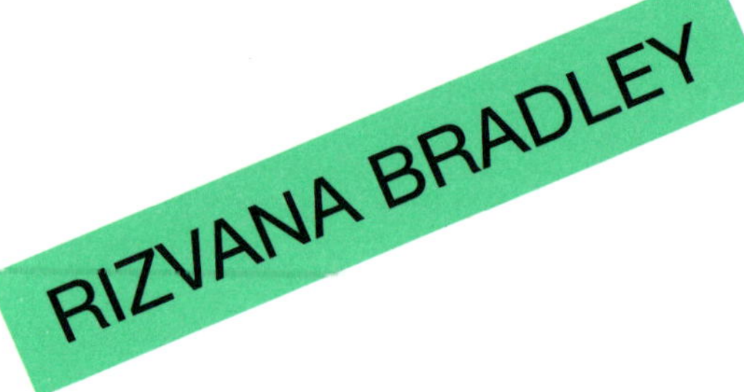

*The grammar of antagonism breaks in on the mendacity
of conflict.*

—Frank B. Wilderson III

And we, here, amid a failure of images.

—Dawn Lundy Martin

Now, more than a year into the pandemic, with the wheels of atrocity once again turning as they should, one might expect most of the obligatory annual retrospectives on 2020's so-called summer of racial reckoning to serve as little more than a kind of punctuation, one that might be anxiously folded into various stories of unity and progress. Representation's injunction saturates daily life to the point of satire: Netflix offers its customers a Black Lives Matter genre, police cars are adorned with historic black political leaders and Pan-Africanist colors for Black History Month, and even US President Biden implores the American people, citizens of a noble if imperfect nation, not to look away from the spectacle of black death, saying:

> We have to look at it—we have to—we have to look at it as we did for those nine minutes and twenty-nine seconds. We have to listen. 'I can't breathe. I can't breathe.' Those were George Floyd's last words. We can't let those words die with him. We have to keep hearing those words.

The trial of Derek Chauvin, the white Minneapolis police officer who murdered George Floyd, was fashioned as the culminating drama of last summer's upheavals. Like the final act of a familiar play whose outcome is always known in advance, Chauvin's guilty verdict was to be the climax of a multiracial saga that had captured our hearts and minds, a cynical reprise of Martin Luther King Jr.'s declaration that "the arc of the moral universe is long, but it bends toward justice." President Biden went so far as to pluck words from the mouth of George Floyd's daughter, Gianna, in his speech on April 20 following the trial: "She said to me then—I'll never forget it—'Daddy changed the world.'. . . Let that be his legacy: a legacy of peace, not violence—of justice." George Floyd's death would not be in vain; it would be the very lifeblood of American democracy, the fleshly renewal of the social contract, a catalyst for the "healing" we need. "Black death functions as national therapy," as Frank B. Wilderson III would say.

This vampiric narrativization, of course, stumbled over the conditions of its making, for it was difficult to reconcile the righteous trumpetings of Chauvin's guilty verdict with the killing of sixteen-year-old Ma'Khia Bryant not twenty minutes later, or of Andrew Brown Jr. the following day. Even as the obligation to repeat these facts marks the fulfillment of a murderous script which is incapable of mourning the life it steals. Even as the recourse to empiricist appeal to common truth or conscience is itself, as Saidiya Hartman might say, "just an extension of the master's prerogative."

Indeed, the manner in which the liberal face of empire has scrambled to exploit the politics of representation this past year betrays a latent desperation as much as an appetite for extraction; what else are we to make of this demand to look, again and again, upon the brutalized flesh of blackness? To look, so that a picture of the world might be preserved, so that the world might be saved—from itself, for itself. Because in fact the precipitate turns that characterized the past year tell a story of anything but progress: the "summer of racial reckoning" was followed by a US presidential election that commentators likened to the deadlocked electoral contest of 1876, the "resolution" of which signaled the end of Reconstruction, trammeling over hopes for achieving what W. E. B. Du Bois called "abolition democracy" and paving the way for the revanchism of racial terror commonly known as Jim Crow. The exuberant celebrations of the outcomes of the US presidential and congressional elections as signaling an irreversible, universally awaited tide of "diversity and inclusion" gave way to the white supremacist raid on the Capitol, which shocked the temperate sensibility of a liberal consciousness that has largely managed to ignore the forms of fascistic sentiment and organization that have been gathering force for decades.

The grating juxtaposition of these political scenes amplifies a discordance which was already evident within those representations of last summer that depicted it as an unprecedented swelling of collective dissent against the global color line. Set aside the rehearsals of unity and progress; to attend truly to the depth and extent of the political impasse from which the protracted morass and escalating perils of the present conjuncture emerge requires a different kind of retrospective. We must turn back to the image of the summer we were given, in the hopes that we might see with new eyes. For the task we face is far more difficult and demanding than embracing fresh perspective; what is called for is no less than an interrogation of the racial constitution of *perspective itself*, and a willingness to turn toward what David Marriott might call the "radically *unwritten*." We must trace the Gordian knot of politics and visuality, if only to glimpse the unraveling it would appear to foreclose.

1

Cologne, June 6, 2020: a young black woman appears in the foreground of a photograph, crowning a sea of people gathered along the banks of the Rhine. Undeterred by the wind that blows her hair back, she holds up a sign that reads "SILENCE IS VIOLENCE," handwritten in black, with "BLM" stenciled in red in the lower-right corner. Marseille, the same day: a close-up shot of the tearful embrace of two black women in the middle of a march, a multiracial crowd blurring behind them. Puerta del Sol Square, Madrid: a black man, suspended above throngs of predominantly white demonstrators clapping in unison, his fist resolutely raised, his body presented as the flag-bearer of the crowd. These photographs, published on the *Atlantic*'s website during the first week of June, are just a few of the great flood of images that circulated during the protests against antiblackness, racism, and state violence

Rizvana
Bradley

that followed the murder of George Floyd on May 25, 2020, a calamity painfully shadowed by the murders of Breonna Taylor and Ahmaud Arbery in the United States in the months just before that. Seoul, Dakar, Rio de Janeiro. Edinburgh, Tokyo, Budapest. Photographs upon photographs. Multitudes upon multitudes.

Contrast these with a second influx of images, which were appearing in the media by the end of July. Solidarity against antiblackness had begun to recede. In the United States, attention turned toward the escalating drama of state repression, most visible in Portland, Oregon, where the Trump administration deployed Immigration and Customs Enforcement, Customs and Border Protection, and other Department of Homeland Security forces to quash the ongoing, predominantly white, protests, in a deliberately sensationalist performance of authoritarian power. These political shifts were accompanied by noticeable aesthetic recalibrations. In publications ranging from the *New York Times* to the *Guardian* to *Al Jazeera,* these images showed a republic in crisis: federal agents in military fatigues and riot gear, the incendiary lights of "flash-bang" grenades and clouds of tear gas. And they showed the civic wounding of protestors: a close-up shot of a white man, his T-shirt pulled up to reveal the bruises left by rubber bullets or tear gas canisters; an overhead shot of a young white woman lying on a medical stretcher, her upper arm lacerated, gloved hands urgently attending to her injuries. The reddened, distressed faces of white demonstrators flushing pepper spray or tear gas from their eyes, or kneeling before approaching state legions, shielding their heads. Such visceral imagery was juxtaposed with images casting the tumult in more hopeful tones, even as a family matter, as with the Wall of Moms interlinking arms, some wielding signs that read "GO HOME FEDS: MAMA SAYS SO!" and "I'M SO DISAPPOINTED IN YOU—MOM."

It would be difficult to overstate the significance of photography and visual media in contemporary political imaginaries, and the Black Lives Matter movement is no exception. Indeed, in his 2016 *New York Times* reflection on photographs that have been associated with BLM since its organizational emergence in 2013, Teju Cole wrote, "Black Lives Matter as a movement originated in images." The rallying cry, "Black Lives Matter," and the diverse forms of political activity to which it has become conjoined are inevitably bound up with the politics of visuality and aesthetic experience. None of these images of collective dissent can be considered in isolation, and not simply because they are all politically and symbolically rendered proximate to the discursive intervention "Black Lives Matter." Each bears and extends the sediment of centuries, a colossal accumulation of racialized visuality.

What is it about these photographs that continues to transfix us? What terrors and insurgencies do they conceal or disclose? It would be easy to see these photographs simply as documentation of protest and oppression, as authentic representations of political courage and commitment. But we must not abdicate, in Frank Wilderson's words, "the power to pose the question." The scale, speed, and ease of the reproduction and circulation of these photographic repertoires and images should direct our attention to the investments and animus undergirding the now global visualization of collective dissent, and of black struggle in particular. If antiblackness is as deep and immeasurable a social antagonism as these vast international mobilizations of solidarity would suggest, then it cannot be presumed that the act of looking has been left untouched by nor innocent of the ubiquity and force of racial violence.

Despite their varied locations, the photographs from early June, which inaugurated the summer of 2020 as a moment of "racial reckoning," share a common representational ambition: to render black life and the brutalities arrayed against it present in ways that elide the structural depth and historical intractability of antiblack violence. By presuming a presence that can only be plotted onto the axes of universality and historical progress, by presuming that antiblackness could ever be exposed or blackness affirmed using the very instruments, maps, and orientations that have been built upon the figuration of blackness as the paradigm for dereliction, these photographs cannot help but eclipse complex, differential expressions of black refusal. The incessant cycling of images of multiracial solidarity alongside intimate images of black grief and pain demands that singular experiences and expressions of black suffering and anger, exhaustion and enervation become sutured to a politics of reconciliation. The viewer is confronted with an image of dissent, but it is a visual dissensus engineered in the interest of social consensus. Whatever fractures divide us, these operations suggest, we are all still at least contemporaries on a common map of political community—citizens of the world, as Kwame Anthony Appiah would say.

The collection of photographs from late July, in contradistinction, involves an almost inverse labor, in which dissensus registers a splintering within a social consensus *already presumed*—a consensus which is so completely taken for granted that even articulating it as a problem for thought elicits disquietude, if not malice. The prominence and care with which the wounded bodies of protestors are displayed in this set of photographs cannot be attributed simply to an intensification of repressive state violence, for it is precisely the extraordinary character of antiblack violence to which the summer's mobilizations were a response. Rather, the aesthetic discrepancy between the images from early June and those from

Picturing
Catastrophe

late July marks the racial border between those who may be *subjects of vulnerability* and those who are *objects of empathy,* between those whose vulnerability marks a violation of bodily sovereignty and an incitement to political redress, and those whose brutalizations can only circulate as social currency within a world which holds them perpetually in arrears. They compose images of bodily vulnerability from which black people are doubly barred, because the injured bodies of the non-black protestors function as synecdoches for the body politic. These are individual bodies, such photographs suggest, which belong to the *national* body: the "whole body, indivisible although clearly divided, that represents the promise of the nation," in Lauren Berlant's words. And if, as Berlant continues, "disruptions in the realm of the National Symbolic create a collective sensation of almost physical vulnerability," then the visual juxtaposition of the protestors' injured bodies with the Wall of Moms reproaching militarized agents of the state as wayward children figures this disruption as a family romance of the nation. These images from late July tilt the narrative arc of "the summer of racial reckoning" toward a riven national kinship, a laceration for which the Biden administration now presents itself as bandage and balm. "This is," after all, "the time to heal in America."

Saidiya Hartman's critique of nineteenth-century white abolitionist sentimentalism in *Scenes of Subjection: Terror, Slavery, and Self-Making in Nineteenth-Century America* and, specifically, her analysis of the libidinal economy of slavery help make clear the imaginative work that both collections of images are doing: they construct seductions of family romance as essential to the fantasy of national belonging. Because, as Hartman argues, "slavery is the ghost in the machine

Rizvana Bradley

of kinship," the image of black death must be serially produced and relentlessly circulated. The nation mends its "familial rift[s] on the bodies cast out as not kin," as Christina Sharpe might say. It is for this reason that Biden enjoins us to look, and look again: the image of black death sutures a wounded nation.

The volatility which constantly threatens to break through the surface of such images underscores foundational breaches within the social order, chasms that run far deeper than political disagreements among contemporaries. "Apocalypse Now and Then" is how Hortense Spillers figures the sense of protracted, yet imminent disaster that saturates the historical present and overruns the photographic frame: "On this landscape of peril and grief, cracks and fissures are divulged that one did not realize could be broached in the first place; gaps in ourselves and between ourselves and institutions, and this spectacle of ruin unfolding on fragile ground underfoot." If one rhetorical gesture were to be singled out from the torrents of media commentary on the summer of racial reckoning, it could be the phrase "in this moment." "What's different about this moment?" a journalist asks in the *Washington Post*. "There is an emerging sense that this time is different," echoes the *Guardian*. Whether this present was seen as the monstrous descent into a racial state of exception or as the first sign of ascendance toward Du Bois's "abolition democracy," the declaration *this moment* would have us believe that these images of black suffering and resistance represent a shared historical present.

If this unspoken pronouncement of contemporaneity held a seductive force a year ago, its allure is considerably diminished in retrospect. For the difficult truth is that those who have been forced to confront what Hartman calls the "afterlife of slavery, whose history is dissimulated in the wake of the non-event of emancipation," know that *here* and *now* are not as self-evident as they first appear. The black diaspora possesses neither spatial anchor nor footing in the forward march of history but instead confronts an interdiction from normative space and time—an interminable displacement of geography and a time without historical arc that renders any simple presumption of *present* or *presence* spurious at best and treacherous at worst.

Strikingly, the most prominent visual displays of black "presence" and of the racial present they are meant to index come to us in the form of black suffering. Such representations are not so much opposed to those which emphasize black dignity or perseverance, resilience, or triumph but rather their condition of possibility and inverted reflection, which is why the transit between the two forms occurs so seamlessly. Writing in 2014 about the murderous images of black death reproduced and continuously circulated online, Mariame Kaba and Tamara K. Nopper critique the ways graphic videos and photographs are used to generate mass political sympathy and mobilize solidarity around black suffering and black struggle:

> One gets the sense that the only way to generate a modicum of concern or empathy for black people is to raise the stakes and to emphasize the extraordinary nature of the violations and the suffering. To circulate repeatedly the spectacular in hopes that people consider the everyday. It's a fool's errand.

Indeed, emancipatory rhetoric and representational tools of civil society are necessarily tethered to "murderous anti-Black projections," as Wilderson points out. The incommensurable difference between the non-black subject who can lay claim to an image of vulnerability and black people who are made the objects of racial empathy throws into relief a deeper structural antagonism. Where this reveals itself as visual discordance, it merely betrays an immanent instability which always already haunts civil society in an antiblack world. Liberal empathy may be regarded as one of countless endeavors to mobilize and contain the antagonism of antiblackness, even if such exertions serially end in failure. Hartman's critique of nineteenth-century white abolitionist imaginaries, which posits "the precariousness of empathy and the thin line between witness and spectator," is no less germane to the present. Is the embattled or ennobled black figure ever truly the subject of the images that saturate our vision? Are these images merely ciphers for those subjects who immediately recognize themselves as their audience?

This war unfolding beneath the facade of the visual requires us to reflect upon representation as constituted by more than what is presumed to comprise an image. As Stuart Hall has argued, "Representation works as much through what is *not* shown, as through what is." Once we begin to recognize the forces of racial (counter)insurgency undergirding the composition of the visible, we may begin to pay attention not simply to what the photographs visualize but to the *racial metaphysics* by which they direct us to see—that which creates the conditions for what appears, as well as what is concealed. What is crucial, in other words, is not merely what can be discerned upon the surface of these photographs, but rather, as Calvin Warren might suggest, "the ontological violence the image enacts," the antiblack metaphysics that undergirds and renders such images legible. These sorts of photographs begin to alert us to a kind of Benjaminian optical unconscious, in which the ceaseless metaphysical annihilation of blackness constitutes what is visualizable through the perpetual displacement of the minor, errant repertoires of black existence. Photographic visuality, in other words, cannot be disentangled from the foundationally antiblack metaphysics of the modern world.

Since the mid-nineteenth century, as Ariella Azoulay describes it, the camera's shutter has opened and closed

Picturing
Catastrophe

"the jaws of history." What can be rendered legible by the photograph comes to index the shape, boundaries, and directives of the political. Photography is deployed to ensure that the political is everywhere and all the time understood as that which can be rendered visible. The photograph is imagined simply as visual evidence of what must be made present, its universal accessibility and intelligibility presumed as ontological fact and ethical right.

For the "others of Europe," in Denise Ferreira da Silva's phrasing, the injunction to transparency, visibility, and legibility has always consummated the union of erasure and morbidity. Directing us to the ways racial violence comes to structure "the protocols and limits" of presence, Hartman argues that "opacity" and "concealment" must "be considered in relation to the dominative imposition of transparency." What is called for is no less than the onto-epistemological work of "rethinking 'aesthetics,'" as Sylvia Wynter put it, and it is a call that has been taken up and responded to in countless ways throughout the black diaspora for centuries. Those of us who have always lived within the dark corners of the photograph must constantly remind ourselves that the concealments, interdictions, expulsions, and contortions of the aesthetic are neither incidental nor secondary to the exigencies perpetually figured as present. The historical cartography of the aesthetic is a killing field.

2

Photography is one of the central means by which the modern world is made knowable. The first two decades of photographic discovery, as Susan Sontag points out, "made possible an ever-increasing spread of that mentality which looks at the world as a set of potential photographs. . . . From its

Rizvana
Bradley

start, photography implied the capture of the largest possible number of subjects." If photography's aesthetics enlist in, or are conscripted into, the project of making the world "frame by frame," as Zeynep Gürsel notes, the formal mechanics of photography can be regarded as technological abstractions which insinuate deeper investments in political subjectivity, veiled though the latter may be. Put simply, we should not neglect the work photographs do in "appropriating the world," as Sontag put it.

It is precisely this appropriative modality of visioning which betrays photography's role in the nineteenth-century world picturing that necessitated its development, as evinced by its earliest forms, from the daguerreotype to the carte de visite, tintypes, and studio portraits, all of which visually played a role in fashioning hierarchies of racialization and in circulating racial knowledge. As Kobena Mercer notes, such visual technologies were instrumental in making "representation central to the politics of colonialism," even as the colonized have serially turned these technologies against colonialism's representational grain. The visual orders of the digital present are no less inflected by colonial and imperial habits of photographic worlding.

The habitus of colonialism requires the myth of origin as much as destiny, a narrational reflex painfully undone in Saidiya Hartman's *Lose Your Mother: A Journey along the Atlantic Slave Route*. In one instance, Hartman reflects on a photograph from a tourist guide for Cape Coast Castle in Ghana, in which the castle's infamous dungeon is shown "crammed with boys and girls from the local school costumed as slaves." The image, which aimed at permitting us "to believe that we could co-exist with the captives, witness their suffering, and remedy their defacement," was nothing more than a failed romance: "The crowd packed in this room would remain without names and faces. That was the nature of the crime that had transformed persons into cargo. It was now impossible to fill in the blank spaces." The photograph is a record of the attempt to stage an impossible reenactment, but in the end, "all the photograph really expressed was yearning."

Hartman's encounters with the archive reveal that there is more at stake than an ethical, political, or epistemic failure of photographic representation. To be clear, the problem is not with photographic representation per se. The issue that ought to concern us here is rather the phantasmatic production of the *something represented* or, more precisely, how this *something represented* is made to appear as if it has emerged from the inconceivable horrors of the *unrepresentable*—"the hell holes of the most horrific conditions imaginable." For Hartman, the violations of history are folded into the extant yearnings of and for those "gone and forgotten," those continuously absented from the archive, yearnings which cannot find a resting place in this world. Absence, in this context, can only be rendered ancillary to some presumed, prior presence.

There are a host of disorderly subjects, practices, relations, affections, and passions that cannot be captured by the photographic medium's indexical, iconic function, and which are therefore cast outside of historical memory. But what is cast out of the frame is never altogether excised. In *Image Matters: Archive, Photography, and the African Diaspora in Europe*, her study of black diasporic subjects, spanning late-nineteenth-century ethnographic images to early-twentieth-century postwar passport photographs, Tina Campt argues that what the frame of the image would seek to displace in fact remains as "affective residues" that touch us in ways which are not readily transparent. These "affective residues" necessarily complicate the repertoires of feeling that are thought to be endemic to the photographic imaginary—in particular, the medium's relationship to something like mourning. Thierry de Duve has written that "photography is probably the only image-producing technique that has a mourning process built into its semiotic structure, just as it has a built-in trauma effect. The reason is . . . that the referent of an index cannot be set apart from its signifier." But what happens to an image when it encounters the traces of what Katherine McKittrick refers to as "black absented presences": that which "cannot be seen or heard or read but is always there"? What are we to make of photography's capacity to lay claim to mourning as both a condition and a function of its aesthetic in the face of the submerged histories and aesthetic genealogies of the enslaved, with their absent or negated "referents"?

Dionne Brand's recent poetic work of criticism, *An Autobiography of the Autobiography of Reading*, opens with an encounter with a photograph of herself as a young child. The first page of Brand's experimental text begins with a peculiar reflection: "There is a photograph of me taken when I was a child. I do not recognize myself, though I seem to remember the day and the event." She continues:

> The little girl, reputed to be me, in the photograph is about three or four years old. It is the earliest and only photograph of this period. They say that I am one of the four children in this photograph; the three others are my sisters and my closest cousin. I recognize them. We are four girls. I am alleged to be second from the left, third from the right. We all have white ribbons in our hair.

The autobiography's initial scene is, crucially, not one of photographic recognition but of *misrecognition*:

> Everyone says the little girl looks like me. I doubt it. I do not recognize myself. Already I am changed in the photograph, since I leave off being myself to follow the directive of the photographer; already I have changed, thinking of composing

Picturing
Catastrophe

myself, for the audience. I now recognize myself as authored, altered. As selected and sorted, from a series of selves for appearance and presentation.

The text enables a return to and a re-inhabitation of a past self, as well as an *imaging* of a past self, from a critical distance. The point, for Brand, is that the photograph does not yield a pure representation of what Roland Barthes calls "photography's *noème*," the *"that-has-been* . . . the Intractable."* Rather, the attenuation of presence and appearance is accomplished by Brand's tracing and retracing of a self that is at once revealed and obscured by the photograph. Ironically, the reader is given an autobiographical account of a subject whose faltering, protracted, even fitful self-appearance calls photographic presence itself into question.

Gradually, we learn that Brand's capacity to see (and not see) herself in the photographic image hinges upon a retroactive (re)discovery of the glimpses of life that existed prior to it—figurations of life and existence that are beyond the image. More crucial than the photograph itself is the mnemonic imagination it stimulates. Brand's quasi-speculative account of this sliver of diasporic history is occasioned by a photographic object which was itself a requisite accessory to an obligatory migration—a fact that draws our attention to the acts of arrangement, selection, and sorting she describes as a social choreography crucial to the making of the photographic mise-en-scène.

By alluding to the ways family members, women especially, are conscripted into a general performance of respectability, Brand captures something essential about the deployment of photographic portraiture as a means of managing national allegiances and civic propriety:

Rizvana
Bradley

"When we take the photograph, we are taking it to send to my mother and my aunt, but also to send to England. . . . England is as much the spectator; and for England, standing behind my mother and my aunt, we must make a good appearance." The picture is stitched to the hope and burden of "making a good appearance" for the metropole. It is clear that this particular photograph, if not this genre of photography, demands the referent (the colonized) be composed for the signifier (the colonizer), fabricated through aesthetic imposition.

As the privileged mediator of the imperial archive, photography has played a critical role in delineating the thresholds and limits of history, as well as of who can and cannot be among its proper subjects.

Brand's *Autobiography* does not reproduce the images she describes. The existence of the photograph only points to the impossibility of her presence within its aesthetic structure. The irony of the inversion is of course that the photograph in which Brand is ostensibly, visibly present, in fact rests upon a structure in which Brand cannot appear, or at least cannot appear to herself, not as a self whose appearance presumes the authority of presence. And yet she is "bound to appear," to use Huey Copeland's turn of phrase. Hence Brand's wry riposte: "Whoever I appear to be is simply that: an appearance."

Those of us who study black radical traditions of experiment and refusal must grapple with the painful fact that every appearance within what David Lloyd calls "the racial regime of aesthetics" is invariably the reproduction of antiblack violence. A radically divergent practice of seeing, an attunement to the fact of black existence cannot be delivered through better or more inclusive forms of representation, as Hartman and Brand show us. Seeing anew necessitates an emergence, as Lloyd puts it, "out of the ruins of representation." Any critical evaluation of the photographic medium's role in materializing race—

or, more precisely, in fabricating the singular raciality blackness is made to bear—must contend with the way photography's spatial and temporal logics have been structured by a metaphysics whose aesthetic regime of picturing depends upon the production of violent gaps, omissions, contortions, and eradications. These are the racial orders of being and knowledge that subtend what Azoulay calls "the imperial archive." As the privileged mediator of the imperial archive, photography has played a critical role in delineating the thresholds and limits of history, as well as of who can and cannot be among its proper subjects.

This is the "violence of presence," as Frank Wilderson and Patrice Douglas have described it, and it is a violence that carries little hope of reparation or redress. For, as Calvin Warren has argued, "antiblackness as metaphysics" establishes "the instruments and framework for binary thinking, the thinking of being as presence." Within this antiblack metaphysics, the black can only be "born into absence and not presence." Thus, because picturing is itself an incarnation of catastrophe, a mechanism for reproducing the violent enclosures of presence, the catastrophe of antiblackness's annihilative ambition cannot be pictured. Photography is merely one of the most salient mediums for the violence of picturing that is general to the modern aesthetic regime; it is no less central to the ongoing racial-colonial war indicted and refused by the Movement for Black Lives than the police, the military, and the carceral archipelago. Photography, in turn, is no less the domain of police power than the city street, the photograph no less a site of carcerality than the prison cell. "Two fatal instruments," Azoulay tells us: "The camera and the gun."

3

The accumulations of images with which this essay opened are not reflections of some objective historical reality which stands apart from the violence of repression any more than the intensified forms of surveillance that have marred the reputation of new visual technologies in recent years. Under the modern aesthetic regime, every visualization becomes a site of enclosure. Yet, even as the photography from the "summer of racial reckoning" could not help but play a part in taming and containing the spirit of "the moment," the visual surfeit brimming from such multitudes will just as surely always overspill the parapets of the frame.

How then do we attend to this visual surplus—as a desire excessive to the image, as an aesthesis that cannot be pictured? How might we begin to recognize its immanent entanglement with the project of abolition, with the collective refusal of every expropriation and enclosure perpetuated by and for the state? The aesthetic discordance gathering beneath the surface of the photographs from the summer of 2020 marks the clash between a *symbolic order* which presumes to present the world as it is (or at least how it is supposed to be), and a *symbolic disorder* that cannot appear within this world as anything other than a problem, even as it holds out the possibility of forms of life beyond catastrophe.

Photography's capacity to glimpse other political horizons is not divorced from its aesthetic regime but a function of them. Photographic techniques of cropping, retouching, and the rendering of perspective, for instance, effectively scale and rescale the world in ways that both expand and reify our sense of the world as such. The question that emerges is: How do we reconcile the radical movement toward *abolition*—which embraces, but cannot be reduced to, political strategies such as defunding the police; closing prisons, detention centers, and military bases; organizing

Picturing
Catastrophe

rent and workplace strikes; and offering mutual aid in the face of structural abandonment—as an ongoing collective project distinguished by a commitment to reimagine and reconstruct social life, if our means of imagi(ni)ng remain bound to a history of photographic representation essential to modernity's enduring project of *worldmaking*?

And yet, any contemporary extension of the Heideggerian problematic of the "world represented as picture" is not and can never be even half the story. For how do we attend to the ones who must continually bear the burdens of photographic overexposure, who are continuously tasked with mending political life while suffering the risks and costs of social morbidity, and who remain subject to an image economy whose phantasmatic projections mandate both the erasure and exorbitant visioning of blackness? How do we accompany those who, in Fred Moten's words, enact a "criminal refusal" of a seemingly totalizing "world picture"? While it is true that we are living in the midst of the terrible culmination of techniques of world picturing, it is also true that those who survive the cataclysms of empire are already, by necessity, fashioning the means of inhabiting what Tendayi Sithole calls "the unmaking of the world."

Perhaps we don't need any more retrospectives, for every effort to return us to an image of the past is one which returns us to the image of the present, to the merciless directives of the racial metaphysics of presence. Perhaps we need, instead, to cultivate a kind of anti-retrospective attention which embraces the declivitous underside that undercuts every enterprise of world picturing, the wounding that refuses suture. To linger with/in this "tear in the world," in Brand's poetics, is to reinvent what it means to see.

Rizvana
Bradley

Image as Currency

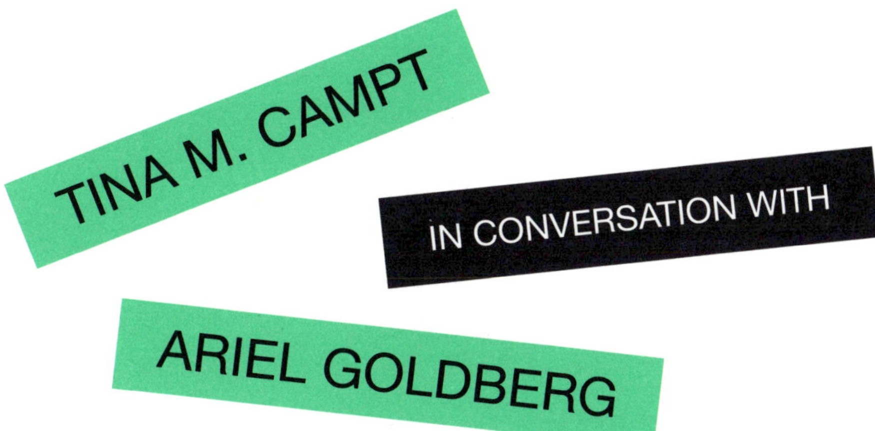

Ariel Goldberg: For this conversation, I have prepared prompts that focus on the centrality of image-making to Tina M. Campt's work. I'll say a few words by way of introduction before inviting Tina to read from *Listening to Images*.

What is image-making as it pertains to world-building, when the scale of vision is infinite? Infinite in that the vision moves across time, particularly the future conditional tense Tina loves.

The power of Tina's writing is an ability to make images come to life, not merely in her own research but in offering modalities of description that empower one's imagination, that trouble what has been taken to be fact—especially inside archives—as well as the imposing orders that govern everyday life. Sometimes, we think about images as a place of loss because we are missing information. I am moved by how, in Tina's work, there's a lot of suffusing of new ways of thinking about how we can be subversive caption writers in our relationship to images. This subversiveness comes about because slowness is a virtue and is achieved through a serialized version of exercises of ekphrasis, of naming and of tending to images across genres of black life, intimate daily modes of beauty, protection, and resistance.

The title *Listening to Images* is not just a description of a process. It is a provocation to all of us, to all interlocutors, to shift images from one intended purpose—perhaps *to be seen*—to another: to be felt, imagined, heard via the affective, haptic, sensorial frequencies. This methodological provocation brings in conditions for viewing and learning, questioning our own subjectivities and the contexts in which images exist and come to life.

I'm also really excited to think about Tina's most recent work, *A Black Gaze*, especially its shift to looking at more contemporary artists, and the tension between vernacular and fine art, which is always alive, and very much a part of this symposium in very fluid ways.

Tina M. Campt: I'm going to start by reading from *Listening to Images*. I am delighted at this suggestion because I've been reading from *A Black Gaze* recently and going back to my earlier work is a pleasure, and it's illuminating because it brought me to the thinking I'm doing right now. This is from the final section of the coda—"Futurity the Remix: #Practicing Refusal."

It was a collection of photographs I couldn't touch, and I'll admit, I'm not really comfortable with that. I prefer to handle and touch photos as much (or little) as an archive or their owner will allow. It gives me a feel for the image, and the contact intensifies the impact and impression they leave on me. In this case, rather than gentle handling, I scrolled, tapped, and clicked in and out, and up and down on my trackpad. This collection of images was a Tumblr—one of the self-made, collaborative, digital archives that have become ubiquitous and addictive, thanks to the technologies of the internet and social media. Having spent two years studying mug shots and prison photo albums, I couldn't help but compare them to this very different archive of twinned images of the same individual posed side by side in two paired images.

But the Tumblr photos shared none of the institutional formality of the rigidly shot, compelled portraits with which I originally compared them. They were not pairings of faces full frontal and in profile. They were not jailed or incarcerated men forced to pose for the camera. They were young black men and women reveling in and lamenting the act of photographic capture as a memento mori. The difference

Tina M. Campt
Ariel Goldberg

enacted in the transition between each photo was a contrast created by an intentional juxtaposition: a juxtaposition that taunts its viewers to "see" a difference and, in doing so, engage the consequences of imposing or resisting the implied narrative that would justify a distinction between them.

#If They Gunned Me Down, Which Picture Would They Use? began as a Twitter feed created in response to the proliferation of negative photographic representations of Michael Brown in Ferguson, Missouri, and (retrospectively) of Trayvon Martin in Sanford, Florida.

> **"They wouldn't show the smiling girl who graduated abroad at one of the best schools in the country. The media would portray me as a hard and mean-looking girl who was asking for it."**

> **"Would they mention my troubled past or that I occasionally smoked weed . . . or would they mention that I was a responsible university student interested in creating a society in which young people aren't getting gunned down due to our fears, judgment, and lack of understanding?"**

> **"They'd make sure my pictures of my achievements not only in academics but in life would never see the light of day."**

Young women and men in graduation caps and gowns, military uniforms, medical scrubs, prom dresses or coats and ties, alongside photos of those same individuals performing menacing stereotypes of black urban life. Refusing to wait passively for a future posited as highly likely or inevitable for black urban youth, the sitters actively anticipate their premature deaths through these photos. In doing so, they enact anterior practices of fugitivity through their refusal to be silenced by the probability of a future violent death they confront on a daily basis. Through these images they fashion a futurity they project beyond their own demise. Rather than fleeing or submitting to a future imposed upon them, they face down the image that would negate the complicated truth of the lives they have lived, in order to interrupt the narrative of their own demise that threatens to extinguish their capacity to claim a life lived in dignity and complexity. Rather than accept the narrative of black urban depravity ascribed to them, their photographic juxtapositions disrupt and disorder the terms of life imposed upon them even in death. This collection of twinned photos simultaneously reclaims respectability and swagger, filiality and disobedience, dignity and rebellion, mourning, loss, melancholy, and lament. They reassemble a photographic archive of dispossession that enacts a future they anticipate will be robbed from them—a future they must image and reauthor in the present in the face of impending death. Their praxis of refusal consists of transforming mundane acts of image making into quotidian practices of fugitivity.

I have argued throughout this book that practicing refusal means embracing a state of black fugitivity, albeit not as a "fugitive" on the run or seeking escape. It is not a simple act of opposition or resistance. It is neither a relinquishing of possibility nor a capitulation to negation. It is a fundamental renunciation of the terms imposed upon black subjects that reduce black life to always already suspect by refusing to accept or deny these terms as their truth. It is a quotidian practice of refusing the terms of impossibility that define the black subject in the twenty-first-century logic of racial subordination.

Refusing the impossibility of black futurity in the contemporary moment demands extremely creative forms of fugitivity. Performing the imperiled state of one's own future through photographs that

Image as
Currency

simultaneously image both who you are and how your life will be effaced in death is at once a refusal and an affirmation of one's capacity to inhabit a future against all odds. It is as brave an act as looking into the eyes of police officers surrounding you, seeing the certainty of a lifetime of incarceration, and deciding to create an alternate future ("line of flight") than the one they have in store. The line of flight depicted by the sitter-subjects of this Tumblr series constitutes a praxis of futurity that simultaneously images and refuses the probability of premature death they confront as their imposed destiny. They redeploy this predictive anterior probability by way of a photographic enactment of death as a fugitive practice of refusal. They are photographic enactments that force us to reflect on the historical continuities between black folks' past, present, and future use of photography to embrace the future they want to see—*now*.

[...]

Like Michelle Koerner and Alexander Weheliye, I too trace this notion of an anterior fugitivity back to the "lines of flight" invoked by George Jackson in his revolutionary classic, *Soledad Brother.* As Koerner writes,

> **Jackson's line 'I may run . . .' announces that fugitivity, rather than simply being a renunciation of action, already carries with it an active construction: a line of flight composes itself as a search for a weapon. Disrupting the opposition of 'flight or fight' that has often troubled the political understanding of fugitivity, Jackson's line affirms a politics where escape is always already a counterattack.[1]**

[...]

This book began with a black feminist mapping of the grammar of black futurity—a grammar of anteriority I defined in the tense of the future real conditional, or that which will have had to happen. I began by describing my accountability to the forms of black feminist capture described by Hortense Spillers as an "American Grammar Book," which continues to structure the lives of black folks in the contemporary moment. As surprising as it may seem at this juncture, I remain committed to a black feminist praxis of futurity and the grammar of the future real conditional. More specifically, I feel a deep accountability to the *had to* of this tense and the necessity of its (grammatically implied) "must." For I believe that the challenge of black feminist futurity is the constant and perpetual need to remain committed to the political necessity of *what will have had to happen,* because it is tethered to a different kind of "must." It is not a "must" of historical certainty or Marxist teleology. It is a responsibility to create one's own future as a practice of survival. The future real conditional is an essential component of a black feminist praxis of futurity as an existential grammatical practice of grappling with precarity, while maintaining an active commitment to the every labor of creating an alternative future. Indeed, it is this grammatical practice of futurity that constitutes my definition of *freedom.*[2]

AG: As you outlined, Tumblr versus Instagram immediately sets us in a different technological temporality, one of a near past, and the quotidian practices of fugitivity of the black radical imagination through this example of #IfTheyGunnedMeDown. The interventions you describe through these images are both analyses of and resistances to the images that were circulating—images of Michael Brown and Trayvon Martin—in the aftermath of their tragic premature deaths. It brings to mind the artist Alexandra

Tina M. Campt
Ariel Goldberg

Bell, who, in a project called *Counternarratives*, did large-scale rethinks of the *New York Times* stories that had presented negative images (in words and photographs) of Michael Brown. Bell edited the printed version in redline as if it were still in progress at the newspaper office, redacted extraneous and racially biased copy and headlines, then used a huge image of Brown's high school graduation in his cap and gown, with the headline "A Teenager with Promise." The picture of Brown replaced both the original story about him and the one that had run next to it, on Darren Wilson, the white cop who murdered Brown. Bell's edited newspaper page and the revision were displayed as diptychs plastered across New York City, which was a really powerful project—in one motion, Bell signaled and decried the racism inherent in US media and suggested a different, more compassionate narrative of Brown's life and death.

I'll bring things back to the consideration of image as currency. In part, the intervention of your book and of your writing creates narratives for images—narratives that are not necessarily present within the archives the images are housed in. For example, in the case of the mug shot, the images haunt the present; they may be from a different time period—the currents around mug shots might seem limited to the state archive—yet the ways these images may circulate are not necessarily defined. I'm curious to hear how you are thinking about image as currency.

TC: I'm super-predictable—I always refer to definitions. So, I'm going to go down that wormhole, where definitions spiral into other worlds, and define some terms and place them in proximity to other terms to think through them. *Currency*—a medium of exchange; being current or up to date; being in demand as a mode of expression. So: a medium of exchange, being in the moment, being in demand as a mode of expression. *Photography*—to what extent is photography a commodity? Then, going backward to go forward, what is the value, based on availability or demand, at which a commodity can be exchanged for other commodities? *Commodity*—think Marx—a thing, an external object, whose qualities satisfy human needs. So: we can think about photography as a commodity that satisfies human needs. When we think about photography as currency, we are obliged to think about its exchange value. We can't think about it simply as an intervention that captures a moment in time; we also have to think about it as a commodity in Marx's sense of something that satisfies human needs that in turn becomes exchangeable or valued—which means thinking about it beyond capitalism, even though it gets inserted into a capitalist structure.

Where I go then, in thinking about these definitions in relationship to photography as currency, is a kind of turn; I go to thinking about images like the Tumblr images, which are asking us to think about what human needs they might satisfy. And when

I'm thinking about black folks, I'm thinking about our need to visualize ourselves in a way that is as complex as the lives that we've been forced to lead, and thinking about photography as an intervention that allows us to depict our struggles in multilayered ways. So, the prompt/provocation of photography as currency drives us to think about photography as a commodity that satisfies certain needs, as well as about the way in which it has become exchangeable (or extractable) for certain forms of value and recognition.

From there, I would speak to the connection I make in my own work, which is a transition from the devalued vernacular photography that has been so essential to black communities in diaspora—that is, making photos that "have no value" to anybody but you—to the kind of work I talk about in *A Black Gaze*—images that are extremely valuable, but at the same time are depicting the devaluation of black lives and black subjects. That's a contradiction that is really important to me in trying to articulate something called a black gaze—how is the depiction of black bodies circulating now? In what ways are contemporary artists disrupting that valuation by challenging us to see blackness differently?

AG: I'm thinking about your thoughts on what human needs might photographs satisfy, the subversive and interruptive elements you've mentioned; and about black life and making images that allow one to be active in their construction and circulation, and disrupt—and refuse—other currents or circulations that are within this Marxist commodity structure of a photography of exchange. I'd be very interested to segue to some ideas within *A Black Gaze* about the movement of images and their interruptive qualities, and especially around how contexts are constantly changing the ways we look at images.

In particular, I'm referring to a theory that you very poetically refer to as the *still moving image*. It has a repetitive quality that gives it the feel of being part of a current and it has practical application—you talk about the work of a lot of filmmakers—Arthur Jafa, Kahlil Joseph—and performance-based work by artists like Okwui Okpokwasili, in whose work you have participated. You have to produce stills of video works or live experiences—like sitting in Deana Lawson's studio and having a conversation with her. These become still images inside *A Black Gaze*, as meditations, as memories, as places to sit and parse out ideas through images. You have a beautiful way of erasing the hierarchies in an image in your very process of writing about them. You write: "The still moving images are images that hover between still and moving images. They're animated still images, slowed or stilled images in motion, or visual renderings that blur the distinctions between these multiple genres. Images

Tina M. Campt
Ariel Goldberg

that require the labor of feeling with or through them." I would love to hear you speak a little bit more about this idea.

TC: *Still moving images* is a term I had to come up with in order to be able to transition from talking about photography to talking about films that do things photography does. It arose from thinking about the technological interventions of people like Jafa and Luke Willis Thompson, who are able to slow down moving images and have us interact with them as if they were photos, and at the same time make still images that move us. It's a kind of double entendre to the extent that it's dialectical. But the real point of it is the simultaneity of stillness and movement. There is a place in between the still and the moving image which is really powerful and extremely moving.

What I'm trying to evoke with this term are questions of what the artist is doing and how they are doing it. How are they able to manipulate the moving image so that it almost seems still and photographic? What is the impact of that on us? What does it mean for us to dwell in that space between movement and stillness? This goes back to ideas I developed in *Listening to Images*, where I was also thinking about spaces in between movement and stillness. That's a space of intensity, a space that demands effort and labor, that demands the balancing of all the various forces that are acting upon us, that are impressing themselves on us, that are compacting us or trying to compel us.

To be in a place of stasis is not necessarily to be at peace or at rest. It's about being able to sustain a relationship to one's environment—a relationship that may involve effortfully buffeting all the forces that are confronting us. With the still moving image in particular, we are being forced to withstand the forces of anti-blackness and work our way to another relationship to them. And that is a space that is not only inhabited by black people—it is a place that certain contemporary artists force us all to be in, and in doing so, it gives us the opportunity to move outside our own comfort level and into a space that might be more generative of a different future.

AG: I love that you say stasis is not about peace or rest, especially in what you describe as one of the main tenets of *A Black Gaze*—that you are inspired by the ways in which black artists render black sociality's "improbable capacity . . . to defy the insistent gravity of white supremacy."[3] That's toward the beginning of the book. Your book embraces difficulty, discomfort, challenges, and you show experiences of dwelling in the space of more transformative moments of stasis as well. A shared project of study. One of them is this beautiful moment that describes a performance of Okpokwasili's *Sitting on a Man's Head*. The piece invites viewers to participate by walking very slowly and entering inside a sort of group meditation. You narrate the experience of moving through this installation and doing something your writing invites people to do, which is to slow down and just be inside the physical experience of looking at images or thinking about all the things that are not visible.

There's something powerful in your recounting this experience with Okpokwasili's work—to quote from *A Black Gaze*, you write that you "became part of the chorus"[4] when you were doing this slow, meditative walking that placed you in a different temporality. To say you had become part of a chorus brings to mind Saidiya Hartman's conception of the chorus as the central framing principle of re-imagining and re-activating black radical life—especially young black women's worlds—in the early twentieth century in *Wayward Lives*. It was exciting, in that moment of reading, to hear an echo of a major theme and thought formation within Saidiya's work become part of your experience of this contemporary artwork. I would love to hear you speak about your collaborations with her.

TC: Collaboration is fundamental to everything I do. Two words that are adjacent for me come to mind: dialogue and inspiration. To me, collaboration is about feeding each other, nourishing each other through creative or intellectual contributions—or I would say gifts. Saidiya and I read each other's work all the time and give each other feedback. So, when I was reading an early version of *Wayward Lives*, the idea of the chorus, which is central to that work, spoke to me in a really important way.

Okwui was also reading early versions of Saidiya's work, and the chorus is central to her practice as well. *Sitting on a Man's Head* has had a number of iterations, the most recent of which saw it evolve from simply a movement practice into vocal practice—a chorus. Sound has become an important element of the project; she's now encouraging people to vocalize—and in vocalizing with others, what emerges is a spontaneous chorus. The idea Saidiya is writing about is a chorus of young women as dancers on a stage, describing the lives of these young women who were seen as wayward but who simply wanted to live their lives in a way that allowed them joy and freedom and autonomy. In *Wayward Lives*, Saidiya writes about people who are literally working in choruses—performance as the best job for them.

But there was also a physical coordination, which allowed them to be together. I think about—and Okwui's work also suggests—the chorus as a vocal entity that has the same kind of coordination challenges as the physical chorus. In a chorus, you have to harmonize, you have to collaborate with the altos, with the sopranos, the tenors. All those people have to come together to coordinate and

Tina M. Campt
Ariel Goldberg

create an internal synchrony. And yet, they are not one—they are a whole but they are not necessarily unified. It is a collaboration. So, I find that to be a rich term in all of these senses.

Collaboration is a really important term to think about, in all of its iterations. What does it mean to be in collaboration with others? How does that offer you a stage on which you can freestyle—but also do that with others? Again, the ideas of the chorus, the choir, are ways of talking about collaboration. We can go back to the Greek chorus and think about it in relationship to a choir. And what is the chorus doing? It is pronouncing; it is commenting; it is giving you supplemental information. It is giving you viewpoints that annotate the main drama of a particular play or a particular set of circumstances. For me, Saidiya's work opens up an awesome and powerful conversation that really takes you places.

Natalia Brizuela: There is something in *A Black Gaze* that is very much about collaboration between the field of scholarship and the field of art practice. In this particular moment, at least in the history of the United States, it seems to me that collaboration between black scholars and black artists is allowing for a kind of disruption of the distance between, and separation of, the past and the future. Your grammatical practice, in both *Listening to Images* and *A Black Gaze*, proposes tenses through which past and future are placed in collaboration and not separated. I wonder if they overlap— this grammatical collaboration and this collaboration between scholars and artists?

TC: You have summarized perfectly what I'm experiencing in the world today. There is an extraordinary collaboration between contemporary artists and scholars because we learn so much from each other. Then there is that grammatical collaboration, in that black contemporary artists are thinking about the relationship between the past and the future. They have to. They cannot avoid it, living in the world right now. That grammatical collaboration—the collapse of the temporalities of past, present, and future—is what we are experiencing as this horrific echo chamber that is our contemporary moment.

That is what has motivated this past year-and-a-half of rebellion. It's no longer a racial reckoning. It is rebellion because of the frequency and the repetition and the brutality of anti-blackness right now. How can one make art and not be in close proximity to that echo chamber? The result is a ricochet between words and images, which is why I had to write *A Black Gaze*, why I had to start writing about contemporary art—because it is speaking to me in terms that are not words. It is speaking in powerful visual registers that confront us with what we are tired of describing. So, we see work like

Simone Leigh's *Loophole of Retreat*, which is a sonic confrontation with the experience of Debbie Africa, one of the Move 9, that places the present and the past in juxtaposition. Jafa's work montages the present and the past in a way that brings us to see echoes of impossibility and possibility, the echo of brutality and pleasure, of joy and abjection. So, when you point to this convergence, I absolutely agree with you. I think it is one of the most productive conjunctures we have experienced in a long time. One thing that I think is really important here is that scholars are listening to artists. We have to listen to artists, and we cannot privilege the word over art. They are mutually informing. It has been my great pleasure, and my great honor, to be a student of artists as opposed to a consumer of art. That's a posture I think we are all being forced into—to be students of artists. And how much richer our world has become as a result.

Robin Coste-Lewis: I appreciate your generosity about artists and what it means to listen to them. I am most moved by your experience and the way you inhabit your own grammar and your writing—it's as interesting to me as listening to artists, if not more so. It's the same thing—I don't see a demarcation between language and image. It's all abstract to me. I wonder if you could talk a little bit about your experience of grammar and temporality in your sentence structures. You're not just talking about past, present, future, or about simple tenses like future past. You have extensive categories of gradation and how you inhabit time in the sentence. It's apparent to anybody who reads your work that this is no accident, that you're meticulous in your consideration of language as an experience of time in history.

TC: My relationship to writing, to language, to tenses and grammar is fundamentally shaped by having lived for seven years in Berlin and studying German for six or seven years. My love of the German language arises from its rigid grammar structure, which I had to learn. I had to learn what the future conditional is. I had to learn about, you know, subjunctive *eins*, *zwei*, and *drei*. That made a deep impression upon me, coming to understand the relationship between time and grammar, how we, as humans, have come up with a structure for referencing the *here*, the *now*, the *what might have been*, the *what should be*, the *what I would like*. Studying and speaking German became a way of understanding my relationship to time and space—and culture. That formative experience of both learning this language and living in it led me to inhabit language in a different way. So yes, I am absolutely, completely self-conscious about every word I write and every sentence structure I compose because I was so alienated from it for a long time. I had to read, write, speak, and teach in German, a language that was foreign to me. It was an extraordinary challenge, so that, once I came back to writing and speaking in my own language, I became very intentional about it. All the things you mention really do come from that invaluable

Tina M. Campt
Ariel Goldberg

experience—as well as from a desire to invite people into that experience because it was so transformational for me.

I did not start out my career writing about images, I wasn't trained in doing the work I do now. I am perpetually learning. As a teacher, my job is to be as clear as possible, and to invite as many people as possible into my thoughts and my processes of thinking. My relationship to German is a relationship of living in translation—and to this day, I still live in translation. That is not to say I live translating myself from a foreign language to my mother tongue, or vice versa. But I lived an experience of having to translate my thoughts or my insights into a language that would reach other people, or that would move other people. To me, that's the most valuable thing we have as human beings—the ability to reach someone else. I'm humbled that you call it generosity—it's just a desire to communicate and to understand how somebody else thinks, or to have someone else understand what I'm saying. It's an intentionality that was born of something else, but it is a life lesson I continue to practice.

1. Michelle Koerner, "Line of Escape: Gille Deleuze's Encounter with George Jackson," *Genre* 44, no. 2 (Summer 2011): 161.
2. Excerpted from Tina M. Campt, *Listening to Images* (Durham: Duke University Press, 2017), 108–116.
3. Campt, *A Black Gaze* (Cambridge: MIT Press, 2021), 99.
4. Campt, *Black Gaze*, 121.

Instruments of Circulation and Resistance

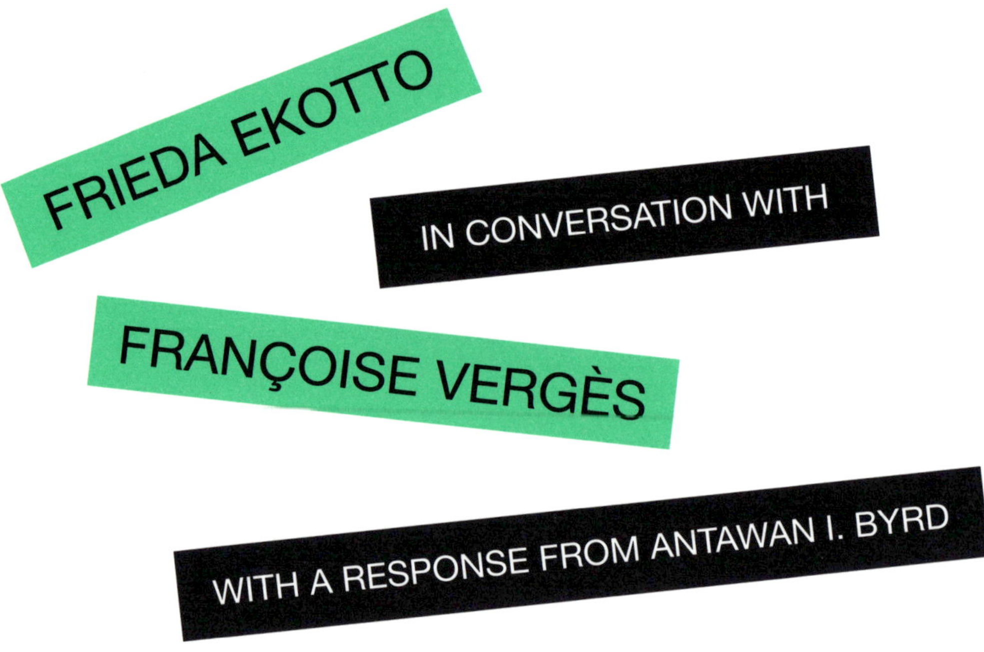

Frieda Ekotto: I want to say something brief about George Floyd. Then I'm going to read a short story I have written about Frida Kahlo. Today, I'm sure these three words—*Black Lives Matter*—have been uttered by everyone around the world. And we have seen pictures of this struggle throughout the world, and even in very racist countries where they don't even like black people, they appropriate the concept of BLM to resist politically.

I ask: Who is George Floyd? We see his image throughout the world now, but nobody knows who George Floyd *is*. He was a father; he was a human being. But we only see a few specific images of him circulating all over. I feel we have stripped him of his humanity. He's dead, but he's not dead. A colleague of mine speaks of how, even when they are dead, the bodies of slaves are claimed by the state. Everyone is claiming George Floyd—but they have stripped him of his humanity. As we think of him, as we see his image, we have to remember that he was a human being, and of course, he has left us the task to continue his resistance.

Tina Campt said something earlier about the visual archive we have created [*see "Image as Currency," pp.151–161*], about how we see images in the archives. We cry our loss—a loss that, as Claudia Rankine writes in her book *Citizen: An American Lyric*, continues to be inscribed upon black bodies and black skin.[1] Until this memory and history are seen, acknowledged, and honored, the violence inflicted upon black bodies will continue, and the dignity due black people will be denied. So, as we use the archives, we have to remember *how* to use them—how to honor lives. I hope people remember that George Floyd was a loving father, a human being—not just a poster in a living room.

I want to read you a story I wrote about Frida Kahlo. I've decided to read it here after listening to what my colleagues have been saying about the art of looking. When we're looking, what do we see? How do we see? This story came to me through watching Stuart Hall discuss the black gaze using the work of Frantz Fanon. He talks about how the black gaze is always sexualized. We see through and beyond the body.[2]

What a misfortune to be a woman!
And yet, for a woman
the worst misfortune is to fundamentally
not understand that she is one.
–Kierkegaard

The Art of Looking
A letter from Frieda Ekotto to Frida Kahlo[3]

Frida Kahlo is emotion, entirely emotion. Kierkegaard's comment has nothing to do with her, this artist, unlike any other. She concerned herself with her being and her feelings. No question, I desire her. She left behind a pictorial legacy in which she grappled with her femininity until her dying breath. For Frida Kahlo, to be a woman wasn't a misfortune; quite the opposite. In every photo, she is dressed stylishly; she is serene, seductive, ready to devour and be devoured. As with every woman with whom I'd like to be intimate, I'm ashamed to admit it, ashamed to say too much, but I admire them both, close up and from a distance. I don't dare say, 'I desire you. I want you.' So, I simply say, 'Oh, I want. . . .' It's a simple phrase, easy enough to say. There is this *pudeur* when I open my mouth, when I say it. These things are not said. We keep them to ourselves. This is my secret garden. I would have surely trembled before her like I did before the great Caribbean poet Aimé Césaire. *Émotion!*

In moments of doubt (like the one I'm having right now), I would have liked to start with an exact date. Something like: 'Frida Kahlo and Frieda Ekotto met in 1986 at the Casa Azúl in Coyoacán, Mexico.' What a beautiful color, the blue of this house, which today still holds a remembrance, a life, a painter's work that crushes the soul with the depth of its artistic expression. Breathtaking paintings are everywhere, exemplary portraits and self-portraits, her colored dresses, her beautiful face, her eyes that speak to me, but also the smells, the feeling of a life crushed by desolation. Since this stay in Mexico during my college years, the Frida Kahlo effect has continued to grow, to transform, to twist and turn and haunt me. She is everywhere and nowhere. She is an element of truth among the story of my family and my country, Cameroon. Everyone seems to know her, especially her experience as a woman involved in a complicated relationship with that other great painter, Diego Rivera, her beloved frog.

As for me, I know her from the inside. It's through her that I began to love my name. My given name, which slides so sweetly between the lips. It's true that Frida Kahlo is a historic name, although for me, she is first and foremost a female bearer of the historical, the political, the philosophical, and a singular painter, in other words an *exceptional woman*, as the teaser for Julie Taymor's film *Frida* (2002) puts it. I would like to touch her, to run my hand across her cheek, to brush her nose, to let my fingers climb up and down hers. I love artists' hands. Something in me is moved when I touch my writer friends' hands. Their long, fine fingers. I'll admit it. I'm dying to touch Frida Kahlo's labia with the tip of my index finger. Frida, I would have loved to love you like a woman loves another woman. I love you so close, so far from your painting. You saw the light of day before me, and I am in the night with you and tomorrow I will see the day. Tomorrow you will look at me with that look you have in the portrait I chose for my office. It's a black-and-white photo. You are the beautiful Frida Kahlo and I am your admirer. A glance at your painting makes me feel as if my heart were being torn from my chest. Your paintings travel the world. Each is different, a particular emotion, infinitely touching, my dear Frida. What emotion, your art, there where you placed your suffering, your humanity.

They are loved, admired. The pain that left you prostrate on your hospital bed for years at a time can even be touched or felt. We admire your exuberant femininity, your many beautiful dresses and magnificent necklaces. We can almost hear them tinkling, yet in that last scene, when she has herself carried in on her sick bed to be celebrated in the gallery, as her husband Diego and the others express their admiration, she appears suddenly, upon her bed in a brightly colored dress, full of life. She is *Frida* as Baudelaire would have put it, 'the celebration of some painful mystery.' Lying on her bed, her face aglow, we forget she is ill, practically dying. Her enthusiasm reminds us that life is nothing but passion and vision.

Whatever she is, Frida Kahlo is first and foremost a result not of destiny, cosmic bad luck, divine will or natural causes, but of a history, a story. And in this history, story, it is impossible to hold her fast within restrictive, impassable limits. Her being and her oeuvre explode into all kinds of possible points of view, which are elusive even as they are affirmations of self. I am Frida Kahlo. *Soy yo!*

I return again to Mexico. This time with Frida Kahlo, German and Mexican painter. I arrive too late, for she is no longer there, only her paintings, which continue to dazzle me, remain. Sublime, this woman who suffered so in her flesh. How to think of her anew, how to extract her from the silence of my soul?

Frieda Ekotto
Françoise Vergès
Antawan I. Byrd

The car accident in which she almost died. The car accident in which I too almost died. Five years old, I lose my classmates in a fatal accident. My father comes with the other parents to claim my body. But I am in the wreckage looking for my schoolbag. I had a pretty, brown leather satchel. We have it still, like a relic among the other objects my family so passionately collects. My father was so moved at my dissertation defense that he told this story with tears in his eyes. 'My daughter, Frieda, my Sulamithe, my mother, was born beneath a bright star. She has been close to death more than once. It's a miracle that she is here today. It does not surprise me at all that she is defending her dissertation on the criminal Jean Genet, a bright star like herself.'

Intertwined at the heart of this plutonic love story are those stories of our countries and our fathers: Germany and Cameroon. It's pointless to revisit this misfortune. There's no reason to—the names Frida/Frieda mark the depths of our wounds. What interests me is our names' trajectories, their confrontations with History. Frida Kahlo, who should be Germany itself, is opposed to it. Frieda Ekotto accepts Germany, which gave her a foundation, a ballast. Colonial history tattoos us beneath our very skin. Indeed, I could now reject this name. I have the choice. I could call myself *Sula*, it's short, it's direct, it's easy to say. It even has two syllables like *Frie-da.*

I was born in Cameroon to a Congolese mother and a Cameroonian father. I come to my encounter with Kahlo, Her Grand Majesty, with my dominated past. The Germans occupied Cameroon. Our common history starts in 1885 around a table in Germany with dignitaries from each European country present and ready to carve up Africa. There was not a single African. So, what should I think of this division? Today the consequence of this great secret meeting is this name I drag around like a millstone. For, even in Cameroon, the new generation no longer knows our country was once a German possession. I learned to love this name because you, too, carried it. But what weight! 1885, the Berlin Conference. The goal is simple: to divvy up Sub-Saharan Africa. Everywhere the inscription of violence; everywhere the horror that wounds each where she is. A common point: Bismarck's Germany. Frida, I would so much have liked to talk with you about this history, our history. I can easily imagine how you would respond to my questions. I know you would study the contours of my sensual lips. That the red necklace I'm wearing today would attract your attention. You would have liked it and you would have winked at me. Your passion, your genius, your desire for Diego who set your body on fire the moment your bodies touched. He kissed all the women who passed beneath his eyes, including your very own sister. You, Frida, you reacted as a jealous woman, you left your beloved frog, finally! But life had fastened you together, and there was nothing anyone could do. He returned to your life like a second husband. That fat, talented, little man, an impossible being, living his life of an artist, forgetting that you, too, had only one desire: to live that life with him. Your artistic oeuvre is as important as his. But that was not the deal. So you found some pretty women, Frida! I know. It's desire, *non*? Your caresses on their buttocks, your soft kisses, wet, warm, hot, your tongue on theirs, your female perfume. Oh! Frida, your look, too deep. I feel it upon me, discretely. I sit frozen in a corner and watch you enjoy yourself.

We are within History. I speak of the past in the present, of the present in the past. Everything mixes together but still remains clear. Frida Kahlo, I desire you, or let's just say I would like to have you in my bed. I'm not being vulgar, this belongs to the realm of the sacred, this woman idealized from afar, in History . . . what we call History? For Frida, a violent passion, infinite suffering. What suffering, my ancestors. This world of lies in which we live. At least, Frida, you had your painting, your brushes, your revolutionary weapons, or as the poet Césaire said, your miraculous weapons!

Frida Kahlo, I ask myself still how to tell you that I am in your small but pharaonic shadow, for I raise you in the depth of a woman's kiss, in the softness of my caresses. There is a picture of you in my offices, in my room, in my office at home. You are in my life, you are important to me. You remind me of your grandeur, your dignity, your passion, your creativity. In the everyday, in my philosophy of the moment, of the now, I see you look at me, smile at me, supporting me. I know that you are there on the complicated path of the everyday, that you accept me as I am with all my contradictions. You, too, were a mountain of contradictions. To want to live means to compromise and to understand the contradictions that define us. I wouldn't know how to get out of bed without your support. When I forget who I am, I breathe a little, and I speak to myself again and again, as Marthe, my partner, recommends I do.

I decided to speak about my relationship with you. But you know, Frida Kahlo, you know that I ask myself often who I am. I move forward in the shadows, slowly, looking for a light to clarify me, to guide me. Yesterday, I spoke with my good friend Nimrod about who I am. He spoke to me about the limits of paranoia. I'm a little frightened, afraid others might think I'm sick. I'm afraid. . . . I know Rimbaud said it, 'I am an other.' Is this true for me? I love talking with Nimrod. He is gentle, tender, passionate. The question of truth remains an important idea in life. To speak the truth, to be true, not to lie to oneself. To let oneself live in this world which eludes me but which I must face. You, Frida, I know how much you suffered, how much you fought to overcome the physical suffering from your accident, but also psychological suffering, you wanted to be a mother. I know that you, in your house, you had children, many children who came for nourishment, who came to give you the smiles you sought in children, other people's children. Me, I am not a mother either. I only raised my late sister Mirabelle's four children. So I am mother by proxy, not as you wanted to be . . . . But I know that you gave so much love to your children, to the children who came to eat at Mamá Frida's house. You waited for them every day. They were rowdy and filled with a joy that delighted you.

In my imagination you are a great woman, a love, a passion; inspiration, I draw from you and your oeuvre.In the end, Hector Bianciotti gives me the tools to drop the 'e' from my name, from in his Académie seat, which the Haitian writer Dany Laferrière will come to fill, and with whom I had the pleasure of working during my first years of teaching. I loved his courses consisting of completely disjointed conversations with students. Bianciotti said that the reason he decided to give up Spanish for French was the French silent *e*. In Italian, as in Spanish, there are no silent vowels. For Bianciotti the day he learned to savor *la lune* in the place of *la luna* was one of great discovery. What did he discover? Silence. And what to discover with Frida Kahlo? The fury that explodes in that silent *e*! More precisely, the uselessness of writing it. But is it so useless? Not necessarily! The *i* in Frida is long—it's there to prolong the vowel in this lovely name! Just like the *h* in Kahlo. Each language has its genius for making words sing. Textual genetics is never transcodable from one language to another. But you're not a woman to do things prudently. Although you're not imprudent, either. Frida is henceforth a Latina name, as is your brilliant victory, your planetary fame with all your images!

I adore you, *calorific* combustible explosive Frida Kahlo,

Your Frieda Ekotto

Frieda Ekotto
Françoise Vergès
Antawan I. Byrd

Françoise Vergès: I would like to speak about the veiled woman, who has become so significant in Europe, and also the bearded brown man, who is constantly under threat of being profiled as a terrorist in opposition to the white bearded man—the hipster—as currency.

Islamophobia provides justification for a permanent state of war and for anti-immigrant, anti-refugee policies. It even enters white ecology, when Muslim women are accused of having too many children and so threatening the environment. How does this visual culture of Islamophobia work? First, a short genealogy of the veiled woman, then the role of white feminism and the question of the veil and war and the instrument of resistance. In terms of a genealogy, Islamophobia is historically anchored in Europe but, in the nineteenth century, British and French imperialism provided new grounds. The French army, for instance, invited artists and writers to be embedded in its "truth." Painters depicted battles and victories over Arab troops, and thus war and the veiled woman became important tropes. I mention painting but in music, poetry, and literature, this question of war also looms large. In 1888, for instance, the British were waging war in Sudan, and claimed their triumph was one of "science over barbarism."[4] The claim that total war was necessary came into play because Muslim populations were seen to be fanatic and savage, and in need of being vigorously subdued and frightened so that they would not rise up again.[5]

Well over a century later, we see similar rhetoric employed whenever Western powers mobilize to "liberate" or otherwise impose their will on nations with largely Muslim populations. We see it again today in Afghanistan, Iraq, and Palestine. It played into propaganda during the Algerian War. In 1958, the wives of French generals organized the unveiling of *Algerian women*. The fact that it was the wives who thought about this "necessity" is significant. In *Algeria Unveiled*, Frantz Fanon analyzed how and why colonial society needed to protect women, given their inferior status. He wrote that it was colonial policy to target the woman so that the rest will follow. Incidentally, the original, French title of *Algeria Unveiled* is the much more active, *L'Algérie de dévoile*, which indicates that it is Algeria doing the unveiling—an unveiling of colonialism and of its own aspiration for independence. Very different from the passivity of "Algeria unveiled."

Jumping to the late 1990s and the early 2000s, white European feminists appropriated orientalist tropes and generated the current vocabulary of Islamophobia. In the late 1990s, in France, Germany, and Italy, white feminists proposed that the veil constitutes Islam's denial of women's rights. In the archives, we find, week after week, letters sent to government ministers, demanding that they pay attention to this question, which led to the series of laws limiting women's right to wear the veil that are in place today in Belgium, Germany, Italy, and France. Governments adopted the vocabulary of Islamophobia and defined the veil as a symbol of the oppression of women by the worst patriarchal system on the planet.

They constructed an oppositional dichotomy of cultures that by nature endorse women's rights and equality between women and men, and those that do not. Of course, these latter societies and cultures are Muslim. The veil became the sign of what must be rescued on the battlefields of the war between civilization and barbarism. And for the white feminist, this became a life-or-death question. This notion—that the veiled woman must be "saved"— was the rubric under which the war on Afghanistan was justified.

The connection between war, the veil, and imperialism is apparent. Today's permanent state of war claims it must unveil Muslim women so they can be free, and the question of freedom is repeated constantly. War campaigns are named for it—recall that Bush Jr. called the war in Afghanistan "Operation Enduring Freedom," and Obama called it "Operation Freedom Sentinel." War is freedom; war brings freedom; war brings freedom to women. And the same logic undergirds the other Wars—on Drugs, Terror, Poverty, even COVID. War must be waged against the virus. War is required to protect women's rights. Peace, then, is a very short interlude between wars, with agreements initiated by white men and signed afterwards by men seated around a table. Peace is a brief lull during which the next war is planned. The belief that warring is human nature has normalized militarization and the weapons industry. The leading countries of Europe—including the one we are in now—design and manufacture and sell weapons of war. This normalization of militarization, of weaponry, brings with it xenophobia and racism. And waging war leaves behind gas, bomb debris, pollution that affects breathing for generations. The soil, the rivers are polluted by what is left behind.

We are told that the veil and the burka prevent women from breathing but the fact that capitalism and imperialism produce difficulty breathing is elided. They provoke suffocation. They produce an economy of exhaustion and suffocation, of exhausted bodies, exhausted land, suffocated forests, suffocated cities, rivers, and oceans. During slavery, masks were placed on the faces of the enslaved, to render them mute and prevent them from breathing.

The universal right to breathe is bound to the dismantling of racism. Preventing breathing is not just about police violence. Of course, that is part of it—"*I can't breathe*"—but, more broadly, it's about the continuous fabrication of suffocation and exhaustion. The World Health Organization says more people are dying everywhere,

Frieda Ekotto
Françoise Vergès
Antawan I. Byrd

every year, from pollution than from any other affliction. And it is invisible: you don't see it, but it kills. So, war produces difficulty breathing, through its economy of exhaustion and suffocation. It attacks the lungs directly—the lungs of the planet and the lungs of the people. In Indonesia today, babies are dying of COVID because they are born with very small lungs. They are more susceptible to contracting the virus because of the poverty they are born into, and the pollution that surrounds them, which leads to asthma and other respiratory diseases.

The image of the veil suffocating women is deployed to mask this economy of suffocation and it eclipses the fact that fighting for the universal right to breathe is a fight against racism. Furthermore, given today's state of permanent war, we should probably consider how we are going to design more refuges—sanctuaries where we can offer safe places to rest and to breathe. Another crucial question surrounds the right to rest. People—migrants, refugees, workers—relate that they are exhausted. They don't sleep well because they're always on the run. Where is the place they can lay their heads on clean sheets and rest?

Rest is forbidden but, at the same time, what would a refuge, sanctuary or oasis from white supremacy look like? How do we write the signs that indicate where the safe roads are, where refuge and sanctuary are to be found? Where one can find false papers, a clean bed, a sense of safety so one can sleep and dream? How do we counter images of violence with images of rest and quietude? And how do we read these signs that must remain invisible? These are like palimpsests; we discover messages beneath what is first seen; under the white texts that try to erase the multi-layered record of what has been written by our ancestors and all the people who can show us the road. We see a map; we don't see sanctuary and refuge at first—but we learn to see them. We learn to read the map differently. Image as cumulative palimpsest. To create a space of peacefulness, where we can think about reparation and its tangled temporality, today we have still to repair the past.

And we have to repair the damaged present. And we have to repair the future because we already know the future is threatened. This tangled temporality makes us think about another way of looking at reparation, focusing not on the damage but only on the repair. We find this effective practice of peacefulness among black women, among Palestinian women, Argentinean feminists, Indigenous women, and Indigenous communities, who create space to rest and to think about radical freedom, to deploy radical imagination, to consider that there have always been possibilities in the darkness of the night of colonialism, as Fanon said. We move. We are Maroons, because one day, yes, one day we will be free.

Frieda Ekotto
Françoise Vergès
Antawan I. Byrd

Antawan I. Byrd: I want to start by posing a broad question—what comes to mind when you hear the phrase that has focused this symposium: *image as currency*?

FE: When I look at images of resistance from the 1960s and then at the Black Lives Matter images we saw throughout the world, I see that those images are the same—which means that between then and now, nothing has really changed. I have this feeling that young people look at the images from the 1960s and think they understand black resistance. That they understand the civil rights movement just by looking at images of Martin Luther King, of Malcolm X, of others. And yet they need to read the history of it. The images are good, but they need to understand how those images came to be.

Now, in the 2020s, the images, the gestures, the pose almost seem calculated to be the same as the earlier images by the people taking them. This to me is striking. I brought this story about Frida Kahlo with me and I'm really happy that I read it, but you see the currency of her self-portrait all over the world. And this is a woman who suffered a lot. What do we value when we look at a picture? I'm always trying to understand what is beyond these images we see.

Particularly when I'm looking at black lives, I see the suffering. The currency for me is suffering. As Françoise says, one day we will be free. I'm wondering how to remove that suffering before that freedom comes. In my work on Jean Genet, that's what I've done as well. Genet suffered a lot. He wrote about the Palestinians, about the Black Panthers, because they were suffering, they were struggling, they resisted. It is this dimension of suffering that I have tried to capture. How do people read that around the world as those images circulate?

FV: Resistance does not circulate as images, but through songs and poetry. Songs are very important for circulating resistance, they are incredibly strong. They resonate, even if you don't understand what they say. They say something that will make you want to act. For me, the circulation of resistance is not necessarily always through images, but often through sound, through music. I always say Bob Marley accomplished much more with his "Redemption Song" than what we learn about slavery from a lot of books. And we could think about a lot of other songs. So, for me, circulation is about bringing together different elements—images, documents, archives. I would say relying only on images is problematic.

AB: I like that you mention Bob Marley, Françoise; and Frieda, I appreciate your 1960s references to Malcolm X and Martin Luther King. Both of your discussions allude to your broader investments in histories of protest and resistance, with references to the Algerian War and imagery produced at that time, during the 1950s and 1960s. And we see very clearly how imagery from Civil Rights struggles of the 1960s parallel images that document racial upheavals over the last two years. Yet, it is also the case today that there are multiple platforms for distributing political imagery and even protest songs. They're being distributed now at a much faster rate than ever before. How do we account for this acceleration in thinking about resistance?

FE: For me, resistance is a philosophical concept. As a post-colonial subject, I feel I was born with that resistance. For me, Françoise, in Paris, is the symbol of resistance. She has been doing this work forever. When I started my graduate work, I was reading her work. So, it's ongoing—and you find Françoise everywhere, in these fast distribution channels; but she's also here right now.

I was thinking about TikTok, how video has done something to still images, that it moves so fast. You see something that lasts a few seconds and you have to react to it. It becomes commonplace—which could be dangerous, too. We have to be careful how we look at these images. During this symposium, we have been talking about looking, listening, observing. It depends on our taking a moment to sort out what it is we want to focus on, because we are saturated with images. And they move very quickly.

FV: I would say that a point arrives, when we speak of resistance, when you have to put your body on the line. Go into the streets, occupy places. We should not forget that people take incredible risks to resist—otherwise we talk about resistance as if it's just a matter of putting something out on Twitter. I find it deeply admirable that there is not one day when, somewhere in the world, people are not standing up and fighting and putting their bodies on the line—in Standing Rock, in Nigeria, in Dakar, in Palestine and, you know, everywhere. Resistance is that.

AB: I want to sit for a moment with this idea of putting oneself at risk. In France recently, there was an effort to pass Article 24 as part of France's "Global Security Law," which is essentially a regulation that criminalizes ordinary citizens who identify and record (via photography) the activities of police officers. So, your body is put at risk, even as you're trying to hold the state accountable. Ariel [*Goldberg—see "Diana Solís: Intimacies in Resistance," pp. 217–219*] spoke about the idea that protest signs could be used to resist detection, that people sometimes hold them up to obscure their identity. That's also an awareness of the kind of risk involved in participating in protests and public spaces.

Frieda Ekotto
Françoise Vergès
Antawan I. Byrd

FV: Yes, holding signs that way is very important, and other techniques you can read about—like using makeup so the camera can't use facial recognition to identify you. But there is an increase in the state's use of tools to forbid that in the public space, to authorize movement and limit demonstration powers. There's a technique in place now—they cut marches near entrances to public spaces. This question of fighting against this re-appropriation of public space is very important, because the desire is to privatize. Gentrification happens everywhere, and it changes the geography. When you move from one safe enclave to another, in between those spaces the state can say there was criminal activity. There is this architecture that forbids the circulation of the body. This kind of control needs to be fought. There are laws now—not only in France but also in England, in Italy—that essentially declare that bodies together are a threat. And that is countered with a license to kill.

AB: I want to transition to address the questions of body and desire. Frieda, I wonder about the role photography plays in your thinking about Frida Kahlo. She was a painter, and most people associate her with her art. But at the same time, so much of her public life was shaped by her presentation of herself through photographs. I know you have a fraught relationship with images of Frida—even though you display them on your office desk—I wonder if you could speak about that.

FE: The question of desire remains important when you're thinking about the body. For me, Frida Kahlo is the epitome of desire. The way she presents herself in every single self-portrait parallels what I was saying about seeing through. It's as though you can see inside her through what is happening to her body, her head. I've always worked on questions of desire in the body, and also sexuality, which is very important. We don't talk a lot about sexuality but it's a must. When we talk about the masses gathering, people touching each other, it's very sexual. It's very sensual. It's beautiful as well. Even if they know they might be killed.

AB: Françoise, I am struck by the parallel you draw between the image of the terrorist and the hipster. Thinking about these ideas of self-presentation and self-styling, could you elaborate on that comparison?

FV: I find the disposition of Afghan men dressed in traditional garb to exude elegance. But in fact, when we look at them, they are shrouded in the perceptions propagated by the white West, so they cannot be regarded as elegant. They cannot be. What is elegance? What kind of masculinity is elegant? And of course, running through that is the question of racialized masculinities—the "good" ones, the "bad" ones. And then, "good" and "bad" femininity, and everything in between, is not even considered.

I've been working on questions of self-presentation, for example in the way slavery is represented in seventeenth-century painting, specifically through figures of men who are smoking. A bourgeois man would present himself smoking, because the production of tobacco relied on the slave labor of plantations. And so, how has the product of slavery disappeared? The conditions of production have disappeared but what emerged is a sign of a masculinity that is acceptable. In contrast, images of Indigenous Americans smoking are regarded as a "tradition" in the history of smoking. This very banal thing—smoking—enters a certain bourgeois self that effectively dismisses other forms of masculinity—for femininity, it's perhaps the same. Now, you have a barbershop on every street corner of Paris today, because it's very important to have a groomed beard. And the poor guy will go there, he'll be profiled. This one has the "right" beard; this one is not "OK." I'm interested now in how anti-blackness and anti-Muslim-ness relate.

FE: You can bring Jean Genet into this, because when he wrote about the Black Panthers, he called them beautiful. Adorable. He desired them. He desired Palestinian men, the way they dress, the way they walk, the way they talk.

Robin Coste Lewis: I really appreciate you talking about the elegance of brown and black bodies, particularly in images of resistance. In my first book, it's so interesting to me that no one talks about the fact that in one of the poems, there is a Sikh man "in his pale pink turban wrapped so handsomely." No one has ever commented on the fact that the first man who appears in my book is wrapped in pink. Do they think that's an accident? In the same poem, there are men who are midwives. Also met with silence. People only want to talk to me about my other work, which is about black feminism, which is great and of course I want to talk about that too. I love what you said, Françoise, about how elegant these men are, yet we're not allowed to entertain or engage that observation. I would love to hear you talk about representations of masculinity that are quiet and gentle and elegant, in resistance images we never discuss. Ariel [*Goldberg—see "Diana Solís: Intimacies in Resistance," pp. 217–219*] spoke earlier about representations of butch masculinity, which was soft and beautiful, like the image you discussed. I think we don't talk about this enough.

Rasha Salti: In Arab studies of feminism, what you see are narratives and representations of women who come from the upper classes who fought—they went to the streets, they mobilized, they fought for the right of women to participate in the political sphere, the right to education, the right to become full-fledged citizens. What is rarely considered is the feminism of the night—and that's why I adore Frida Kahlo, because she incarnates the feminisms, or the feminist struggles, of the cabarets, of the seedy stages. In the history of the Palestinian struggle, there was an incredible belly dancer who was smuggling weapons to the revolutionaries in 1936. Asmahan was a famous singer and had a very active political life that led to her assassination. Frida Kahlo's appropriation of Indigenous aesthetics, of bordello aesthetics; her nakedness, the way her body was harnessed to function evokes this for me.

Natalia Brizuela: Listening to you, I kept thinking about scale. Françoise reminded us that rest is a form of freedom and that there can be no freedom without rest, but also that resistance involved putting your body on the line. With both of these ideas, there is a question of scale, because we tend to associate and think of resistance and these mass movements as huge waves—which they are. But to bring it down to the scale of the body—Frieda, you began by saying we should remember that George Floyd is not just this image that circulates around the world; he was a man. He was a father. Then you offered a reading that brought the question of freedom and resistance down to the scale of your body. You were talking about Frida Kahlo but that story is so much about you, and about a certain quietness and rest in female desire.

FV: I call this an economy of exhaustion. Capitalism exhausts the body; it depletes the life force, so rest becomes vital. This isn't just about allowing your exhausted body to fall into bed—it's also about the way housing is being built, for example migrant camps where rest is difficult or impossible. So, there are those who can rest—we see this with the pandemic, those who have a place to rest, a garden, perhaps—and those who cannot. It becomes a question of health, of constructing the body. Constructing the lungs. Rest is connected to breathing and the collective possibility of peacefulness, alone or with other people. Everything about capitalist economy is calculated to make this more and more difficult. Opportunities to create peacefulness are increasingly narrow. There are fewer spaces to rest in, less time to allow for rest. There remain opportunities—when you go for a run at night and so on, and when people come together around food. I'm always struck by the way cooking and eating together often bring peacefulness. You know, you cannot cook and fight. But we have seen in camps in France, or in Italy, how, when food is distributed, the cops will come and urinate in the food, because there's something about this forbidden moment of people sitting together—in the street, but nonetheless in a moment together, eating. That cannot be allowed. It must be inhibited. Everything is about suffocating time.

To resist means having time. Time to think, to plan the strategy, to plan the counterattack, to write your manifesto, your poem, your song, to discuss ideas with friends. You can't just march into the streets unprepared. Sometimes it looks that way but there is always lengthy preparation and organization. Those of us who have organized marches,

Frieda Ekotto
Françoise Vergès
Antawan I. Byrd

as I have done many times, know that having the time for all of this is an absolute necessity. To me, the restriction of time is part of this economy of suffocation and exhaustion, and we have to fight it.

FE: Françoise, I read some of Fanon's writing that has been discovered recently. He wrote chapters and chapters about exhaustion, about the lack of breathing properly, and the need to rest and to regenerate the body. Listening to you, I think Fanon would be so proud of you.

1. Claudia Rankine, *Citizen: An American Lyric* (Minneapolis: Graywolf Press, 2014), 134.

2. Stuart Hall in *Frantz Fanon: Black Skin, White Mask*, a film by Isaac Julien (1997).

3. Translated from the original French by Emily Goedde.

4. Winston Churchill, *The River War, Vol. II*, (London: Longmans, Green, and Co., 1899), 164.

5. Churchill, *River War,* 248–250.

The Photograph between Trace and Evidence

ELIAS SANBAR

IN CONVERSATION WITH

LÉOPOLD LAMBERT

Elias Sanbar: What I would like to bring to the table is another way of looking at, deciphering, or reading photographs. My method will be to consider groups of photographs and reflect on the knowledge that can be extracted from them. Some of these images date back to the nineteenth century. When we are confronted with antique images or objects, we have a tendency—and it is incorrect—to imbue such objects with an attribute of rareness, which leads to conferring on them commercial value.

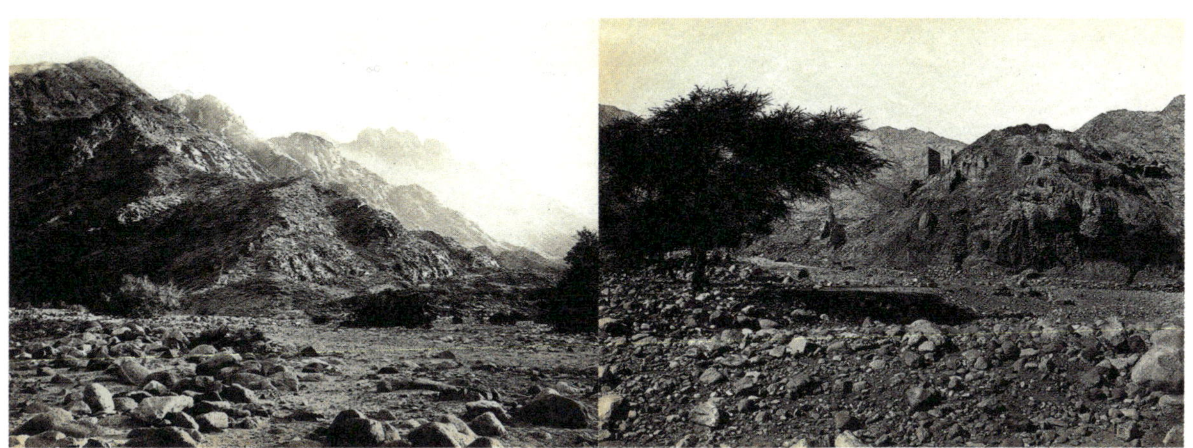

1. Left: Francis Frith, *Mount Serbal*, 1857; right: Francis Frith, *Ruins of Paran*, 1857. Private collection of the author.

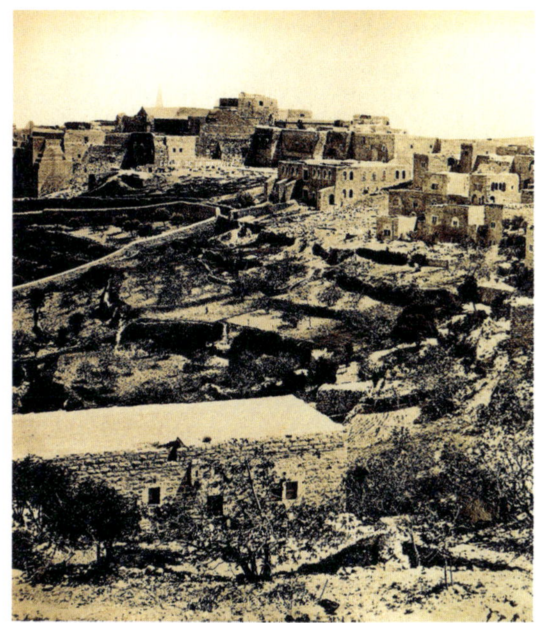

2. Francis Bedford, *Bethlehem*, 1862. Private collection of the author.

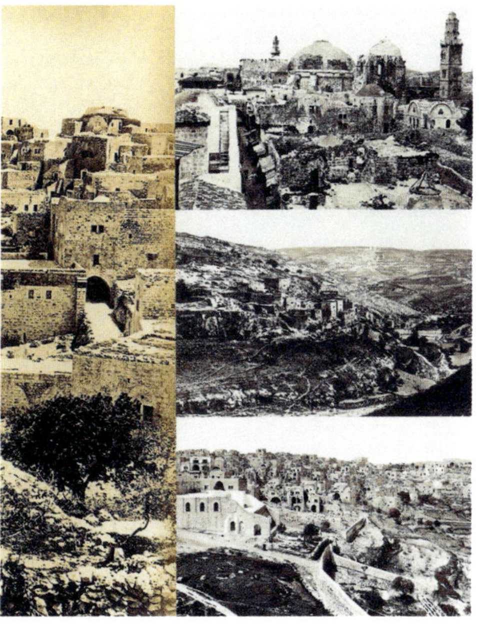

3. Left: Tancrède Dumas, *Bethlehem,* c.1880; top right: Francis Frith, *Street of the Church of the Holy Sepulchre,* 1857; center right: John Crumb, *Kiryat Jearim,* 1860; bottom right: Frank Mason Good, *Bethlehem,* c.1870. Private collection of the author.

The pictures I am speaking of have been printed in their thousands—they are not rare. I insist on this point to underscore the fact that such pictures shaped how Palestine and Egypt came to be regarded among thousands upon thousands of people in the West at the time of their circulation. They are not uncommon anecdotal pictures; rather, they evince very deeply pervasive perceptions of the Holy Land, as it was referred to then, in the West. I will approach this idea through five ways of reading such images. This method is not unique—I'm not developing an exclusive theory of reading images—but I suggest this one *form* of reading, which is mine.

Léopold and I thought about the title of our conversation, and we chose *evidence*, specifically because of its meanings in English—"proof"—and in French, but we also chose trace, specifically because it implies "clue," and the possibilities of deciphering and understanding that the word opens up.

This first pair of photographs [Fig. 1] shows two views of Palestine at the beginning of the second half of the nineteenth century. The first is of Mount Sinai—according to Abrahamic tradition, it is here that God spoke to Moses and delivered the Ten Commandments.

These photos [Figs. 2, 3] show deserted territory, as if it is a ruin, almost as though there has been an earthquake. This manner of representing the Holy Land was common for the Anglican Church, and while these photos predate the birth of the Zionist movement—which eventually led to the establishment of the State of Israel—they nonetheless incarnate the drive of Anglican photographers to prove that Darwin's theory of evolution is baseless. In effect, what these pictures are evidence of is a peaceful crusade—as opposed to the crusades of the Middle Ages. The fundamental idea that emanates from the many thousands of these pictures, of which I am showing only a very few, is to demonstrate that this territory, the "holy land," is abandoned to desolation by its children. It is neither nature, nor cataclysm, nor economic conditions that have brought this land to ruin; rather, that responsibility is laid at the feet of its inhabitants.

Based on this, there arose a new idea, which carried considerable currency until 1948—namely, that Palestinians were, in effect, squatters in the land of Palestine, that holy, happy land where the Ten Commandments were revealed to humanity. Consequently, another terrible, totalitarian idea was laid upon the first, this one specifically endorsed by the colonial powers. This was that the redemption of the land was the priority, rather than providing support and care for human beings. And, the argument went, this land could only be redeemed if it were cleared of those who neglected it. This

Elias Sanbar
Léopold Lambert

same notion brought about the expulsion Palestinians from their land in 1948. Zionism was not yet a factor at the time I am referring to; the representation of a "holy land" that beckoned redemption, however, was strengthened and disseminated by a religion whose mission of saving souls was thus redirected to redeem a territory. The notion of the cleansing of land becomes all the more significant with the arrival of the Zionist movement and culminates in the Nakba of 1948. Its origin is incarnated in these photos.

When we consider other photographs taken of the same territory in the same period, such as for instance these capturing the orange groves of Jaffa [Fig. 4], we see a far cry from the abandoned desertic landscape of destruction from the previous set. We see children, people, inhabitants—the so-called destroyers of the land—going about harvesting their crops. These pictures are very significant, yet they could not counter the prevailing Western notion of the abandoned Holy Land. They are beautiful, moving, full of emotion—but they appeared after the idea of desolation and destruction had already been deeply implanted. Furthermore, the missionary movement in Palestine claimed these photos were lies. They saw as real only the images of destruction of desolation.

In this pairing of images [Figs. 5, 6], we see at left an Indigenous woman near the US-Mexico border and, at right, a woman from Bethlehem. The two pictures are troubling because they date from the same period and were taken 6,200 miles apart. They are not by the same photographer but, in effect, they construct the same perception. The common element is each photo's background, namely the setting and objects on display. What is this background intended to signify? Consider this other, far rarer picture [Fig. 7], also "ethnographic," with similar decorum, taken in an apartment in Beirut by a French photographer—who, in this case, forgot to draw the curtain and hide the reality of the studio. It is uncommon to find evidence of such fancification, or fabrication of decor. So: What does this decor say?

First, all the subjects pictured are dead. It is perhaps banal to note this, but it indicates that these persons are interchangeable. It is rather the background or decoration that points to the fact that its elements are indices of a world that is fated to disappear. In other words, these three photos capture the disappearance of a culture. This photograph of a mother and child [Fig. 8] stands in contrast with the three "ethnographic" images. While the woman is dressed in traditional garb, and evokes the canonical "mother and child" of Palestine, at the moment of capture, she is not considered dead by the photographer—Khalil Raad, himself Palestinian—rather, she sparkles with life. We see, then, that the first three images, taken by French and American photographers, herald the imminent erasure of their subjects, whereas the Palestinian photographer does precisely the opposite.

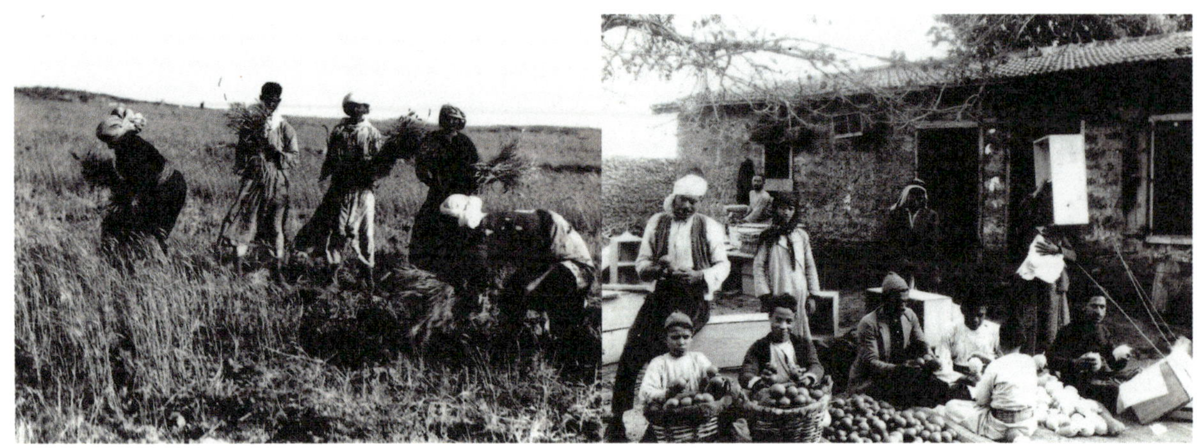

4. From Khalil Raad's *Works and Days*, c.1920. Private collection of the author.

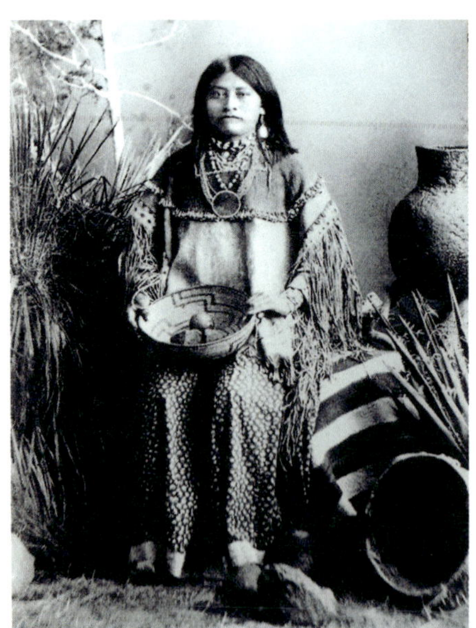

5. Photographer unknown, *Daisy*, c.1880. Private collection of the author.

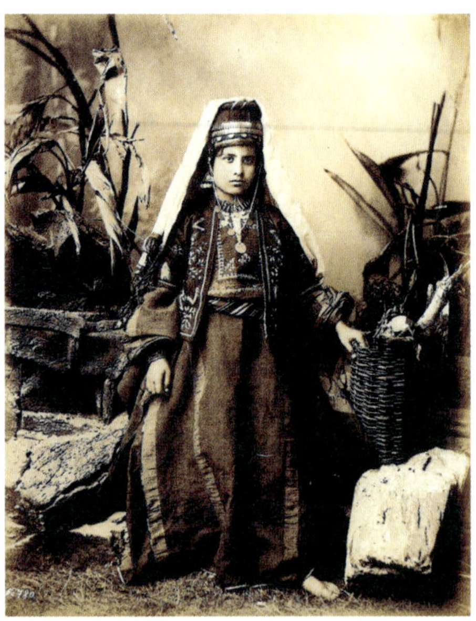

6. Maison Bonfils, *The Bride of Bethlehem*, c.1880. Private collection of the author.

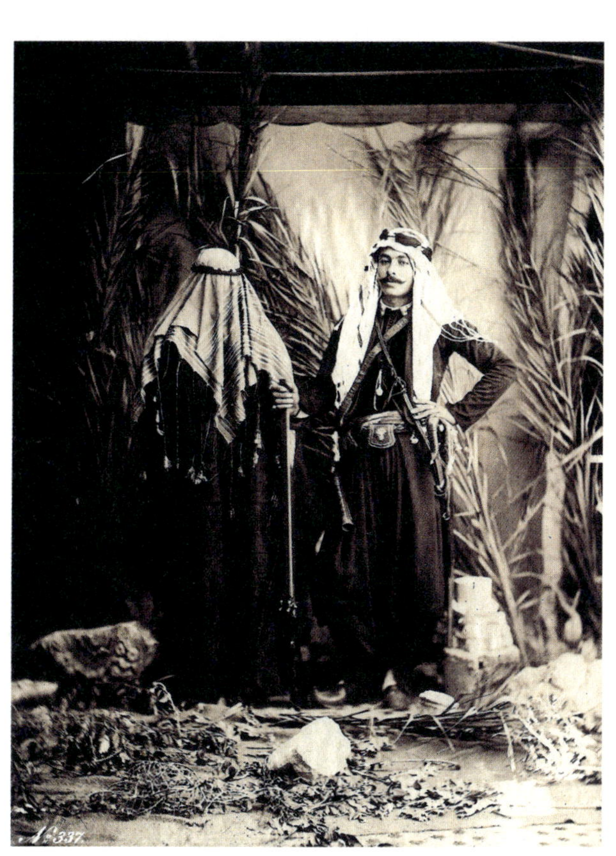

7. Maison Bonfils, *In the Bonfils Studio,* c.1880. Private collection of the author.

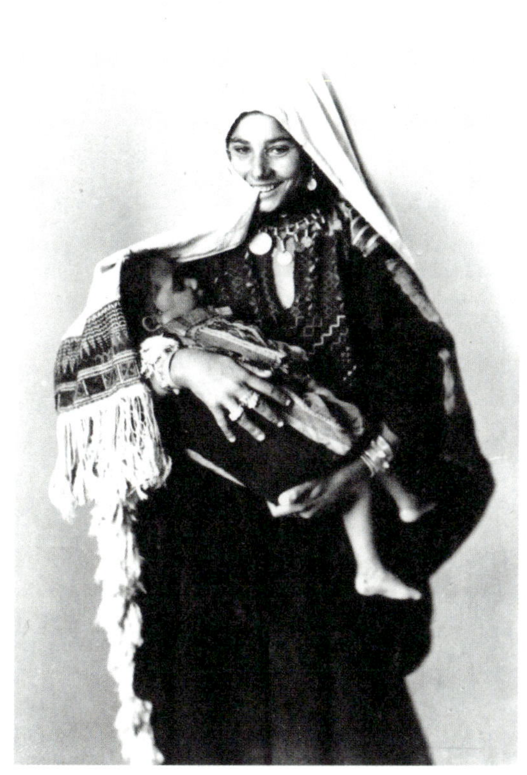

8. Khalil Raad, *Motherhood,* c. 1920. Private collection of the author.

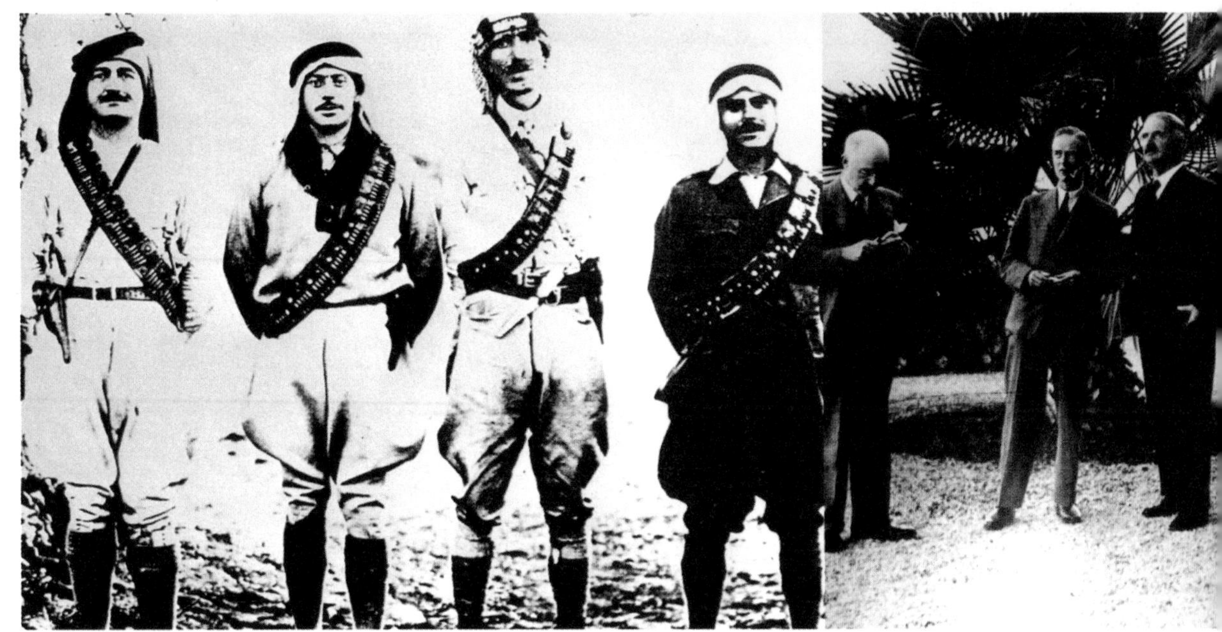

9. Left: Photographer unknown, *Fawzi al-Qawuqji and his Lieutenants,* fall 1936; center left and right: Photo Maison, *Lord Peel and the Members of the Royal Commission for Inquiry,* November 1936; right: Augustin Casasola, *Pancho Villa in Ciudad Juàrez,* date unknown. Private collection of the author.

This group of pictures [Fig. 9] prompts a reflection on the idea of *"temps de pose"*—instantaneous capture—and the experience of time that the photograph incarnates. On either side, we see groups of people who were photographed in the same time period, the 1930s. On the right is a group of revolutionaries in Mexico with Pancho Villa and, on the left, a group of Arab guerillas, with the mountains of Palestine in the background, during the Great Revolt of 1936 against the British Mandate in Palestine. The two photographs in the center depict several men at a garden party at the residence of the British High Commissioner. What we have, then, are images of two groups of men who are aware that the men in the two images in the center want to erase them. The men in the middle want to drive the others out of the schematic of time, while they represent the British Empire, which they understand to be perennial.

Despite the formal disposition of the revolutionaries posing for the photographer, the photos in the center are in fact more staged: they are intended to suggest an spontanenous, casual gathering and convey the pretense that none of the men were aware that they were being photographed. They have the luxury of striking a pose. In contrast, the photos on each side capture groups of people who know that they are on the verge of disappearing, and their presentational disposition seeks to assert that they still exist. They do not pose for so much as confront the camera; in that confrontation, they are pausing the

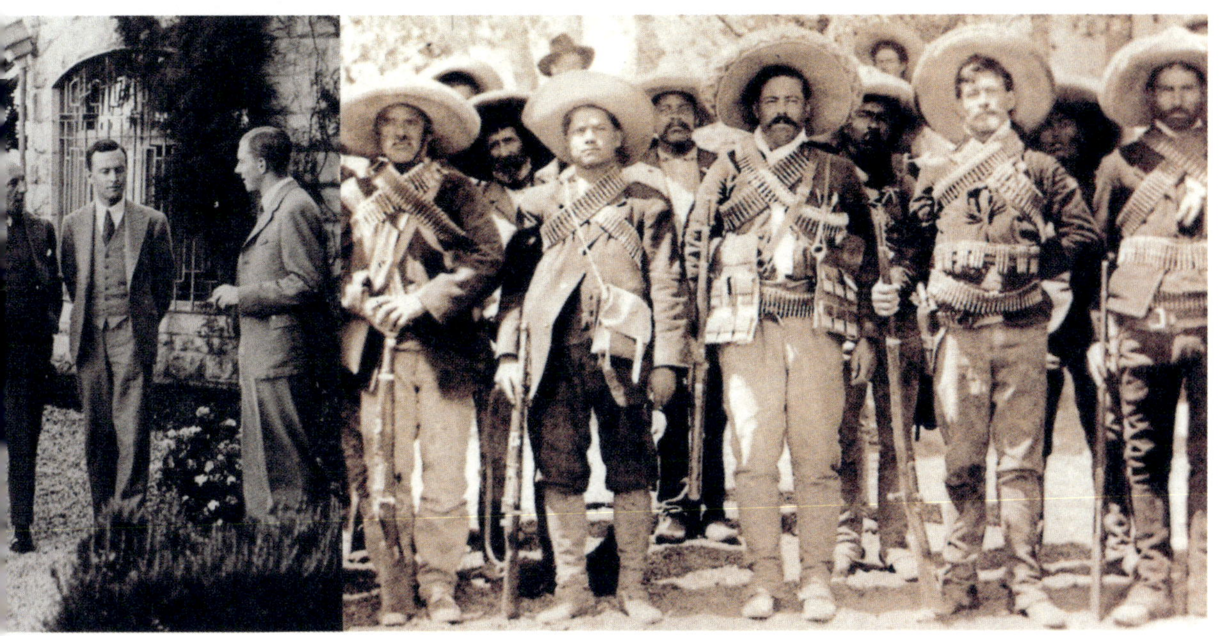

unfolding of their destiny and of time. The relationship to time becomes evident when we consider the requisite effort to embody a relaxed casualness and "conviviality in the High Commissioner's garden" by these colonial representatives who were convinced that their empire would last forever. They are not anxious that they will be expelled from time.

These images [Figs. 10–12] depict everyday life in Palestinian society, which circulated rarely. I have deliberately mixed subject matter—a masquerade ball, a picnic in the countryside. These photographs were taken at the same time as the photographs of the armed insurgents and of the British High Commissioner's garden party. There is a tendency to think that, during wartime, all other social activities are halted, but in reality normal everyday life and war take place at the same time.

This photograph moves me deeply [Fig. 13]. As a child, I was transported in such a truck, when we Palestinians were driven out of our land. This is a picture of our expulsion. It is the endpoint of the process that began in the images taken a century earlier: the expulsion of people from that land that had to be "redeemed."

Here another photograph—a very rare one, as they have for the most part been destroyed—of expulsion by sea [Fig. 14]. For a long time, it was claimed Palestinians sought to drive the people of Israel into the sea. These images show the Israelis enacting that threat on us. My father was forced to leave like that, in a small boat.

These are photographs of the refugee camps where we settled immediately after our exodus. They were set up under the mandate of United Nations resolutions and administered by an institution that took charge of the lives of the refugees until the moment they could return to their homeland, as was essentially stated in the writ of the resolutions. This picture [Fig. 15] represents an aesthetic of misery and was taken so that the institution could justify its annual budget and demonstrate its mission, with accompanying reports listing its activities. To evince its achievements via photographs, the institution commissioned renowned photographers—in this case a well-known Swiss photographer—to document the lives of the refugees, bringing about another aesthetic approach to the disappeared territories. The culture and the territories of Palestine were now depicted as though they had been transported into exile—and, in an unconscious way, the photographers reproduced the canonical aesthetics of the Holy Land. These men are "Peters." And this woman is the "Blessed Virgin with a child" [Figs. 16–18]—in camps populated almost entirely by Muslim Palestinians. These photographs seem to convey that the nation of Palestine has not disappeared but has merely been displaced. From the point of view of the deported Palestinian population, their homeland was not under occupation, rather, it was inundated. But where are the images of this inundated country? Representations such as these contribute to the erosion of the rights of Palestinian refugees to return home.

Finally, here are some photographs that are totally unbelievable [Fig. 19]. They were staged in the south of Lebanon in the 1970s by Palestinian freedom fighters, with the intention to appeal to world public opinion. At that time, there were numerous revolutionary movements engaged in struggles of liberation, drawing inspiration from Lenin's assertion that there can be no revolutionary movement without an underlying revolutionary theory. The Palestinian refugees had no revolutionary theory. They just wanted to go home. But we needed to have a revolutionary calling to mobilize. In Communist theory, the means of production had to be transformed. So, in a very mechanical, perfunctory way, these pictures have been composed to express more than just the desire to return home, they suggest a transformation of the society— in this case, of its production of wheat. What is striking in these photographs is a detail: the workers are using a sickle to harvest the crop, though contemporary machinery was widely available—in 1973 and 1974, no one was harvesting wheat with the sickle. To demonstrate the revolutionary spirit, however, one of the central symbols of Communism had to be invoked.

Elias Sanbar
Léopold Lambert

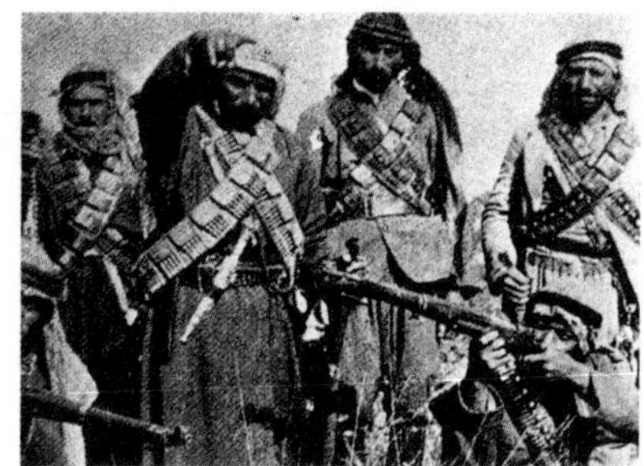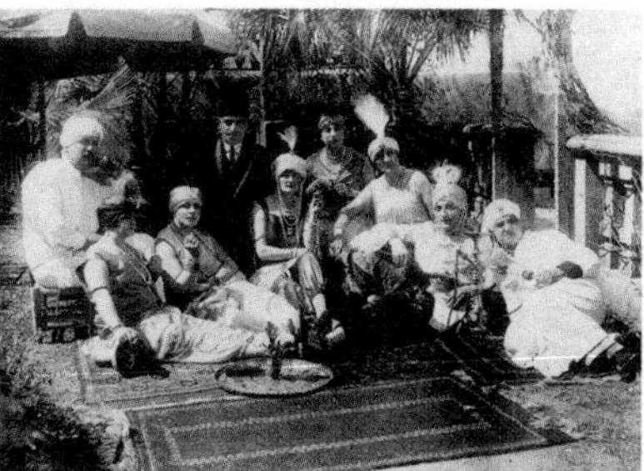
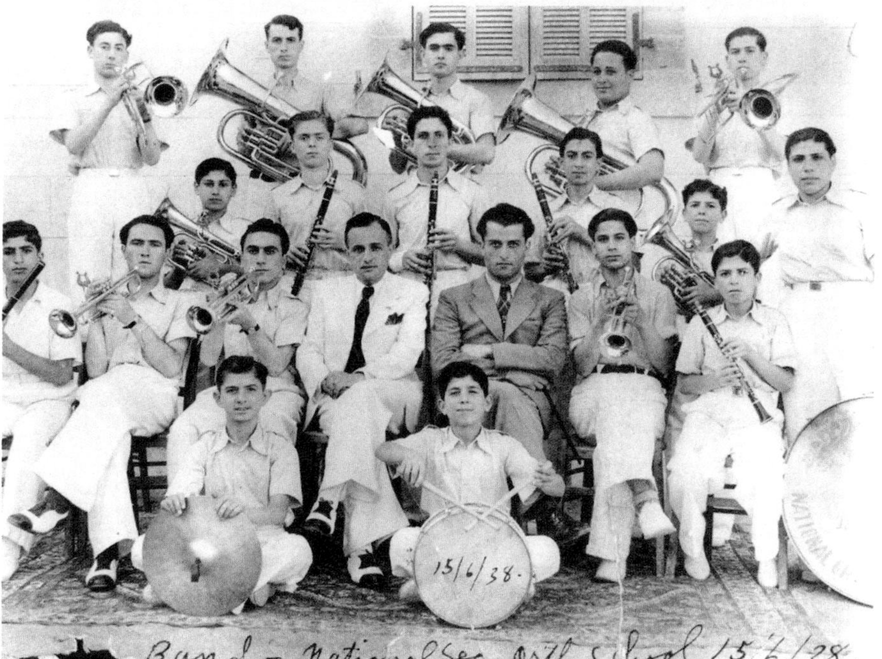

10. Top left: Photographer unknown, *Palestinian Guerrillas,* c. 1936; top right: Rachman, *Masquerade Ball at the Home of Alfred Roch,* 1924; bottom: Photographer unknown, *Fanfare in Jaffa,* June 15, 1938. Private collection of the author.

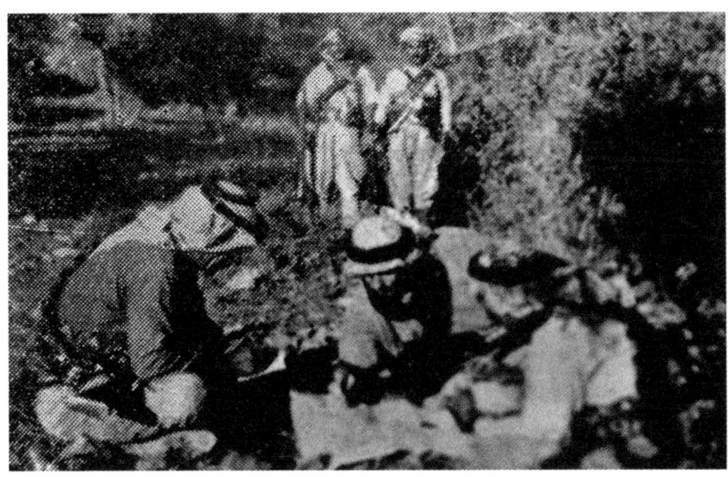

11. Photographer unknown, *Scene from the Guerrilla Front*, c.1936–1938.
Private collection of the author.

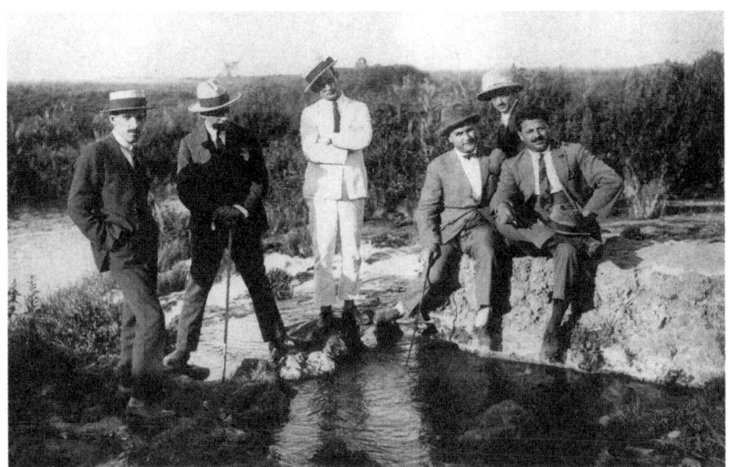

12. Photographer unknown, *Hanna Franji and His Friends in Jericho*, 1921.
Private collection of the author.

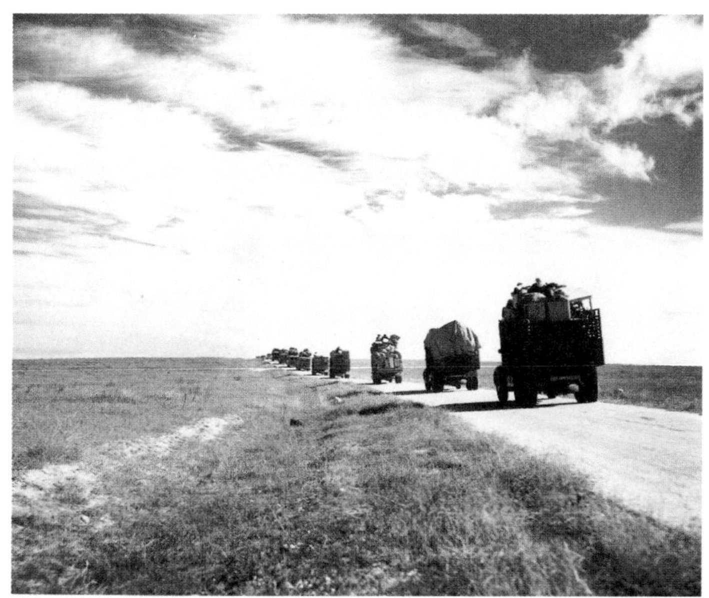

13. Photographer unknown, *Toward Exile,* 1949. Private collection of the author.

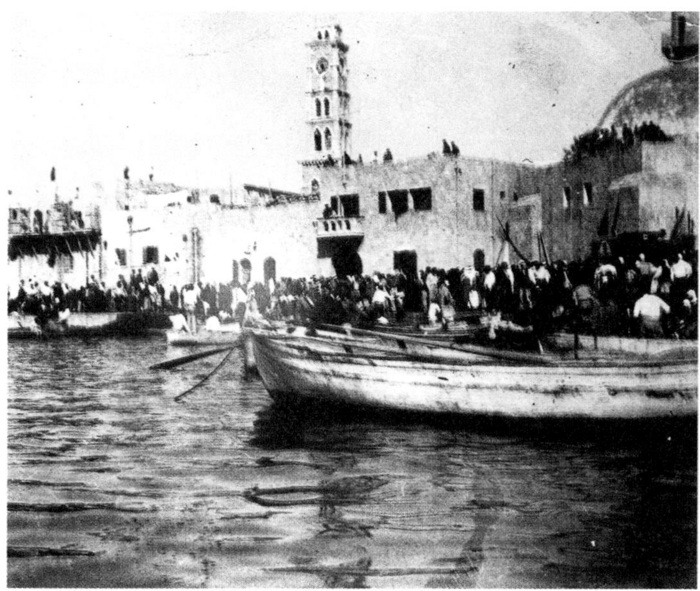

14. Photographer unknown, *The Fall of Jaffa, Thrown into the Sea,* April 1948.
Private collection of the author.

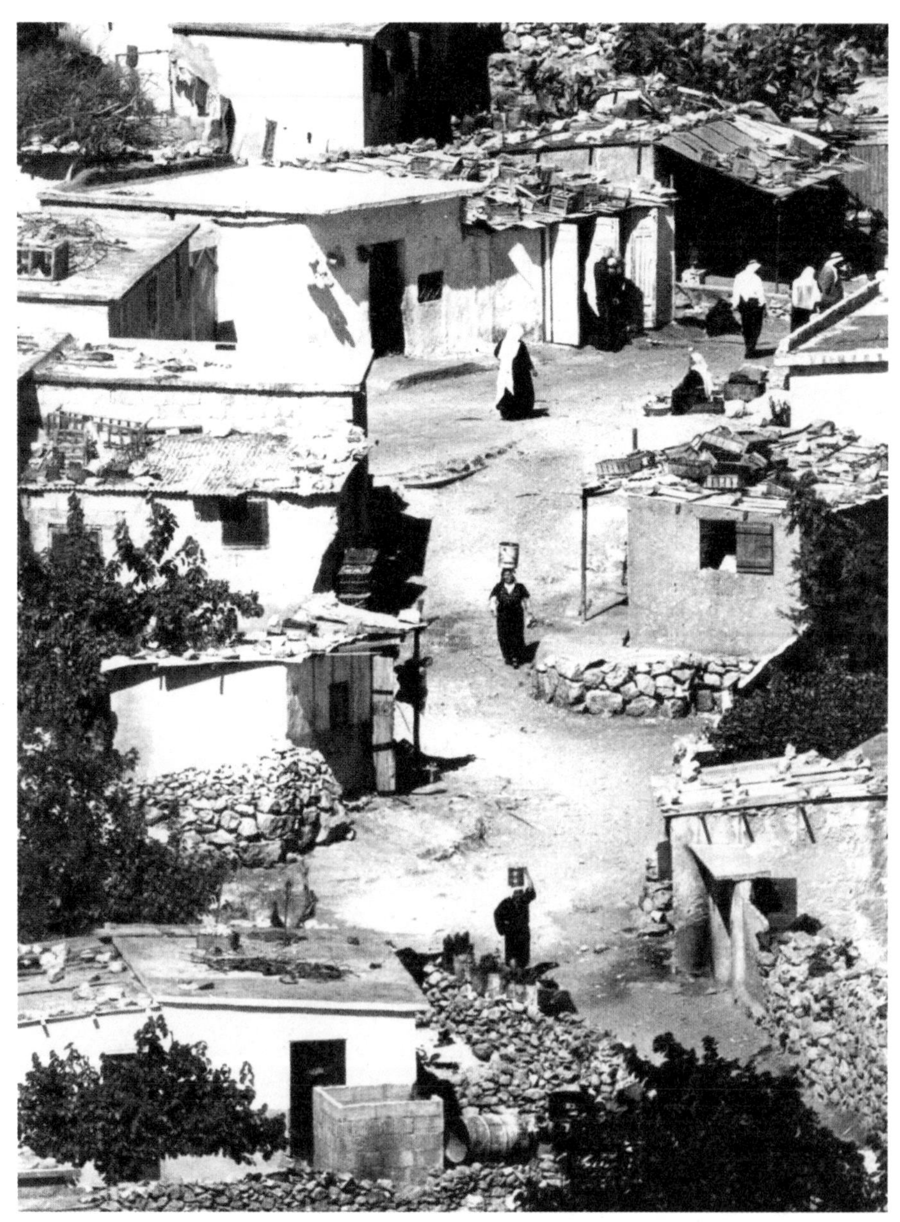

15. *The Dheisheh Camp, West Bank*, UNRWA archive, c.1950. Private collection of the author.

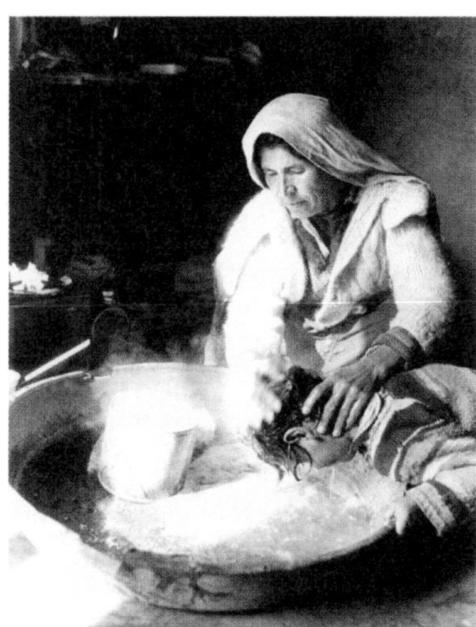

16. *The Baqaa Camp, Jordan,* UNRWA archive, c.1950. Private collection of the author.

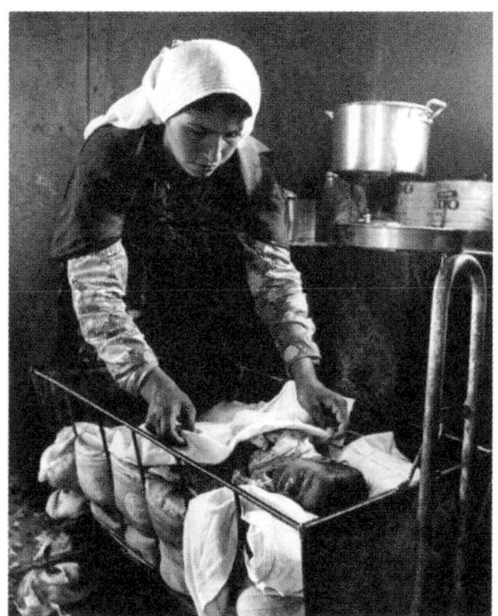

17. *Swaddled Child, Baqaa Camp,* UNRWA archive, c.1950. Private collection of the author.

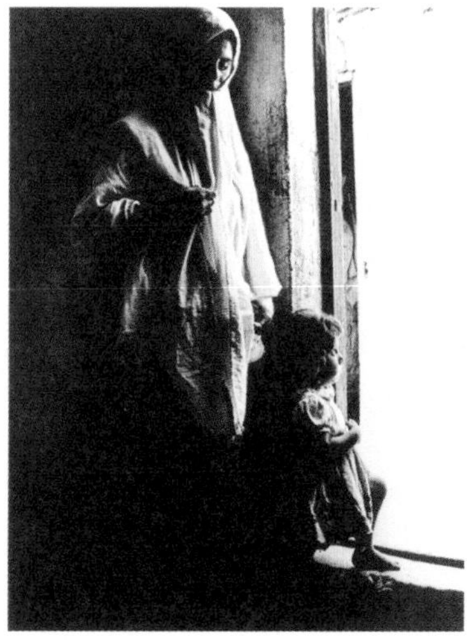

18. *Mother and Child,* UNRWA archive, c.1950. Private collection of the author.

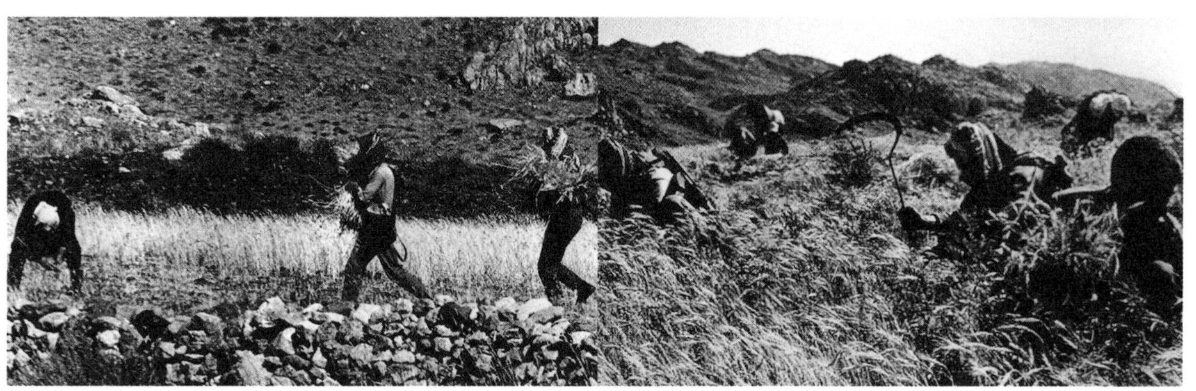

19. Hani Jawhariyyeh, *Harvests, South Lebanon,* c.1968–1969. Private collection of the author.

Elias Sanbar
Léopold Lambert

Léopold Lambert: As Elias mentioned, he and I like this notion of *evidence* very much. In French, we would translate it to *preuve*, which is "proof," while *évidence*, is "obviousness"—this double signification, "the obviousness of the proof," is a motif we both wanted to explore. I want to consider critically the idea of evidence—how it is being used, to whom it is directed, who is using it and to what purpose—as well as recognize that the act of producing proof can be very risky, especially in the conditions of colonialism like those that exist in Palestine.

These photos [Fig. 20], taken by Muhammad Awad, show the photographer targeted by an Israeli soldier—we can see the canister of tear gas the soldier has launched as it comes toward the camera. Thus, we can see quite clearly how documenting colonialist activity brings with it considerable risk for the person conducting that documentation, who here is targeted and attacked. I want to place this idea alongside an understanding of when one has to be on the side of forensics—which was explored earlier today by Samaneh Moafi [*see "The Witness without a Camera," p. 235*]—and more generally how forensic architecture can contribute to this conversation. I propose to situate these questions using the theory Jacques Vergès expounded in *De la stratégie judiciaire*, that of "rupture defense," which challenges the terms of the judiciary and transforms the courtroom into a forum.

We must ask under what conditions it is appropriate to take up this position of not accepting the rules of the game, or of presenting certain kinds of evidence, which may be fabricated. If one judges that going along with established procedures is the more damaging route, then one should not accept them. It was when he defended Algerian revolutionaries, many of whom were women—notably Djamila Bouhired—that Vergès developed the strategy of rejecting the authority and legitimacy of the court in which the trials were taking place.

I am not approaching this subject in order to argue that one of these paradigms is better than the other. Rather, I ask: When should one employ one or the other? I suspect the majority of people here have not viewed the video of the police murder of George Floyd and did all they could not to see the photograph of little Alan Kurdi, who died on the Turkish seacoast when he tried to flee Syria to come to Europe. We do not need to see such images to recognize the structural, racist, and colonial violence that brought about the death of these individuals.

This, then, is an example of images that do not help the struggle. Elias pointed out the production of photographs that support particular ideological agendas. I find it significant that sometimes, photographs of colonialist propaganda do not support the

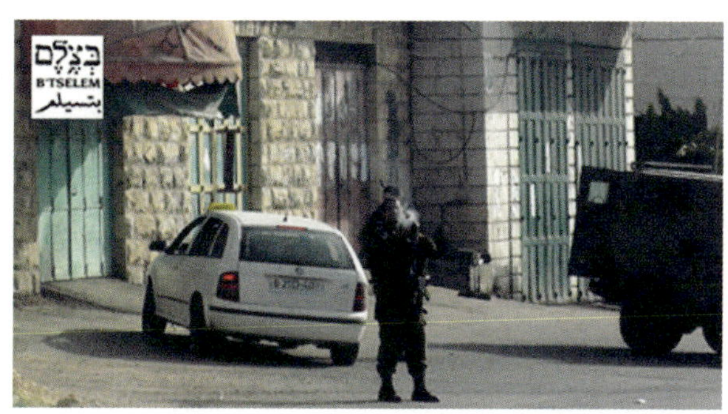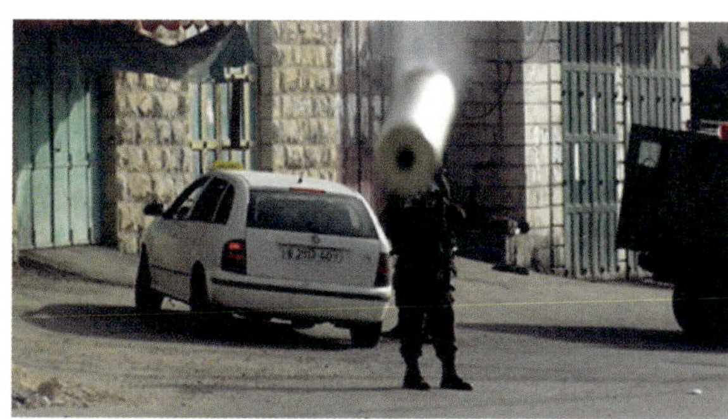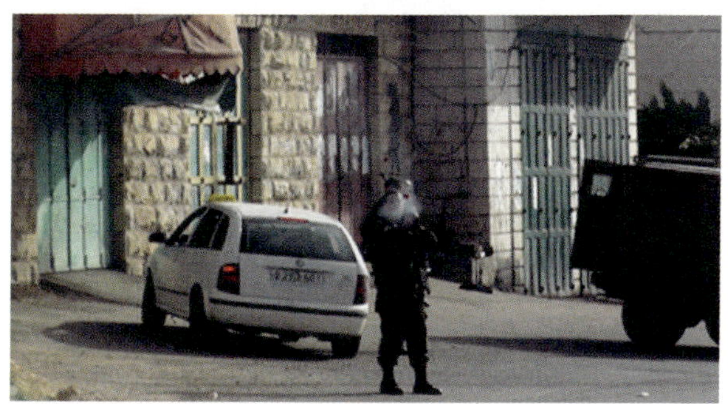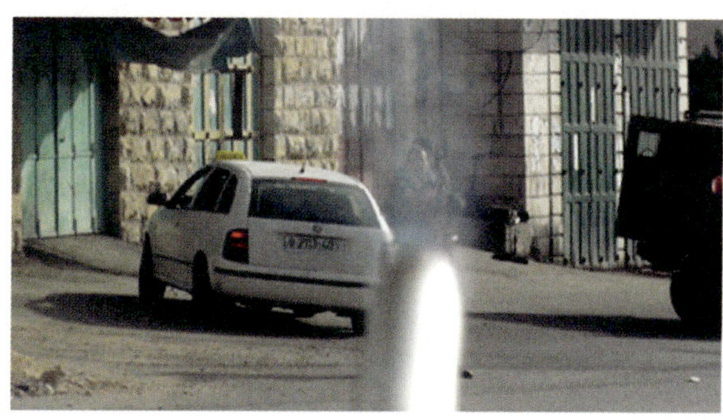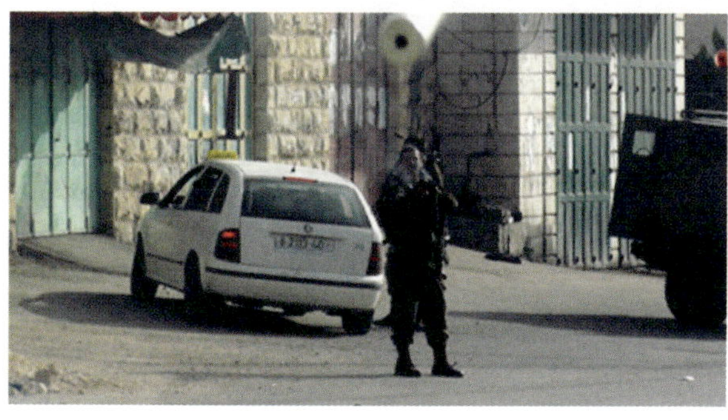

20. Muhammad Awad, *B'Tselem*, 2013. Source: YouTube.

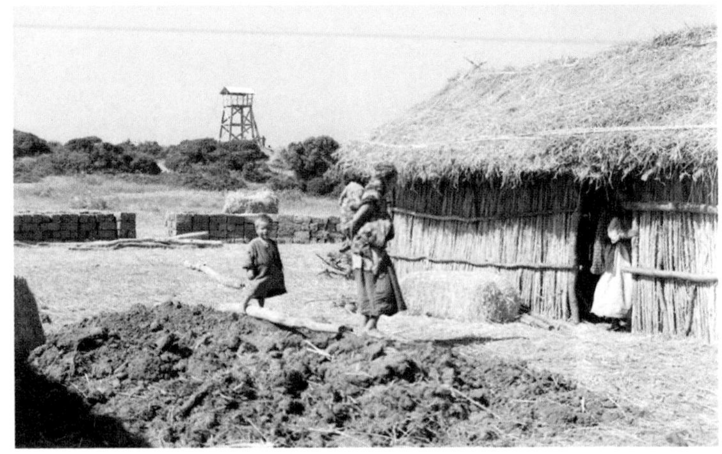

21. "Regrouping" camp in Algeria during the Algerian Revolution (1954–1962, ECPAD).

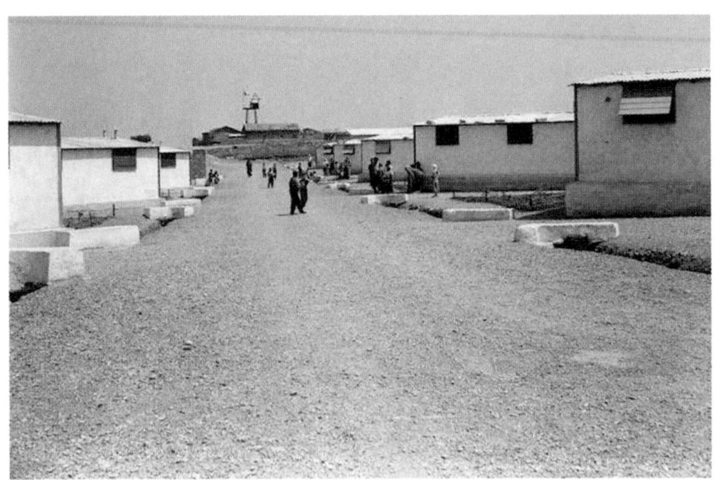

22. "Regrouping" camps of Cheria et Sidi Madani in the Blida region, Algeria, during the Algerian Revolution, 1959 (Rault/SCA/ECPAD).

colonial project. These two pictures are of Algeria during the war of independence [Figs. 21, 22], during which two million Algerians were driven out of their territory between 1946 and 1962. I find it very impactful that the photo on the left was taken only six years after the similar expulsion of the Palestinian people from their land in 1948. These pictures were taken by the French army to show that the people from the villages had been resettled in artificial villages and so "everything is fine."

But, as Elias has outlined, we must look at the setting. In both of these photos, we see in the background watchtowers from which the population was monitored. These are prison camps, under military control—where, I would add, there was very high child mortality. These photos do not fulfil their function as propagandistic proof of the humane treatment of displaced villagers—they are evidence that this is a prison. To link this back to the Nakba—the expulsion of the Palestinians—here we have a series of photographs by the French photographer Bruno Fert [Fig. 23]. Elias spoke earlier about absence. Here, we see Palestinian villages that were depopulated and destroyed in 1948. There is a tendency to forget that, a few months before the declaration of the State of Israel, the expulsion of Palestinians had already begun during the British Mandate. As an architect myself, I find architecture as trace evidence is highly compelling, in that it allows ruins to reflect two stories—one of which is the historical background of a Palestine that existed, that was a functioning society, that had a quotidian life. The second story is of the destruction of that Palestine. It shows ruin and erosion but, in the context of the Nakba, it is a reflection of ethnic cleansing and of villages destroyed, emptied by paramilitary and Zionist groups that, later, formed the Israeli Army.

So, traces of architecture are a form of evidence. Moving on to these photos, also by Fert [Fig. 24], we see the absence of architectural traces functioning as evidence. The double history of Palestine contained in its architectural remains means that, sometimes, such evidence of the destruction of Palestinian villages can be damaging to the Zionist narrative. Thus, not only the village but also its ruins must be erased. Hence this series of photos, which show places where all traces of destroyed villages have been removed, suppressed, deleted. Yet, the absence of something can be very obvious proof. In this set of images [Fig. 25], we see what remains when photos like the previous set do not exist—which is to say, if these villages survive based only on the legend of their depopulation and destruction. Here, Fert presents names of villages accompanied by their latitudinal and longitudinal coordinates and the dates of their depopulation.

What, then, is left over when even pictures are no longer extant? If we exit the register

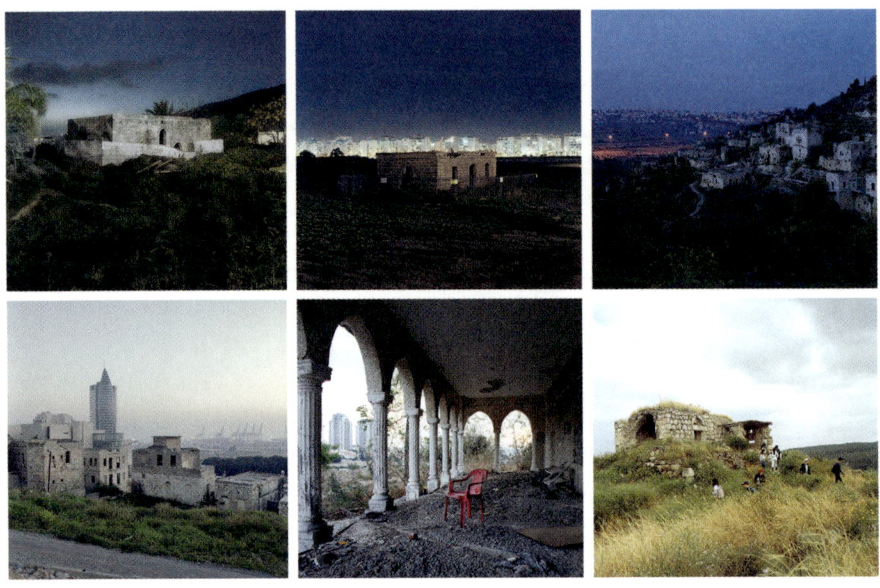

23. Bruno Fert, from the series *Les Absents*, 2015. By permission of the artist.

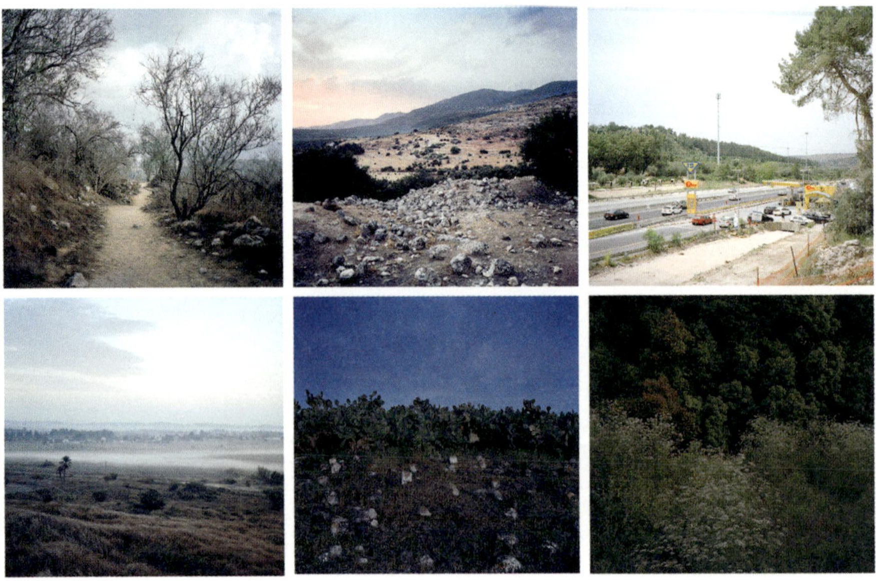

24. Bruno Fert, from the series *Les Absents*, 2015. By permission of the artist.

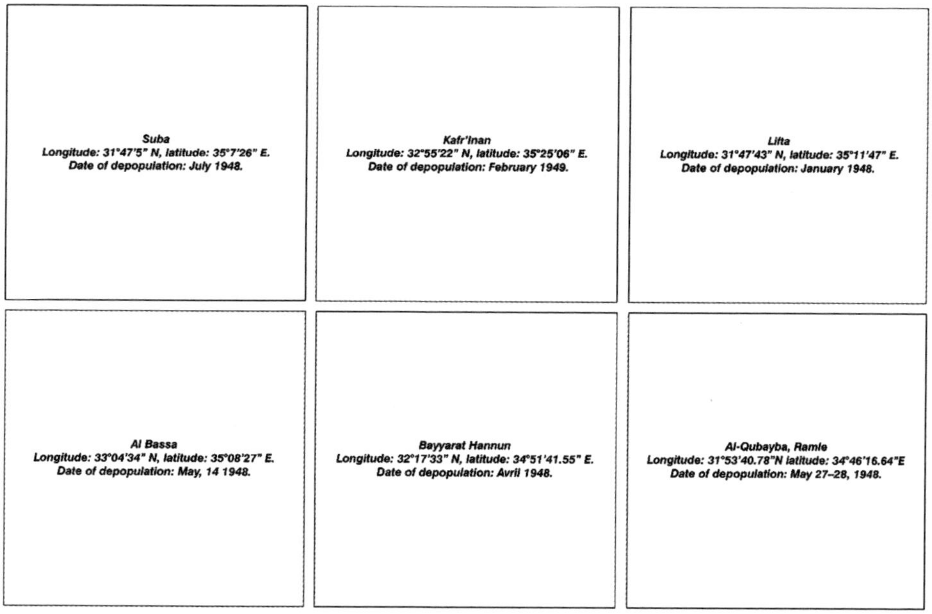

25. Bruno Fert, from the series *Les Absents*, 2015. By permission of the artist.

of evidence and remain in the context of trace, we find ourselves in something akin to rupture defense—the phantasmic evidence of these disappeared villages accompanied by the fact that they are geographies that still exist, that maintain a future potential for the return of Palestinian refugees to their home.

As a final thought, I turn to these images [Fig. 26], which insist on maintaining traces via artistic interference and which embrace political subjectivity. The cactus is a symbol both of Palestinian life and of the patience of the Palestinian people—in Arabic, صبر [s-b-r] forms the root of the words صابر [*sabaar*]—"cactus"—and الصبر [*al-sabr*]—"patience." In many instances, cacti are the last extant witnesses of disappeared Palestinian villages. These witnesses and this artistic intervention, I think, provide a launching point for continued discussion.

Samaneh Moafi: Léopold—I would like to learn more about the way you conceive of the forum. There is a range of forums we can think about—the criminal court of law, the people's tribunal, the public inquiry—these are the legal ones. We can add to that the exhibition, the gallery, this forum where we're sitting now. What is evidence, what is a proof, if it is outside the context of a forum?

Natalia Brizuela: I keep thinking of a word that I know is very significant to Palestinians, which is *sumud*—"steadfastness." This is a notion that has become seminal to Palestinian discourse since 1967. And the temporality of steadfastness complicates the past as well as the future. I wonder if you could talk about *sumud*—its temporality and its relationship to the different forms of temporality you trace in the photographs you shared.

ES: What you say, Samaneh, concerning legal procedures is fundamental. But, in this exercise, I don't believe we used this question of evidence and clues as evidence for the context of a tribunal. The conflict here is different than that of the negotiation of law and condemnation. We're speaking here about pictures and the traces of evidence we can see in them. I have been engaged in the international tribunal approach for twenty years—but here we are speaking about photographic elements can help us to find a certain interpretation. So, around the images of destroyed villages, I wrote a text on absence. My approach was to explore the points at which absence is more apparent than presence. That is the fundamental element of my book and that is why I asked the photographer—and he agreed—to title the book *Presence—Absence—Presence.* The void of absence leads to invisibility.

Elias Sanbar
Léopold Lambert

This leads to the second question, which points to the two pillars of Palestinian

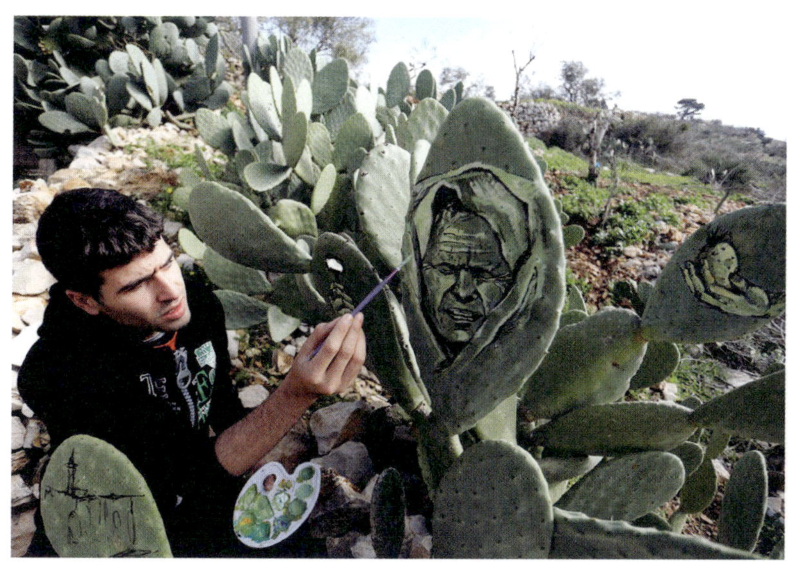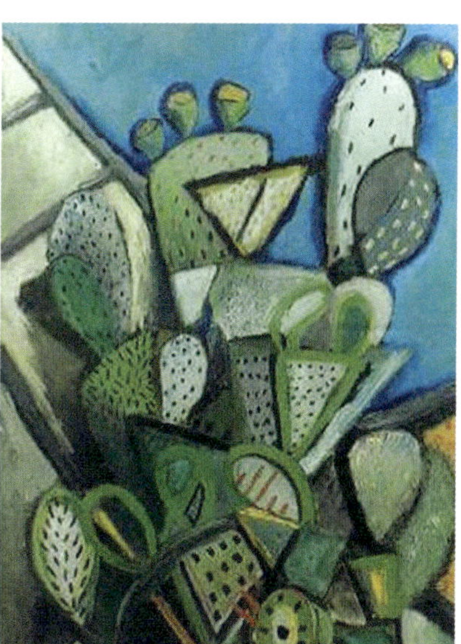

26. Left: Palestinian artist Ahmad Muhammad Yasin at work, 2016; right: A painting by Palestinian artist Karim Abu Shakra, 2015.

resistance. Natalia, you invoke the Occupied Palestine of 1967—but those of us who were expelled in 1948 are not in the *sumud*. We want to go back. The idea of *sumud* is linked to the situation of the Israeli occupation, under which people were not forced to submit to the being driven out of the territory as we were in 1948. The Palestinians of 1967 are rooted into their territories. So, *sumud* is a question of being rooted to a territory. For us, the refugees, if over the last seventy years we were to accept for one minute to fix ourselves in place, our exile would become final. We are condemned to living perpetually in flux until we can return home. It is this displacement, or movement, that has saved us. That is a fact. And that is in part because we provoked a lot of mistrust—countries, including Arab countries, don't like nomads, don't like people moving around. They want to know where to put people, how to control them, how to fix them in categories, monitor what they eat, determine what they do. We are a population that is in constant movement, we're not fixed anywhere. This is also something that contributed the development of mistrust and a destabilizing misery for Palestinians in countries that have very fixed ideas that oppose this kind of movement, and we were thousands, hundreds of thousands of individuals, some of us were armed revolutionaries. This implied destabilizing state structures although that was never intended. So, in short, we have two destinies as Palestinians. It is lucky we have communities in *sumud*, because without them, Gaza would have been emptied. But those of us who were displaced should not stop our drive to return home.

LL: My point is precisely about recognizing in which forums we produce proof. In the case I presented, I do include the forum of the courts. In that context, there is a set of rules that very much works with the production of evidence and that is very much worth considering as what I call "playing the game." In other instances, however, in which the forum is not established within a specific set of regulations—like, as you said, the context we are in here—I think there is a certain kind of premise on which we can assemble something that is not possible on a larger scale.

There is an organization in France that works with forensic architecture. They conduct investigations—like you do, Samaneh but in different forms—of the police murder of Adama Traoré for *Le Monde*. This, for me, is typically a manner of the production of evidence that is more harmful than it is useful over the long term, insofar as it essentially embodies a very objective, or let's say science-based medium to say what Traoré's family has been saying for years now in the fight for justice.

So you have this white, leftist newspaper saying, "OK, this is what happened, this is what we agree is the truth," while that has been said for years by the families. This, for me, is highly problematic. But, if that took place in a court of law, it would be a very

Elias Sanbar
Léopold Lambert

different story because it's a different forum than that of society at large, or of the readership of *Le Monde*. It's all a matter of evaluating in which forum we are situated and deciding strategically whether we are going to adopt the approach of playing by the established rules, or of refusing those rules.

ES: The photos Léopold showed of the cacti bring to mind a text that appeared in a review of Palestinian studies that I have been in charge of for the last thirty-six years. I asked the Mexican author Carlos Fuentes to write an article for the magazine. He asked what I wanted him to write, and I requested that he tell us something about the Indigenous people in Mexico. He wrote a piece about an Indigenous economy based on fish and fishing—everything was organized around products of the sea. Rather than killing them, the invaders drove them away from the seashore. In the end, they were left high in the mountains, where they could not survive. Their economy—their life—was based on the climate, on fishing, on the land by the sea. When they were driven away, into camps, they committed collective suicide by eating cactus figs. We Palestinians have not consumed toxins but our expulsion from our land was meant to be final. For more than a century, we have fought to survive. There are still people who do not like us very much. We have been exiled from our land but nobody says Palestinians do not exist. We are still here.

THE ERRANT PHOTO ALBUM

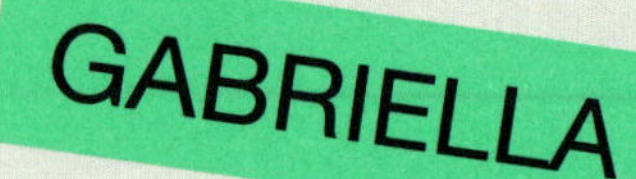

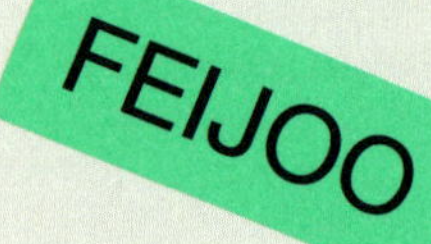

The Errant Photo Album is a recurring format for this edition of the Triennial of Photography Hamburg. The contributions printed in this volume were delivered during the Lucid Knowledge symposium, and sibling entries by the triennial's partner curators can be found on *Allegories of the Visible*, the triennial's digital editorial platform, which visits the theme of currency through a constellation of ideas on the mediatory status of the image and its strategic possibilities for knowledge, echoing the guiding aims of the symposium.

For Lucid Knowledge, the Errant Photo Album took the form of a modest prompt: an invitation to contribute a single photographic image to what would become a collectively authored photo album. Despite this ostensibly forthright request, in listening to our interlocutors' contributions we soon found that the story of an image is sometimes best told in its absence, or through the serializing of several images. In bringing together these texts, we seek to connect the project with the constitutive process of organizing a family photo album. Itself a sensory form of value-making that registers the perspectives and desires of multiple generations and temporalities, the family photo album is a format in which personal and historiographic efforts of preservation overlap in the task of building and claiming memory and meaning from disparate sources: it is a compelling space from which to ruminate on and perhaps refute inscriptive values of photography as currency.

The textured considerations that thrum here pose a set of questions around our relationship to images as material and semi-material things conveyed across geographies, archives, pages, mantelpieces, and servers. If captions tell a particular story of dispersal and circulation, how can moments of solidarity form around the recovery of photographs, or in the search for information and, crucially, context? How do visual glitches provide critical entry points into the processes by which images are made to witness or stabilize conventional knowledge formations? And what do we gain from setting aside learned patterns of interpreting photographic images and following "errant" modalities instead?

With associations of roaming or itinerating, "errancy" evokes Édouard Glissant's poetics of the errant. For the Martinican writer and philosopher, errantry emerged in contrast to movements of conquest and uprooting; challenging impositions upon language, self, and identity; and transforming compact nations and edicts through processes of creolization and diasporic formation. Significantly, Glissant described errantry as the knowledge of an insistent relationality that brings one to renounce the idea of universality and other such worldly summations: "The tale of errantry is the tale of Relation."[1]

Proceeding from Glissant, the Errant Photo Album considers images as deeply relational entities. Its format invites thinkers to participate on various levels, as nominated storytellers of a multi-subjective photo album. Witnessing the unexpected resonances that have emerged in the shaping of this album has been a deeply moving experience.

1. Édouard Glissant, *Poetics of Relation*, trans. Betsy Wing (Ann Arbor: University of Michigan Press, 2010), 18.

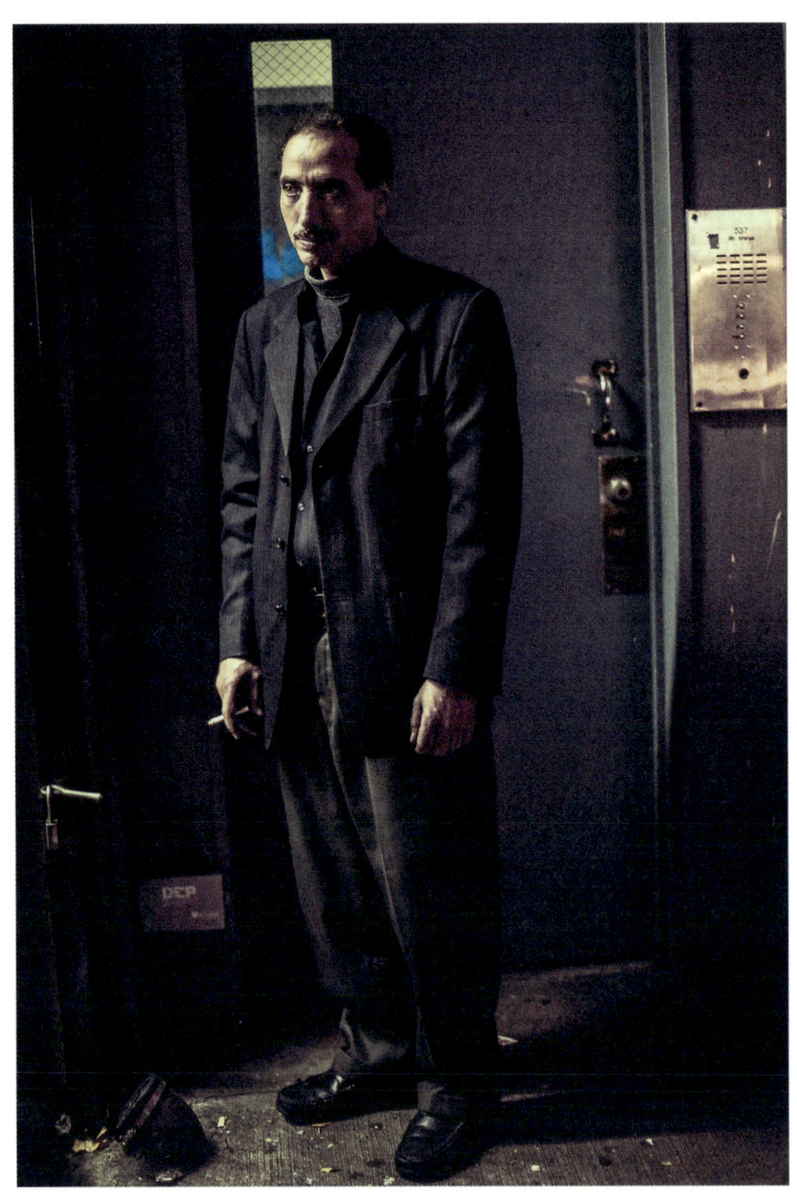

Tala Hadid, *Sabri, 38th Street*, 2013. Courtesy of the author.

SABRI, 38TH STREET

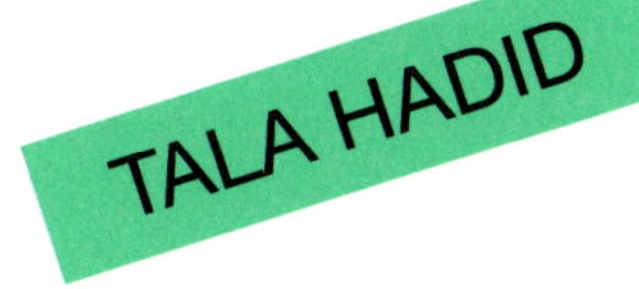

From an old folk song
A couple of slaves fell on the roof
Of our house in Baghdad.
They were tied with a rope,
Back to back,
Wearing torn white clothes
And weeping.

I believe they were waiting for a ship, sailed by pirates
I believe they were staring at a horizon of trees.
I believe they were thinking of a distant island.

When I climbed to them and released them from the rope
They lit up in flames in my hands
And turned to ash.[1]

–Fadhil Al-Azzawi,
"In Captivity"

Sabri, let me tell you how it all began. January 2008, icy winds hurtling down 9th Avenue. The door on 38th Street betrayed nothing, scuffed wood painted grey, unremarkable and dirty. Next to it the bodega, run by Dominicans, the one where you'd go to buy your cigarettes. Through the door, on the other side, the heavy red curtain, a portal to the hidden place where our mostly silent relationship began, and where night floated in what seemed like an eternal suspension. It was a closed circuit, a "place without place,"[2] as Michel Foucault would write in his description of those strange and liminal spaces he called heterotopias. Behind the door on 38th Street, the ground disappeared and time stood still; all was possible as the outside world dissolved and another dimension opened up. But I digress. Let me pick up where I left off. That late afternoon in January, I had come to meet Merzak and Lali. The meeting had been set up by a friend who was planning on curating a show on recent immigration to New York. He had asked me to make a video piece for the project. He said that Merzak and Lali held the key to a whole network of recent Arab immigration to the city, he said that he'd heard there was a heroin epidemic raging in the community. I said, "I'm not really interested in doing a portrait on addiction" but I went to the meeting anyway, curious to see what I would find. And in my shoulder bag: my camera.

"Everything is allowed here, except for penetration."

I had nodded, stupidly, not quite sure if I had understood correctly. Merzak and Lali, husband and wife, sitting casually side by side on an old sofa, had explained that their place was a "cabaret-bar" and that I could start photographing that very night. We were in the basement and, every once in a while, young Eastern European women in casual day clothes passed by down a corridor that led to different hidden rooms. Later, I would discover how it all went down, the strict economy of the place: Russian and Polish girls for American clients downstairs ($400–$500) and the less expensive freelance system in the cabaret upstairs, with a mainly Arab worker clientele. Eventually, I came to understand that for the men upstairs it wasn't so much sex they were after but alcohol, and solace from the reality of working life in America. And so, it was upstairs I wanted to be, where I was welcomed with grace and curiosity by those who passed through and those who remained, and where I would later, as you know Sabri, not make a film, but take a series of photographs.

"Have a drink on the house." The meeting with Merzak and Lali was over. I stumbled up the stairs and found a corner at the bar. The low hum of background music, the murmur of voices. I placed my bag on my lap and could feel the heaviness of the camera on my knees. My eyes adjusted not just to the light—red hues, dark corners—but to the men around me. Some, I noticed, your compatriots, were from Yemen.

I call image that which in any field of the visible escapes communication—all that which grows in the image. It is in the visible that something is hollow and escapes the reduction of its presence to what it shows. Jean-Louis Comolli says that when he starts a film, he first determines what he is not going to show. Why can we look endlessly at paintings that have been around for centuries? Because they continue to grow inexhaustibly.[3]

You told me, Sabri, not to photograph you. The interdiction was hard to swallow because when I first saw you, I was struck. I was smitten. I couldn't stop looking at you. It wasn't just your gaunt face, or your eyes that burned with intensity, or the fact that you came most nights, for nearly a year, dressed in the same crumpled suit, carrying the same small briefcase. It was something else that I saw, perhaps a recognition of what was hidden inside you. And so, I submitted to your demand and turned my camera elsewhere. For weeks I photographed those who would let me—the girls, the workers, the soldiers passing through town, the musicians, and the barflies. And yet, you were always there, just outside the frame. You can't imagine my surprise when, one night, with the camera against my eye, I felt your hand on my shoulder. "Do you need help?" you asked as you lifted your cellphone to direct its light onto the Egyptian woman against the wall whom I was photographing. I couldn't believe it. You had been watching me for weeks—or, rather, you had been watching the act of photographing. And even if you had forbidden that your own image be taken, you slowly got closer. From then on, you were always nearby, just at the edge of sight. Sometimes you helped, graciously offering to carry a bag or hold the camera. I was grateful, especially for this silent bond that grew between us.

One night, I asked about you. I approached the group of young men from Aden and asked them who you were. It was a short conversation; they leaned in over their drinks and whispered. They said you were from Sana'a. They said you had been arrested after 9/11. And that you had been taken away to some site—an airport? A hangar somewhere? They didn't know the details. They said that you were gone for weeks. They said that when you returned you never called home again, too ashamed to speak to your family in Sana'a. I wasn't sure if the story they told was true but it stayed inside me, like a burning secret.

Years later, I stumbled on a report that had been released in 2007 and I thought of you, Sabri. The Center for Human Rights and Global Justice at the New York University School of Law had released a firsthand account from a survivor of enforced disappearance and torture at a CIA "black site." The man describes in grueling detail the horror he endured. He was from Yemen, from Aden. He said he had been driven to the airport and put in a room. There, he was stripped naked and tortured. He said his torturers were dressed head to toe in black; he said they were wearing black masks and had surgical gloves on their hands. He said that one of them was taking photographs of him during the ordeal.

Sabri. In Arabic the name comes from the word *sabr* (صَبْر) which means "patient," "enduring," "spiritually steadfast."

My father, Foulath, left Baghdad at seventeen and, after the imprisonment of his father, never returned. He hardly ever spoke of the city, the wound too deep. But it lived in him always, the arteries of its streets spreading deep throughout his body. Later, during the war, when the bombs dropped over the city, it was as if each explosion pierced his flesh. Baghdad/Sana'a: cities that can never be lost. And so, you found yourself in America, on this island at the meeting of the Hudson River and the Atlantic. But inside you another city: Sana'a, founded by Shem Ibn-Nuh, son of Noah, surrounded by a ring of mountains. Cities that can never be lost.

Months passed; I can't remember how long. I had been spending about four nights a week at 38th Street, in a vortex. It was on one of those nights, the camera in my hands, that I looked at you across the bar and you nodded your assent. We went outside. It was 3 a.m. We stood on stained concrete littered with trash. You took a drag of your cigarette and looked at me, and then you stood still, a quiet pose. You turned your head; I lifted my camera. In the photograph, it's as if all the sounds of the city have been sucked away. Just you. Or a shimmering imprint of you. Now, another kind of sound emerges, a constant hum, a voice. Yours? Your presence fills the frame completely. Is this what Mondzain meant when she wrote about an image's inexhaustible growth? The movement emanates outward from within you, a lifeforce, that ineffable thing that can never be fully grasped or denied, unfolding in time. It's a gift, through the lens, from you to me, to them, to us—the unseen thread traced from there to here and back again. Here, on this street, on this corner of the city, after everything you'd been through, dishonored in the Land of the Free, we came together and carved out a space, which we then framed, and where you stood, inexorably there, with your past within you and the future, like an open horizon, yet to come.

1. Fadhil Al-Azzawi, "In Captivity," trans. Al-Azzawi and Khaled Mattawa, *PROMETEO, Latinoamerican Poetry Magazine*, 84–85 (July 2008).
2. *Des Espace Autres* published in *Architecture / Mouvement/ Continuité*, October, 1984, based on a lecture given by Michel Foucault in March 1967. Translated from the French by Jay Miskowiec.
3. Briankle G. Chang, "An Interview with Marie-José Mondzain: What is an image?," *Inter-Asia Cultural Studies* 20, no. 3 (September 2019): 483–486.

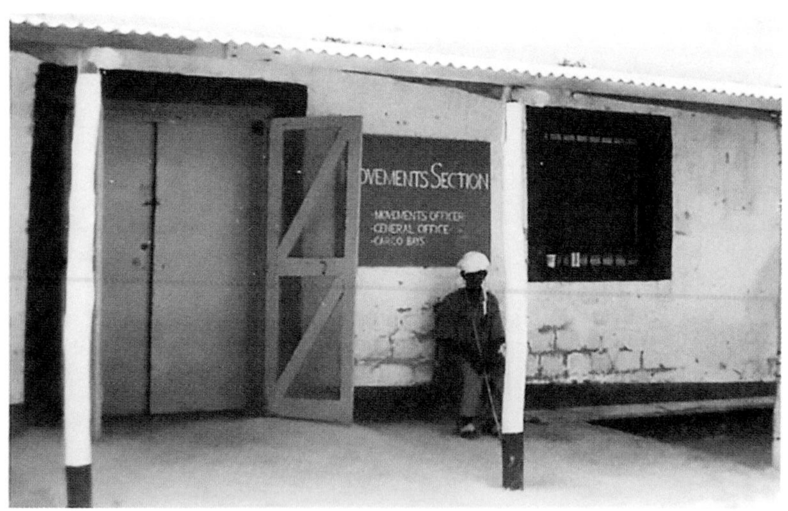

Chowkidar sitting in front of the Movements Section, RAF, Sharjah. Circa 1966. Personal archive of David Stevens, former RAF Sharjah, c. 1960s. Source: The Professional Pilots Rumor Network.

THE CHOWKIDAR: EPISTEMIC MARKERS AND TRANSNATIONAL LABOR FLOWS

UZMA RIZVI

I came of age in a discipline that taught me how to *see* using photographs of archaeological excavations, pottery yards, the dig house, and/or some building that was attendant to the systems of coloniality. Inevitably in these images, there was standing—either on the side, in the background, or deep somewhere in the crevices of the site—a chowkidar. The word *chowkidar* comes from the Urdu words *chauki*, which is an outpost, and *dar*, which means "keeper"—and so this "keeper of the space" between the outposts, the caretaker, seemed to have an omnipresent role. And yet, we were taught how to *unsee* these figures by never mentioning, indexing, or articulating their presence. It was as if they did not exist within the frame or framework of archaeological visions. We were only ever alerted to the presence of the body when we needed epistemic reference; it would be

at that point that our professors would say, "You can gauge the height of the extant wall if you use the chowkidar for scale."

Being taught to erase figures in the colonial frame is not a new game. This is precisely the insidious and violent form of the colonial gaze that manifests itself in contemporary archaeological practice. In this short moment, as we sit with this image, I want to speak about how we see what is being erased, and the complexity of narratives that emerge from the existence of a brown body. I want to linger in that complexity as it also accentuates how we, as brown bodies, through that gesture, are taught by the academy to erase ourselves, trained as we are in maintaining the power of the colonial gaze over our own research. Colonial violence is multi-scalar and it

transcends time; it is precisely how in one moment, the ancient, historic, and contemporary are simultaneous. It is why I connect the deep past to the present in my own work, because to undo that violence, my critique must also attempt to be multi-scalar and to transcend time.

The image I am sharing is not mine. I did not take this image, neither do I personally know the person who took this image nor the person in the image. I selected it because it is a commonplace *type* of image, a trope of colonial nostalgia—one that mimics ethnographic and archaeological epistemic markings. This is not an image presented by an anthropologist but, rather, one delivered by a soldier of Empire. One could say I "excavated" it from the online website entitled the Professional Pilots Rumor Network, under the subsection Aviation History and Nostalgia. Or perhaps this image chose me. In a text published in 2012 on *e-flux* related to an exhibition on animism, Anselm Franke states: "The future is now behind us, and the past approaches us from the front."[1] The text made me consider the following question: What does it mean to be approached by the deep past? In designing research methodologies, a basic assumption is that we, as archaeologists, approach the past. But what if, for a moment, we consider that it is not we who determine the outcome of our research, but rather, it is a negotiation/mediation/ collaboration/conversation, perhaps even a dance, among many different human and nonhuman stakeholders/participants. When I think back to how I met this image, I had certainly scrolled right by it. It was the figure of this gentleman who beckoned me back, who said "Hello," who asked me to see him, even if I could never fully do so. The quality of the image is low-resolution, suspect; the inability to see particular facial features is part of the nostalgia. It is like our memory of this figure has a form and a type, but the individuality of the person is not recorded. This happens often with images of chowkidars at archaeological sites as well, where it is mostly their height that is relevant to the photographer for scale. By selecting this image, I wanted to step away from the archaeological site to see the same figure of the chowkidar within a different context— somehow still as a figure but examining how that figure indexes a complexity that is held within their body. Still an epistemic marker, but of a different sort—one that shifts this body into a different narrative current, still linked to the violence of coloniality but this time speaking to a particular heritage of colonial transnational labor flow.

This image is from the personal archive of David Stevens, formerly of the Royal Air Force, stationed in Sharjah, and, according to the publicly accessible online post, was taken in the late 1960s. A building fills the background; interspersed posts interrupt the flow and frame the doorway that seems to be the focal point. To the right of the double doors, slightly hidden by a screen door, is a board that reads, "Movements Section: Movements Officer, General Office, Cargo Bay"—clearly a building integral to the logistical support of the RAF. Under the bottom right corner of that board sits a

gentleman, upright, both feet squarely on the ground, hands in his lap, holding a long staff in a relaxed position and wearing a loosely wrapped *pagri*. We get the sense that perhaps the teacup on the windowsill may be his, that it was put away for the photograph. He seems so generally familiar, and yet, we still cannot see him.

That the body in this photograph is not easily provenanced in its context grants me space to think on the relationships between epistemic markings and transnational labor flows. Specifically, I want to think about what it means for us to see a brown South Asian body as the chowkidar, guarding a RAF building, on a Gulf Arab landscape, specifically in Sharjah in the 1960s, which means prior to the formation of the United Arab Emirates (UAE) in 1971. Perhaps through that seeing, we may become more attuned to the history and heritage of a particular form of labor; a colonial history we have all been taught to unsee within specific contexts. Perhaps it is through *that* seeing that we will recognize the internalized schemata of colonial racism, filtered through classism and sexism, that allow us to place particular kinds of brownness into hierarchies of acceptability, commensality, and wages even within the landscapes of the Global South—and here, I'm specifically thinking of domestic and manual labor in the Levant and North Africa. By paying attention to the history of transnational labor flows set into motion by the various colonial powers, in order to "help" their officers in various locations around the world, we begin to see networks

of exploitation manifest and maintained in the contemporary world. And, as Arundhati Roy once said: "Once you see it, you cannot unsee it."

The inherent complication of the UAE presents itself here. The Trucial States were never a colony nor a protectorate, and yet, due to their highly entangled relationship of protection with the British Empire, the impact of colonialism maintains itself on the landscape.[2] The perversity embedded in the violence of colonialism is felt acutely in the UAE. It is at once a landscape that maintained a colonial infrastructure and military that was supported by labor from other colonies and, as of 1971, a home to a rebranded elite that has resulted in what is now called a high-income post-colony. The usual binary formed through the relationships between a colonial power and a local/indigenous population is complicated by a third population of migrant workers to that colony/non-colony, this one non-British.[3] This includes non-Gulf Arab, and South Asian and Filipino immigrants, first coming in primarily for blue-collar positions such as manual and domestic labor but then, via transnational flows of labor, in professional positions as well.[4] This was further complicated by the pre-existing Indian Ocean mercantile communities that had been based in the Gulf [5] since the late nineteenth century.

In my own work in Sharjah, I've come across many brown men of South Asian descent with whom I have driven across the landscape to conduct archaeological surveys.

In our conversations about heritage and history, I am always struck by how many of them have lived in many different locations, on US military bases and in other Gulf countries. Their bodies move among and between, tracing colonial pathways of labor exploitation. And then there are those who have lived on that land for generations—sometimes as far back as four—and yet, they hold passports that link them to Bangladesh. Never having been to the places of which they are told they are citizens, their sense of belonging hovers in these liminal spaces, marking their existence from one work visa to the next. If they stopped working, they would be sent to whichever countries issue their passports—countries and landscapes they have not belonged to for generations. And so, they must work, and continue to work, and ensure they do not stop working to maintain their homes, their sense of belonging and experience. I often find these conversations and bodies in the crevices of sites, or on the sides of buildings, watching, caring, and erasing themselves just to survive. As one of them recently told me, "Here, it's more important not to be seen, but if we aren't here, they will let us go for not doing our job." These bodies live in a contradiction of existence—to be simultaneously seen and un-seen. The gentleman continued: "If we were not here, then this area would not be cared for, and so it is important work. This is the work of the chowkidar."

1. Anselm Franke, "Introduction—'Animism'," *e-flux journal* 36 (July 2012), https://www.e-flux.com/journal/36/61244/introduction-animism/.

2. James Onley, *Britain and the Gulf Shaikhdoms, 1820–1971: The Politics of Protection*, CIRS Occasional Paper 4 (Doha: Center for International and Regional Studies, Georgetown University School of Foreign Service in Qatar, 2009).

3. Ronald Boyle, "Language Contact in the United Arab Emirates," *World Englishes* 31, no. 3 (2012): 312–330.

4. Naomi Hosoda, "*Kababayan* Solidarity? Filipino Communities and Class Relations in United Arab Emirates Cities," *Journal of Arabian Studies* 3, no. 1 (June 2013): 18–35; Karen Leonard, "South Asian Workers in the Gulf: Jockeying for Places," in *Globalization under Construction*, eds. Richard Warren Perry and Bill Maurer (Minneapolis: University of Minneapolis Press, 2003), 129–170.

5. Neha Vora, *Impossible Citizens: Dubai's Indian Diaspora* (Durham: Duke University Press, 2013).

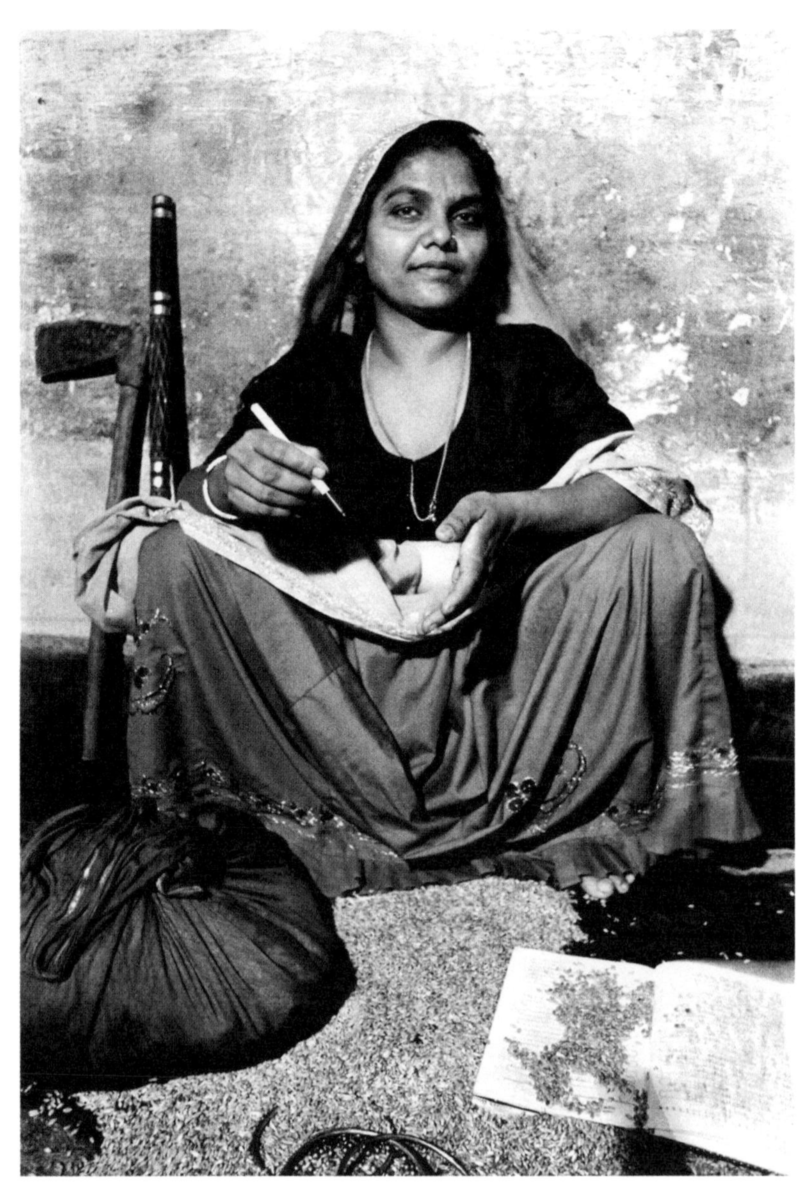

1. Sheba Chhachhi, *Shanti—Staged Portrait 1, Dakshinpuri, Delhi, 1991*, from *Seven Lives and a Dream*. By permission of the artist.

SCRIBAL SUBJECTIVITIES: ACTIVATING THE SILENT AND THE SPEAKING PARTS OF A WOMAN'S LIFE

NANCY ADAJANIA

Sheba Chhachhi was radicalized by the Indian women's movement of the 1980s. Her photographs of that period have become iconic images in the history of Indian feminism; they memorialize the groundswell of protest as women poured into the streets, demonstrating against dowry, rape, and discriminatory legislation.

At the barricades, Chhachhi acted as a documentarian, photographing newly insurgent women who were claiming public space, articulating their position as citizens subjected to social and political oppression. At the opportune moment, she would vault into the demonstration, slipping from the roles of observer and documentarian into those of partisan and participant.

In the gestures of Chhachhi's women protestors, Delacroix's *Liberty Leading the People* and Kollwitz's tormented mother figures live again. But such revolutionary-heroic visual rhetoric, while negating the clichés of female passivity, created another stereotype: that of the female militant with clenched fists and raised arms.

Aware of the limitations of documentary photography, Chhachhi consciously critiqued her own decade-long practice by "constructing" her photographs in the 1990s.

During this phase, she produced staged portraits of fellow feminist activists. *Seven Lives and a Dream: Feminist Portraits* (1990–91) grew out of her discontent with the instrumentalization of the act of protest as a clichéd vocabulary of resistance. Chhachhi broke the contract of specialization governing the orthodox relationship between photographer and sitter, replacing it with a cooperative model of representation. Carrying forward the negotiated mode of self-representation available in the transactions between sitters and photographers in the popular tradition of the bazaar photo studio, she invited her protagonists to play an active role in choosing their scenography, including the props and the performative gesture.

In *Shanti—Staged Portrait 1, Dakshinpuri, Delhi, 1991* [Fig. 1], the woman activist Shanti, the author of a number of feminist songs, appears with her clothbound diary or notebook, and her pen. Chhachhi describes her as an incredible street theater performer, singer, and dancer. A migrant from Rajasthan who was widowed early, Shanti worked with Sabla Sangh and Action India in the resettlement colonies of Delhi on health education, domestic violence, and consciousness-raising, as well as other feminist issues. Her self-presentation places her writing material against an agrarian setting: an axe, anklets, and grain spread on the ground.

In a second photograph, Shanti wields an axe instead of a pen [Fig. 2]. Common to both portraits is the diary or notebook in which she puts down her thoughts and composes her songs. Intriguingly, I find that most of the protagonists in

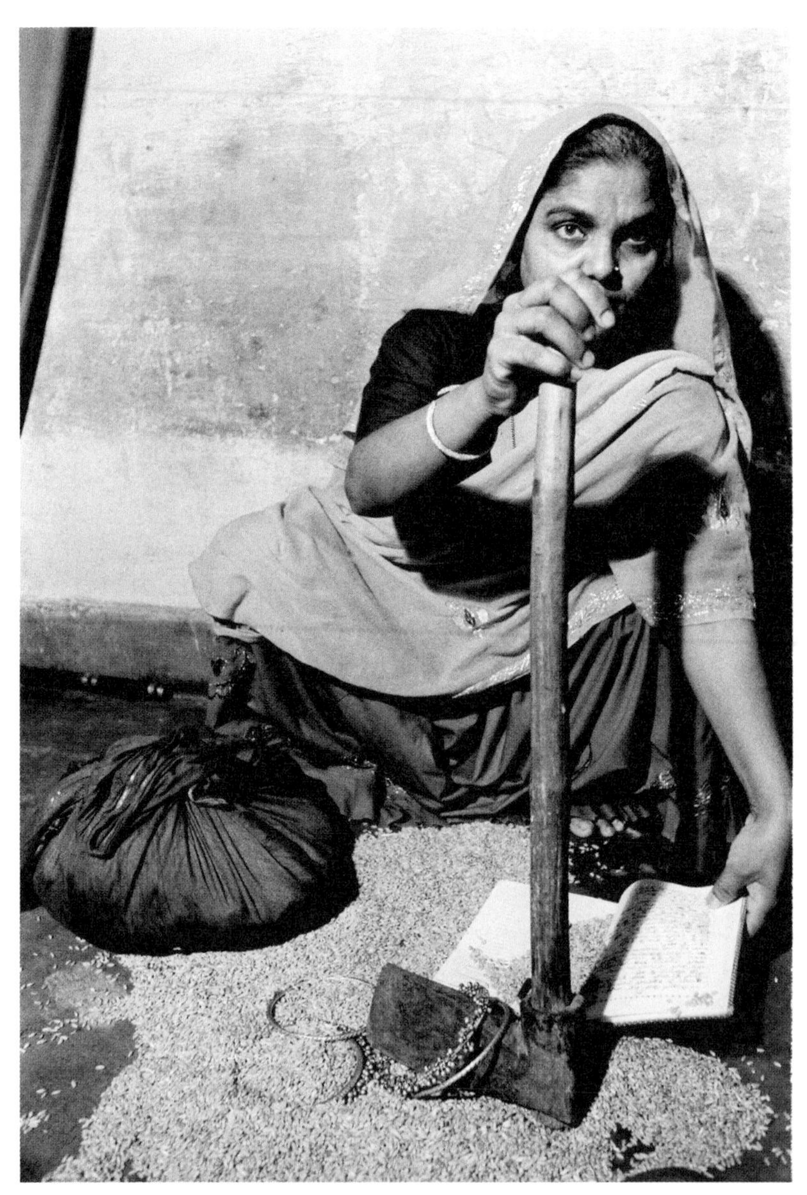

2. Sheba Chhachhi, *Shanti—Staged Portrait 2, Dakshinpuri, Delhi, 1991*, from *Seven Lives and a Dream*. By permission of the artist.

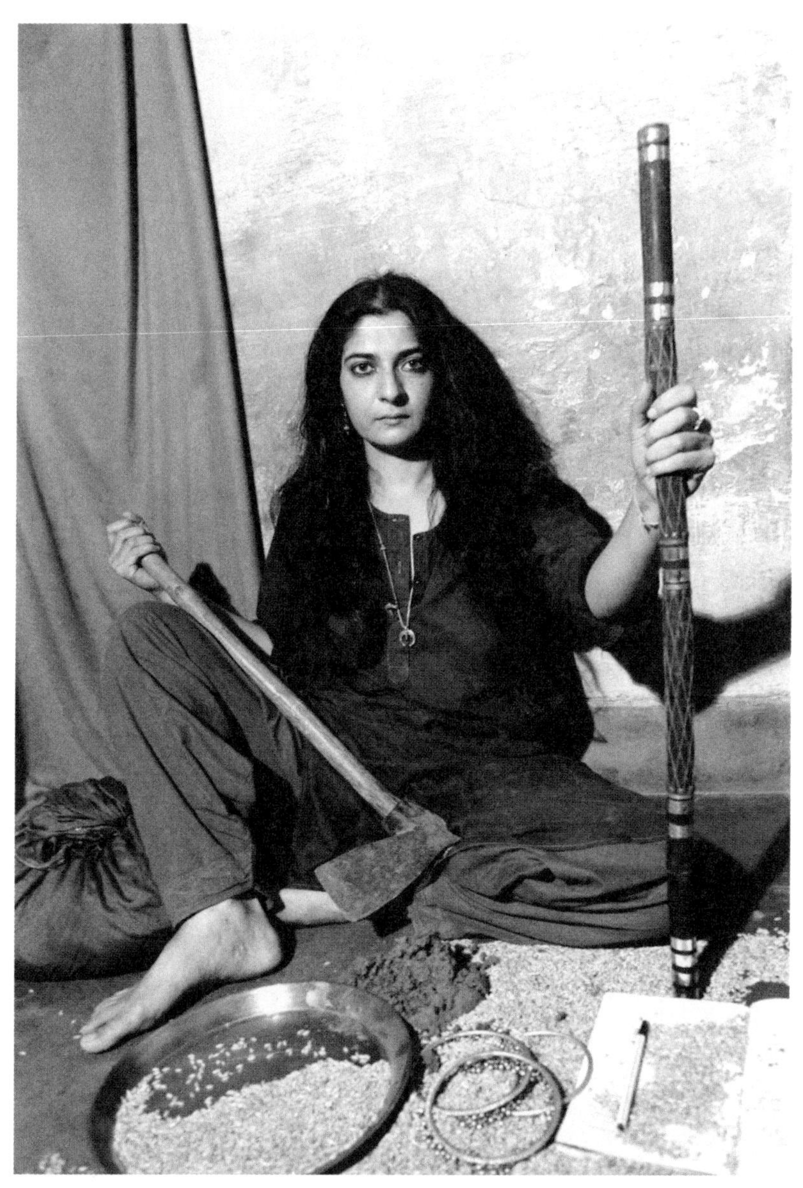

3. Sheba Chhachhi, *Sheba—Staged Portrait, Dakshinpuri, Delhi, 1991*, from *Seven Lives and a Dream*.
By permission of the artist.

Chhachhi's photographs from the *Seven Lives* series insist on presenting themselves with their diaries or notebooks. The diary is a trope of self-assertion, a mode for the production of a self. It signifies that women's time and labor has value, and that their writings articulate experiences worth recording and preserving.

As I researched further, I realized that the women's group Jagori [Awaken, woman], of which Chhachhi was a co-founder, had published its first notebook in 1988. The notebook, as a symbol and tool, was to become a leitmotif of the women's movement, a mnemonic device to activate both the speaking and the silent aspects of women's lives.

As the literary theorist and feminist philosopher Gayatri Chakravorty Spivak has argued repeatedly, however, the ground must first be prepared for the subaltern to speak. Feminist solidarity did not come into being fully formed, unstriated by difficulties of communication, nor infused with an unproblematic common purpose. On the contrary, it had to be shaped by wrestling with differences of class, education, and caste. It is useful to read Jagori's retrospective field notes in this context:

> In 1989, we created the notebook *Mujh se tujh tak* [From me to you]... [which] explored the multiple meanings and dimensions of friendship between women—the sharing, the companionship, the intimacies, the excitement of entering forbidden territories of loving and living.... In the first notebook, it was the Jagori team [comprising middle- and upper-middle-class, English-educated women] that worked on it but this time it had moved into the hands of the community health workers. They wrote the poetry and drew the visuals—in their homes, in the slums and in collective workspaces.[1]

In bringing together loose sheets of paper on which women activists had charted out the itinerary of their lives, written poetry on the run, or recorded experiences in the field, the notebook legitimized all these as valid expressions.

Shanti, in turn, took a photograph of Chhachhi in the same setting [Fig. 3]. Chhachhi's chosen performative gesture mimicked Shanti's: they are both seen to be wielding the axe in their portraits. This performative swap should not be read as a simple case of overturning the elite gaze or equalizing locations: indeed, the mismatch between the women's social locations cannot be magically erased by the enactment of an easy exchange of places. If anything, the differential of social, cultural, and economic capital between the two actors is accentuated. We are reminded, also, that a difficult solidarity is achieved, with a great deal of affective labor having been invested by both Chhachhi and Shanti in sustaining their relationship. Chhachhi often speaks of building relationships with her sitters while referring to her staged portraits. One of the etymological meanings of *relationship*, derived from the Latin *relatus*, is "to be narrated." The act of narration is manifested in Chhachhi's portraiture, but also in the pamphlets and diaries of women's groups such as Jagori. And Jagori's activities, in turn, must be seen in the larger context of feminist publishing in the 1980s, of both oral histories and academic treatises.

Urvashi Butalia and Ritu Menon founded Kali for Women, the first feminist publishing house in India, in 1984. The first women's magazine, *Manushi*, co-edited by Madhu Kishwar and Ruth Vanita, had already begun life in 1979. In one of the staged portraits, Butalia looks like a prose DJ with a bank of typewriters. The props and scenography of this portrait differ from the portraits of a subaltern woman like Shanti, but they all assert, regardless of class differences, the women's desire to express themselves through the written word. They appear as scribal subjectivities presenting themselves in the act of rewriting and re-editing their life-scripts.

The most prominent strain within Indian feminism in the 1980s was an activist one that confronted the executive and judicial establishment on issues of manifest violence against women. According to the feminist historian Radha Kumar, the activist aspiration, whether Gandhian, Maoist, Socialist, or Communist (most feminists belonged to one or another of these ideological camps), was to transcend the self.[2]

> At the same time, as Kumar says, this image of selfless sacrifice conflicted with the feminist view that ideals of feminine purity and selflessness were a part of the structure of women's oppression. In a way the conflict was resolved by pushing

it into abeyance, through focusing on forms of violence against women, rather than the less obvious ways in which they were oppressed.[3]

In these staged portraits, we see how Chhachhi critiques such an idealization of selflessness and sacrifice as a vestigial reflex of the patriarchal structure of consciousness by securing what I would call a field of ludic autonomy, of intimacy and pleasure, which neither the patriarchy nor the activist orthodoxy would sanction. She was able to resolve the conflict between achieving social-juridical reform and ensuring autonomy—not by pushing the latter into abeyance but by generating a space through staged portraits, one in which her feminist sisters could express their activist and ludic energies in equal measure.

1. Jagori, *Living Feminisms—Jagori: A Journey of 20 Years* (New Delhi: Jagori, 2004), 27.
2. Radha Kumar, *The History of Doing: An Illustrated Account of Movements for Women's Rights and Feminism in India, 1800–1990* (New Delhi: Kali for Women, 1993), 114.
3. Kumar, *History of Doing*, 114.

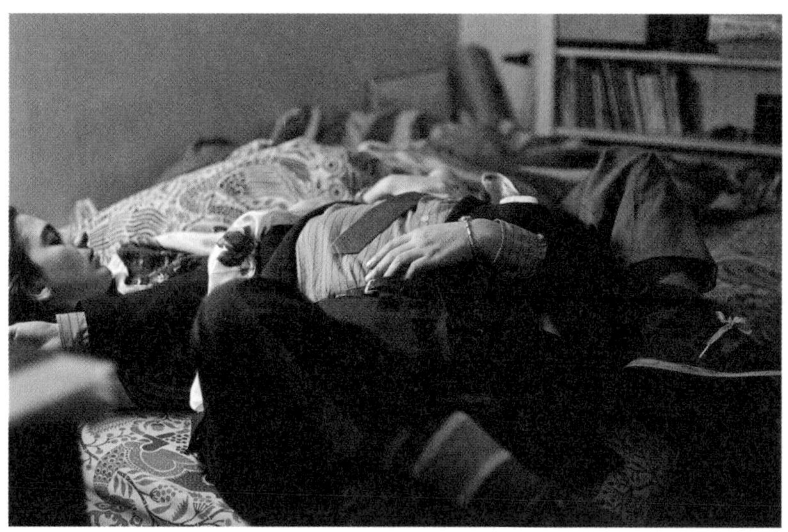

Diana Solís, *Karen and Diane*, Chicago, 1980s. By permission of the artist.

DIANA SOLÍS: INTIMACIES IN RESISTANCE

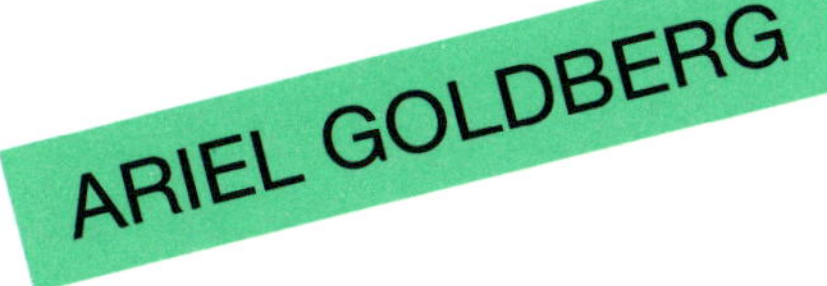

Two friends of the photographer Diana Solís lay intertwined on the bed of her Chicago apartment in the early 1980s. Karen is below, in profile to the left; Diane, on top, her head dipping back, off the ledge of Karen's waist. Diane's chin starts to blur as the depth of field of the camera lens grows incrementally. Karen's hand appears to rest at her collarbone, above the curve of Diane's chest, perhaps loosening the knot of her skinny tie. Diane's jacket is unbuttoned, drifting with her tie to the side of the parallel stripes of her collared shirt, as if her outermost clothes are drowsy too.

I imagine Solís quietly crouching near the corner of the bed, hoping the sound of the shutter won't disrupt their fluid entanglement. Of course, there is no flash. Her perspective is level with their bodies; Solís's camera meets her friends, sharing their warmth. Solís's bedroom anchors the image, diagonals drawing us in, with a bookshelf and cluster of rolled-up art supplies.

Solís was in her mid-twenties when she took

this picture; she was studying photography at Columbia College while working part-time as a photojournalist for local periodicals, such as the *Chicago Tribune*. At the time, she also worked as an educator at grassroots projects like the Latino Youth Alternative High School, where she mentored students who left the local public high school that was at the center of student-led protests demanding black and Latinx history in the curriculum, an end to police harassment, smaller class sizes, and improved facilities. Diane, the figure pictured in the classic butch attire of a full suit, was also an out gay teacher at Latino Youth. In another image from Solís's archive of a group of students studying, there is a note from Diane on the blackboard, asking Solís to call her.

Diane's hand rests down by her belt buckle, the tips of a few fingers disappear at her waistline. The lovers are near the edge of the bed, so their shoes can stay on; even at the end of a long night, their outfits are realized in all their glory. Karen's argyle socks sneak out from her New Balances;

practical shoes for a printmaker, who contributed to the production of many a protest sign as a member of the Chicago Women's Graphics Collective. New Balance, a stable sneaker logo, offers a conduit of familiarity: the nowness of looking across the forty-year or so divide between our present and theirs.

I first learned of Solís's work through her longtime friend and collaborator Nicole Marroquin, who is also an interdisciplinary artist and educator living in Pilsen, a neighborhood in Chicago. Nicole and I met at the Magnum Foundation's Photography Expanded: Counter-Histories in 2018, a symposium in New York building on similar themes as this Lucid Knowledge symposium. Nicole mentioned she was working with Solís to digitize more than seven thousand images and ephemera Solís had stored in a friend's basement for over twenty years. A year later, I visited Pilsen to meet Diana, and the three of us spent several days in Nicole's living room looking at the initial scans of Solís's wide-ranging body of work, including images of muddy rugby games, the 1979 Festival de Mujeres in their neighborhood of Pilsen, marches to protest the assassination of local labor leader Rudy Lozano, Latina nights at gay bars, and then portrait studio sessions in Solís's apartment above another gay bar.

From the late 1970s through the late 1990s, Solís's camera moved across the thresholds of public and private, seamlessly recording such events as Encuentros Feminista Latinoamericana y del Caribe, and mothers and daughters, friends and family of Solís, posing for her within their homes in Pilsen. Faced with the challenge of choosing a single image to speak on for this Errant Photo Album, I am reminded of an image not reproduced here: a self-portrait of Solís, in which she holds up a loupe above her eye, considering an edit from a roll of film. The more intimate, late-night image of Karen and Diane corresponds to yet another image, this one from protest documentation from 1979—the edge of another decade—where signs read: "Government out of Bedrooms, Cops out of the Bars."

Some protestors even cover their faces with their signs, perhaps skeptical of Solís's camera. Which leads me back to how the picture of Karen and Diane on Solís's bed also evades being a full-frontal portrait; the picture is not meant for identification or to mark a milestone. The image dips in and out of blurriness. Karen's eyes are closed, though we don't know if she is asleep or just resting. The animal-and-plant print on the bedsheets swirls and tussles, mixing with the patterns of their clothes, in harmony with their puddle of embrace. The fabrics become a busy wallpaper of a photo studio turned on its side. Is that a scarf with flowers? A paisley blouse? A snakeskin texture on the belt?

In lesbian and queer spaces, taking pictures is still a tentative affair, as the camera at times resembles the eye of the state, the capture of the social media corporation, or the media spectacle; in the early 1980s, cameras reckoned with these conditions perhaps more explicitly. Those who went out to gay bars risked their safety on a myriad of levels. Solís strategically found ways to blur images or hide faces, to offer a record of energized gathering but respect the desire for anonymity. The softness of an exposure just a few fractions of a second slower than sharpness renders the love that the state fears and tries to criminalize. If this image was presented to software trying to read its contents, I wonder how it might resist detection—an exclamation point in a triangle, avoiding immediate recognition.

The range of Solís's photographic work covers numerous genres, not to mention a twenty-year hiatus from photographing to develop a career in painting and illustration, murals, and large-scale public art installations. One through line in Solís's practice is her work as an educator, as she supports multiple generations of artistic communities in Pilsen, where she grew up and still lives and continues to teach art through public schools as well as adult education organizations. Pilsen is a historically Mexican American neighborhood that continues to be a center for grassroots feminist Latinx and youth organizing in the Midwest region of the so-called United States. Solís's work resists the persistent historical erasure of Latinx culture from broader US culture, as well as the displacement longtime residents face from gentrification. Solís was born in Mexico and came to the United States as a young kid, then lived in Mexico City in the 1980s; she is a prominent figure in the cross-pollination of queer Latina visual and literary arts and organizing across the imposed US–Mexico border.

One future home for Solís's photographs is the Chicana por mi Raza Digital Memory Collective, a digital humanities project, where her images will be accompanied by detailed captions hyperlinked to other relevant archives and made available to the general public and academic researchers alike. To begin this work of making Solís's photographic archive accessible, in spring 2021, Nicole Marroquin created and taught a class called Art in Communities: Activating a Queer Latinx Archive at the School of the Art Institute, where Marroquin is Chair of the Department of Art Education. The class partnered with Latitude, a local community-based digital photography lab in Chicago where students learn, hands-on, the technical and practical processes of archiving. Students scanned Solís's negatives at Latitude and met weekly with twelve guest lecturers: scholars, activists, and artists who are involved in various modes of engagement with Solís's photographic work.

When I visited Marroquin's Activating class, I shared some images from Solís's work that is at the center of an exhibition I am developing, "Images on which to Build," which considers how queer photographic practices both created and documented spaces for learning in various overlapping grassroots activist struggles that took place from the 1970s through the 1990s. Solís participated in the numerous social and cultural works she was also documenting, often teaching photography workshops within the organizations or at the Encuentros. Solís's narratives around her archives run through intergenerational conversation and collaboration.

There is a circuit throughout Solís's work: the energy—and power—of organizing that's happening in her pictures is also happening in the careful work of re-presenting her pictures. As María Cotera, one of the founders of Chicana por mi Raza, asks in an essay for the anthology *Chicanas Movidas: New Narratives of Activism and Feminism in the Movement Era*:

> Is it possible to interrupt the erasures of the archive/knowledge system . . . Can we challenge the power relations between scholars and their objects of study that all too often render silent the multitude of voices and articulations that cannot be contained in a single coherent narrative?[1]

In our "retinal age," we are overloaded with digital images, in particular an influx of images of trans and queer life that are challenging over a century of mainstream visual culture dominated by white heterosexuality as the norm. Increasingly, I find I am drawn to a slower time—one of late twentieth-century analogue documentary work, rendering the currents of trans and queer life, of images that are not lost, of images that are not devoid of context. Solís frequently gives talks on her photographic archive, detailing actions, organizations, events; her images activate not only memories but offer crucial information, as messengers of continuity in struggle. Her images are more exciting than any textbook a student could ever hold.

I find synchronicity in Diane's right leg that crosses, shin just above the knee over her other drooping leg, and how Karen's legs mirror this arrangement, a current moving them together as their bodies rest. After listening to Diane in a Chicago Gay Oral History Project video online (the virtual component of *Out and Proud in Chicago*, a 2008 book edited by Tracy Baim), I imagine this picture was taken after she emceed a Lesbians of Color poetry reading or after playing in the pool league she organized for over fifteen years. As much as I try to zoom out and offer a view into the other sheets of negatives in the folders, this image of the lovers in bed comes loose from Solís's archive to take us to when a night becomes soft, when a bed is a couch. Their full body contact in proximity to Solís and her camera proposes infinite coordinates of touch, while fully clothed for going back out into the world.

1. María Eugenia Cotera, "Practices of Chicana Memory before and after the Digital Turn," in *Chicana Movidas: New Narratives of Activism and Feminism in the Movement Era*, eds. Dionne Espinoza, María Eugenia Cotera, Maylei Blackwell (Austin: University of Texas Press, 2018), 306–307.

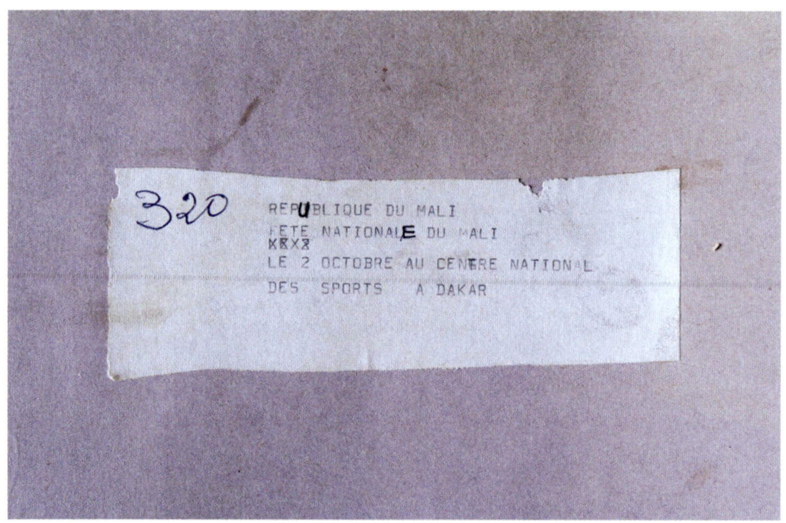

Item photographed by the author while conducting research at the National Archives of Senegal.

INTANGIBLE

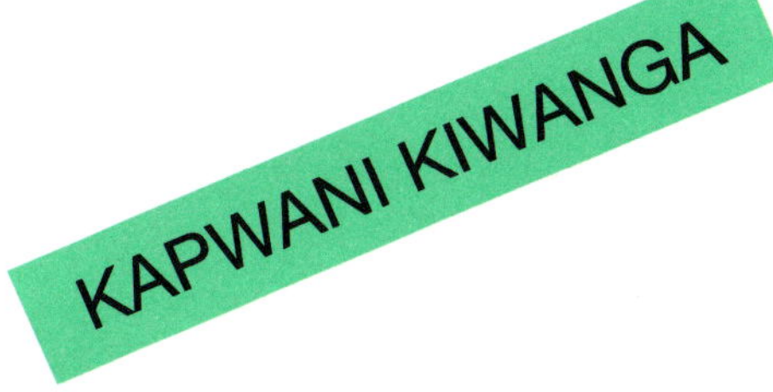

320
Republic of Mali
Malian National Holiday
October 2
National Sports Center in Dakar

I took this photo in 2012 in Dakar, Senegal.

It is the back of a photograph I wanted to recall. That I had lingered on. That I found held something; some information. Something intangible transferred from the paper I held in my hands.

I had plunged myself into the National Archives of Senegal, looking at images of the period of the late 1950s and the 1960s, when a number of African nations obtained independence. I did not know what I was looking for. But I looked and looked. Image after image. Black-and-white. Some with inventory numbers. Some without names. Some with descriptions. And some without.

My gestures—dusting off, pulling out, squinting, turning over, replacing, closing, returning—are known to many who wrestle with the archive, iconographic or otherwise.

Out of this time spent in various archives in Dakar grew my ongoing project *Flowers for Africa,* as well as my unsettled relationship with light and its capture. With this project, I intentionally reach beyond the historic image. It is my attempt to think of a new archive. To privilege the shifting sands of interpretation is what feels the most generative; the best chance one has of attending to, or leaning into, a place of liberation.

In *Flowers for Africa*, the authority of the archival image is replaced with floral arrangements. Bouquets, boutonnières, garlands, and centerpieces, present during key moments in African independence and captured on film—still or moving—are shown to florists, who appropriate them in their own compositional language.

These restaged compositions are interpreted from archival images. No artifact accompanies the work. The replicant sculpture of cut flowers and foliage is left in an exhibition space to dry out and wilt away over the course of the exposition. No attempt is made to maintain their freshness. They are destined to follow their natural course of decomposition. They slip away from the status of factual evidence and become fallible witnesses. They hold and defend a space of possibility, rethinking and letting go. Becoming. Constantly becoming.

320
Republic of Mali
Malian National Holiday
October 2
National Sports Center in Dakar

I lingered on the image on the other side of this caption for its intangible pull. I saw flowers I could not touch or smell. I was not too sure of their form, could not distinguish individual flowers from the collective mass. Their hues resisted identification. Most were collectively assigned to the gradients of black and white. They were centered in the frame yet, somehow, they pulled me *hors cadre*—outside the frame.

The flowers were not meant to be subjects. They were meant to be decorative, to add a celebratory atmosphere. They were intended to serve. Although present and visible, they were accessory; secondary to the authority of the frame. Yet their presence pushes the imagination to enlarge the frame of consideration beyond the photographed scene. Their intended role refused subservience and pointed beyond in solidarity. Beyond the National Sports Center of Dakar, into the streets to roam and observe what filled the bowls of the citizens of the newly formed republic of Mali as they ate—or did not eat—an evening meal. These floral arrangements offer a portal beyond the site of power and officialdom, to the everyday laboratory of living independence.

The flowers of *Flowers for Africa* are changed by light; they age and fade. They are not transformed by light into the statuary of a photographic image. They are a verb, just as independence is an ongoing, everyday process of negotiation that necessitates care.

320
Republic of Mali
Malian National Holiday
October 2
National Sports Center in Dakar

During my creative process as an artist, I have spent a fair amount of time in archives. The iconographic annals have often been ones of discomfort for me. It is more than just the archive that unsettles me. I have begun to believe this is my own particular brand of photophobia. Not a physical discomfort in my eyes due to light sensitivity but rather an ardent distrust of light when used to arrest, to stop, to fix.

In Simone Browne's 2015 book *Dark Matters: On the Surveillance of Blackness*, she analyses historical and contemporary examples of surveillance of blackness. She looks at how global concerns of increased surveillance are linked to a historic apparatus of antiblack "tracking." It is through her work that I became aware of the eighteenth-century New York City lantern laws, which mandated that enslaved persons carry lit candles if they moved about the city after dark unaccompanied by a "white" person.

These laws thus made light a supervisory device—any unattended slave was mandated to be illuminated. This legal framework marked black, mixed-race, and Indigenous persons as security risks in need of supervision after dark. In this way the lit candle, in panoptic fashion, sought to "extend to the night the security of the day."[1]

Light enables sight but it is the reception, transformation, and interpretation of light's electromagnetic waves that allows one to see. It is with an emphasis on interpretation that I return to the process of *Flowers for Africa*, in which it is the florist's interpretation of the archival image that is at play. No single recreation of a given floral arrangement will ever be the same. Each depends on which flowers are available, the season, and the taste and life experience of the florist. Each puts interpretation first and foremost and sheds any pretense of historical accuracy or authority. Such interpretation frees light's wavelengths from the original celluloid or digitized pixels. It releases it and surrenders it to atmospheric pressures and varying air densities.

Michel Foucault reminds us that the act of viewing can become an exercise of power when it becomes the gaze—another reason the photographic archive can be an uncomfortable place in which one can unwittingly become party to the violence of viewing or image-taking. Foucault describes the gaze not as something one has or uses; rather, it is a relationship into which one enters.

Marc Garanger, a French conscript stationed in Algeria during the Algerian War, took approximately twenty thousand portraits of Algerians. In 1960, he produced portraits of Algerians living in internment camps under military supervision around Aïn Terzine in order to create identity cards. The camp commander ordered that women be photographed without the veils they wore in public. Unaccustomed to showing their full faces to anyone outside their intimate circle, they stood before Garanger's camera exposed as never before.

Their unveiled photographic likenesses expose these women in perpetuity. Statues of light, weaponized to exert control.

I have found myself participating in the violence of viewing stolen light. Unprepared, I have stumbled upon such images. Anger arose, for I had not asked to be an accomplice. Such situations occur from time to time when one engages with archives. Yet, each time this occurs, the sting is no less virulent.

In Harun Farocki's 1988 film *Images of the World and the Inscription of War*, speaking in relation to Garanger's images, the narrator states:

The veil covers mouth, nose, and cheeks and leaves the eyes free. The eyes must be accustomed to meeting a strange gaze.

The mouth cannot be accustomed to being looked at. . . . A mouth, to be able to taste something, must come close to its object. The eye, to be able to see, can remain at a distance from its object.

In Garanger's photographs, one is reminded that the gaze, however violent, is often met. If sight can be commanding, it can equally resist.

As I progressed with *Flowers for Africa*, I came across a newsreel depicting members of Algeria's first sovereign government, the Provisional Government of the Algerian Republic, led by the party president, Benyoucef Benkhedda, as they arrive in Algiers in convoy on July 3, 1962—the date on which France officially recognized Algeria's independence.

The resistance I found in the eyes of the women photographed by Garanger came back to me when I saw a bouquet of flowers, held triumphantly in hand, as the convoy rode through the streets.

320
Republic of Mali
Malian National Holiday
October 2
National Sports Center in Dakar

I will allow you to imagine the photo on the other side. In so doing, I ask you to resist the desire to capture light to serve authority.

1. Jeremy Bentham, quoted in Simone Browne, *Dark Matters: On the Surveillance of Blackness* (Durham: Duke University Press, 2015), 24.

ALL THE FAMILY PHOTO ALBUMS SHOW ME

ANDREAS SCHLAEGEL

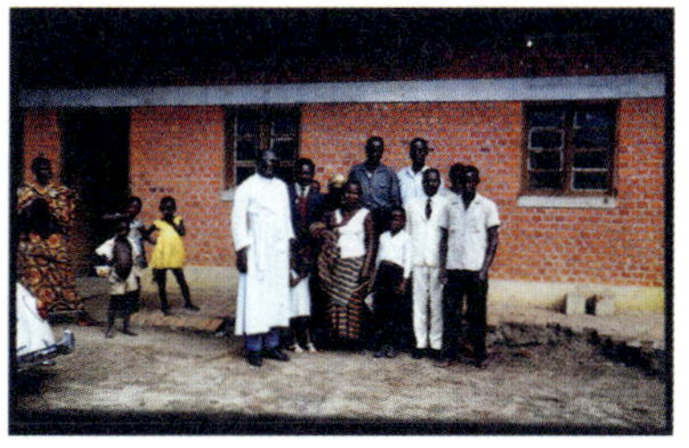

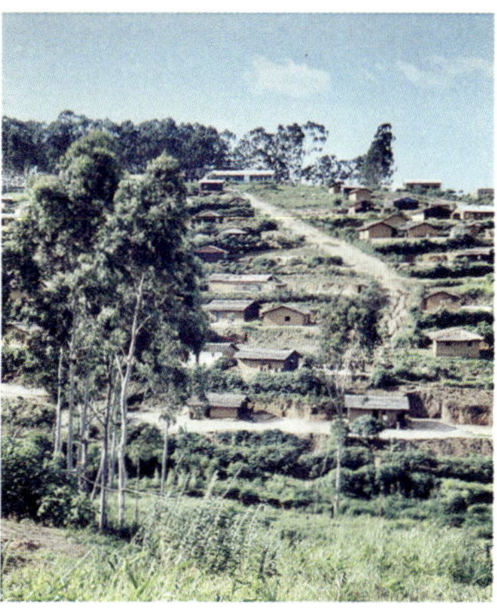

I have taken the title of this series of reflections on photo albums literally: What is an errant photo album? How does it err? Does it wander away? Does it go off the right track? Does it go AWOL?

A photo album is not an archive; rather, it is the domain of the amateur, the enthusiast. A family photo album is a homemade greatest hits compilation (and is at least as obsolete as that genre). Its appeal—and what separates it from digital photo albums on mobile phones—lies in its creation of its own narrative. It represents the preferred family story told at the time of its compilation; a form of bourgeois (or petit-bourgeois) self-historicization—if not hagiography—in the form of a photo novella. An agglomeration of trophies, of confirmations of feelings of self-worth.

The mere mention of the term *photo album* takes me straight back to my parents' house, where the story of our family is made manifest in row upon row of heavy, leatherette-bound volumes, labeled with dates, sometimes locations, chronicling our nuclear family in events, birthdays, weddings, travels—today spanning more than half a century in carefully selected and devotedly arranged images.

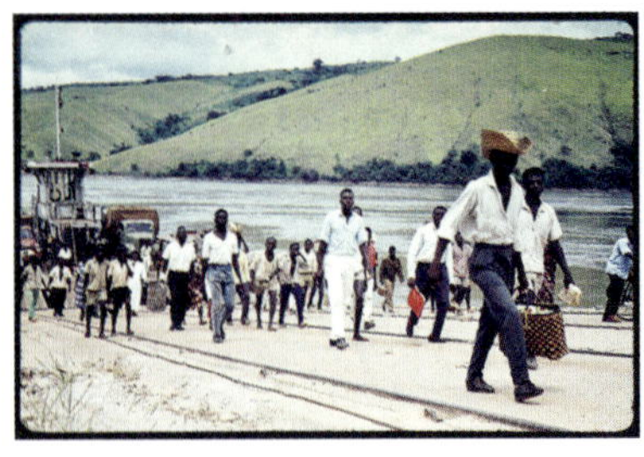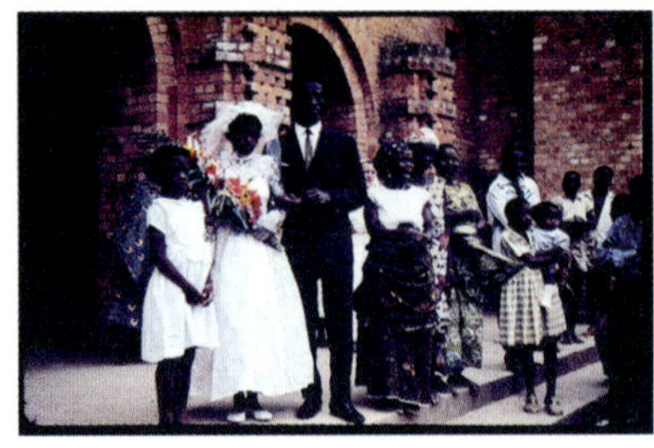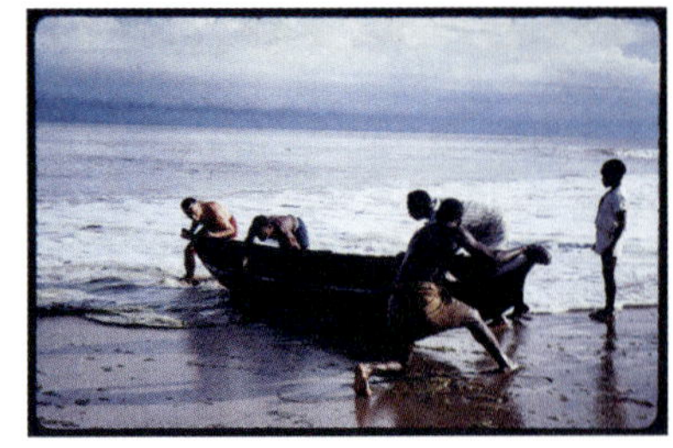

Both my parents are enthusiastic photographers. This hobby shaped their relationship, as a device for framing moments, generating the narrative that creates a sense of a perspective on reality. The beginnings of their relationship were only later rendered in albums; initially, that period was documented in thousands of slides. The story of their relationship and the story of our family, as I imagine is often the case, is primarily a story told in photographs.

It begins in what was then the Belgian Congo, where my parents first met, fell in love, and were married. Where they started a family; where their first child was born. Me. From 1964 through 1967, they lived first in Kinshasa, then in Leopoldville. I was a year old when my parents departed and settled down in southwest Germany, thus I don't have any memories of that time.

My father was appointed a telecommunications engineer for the United Nations Development Program, whose mission was to improve the national telephone system in what was then the Belgian Congo and to train engineers in maintaining and expanding its local networks. He received an advance, which he invested in a camera—a Leica M3, whose portability and versatility reflected the sort of pictures he aspired to take.

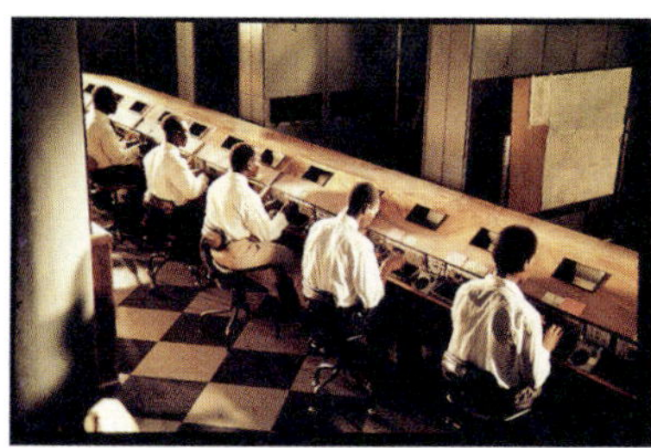

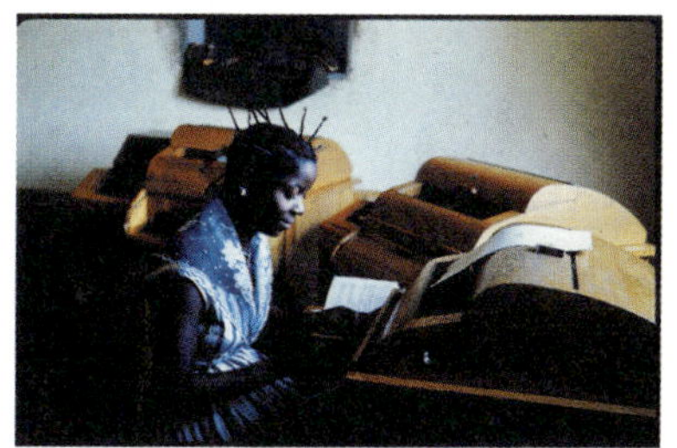

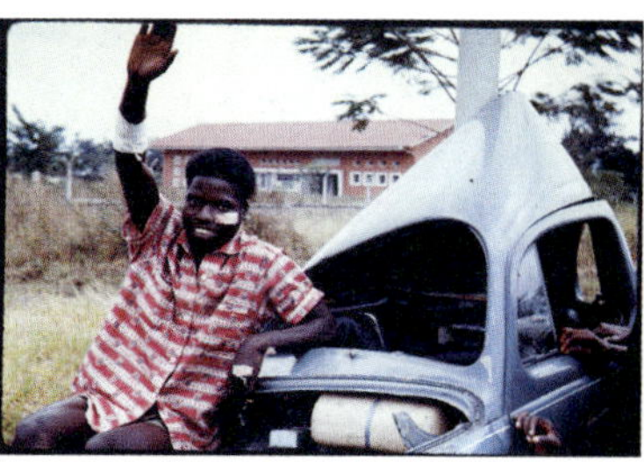

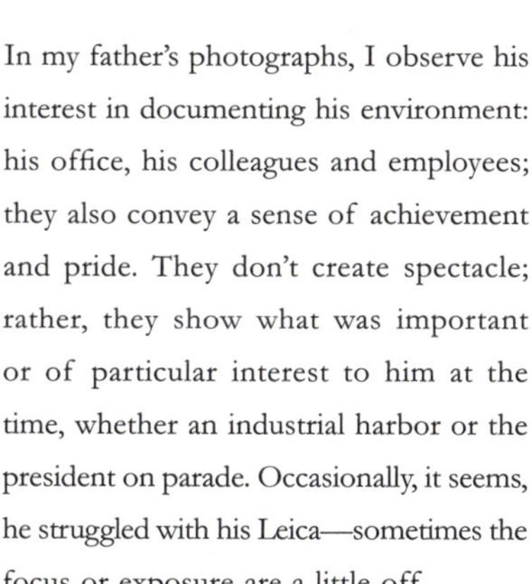

In my father's photographs, I observe his interest in documenting his environment: his office, his colleagues and employees; they also convey a sense of achievement and pride. They don't create spectacle; rather, they show what was important or of particular interest to him at the time, whether an industrial harbor or the president on parade. Occasionally, it seems, he struggled with his Leica—sometimes the focus or exposure are a little off.

My mother fled a dominant father and the pervasive sexism of the working environment in the Federal Foreign Office in Bonn, the West German capital, where she worked as a translator. Responding to a posting on the bulletin board, she applied to become the official translator for the German Embassy in Kinshasa. As my father did, she received an advance and—also like my father—decided to purchase a new camera with it. She chose one that had just come on the market: a Pentax Spotmatic, a single-lens reflex model, intended for the affluent amateur and marketed for its ease of use due to the novelty of a built-in light meter.

With its quick and easy operation, the Spotmatic informed my mother's organic approach to photography. It became an extension of her body. She easily assumed the role of photographic director, arranging objects of interest; her taking pictures created something of a spectacle. She danced the dance.

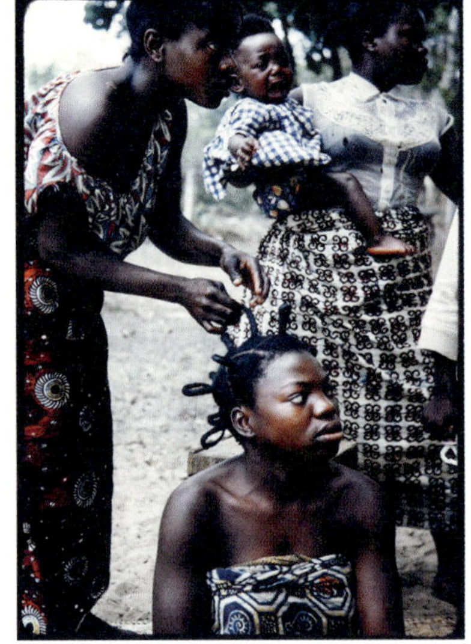

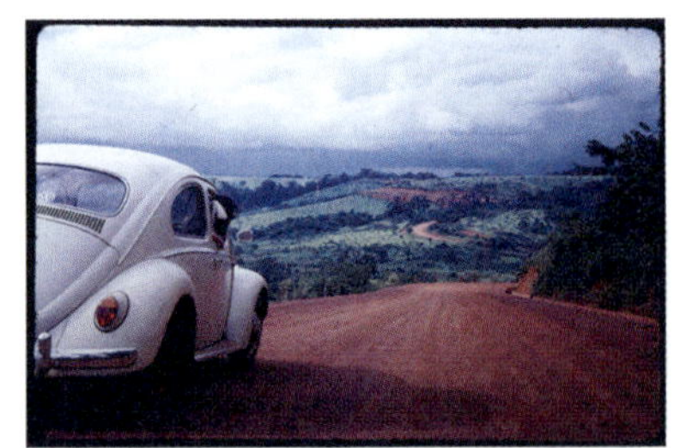

In her pictures, I sense a mixture of naivete and cunning; a desire to capture sunsets, landscapes, flowers, children, people, all that might be seen to represent an idea of beauty. I often wonder about stereotyping in her pictures, but my observation that the way she gets close to—nearly intimate with—her subjects is sufficient to subvert this notion. "People approached me and asked to have their pictures taken," my mother would say. She didn't hide behind her camera; there was no need to sneak pictures. She still takes photographs; to this day, I receive sunrises and sunsets, often with the caption "So beautiful."

It is no surprise that my parents bonded over their enthusiasm for photography. They took pictures incessantly—first of everything else, then increasingly of each other. Neither of them had any intention of producing artistic images. Proud though they were of their pictures, they rarely presented them to anyone outside their immediate family.

As a child, I loved to see their slides. The ritual of pulling down the blinds, plunging the living room into darkness, setting up the slide projector, and draping bedlinen over the bookshelf for a makeshift screen.

Part of the attraction was in seeing my parents' former selves—the young couple in love; part was in observing how, upon seeing the projected images, they relived their memories. Some they would not care to share; others they would. New stories emerged every time. A snake that took my mother by surprise on a hike in the countryside grew larger with each retelling.

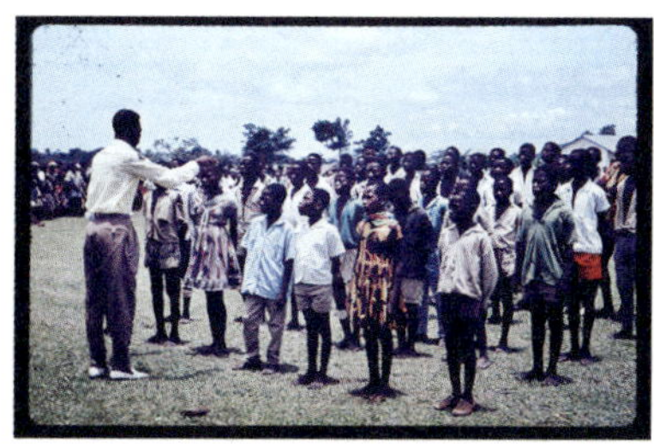 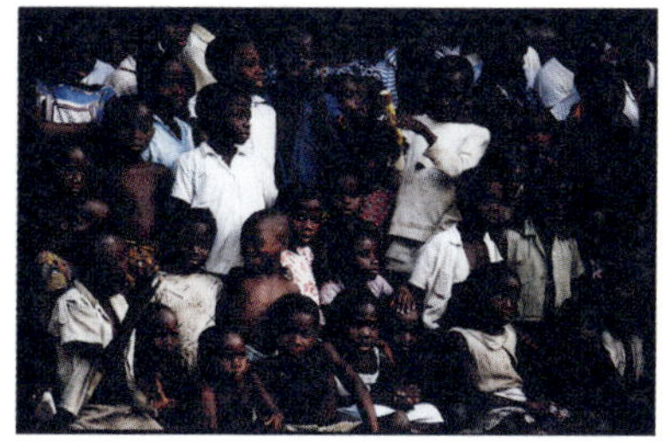

One of these evenings, however, turned into a disaster. The projector and screen were in place and we kids were giddily seated on the sofa. My father inserted a tray into the projector. The first image showed a chaos of bodies on the back of a truck. He quickly forwarded to the next slide. More carnage: corpses on a street. A series of images of atrocities followed, as my father hectically shuffled through the slides as quickly as the mechanical system of the projector would let him, in a doomed attempt to save the already ruined moment of family harmony. In a panic, my mother shoved us out of the room.

The evening ended with us kids in the bedroom, in tears of confusion and angst over the abominations we had been exposed to. We overheard heated arguments in the living room. The cabinet crammed with slides was declared verboten for us. And we obeyed. We forgot and we didn't look back. My siblings don't remember this incident anymore.

A few years ago, upon reading David van Reybrouck's book about Congolese history, struggling to make sense of the complexities of the Congo crisis, I felt a near-physical jolt of recollection, and those images from my childhood, seen so briefly, were back.

But now I knew where to look. I wanted to see them again and to understand what had happened.

My parents still live in the same house and the cabinet stands in the same place. After asking permission, I opened it. The slides were gone. My father explained. He didn't want to live with those images anymore. I was too late.

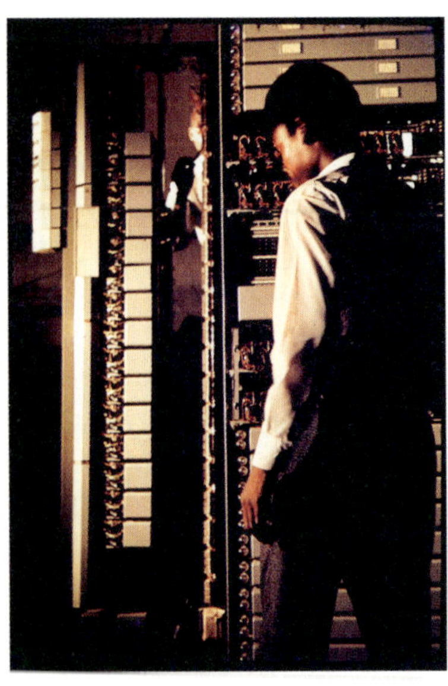

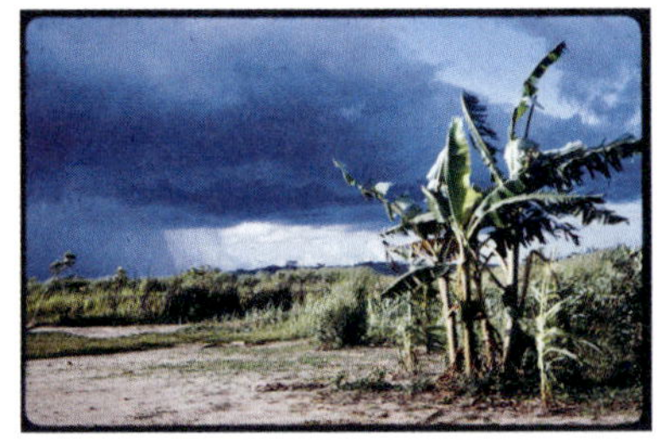

But my father could still tell the story of the violence he witnessed while in Stanleyville, now Kisangani, Congo's third-largest city. How he and his colleagues had been there, working on telephone lines, then holed up in a hotel room, hoping to escape the mayhem raging in the city. First, Simba rebel warriors had attacked and killed Belgian farmers, then anyone they associated with the central government: officials, the evolué (Congolese people who lived the "white way"). My father explained that the Simba—the "lions"—were young men loyal to Patrice Lumumba, the democratically elected leader of the Congo who had been killed on the orders of the CIA three years earlier. The warriors were high most of the time, cruel and unpredictable. They used traditional weapons and invoked magic rituals that made bullets pass through their bodies as if they were made of air, thus rendering them invincible. Their magic was very strong. Soldiers from the national army ran away in fear.

The Simba rampage formed the pretext for a second wave of even worse violence—officially inflicted by the government army, but more so by Belgian troops and to an even greater degree by South African mercenaries, who had no respect for the lives of the local people.

When, after days of mayhem, silence fell and no more gunfire was to be heard, my father mustered up the courage to leave the hotel room. As he stumbled into the streets, he took out his camera and started taking pictures of what he saw.

The corpses on the truck I remembered from my childhood experience were those of Simba warriors. They probably weren't victims of the most recent attacks but had been killed in previous violence; as they could still fight as spirits, their bodies were brought along by the truckload into battle. The truck my father photographed stood by the roadside, abandoned by its driver, who presumably fled from the mercenaries. Their unimaginable degree of racism and disrespect for human life was displayed in its gruesome effectivity, a merciless, systematic slaughter of any local they came across. It was the traces of this massacre that my father was witness to.

Of all the slides of that day, only two images have survived. One is deceptively peaceful. We can't see the face of a man lying shirtless on the grass of a lawn, framed by the foliage of palm trees. A white wall in the back suggests a mansion, adding to the oneiric quality of the image—a moment of movement suspended not only by the photographic process. I would like to believe he could be sleeping. I know he is not. A low wall divides the photographer from the scene, as if he were spying on something not meant for his eyes: a private, intimate moment. The film was damaged: perhaps sand in the camera has inscribed the three parallel scratches that appear on the image.

My father couldn't tell me who the man in the picture was, and it's impossible to say to whom he fell victim. When I see this picture today, I find it utterly frustrating that I cannot know more about it. It's an unresolved issue. It's not my picture—I didn't take it—but I have it now. And I have chosen to take responsibility for it. I cannot escape its weight—not because of the presence of a dead man, rather because in looking at his body I grasp that this photograph concerns everyone who is confronted with the image it presents.

Of the roughly six thousand slides they took in Congo, my parents selected and kept only about two thousand—the good memories. The stuff of their nightmares they edited out. Of those remaining slides, I selected two hundred to explore further. I selected no family pictures, only those that gave me the impression the photographer, my mother or father, had a genuine interest in what or whom they photographed; that, in taking the picture, they were trying to hold on to something, that they wanted to explore further. Just as I am trying to explore.

When I look at these pictures, I try not to evaluate them too much. I viewed the slides with my parents and recorded our conversations. It took us two days. It located the pictures firmly in my parents' narrative.

But theirs is not the whole story—and this is the dilemma of the photo album.

A large part of the story is missing, and I want to find it. Perhaps I will take these slides back to Congo. Would they be of any interest at all? I could circulate them—but in doing so, do I ascribe to them a new and different sense of value? Ideally, I would imagine these images could generate a new conversation, whose starting point—my slides—can be left behind. A new, errant photo album.

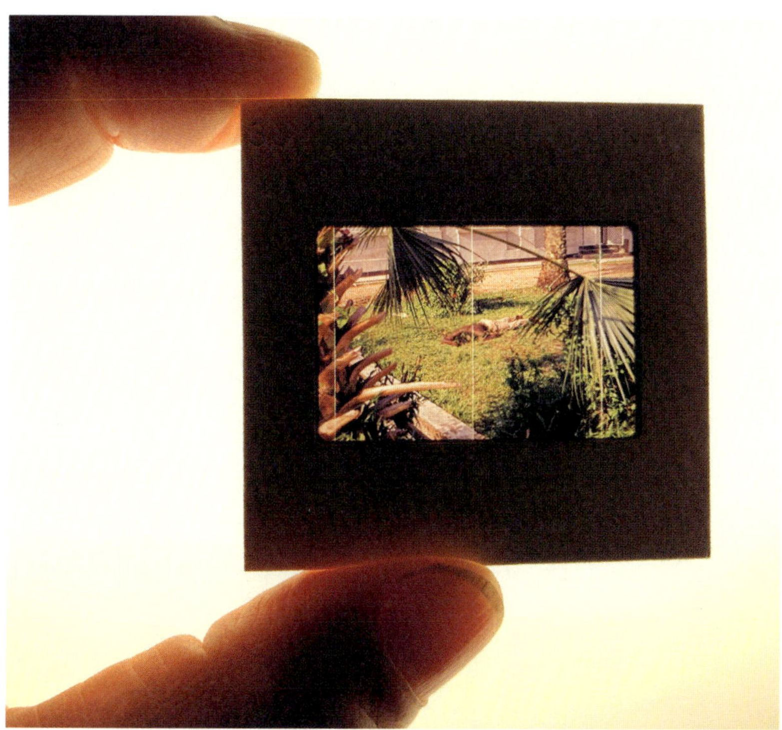

All photos courtesy the author's parents.

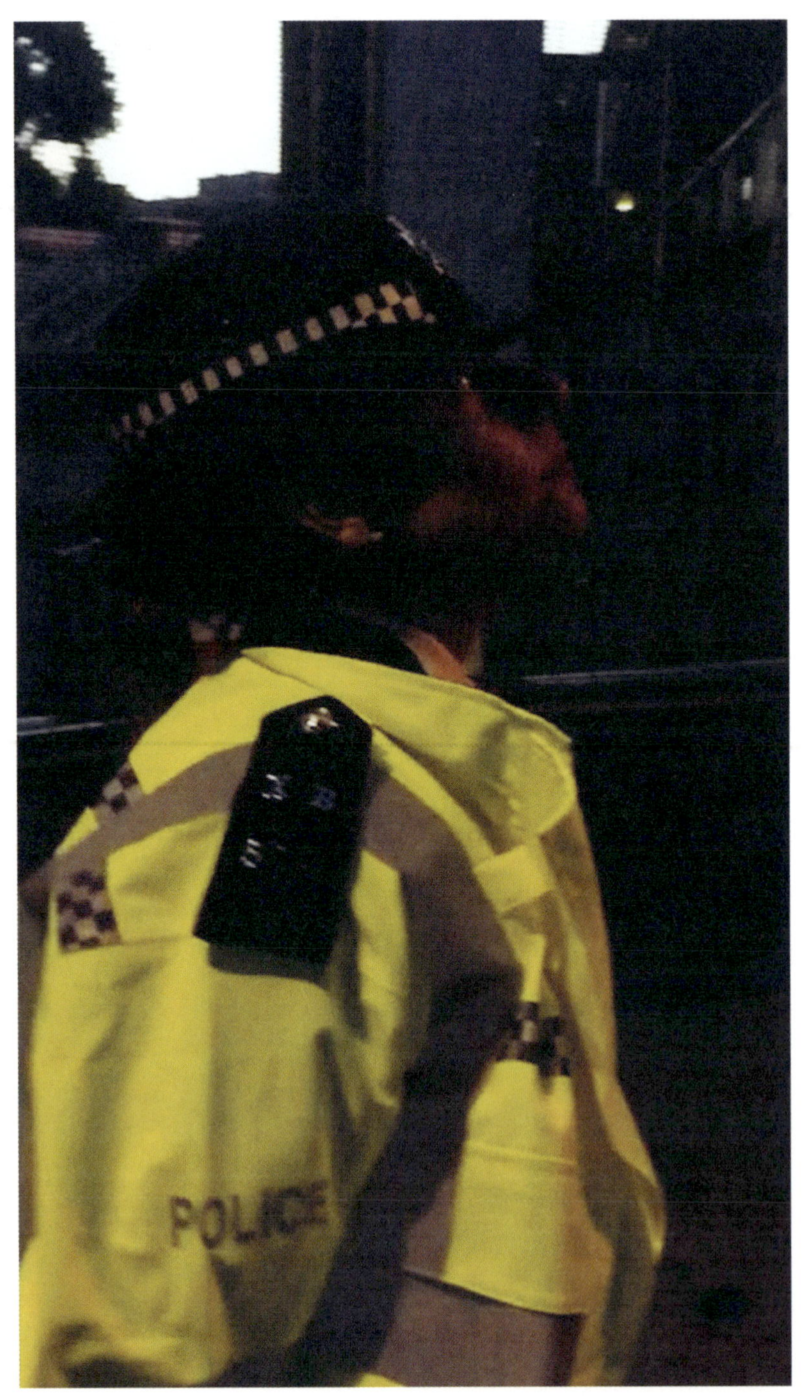

1. Still from Reuters copyright phone footage from near Grenfell Tower. June 14, 2017.

THE WITNESS WITHOUT A CAMERA

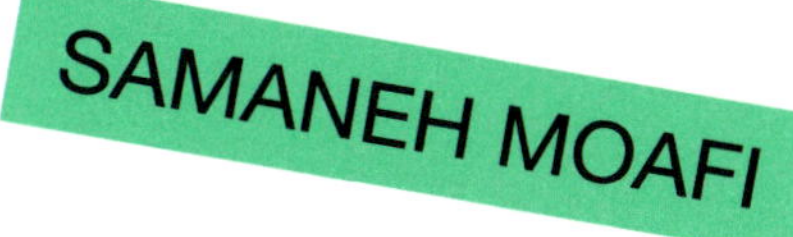

Bearing witness holds particular meaning for me—an immigrant, a woman of color, and a member of the UK-based research group Forensic Architecture. At the request of our collaborators—legal teams, human rights groups, and those subjected to state and corporate violence—we at Forensic Architecture probe into footage most often captured by amateur videographers; everyday people who suddenly find themselves witnessing crimes. We know that every frame of every minute of every such video is likely to hold information that is invaluable for determining accountability. Hence, we do our work with the utmost care, moving back and forth between frames, examining each for hundreds of minutes, if not more.

At times, I find myself arrested by a video. This still frame, for example [Fig. 1], shows a police officer in a night uniform, holding a cordon tape. She looks away from the videographer—away and upward. In the frames that follow, the camera pans the surroundings. A dozen or so residents are gathered behind the police barrier. They,

too, are looking up. The videographer herself would have been among this group. Why did she film the witnesses and not the scene they were witnessing?

We geo-located the video to a spot near the Latimer Road tube station in the London Borough of Kensington and Chelsea. The timestamp is 4:14 a.m., June 14, 2017—the night a fire broke out in Kensington's twenty-four-storey Grenfell Tower. Seventy-two residents of the complex lost their lives, the majority of them brown and black bodies. Migrant bodies. Among them, thirty-two from the Middle East and North Africa. Nine from East Africa. Five from West Africa. Five from Bangladesh.

Another video, recorded from the same spot an hour earlier, documents the fire as it wraps around the building. The only part of the tower yet to catch flame at this point is a small wedge on the west face. Halfway through this clip, the videographer zooms into this unburnt section, as if trying to realize something using the screen of her smartphone. She then indicates what her

camera has been capturing. Her index finger enters the frame and points to a window on the twenty-third floor. Blurred among the pixels of the zoom are the silhouettes of two bodies, trapped beneath a roof engulfed in flame. The silhouettes move and we realize they are alive. It feels as if they are looking down toward the witnesses on the ground.

It is, then, an hour after this that the videographer starts filming the witnesses around her. The morning after, she shares what she witnessed with her smartphone camera on a social media platform. Circulating virally, her videos are a site where evidence and testimony collapse in on one another. Eyal Weizman, my colleague and the founding director of Forensic Architecture, has written about the way the introduction of such images in court trials leads to complications that are aesthetic, political, and ethical.[1] This occurs not because the image provides a stable and fixed alternative to human uncertainties and anxieties but, rather, because the complexities associated with testimony—that of the subject—echo in the image-object.

A few years after the Grenfell catastrophe, amid our investigation of the August 4, 2020, explosion at the port of Beirut, I found myself arrested by another video. It shows in its foreground blazing sunshine cast on the rooftop of a grain silo in Beirut. Trapped in the summer sun are the shadows of two workers, one holding a smartphone. The videographer's colleague steps away and pulls him back, while his filming of the warehouse continues. The fire escalates within seconds. Thick smoke clouds billow out of every opening. As it falls to the ground, the phone captures the sound of an explosion. It continues recording for a few seconds, then stops. In effect, the video is the final self-portrait of a worker.

On examining the frame closely, we located the source of the explosion to the northwest area of the warehouse. This helped us cross-reference the worker's video testimony from the silo with another taken by a skilled migrant worker who was filming from a mid-rise building located farther away and near the Saint George Hospital. We used the smoke clouds rising from the warehouse—their shape, color, and source—to cross-reference several video testimonies from around the city: a balcony of a residential tower, a rooftop bar, a port walkway, and a boat at sea. Our 3D reconstruction of the explosion pieced together people's testimonies and generated a poly-perspectival model.[2]

We used the 3D model to bring together accounts from within and without the site of the explosion, those anchored in the short few minutes between 5:54 and 6:08 p.m., and those recorded months earlier. This helped us determine the precise layout of the materials stored inside the warehouse. The findings of our investigation were later used as evidence by Human Rights Watch in their August 2021 report, which held several members of the Lebanese political class accountable for crimes including homicide with probable intent, unintentional homicide, and environmental pollution. Our reconstruction of what was stored in Beirut's port is tethered to the video testimony of two workers who risked (and lost) their lives to film a warehouse seconds away from total destruction.

Let us shift from their work back to the two silhouettes trapped in toxic smoke, standing at the window of their twenty-third-storey flat in Grenfell Tower, witnessing those who are witnessing them on the ground. They are *witnesses without a camera*; subjects lacking an image-object. One effect of trauma is that it often causes some understandings of situated experiences to be lost. In many cases, it is seemingly unimportant details that allow for the piecing together of witness accounts. In the absence of video testimony, alternative evidentiary methods are a necessity. Over the course of half-a-dozen projects, Forensic Architecture has developed a specific interviewing technique for this purpose. We call it "situated testimony."

These renderings [Fig. 2] are from a 3D model of the home of Rashida, a survivor who was housed on Grenfell's fifteenth floor. Using our technique of situated testimony, we used a large monitor to share the model with Rashida. We helped her navigate its every corner and recollect her memory of details such as the shape and size of the furnishings and their arrangement in the space. We modeled her recollections as she described them. Via this process, she remembered the events of the night with greater resolution—including a moment when she was standing near the window. Such situated testimony allows witnesses of the tragedy to move between egocentric and allocentric perspectives—respectively, the scenes as they experienced them at eye level, and a perspective that allows them to see themselves in relation to their surroundings, which triggers memories of the objects, colors, sounds, and smells that enveloped them at the time of the event. Rashida, for example, was able to recall the thickness of the smoke when she first smelled it, and the direction in which it was moving.

We have spent over three years reconstructing and piecing together the recollections of Rashida and other witnesses of the fire in the 3D model.[3] To date, our work has empowered individuals to remember the details with greater accuracy. We have yet to share the findings of this ongoing research, however. Throughout Phases 1 and 2 of the Grenfell Tower Inquiry, a forum created to examine the circumstances leading up to and surrounding the fire, several survivors and bereaved families have submitted their testimony. Suggestions that institutional racism, classism, and religious discrimination contributed to the loss of life in Grenfell are on the table. A great deal more needs to be done and the quest for justice continues. The production and presentation of architectural evidence anchored by the testimonies of witnesses, with or without a camera, might be an opening for the quest.

1. Thomas Keenan and Eyal Weizman, *Mengele's Skull: The Advent of a Forensic Aesthetics* (Berlin: Sternberg and Portikus, 2012).

2. The Forensic Architecture team working on the Beirut Port case includes the author (Researcher in Charge), Lola Conte, Nicholas Masterton, Kishan San, and Robert Trafford.

3. The team at Forensic Architecture working on the Grenfell Tower case includes Eyal Weizman (Principal Investigator); Robert Trafford and Christina Varvia (Project Coordinators); Nour Abuzaid, Alican Aktürk, Manuel Correa, Ebrahem Farooqui, Franc Camps-Febrer, Zac Ioannidis, Lachlan Kermode, Nicholas Masterton, Sarah Nankivell, Simone Rowat, Nathan Su, and the author.

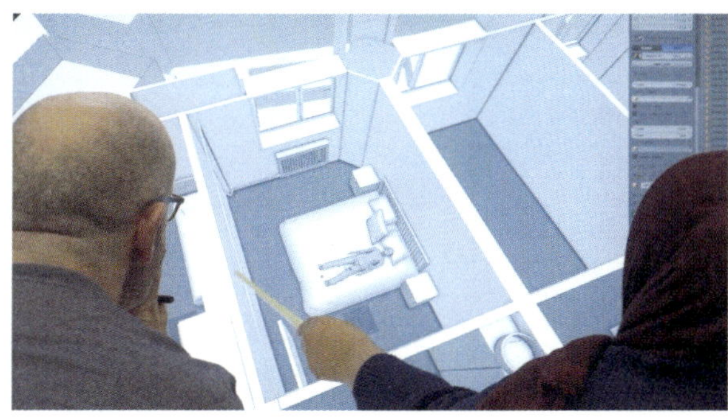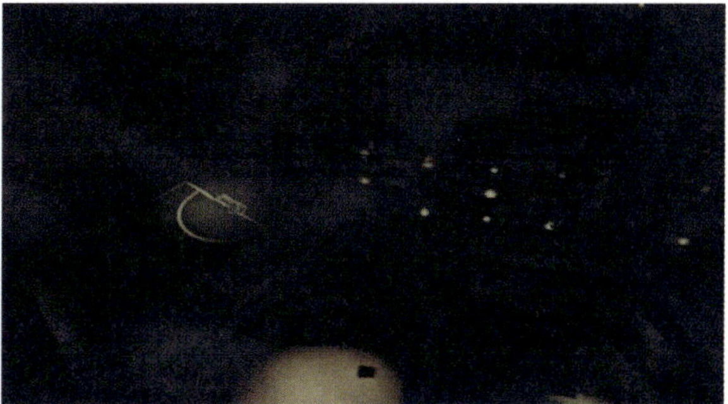

2. Renderings from situated testimony on the fire at Grenfell Tower. Courtesy of Forensic Architecture, 2021.

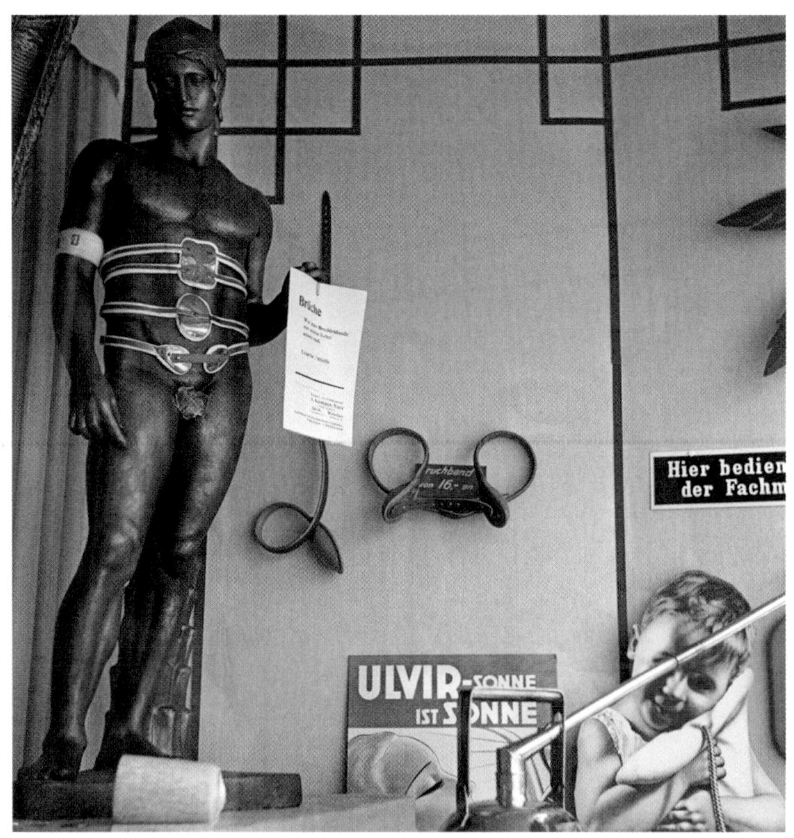

1. Herbert List, *Apoll mit Leibbinden*, 1936. © Herbert List—Magnum Photos / Herbert List Estate Hamburg. By permission of the Museum für Kunst und Gewerbe Hamburg.

IS APOLLO GAY? HERBERT LIST'S REINTERPRETATION OF MALE BODIES

ESTHER RUELFS

Strolling through Zurich in 1936, Herbert List trains his lens on the window of an orthopaedics shop [Fig. 1]. He allows the glass to disappear almost completely, along with the various products displayed in the foreground, of which we see only snippets framing the picture. Instead, he focuses on a statue of Apollo outfitted with hernia belts—sixteen Swiss francs for a double-sided belt. List has made the replica of a Greek sculpture his main motif, and it thus becomes the focal point of his erotic take on the scene.

Since the 1920s, the shop window has generally been a space occupied predominantly by female mannequins. Window dressing and the shop-window mannequin, developed during that era into a mass medium, with the appearance of new periodicals on the art of window dressing and the emergence of the profession of window dresser. The rise of the medium involved the gradual eclipse of the kind of "outdated" window displays captured by List by the advertising strategies of the modern consumer world. Mechanical works of art disappeared, as did realistic wax figure mannequins ("relatives from Castan's Panopticon"[1]), to be replaced everywhere by streamlined, abstract figurines designed—according to the prevailing logic—to boost the urge to buy. List takes a deliberately anti-modern stance in his choice of shop windows, photographing old-fashioned arrangements in various orthopaedics shops, a flower-shop window adorned with a wax figure, a sailors' outfitter in St. Pauli, and an art supplies shop displaying an assortment of body models. All of these were shops that could no longer keep up with the pace of modern urban life. List portrays these quirky small businesses with a sure eye for the absurd and the peripheral. And the windows of all of them reflect a specific construction of the body and of gender.

It is significant that shop-window mannequins are usually female. This is a central consideration in various articles that appeared in the illustrated magazines of the 1930s outlining how to give them a lifelike look. The aim is to beguile the male observer with these "queens of the shop windows," to which "many a man has gradually lost his heart."[2] But List inverts this situation in his shop-window photograph, which manifests instead his specific interest in the male body, emphasized as a sexual entity constructed through various cultural attributions. The ancient youth is here the object of his queer gaze. As a result, the hernia belts and bandages take on a new life, morphing from medical aids into leather shackles.

This image is part of a series of shop window photographs taken by List between 1930 and 1938 and offered to the Swiss magazine *Du* and to his photo agency Blackstar in a letter dated 1948 as a series titled "Märchen am Rande der Straße" [Streetside fairy tales], complete with captions.

My erotic reading of that image is underscored by another photograph List took—a display in the window of a sailors' outfitter [Fig. 2] offered in a series together with other shop window photographs, including that of the orthopaedics shop.

"He stands as straight as a poker, for he has swallowed a stick. A bearded Adonis, furnished with the attributes of masculinity: captain's hat for 2.95 and knives for 0.95 and 1.25. For 2.50, he'll give you his immaculate jacket."[3]

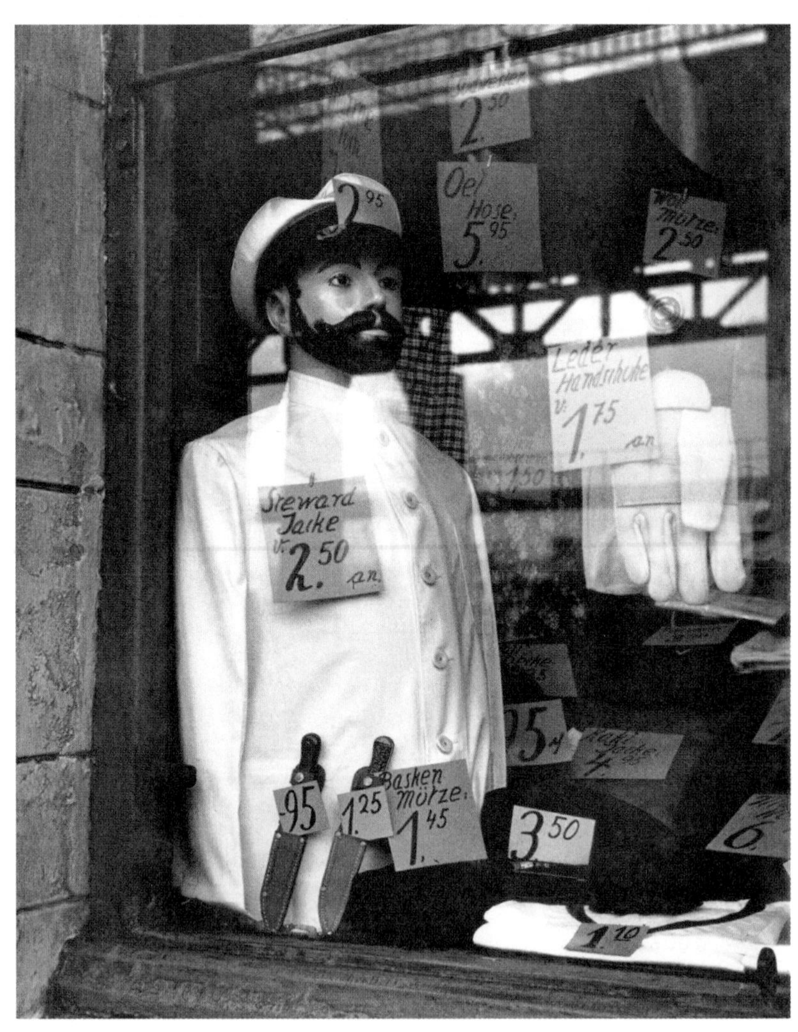

2. Herbert List, *Seemansbedarf, Hamburg*, 1930. © Herbert List—Magnum Photos / Herbert List Estate Hamburg / Agentur Focus.

The photograph of the orthopaedics display ties in with List's interest in antique sculpture. He delighted in teasing out the subliminal eroticism of classical art and provoking an erotic way of looking at well-known artworks. A prime example is his photograph of the "Statue from Antikythera," taken in Athens in 1937 [Fig. 3]. He photographed the torso of the sculpture from behind, in the courtyard of the Athens National Museum. The marble of the buttocks and waist had been corroded by long years in the sea before it was recovered. List made calculated use of the varied surface textures—rough, weathered stone versus smooth marble skin—to create a lifelike effect in his image. An enthusiastic viewer might imagine the marble surface as real skin dusted with sand. The play of light and shadow turn the figure's back into vibrant, pulsating flesh, while small cracks in the marble surface have the look of fissures in a living dermis.

List proceeds in similar fashion in his 1946 photograph of Michelangelo's "Slave," rendering manifest the implicit eroticism of this icon of Renaissance sculpture [Fig. 4]. The photograph, which List shot in the war-ravaged Munich Academy of Art, shows a plaster cast of the sculpture and emphasizes the erotic tension and the beauty of the body. The completely relaxed face of the "slave" and his closed eyes can be interpreted by the viewer as sleep, death, or rapture. This facial expression, as well as the playful gesture with which the prisoner grasps the shackle around his ribcage, are a contradiction of the motif of bondage. The

light, slanting sharply from the upper right, sweeps across the body and accentuates the missing piece of the upper arm, which stands in sharp contrast with the intact remainder of the body, on which scratches on the plaster resemble small skin lesions.

The Apollo Belvedere, on which the sculpture in the shop window was modeled, and Michelangelo's "Slave" had already become devotional objects of Western homosexual[4] culture around 1900, and replicas of them could be found in private areas of the homes of numerous homosexual men in Germany.[5] Michelangelo's sculptures also appeared as reproductions in the first homosexual magazines in Germany such as *Der Eigene*, *Die Insel*, and *Die Freundschaft*. Even beyond homosexual culture, the erotic allure of antique statues was recognized and caused much moral anxiety, so that even at the beginning of the twentieth century anyone under the age of eighteen was forbidden from entering Munich's Glyptothek.

Particularly in his photographs of sculpture, List addresses a stimulus aesthetic that places the accent on the artworks' sensual, imaginary, and erotic appropriation. His photography evokes the dream of actually touching the seductive artwork. List draws the viewer in, thus rejecting the conventional, distanced reading of "high art" that stamped as "wrong-headed" any admission of erotic appeal. Georg Friedrich Wilhelm Hegel had already warned against "pawing at the soft marble parts of the goddesses"[6]; ever since the

neoclassical period, "certain subjects and modes of presentation [were] categorically excluded" from the realm of the aesthetic.[7] This included anything that might trigger "sensual pleasure" and enjoyment and thus put disinterested appreciation of the art at risk. Instead of "disinterested appreciation," however, List explicitly advocates a stimulus aesthetic, devoting himself to areas that are excluded from the realm of high art: kitsch, popular culture, and art that "touches."

The art of antiquity is endowed with an air of desire that relates to a society and its ideal form of social conduct or accepted homosexuality. In this sense, List's erotic view of the body and his attempt at a photographic Renaissance is also a political project, namely a gender political endeavors.

I first encountered the orthopedics shop photograph in 1999 while conducting research, and it was my first purchase for the collection of the Museum für Kunst und Gewerbe Hamburg (MKG) in 2012. It made me realize that parts of List's work only became visible with a gaze trained on gender issues in the 1990s and 2000s. And it brings to light a blind spot in the collection of the MKG. Founded in the nineteenth century, until at least 1988 the collection had been devoted primarily to male, German and US photography, and for which issues of gender politics had played no role.

Every generation looks at a collection differently and collects things that may not have been deemed important by

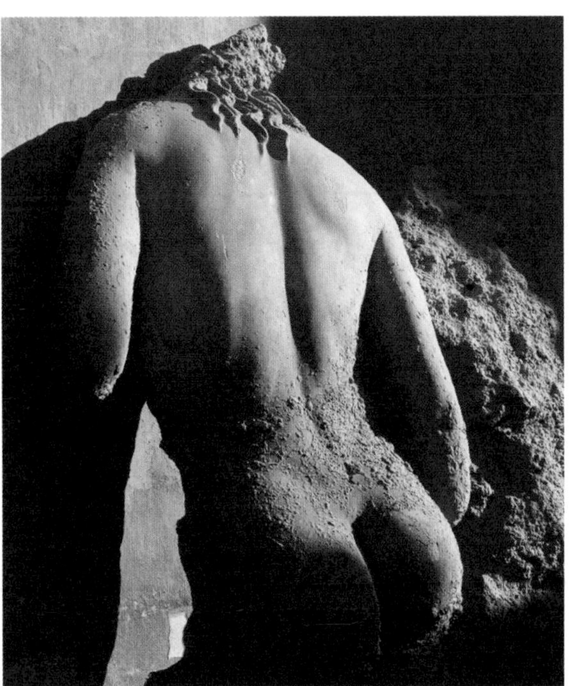

3.Herbert List, *Marmorstatue aus Antikythera,* 1937. © Herbert List—Magnum Photos / Herbert List Estate Hamburg. By permission of the Museum für Kunst und Gewerbe Hamburg.

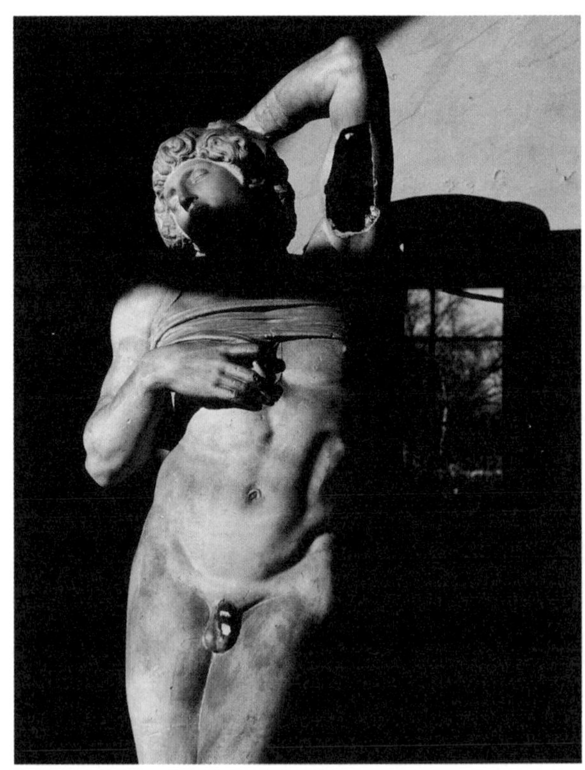

4. Herbert List, *Gipsabguss des Sklaven von Michelangelo*, 1946. © Herbert List—Magnum Photos / Herbert List Estate Hamburg / Agentur Focus.

their predecessors. Our collections today should represent more than they have done to date; they should, for example, include women photographers on an equal footing with their male counterparts and they should become more diverse overall. In this way, they can both reflect and drive change in our society.

1. I refer here to Castan's Panopticon waxwork museum in Berlin, Wiki, "Einfach Puppe!," *Das Magazin* 89 (January 1932): 6781.

2. Wiki, "Einfach Puppe!," 6779.

3. Herbert List, *Kleine Maerchen am Rande der Strasse, drei Manuskriptseiten*, Herbert List Archiv, Hamburg.

4. Note that, in light of contemporary sensitivities around usage of the term *homosexual*, I use it to describe cultural elements in times before the term *gay* became common parlance.

5. Andreas Sternweiler, "Kunst und schwuler Alltag," in *Eldorado. Homosexuelle Frauen und Männer in Berlin 1850–1950, Geschichte, Alltag und Kultur* (Berlin: Berlin-Museum, 1984), 76. Exhibition catalog.

6. Georg Friedrich Wilhelm Hegel, *Ästhetik*, ed. F. Bassenge, vol. 2, Frankfurt am Main, 1965, 14f.

7. Thomas Hecken, *Der deutschen Begriff "populäre Kultur*, 14. See in particular the chapters "Gegen Reize" and "Für Reize."

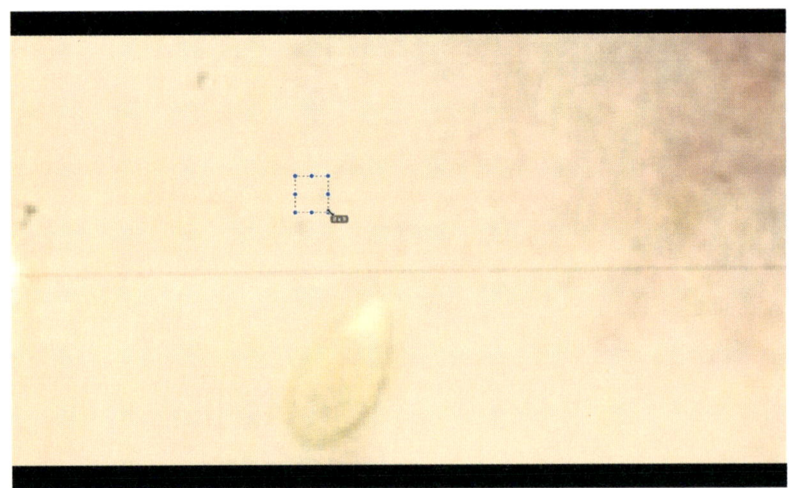

1. Doreen Mende, *Reiterating an Itinerary to Translucency (1982/2013)*, 2021. Screenshot from a research video. By permission of the author.

REITERATING AN ITINERARY TO TRANSLUCENCY*

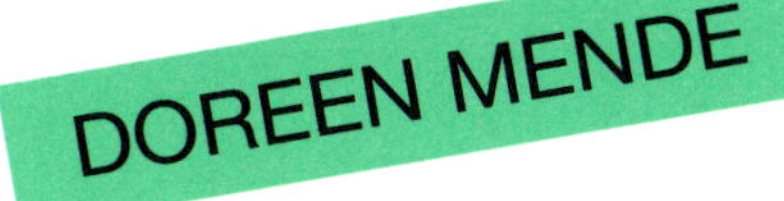

There is vulnerability. Nakedness. A myopia in vision necessitating eyeglasses. But no myopia in thought. I trust. I think. I assume. Since I wish for thought beyond vision as reason. Beyond knowledge as evidence. Because what I can hear is an echo. A traveling vibration. Sent by a delegate of solidarity. Delayed in arrival. And still arriving. From gestures, acts, encounters, misunderstandings, and promises of a political friendship. I can hear the excess of silence between the letters on this very page. Arriving in my eyes through the blurs-yet-lines of the vast pixel-grid across this screen. Across the glitches of this digital transmission: I can hear the undocumented clicks of the camera shutter reporting from the intimacy of a gaze. Yet, never fixed into a frame. Gazes without clicks accompany this political friendship—or, a geopolitical coalition installing a fabric of practices between a people's movement unfolding in the so-called Global South in Beirut, Aden, and Tunis providing locations for Palestine-in-exile: in distant proximity, during the global Cold War, a political friendship with a state-socialist union of photographers in the so-called Global East of East Berlin, or GDR—the German Democratic Republic. If there was a divided world in the North, then there was a divided world in the South. Yet, where can a delayed delegate of political friendship speak from today?

Between the East and the South.
An East-South conversation.
Intertwined in politics of memories.
While displaced into pixels.

A friendship in resonance with the call for antifascism, anti-imperialism, and anticapitalism as lubricants for a world coalition of internationalism by means of photography. A friendship departing from the early 1980s—when the world spoke in binarisms through the global Cold War. A friendship that produced photographic records that were traded as a currency for liberation—confronting and opposing the logics of primitive accumulation through images.

A friendship between the East German photographer Horst Sturm and the Palestinian photographer Youssef Khotoub, the latter one of a group of not more than twenty who refused to comply with the logic of primitive accumulation through images. He reckons with a political economy of refusal in 2011 when he says:

> I was staying in the Al Damoor near Beirut. It's a place that was full of bombardment at that time. I just got out of there and took a lot of pictures of bloodied bodies and the destruction there. French cameraman and photographer met me at that time and offered to buy my work . . . my film and pictures . . . . I refused to do so . . . and I said as usually . . . you're the only one that I won't sell my pictures . . . usually he would buy them for one hundred dollars . . . hundred dollars at that time. The Frenchman offered me three hundred dollars for the pictures of Al-Damoor and I refused to sell them to him; then he called me a stupid man for not selling.[1]

There is exhaustion.
The need for a rest.
There is more exhaustion.
Close to the limits of the human.
And to the limits of photography.

Drops of liquid have become manifest on the skin which is composed of silver bromide crystals. Washed and fixed by sodium and ammonium thiosulfates. Chemicals promise to compose a skin for embodiment that, according to Laura Marks, would emerge from the image as a vector of representation. Yet, we must avoid by all means possible the tempting spectacle of visual representation. Because, what we need for this photograph, which portrays a Lebanese-Palestinian photographer-bodyguard called Khaled, who was nicknamed "Mein Sandokan" by Sturm in 1982, and is portrayed here sitting on a bed in a hotel room of the Beau Rivage in the Ramlet al-Baïda district located near the Rock of Raouché at the Corniche of Beirut . . . . What we need for this photograph is what Tina M. Campt considers "the endlessly generative space of the *counterintuitive*."[2] This method, suggested by Campt in *Listening to Images* will be my principle to rehearse, to perform and to exercise, dear reader, the fourth iteration of not exhibiting this photograph as representational evidence of solidarity, but rather, as an itinerary to translucency. This fourth iteration of not exhibiting this photograph as a representational frame. It is another exercise of engaging with an "incurable image," as Tarek Elhaik proposed to think an image in the afterlives of colonization. Yet, I need to clarify one point: both Elhaik and Campt "open up the radical interpretative possibilities of images and state archives we are most often inclined to overlook, by engaging the paradoxical capacity of [. . .] photos to rupture the sovereign gaze of the regimes that created them . . . ."[3]

Whereas, this photograph here— of which we now see merely

pixels,
glitches,
smudges,
creases,
monochromes,

on a home-scanned .tiff file operated in Preview.

This photograph of Khaled in a room of the Beau Rivage in Beirut was taken on the other side of power: on the side of revolutionary beliefs to fight imperial modes of capitalist occupation as a method to fight settler-colonial violence within the global Cold War, yet this opposition had already started decades earlier with the French and British Mandates inscribing the coloniality of being into forms of Levantine life. The present contribution, which also is the fourth iteration of not exhibiting this photograph, is a further rehearsal of refusing to curate this photograph in the professional sense of curating: here, I mean curating as structural violence, when making public means the deformation or extraction, the ab- or misuse, likely without intention, of an entrusted souvenir of struggle, taken in a moment of quietness and vulnerability and study. Such curatorial refusal confronts the desire to expose the photograph as a shortcut, transfixed, or framed object on display.

In previous iterations, I have shared this photograph in public as

a poem,
a public reading,
an image-complex.

Always with the need to avoid, by all means, allowing this image to be absorbed and dominated by a normative / racializing / classifying / codifying gaze that cannot do otherwise than merely look at this photograph through the political economy of representation as capital, as racial transaction in a post-1989 world.

Later on.
There will be a gun.
Resting on a bed.
And a book on photography.

A manual to use the Pentacon Six professional photo camera from the GDR. This title, *Pentacon Six*, reminds me so of my father, who used the same *profi-camera* for three decades.

There is a war of independence.
Against a settler colonial state.
Amidst a global Cold War.

In which also solidarity
cannot be separated
from the binarism of that war.

Yet, we have not learned enough that the "true place of the filmmaker is in the AND," as Serge Daney once said. The *AND, A–N–D*, is not an expression of

2. Doreen Mende, *Reiterating an Itinerary to Translucency (1982/2013)*, 2021. Screenshot from a research video. By permission of the author.

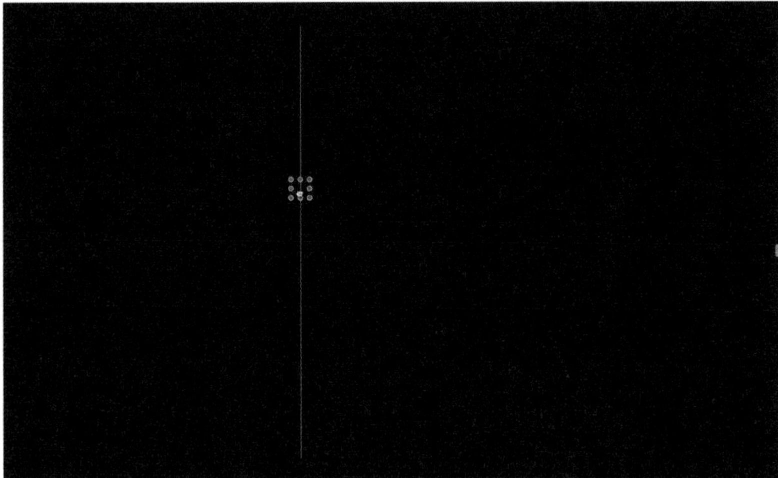

3. Doreen Mende, *Reiterating an Itinerary to Translucency (1982/2013)*, 2021. Screenshot from a research video. By permission of the author.

arithmetic summation or accumulation. But an ongoing stammering—between here *and* elsewhere, between now *and* then.

An ongoing search for a non-binary speech.

For utterances with the capacity to unsettle the categorical imperative of binarism of separating East from West from South from North: it is in our language that we can start to rehearse a non-binary articulation to counter the intuitive.

Because the intuitive too often
only acts from or reacts to
the structured normative order.

The intuitive is closer to
the unconscious as a master
than to
consciousness as emancipation.

What would such an "endlessly generative space of the *counterintuitive*" need—to emerge? Let me return to such *stammering* in which the AND between here and elsewhere, between you and me, wonders and wanders. Such stammering has occurred so many times. I remember myself stammering. I remember myself listening to my absence of words in public talks, conferences, exhibition tours, and sometimes even kitchen conversations about a politics of antifascism traveling from a one-state socialism that has German in its name as constitutive of solidarity, of a political friendship with a people in struggle. At the same time, I remember the stammering voice of a fifty-five-year-old

man from Ramallah looking at photographs like this one who cannot speak, who is searching for words, whose voice trembles, for whom words are not enough to capture

A memory without history.

I also remember a woman from Leipzig whose voice trembles from anger and distrust, from depression and betrayal by a political project of internationalism. In the current political climate, when right-wing parties are re-elected to the federal government, the stammering trembling voice opens towards an "endlessly generative space [for] the counterintuitive" that is exorbitantly populated by a quietly *past disquiet*;[4] this narrative unsettles normative structures of memory constituting the debates over the end of the white West.

Yet, instead of trembling and stammering, there is a voice continuously rehearsing a counterintuitive practice.

One has disappeared.
While the former is still waiting.

* This research video [Figs. 1, 2, 3] is the fourth iteration of a refusal to publish, to exhibit, to curate, to display, or to make public a color photograph that reads on verso, "K[h]aled. Beirut. PLO. 'My Sandokan' for My Security. At the Hotel." The color photograph, which I digitized with a home scanner into a .tiff file more than ten years ago, was taken by the noted East German press photographer Horst Sturm in a hotel room of the Beau Rivage

in the Ramlet al-Baïda district, which is located near the Rock of Raouché near the Beirut Corniche. Until the summer of 1982, the Beau Rivage accommodated international guests of the Palestine Liberation Organization (PLO); among them, on a number of occasions, was Sturm. Under the political premise of international solidarity with Palestine—to which the Union of Journalists of the German Democratic Republic contributed as much as the state press agencies of Poland, Czechoslovakia, Yugoslavia, and Algeria, as well as independent militant filmmakers and journalists from Japan, the Federal Republic of Germany, Italy, the United Kingdom, and France—Sturm traveled several times to Beirut and other locations for a series of photo-educational collaborations with the Photo Section of the PLO. Not only its history, but also its memories do not exist in any intellectual/public debates of the present.

In the early 1980s, Sturm worked together with a group of Palestinians on the development of a new visual grammar to internationalize the Palestinian cause and present it to the world by means of photography. Over several years, they would meet in Aden, Beirut, East Berlin, and Tunis for training in photography as a social-political practice. It is nothing new to remark that Yasser Arafat, the PLO's political leader at that time, was a keen photographer who understood the power of a militant image. Apart from a few women, among them Marleine Bradely, Jivira Goef-Hadadine, Yassira Kubbeh, and Leila Zakaaria who participated in the collaboration over its six-year duration, largely Palestinian men joined the educational program that Sturm conceived around the practice and theory of photography. Most of them had been trained in their teenage years as *fedayeen* (freedom fighters) during the 1970s but had been wounded in the battlefields: they replaced the gun with the camera under a political economy aiming toward a worldwide communist revolution.

In the early 1980s, the PLO was in search of a new visual grammar to speak for the Palestinian people, one that would communicate in a different way than that possible using the revolutionary image. In collaboration with photojournalists such as Sturm, and based upon the promise of trans-communal comradeship, they developed a visual grammar that shifted the revolutionary image—i.e., the motif of the almost exclusively male, heroic fighter, often portrayed with gun in hand— and transformed it into the humanitarian image, employing motifs such as the crying mother or the lonely child in a bombed-out environment. Thus, I would argue that socialist state solidarity prepared the conditions for the globalization of the humanitarian image; furthermore, I would argue that the socialist globalism of the GDR prepared the conditions for the visual grammar of humanitarian violence that still falls under the promises of socialist internationalism, while global neoliberalism lubricated the political economy of humanitariansim. This is what bothers me; it evinces the need for decolonizing solidarity.

1. Youssef Khotoub, 2011, in *Itineraries to Translucency*, a research video that forms part of Doreen Mende, "The Itinerant" (PhD thesis, Goldsmiths, University of London, 2013).
2. Tina M. Campt, *Listening to Images* (Durham: Duke University Press, 2017), 6.
3. Campt, *Listening to Images*, 5.
4. See Kristine Khouri and Rasha Salti, eds., *Past Disquiet: Artists, International Solidarity and Museums in Exile* (Warsaw: Museum of Modern Art in Warsaw, 2018).

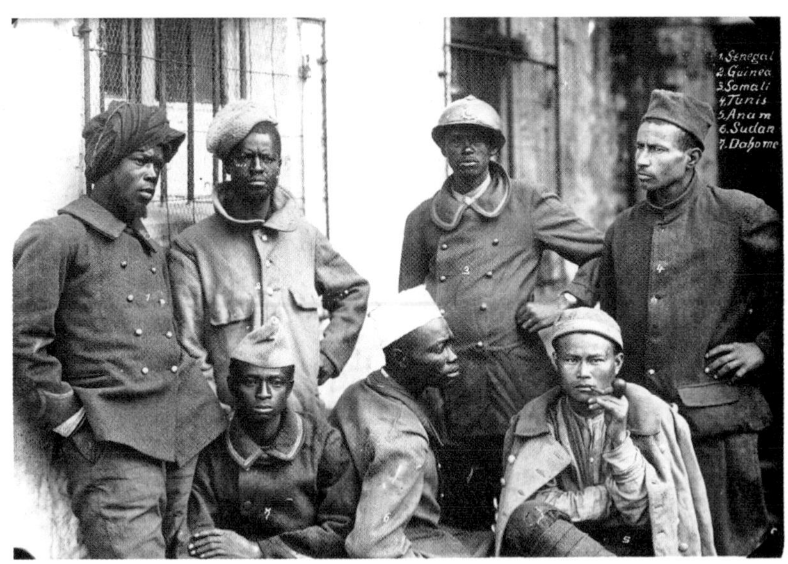

1. *Französische Kriegsgefangene* [French prisoners of war]. Source: Federal Archives of Germany (Bundesarchiv, Bild 146-1999-002-00 / Fotograf: o.Ang.).

LOOKING FOR LOST CAPTIONS, OR HOW I FOUND ANCESTRAL SOLIDARITY IN CYBERSPACE

TUAN ANDREW NGUYEN

Chapter 1: The Photograph

This is a photo taken in 1917 in a POW camp by a photographer in the German Army [Fig 1]. We can assume, by the handwritten notation on the right side of the photograph, marked carefully with a number that corresponds to each "subject" in the frame, that the subjects are colonial soldiers from these respective locations:

1. Senegal
2. Guinea
3. Somali—I am assuming this is French Somaliland, which is now known as Djibouti
4. Tunis: Tunisia
5. Annam, which is the name given to the central part of Vietnam by the French during their one hundred years of colonization
6. Sudan—I am assuming this is French Sudan, which is now part of Mali
7. Dahome—now Benin

I've looked at this image for hours and hours on end. I've zoomed in and zoomed out hundreds and hundreds of times, exploring the details of each character as well as the spaces between them.

I look at the image and I think:
What was the relationship between these men?
Did they share a common language?
Maybe they might have communicated with one another in their own creolized versions of French?
Did they share stories?
Did they protect each other on the battlefield?

Is this the image of solidarity I had been searching for?
Were these soldiers acknowledged beyond this photograph?
What were their names?
Did they ever find their way home?

Chapter 2: From Instagram to the Archive

I had been looking for images of solidarity between colonized peoples for several years. As I was scrolling through my Instagram feed a couple of years ago, I came across a black-and-white image of seven men. Black and brown soldiers. From the uniforms, it looked like it was taken during a European war.

Then I noticed a few hashtags below the image: #WWI, #colonialtroops, and a few more I can't recall. I was drawn to the Vietnamese character smoking a pipe in the corner. I screen-capped the image and would eventually lose it in the over thirty thousand images I have on my phone.

For months, my research assistant and I scoured the internet to find the source from which the image came, possibly an archive or a collection somewhere. But we always came up short.

For an exhibition, I wanted to pair this image with another image I had found. One from a personal archive of a man I befriended in Dakar, named Jean Claude Do. He is in the center of this photo [Fig. 2], taken in 1958 during a Vietnamese Lunar

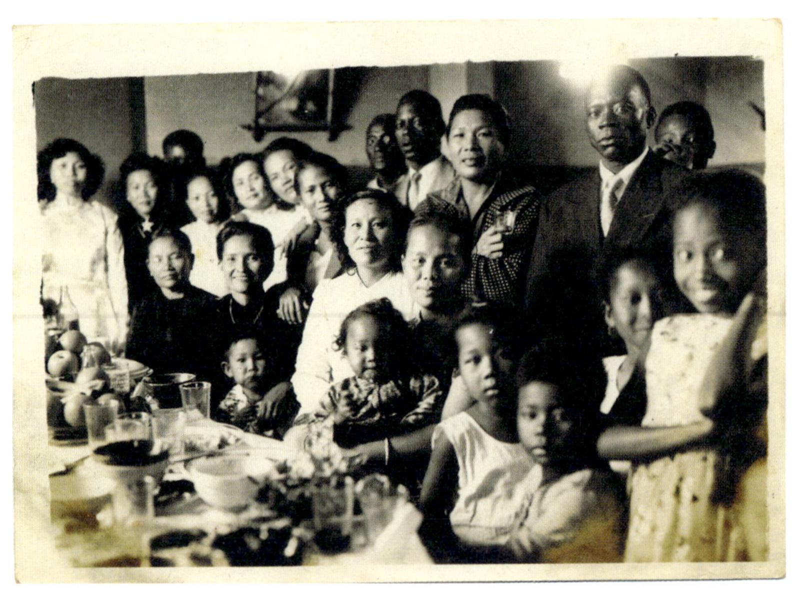

2. Tet in Dakar (seated, third left). Courtesy Jean Claude Do.

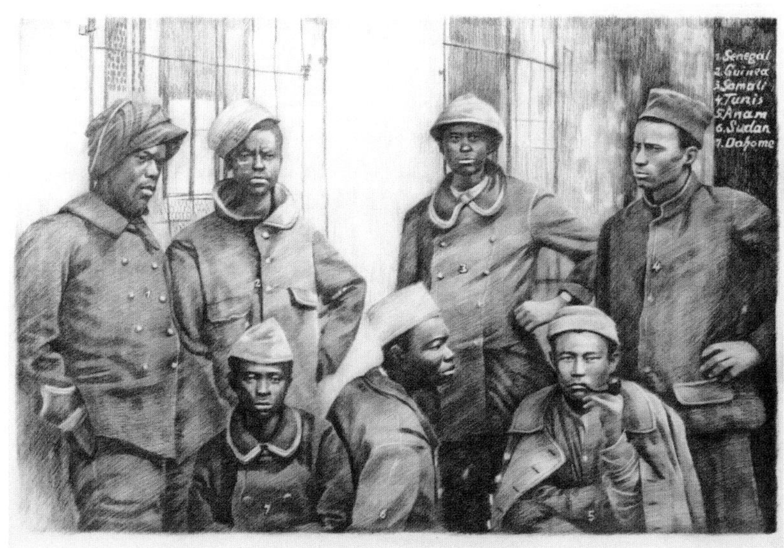

3. The author's pencil drawing of Fig. 1.

New Year celebration in Dakar, Senegal. Most of these men were colonial soldiers of the French Army who were stationed in Indochine to squash the Vietnamese uprising against the French. Their wives and children migrated to Senegal after the French were defeated in 1954.

So, lacking a high-resolution version of the World War I POW image, I decided to draw the image, using pencil on paper, at a fairly large size—approximately sixty by eighty centimeters. Of course, because the digital image I found was so low in resolution, I had to speculate on the details and the parts of the low-res image that didn't hold together when I blew it up.

When the drawing was complete [Fig. 3], I photographed it and while I was cleaning it up in Photoshop, I had a sudden thought to throw this photo-of-the-drawing-of-the-photo into the internet image search function . . . and *voilà*! Through a series of links, we found the image in the Federal Archives of Germany. The image comes up on the search with this title: *Französische Kriegsgefangene* [French prisoners of war].

On the detail page, the archive title translates to English as, "Prisoners of War: Colored Soldiers from French Africa." There is a caption at the bottom of the page that reads: "Some types of 'culture bearers' of the Entente [otherwise known as the Allies] from the last battles in Champagne. 'Culture bearers' from Senegal (1), New Guinea (2), Somali (3), Tunis (4), Annam (5), Sudan (6), Dahome (7). O.H.L."

"O.H.L." stands for *Oberste Heeresleitung* [Supreme Army Command]. The date is noted as June 1917.

I wondered about the caption. There seemed to be a lot of question marks here. Then I remembered the Wikipedia entry at the bottom of this image that remarks: "This description has been identified as biased or incorrect: racist."

So that completely undermined everything I thought I knew about this photograph. Who took the photograph? ("o.Ang," which appears where the name of the photographer should be given, is a German abbreviation for *ohne Angabe von Grunden*, which simply means that there is no information available.)

Was it taken in a POW camp?
Were they prisoners of war?
Or could they have been colonial soldiers about to go into battle?
Was this image even photographed in Germany?
Were these men posed?
Did they know each other?
Were they friends?
Why does this photograph look like a spread from a fashion magazine?
Why did they all look so cool and calm and composed?
And would these men find their way home?

Chapter 3: A Love Story

This photo [Fig. 1] was found in the personal archives of Luc Baudin after his death in 1945. Baudin, who had learned photography from years of working in his father's portrait studio in Bordeaux, later moved to Paris to start his own career. While in Paris, he came across Edward Steichen—noted as the pioneer of fashion photography—while Steichen was photographing women's gowns for designer Paul Poiret in 1911. Baudin wanted to be Steichen's assistant but Steichen dismissed him, saying that Baudin didn't quite have the eye yet.

Years afterward, during World War I, Baudin was drafted into the army but managed to find an assignment as a war photographer. He had leanings towards darker men and found interest in following the colonial soldiers of the French Army instead of photographing the French soldiers. For this he was reprimanded multiple times.

Baudin admired a soldier from Guinea named Aboubacar, who absolutely refused to be photographed. On a bright autumn day, before the colonial troops were to be deployed for battle, Baudin befriended several other soldiers and asked them to pose together with Aboubacar, for this photograph. A photo that Baudin never submitted to the military but instead kept to himself.

The discontent on the Guinean soldier's face remains evident.

Years later, having become a respected photographer in his own right, Baudin was asked to contribute a major photographic

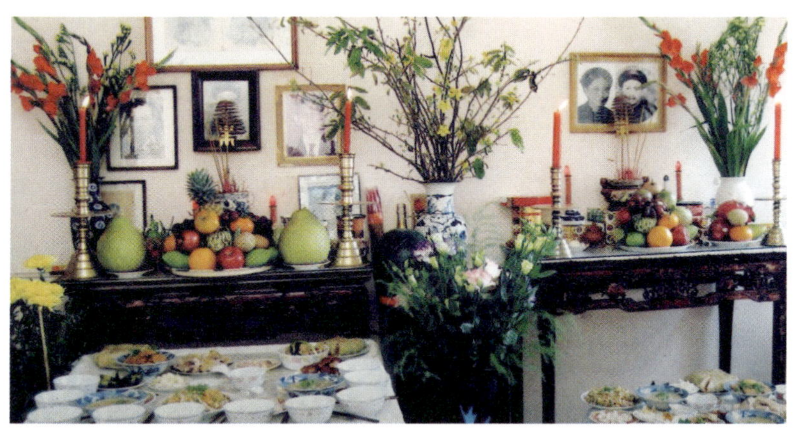

4. The author's grandmother's altar.

spread for the first issue of *Elle* magazine, which launched in 1945, but Baudin unfortunately died a couple of months before he could realize this project.

Baudin's photographic archive of over two thousand images was sold for 1,000 francs in 1954 at a local auction. It was purchased by a German collector, who would eventually gift her collection to the German Federal Archives.

Chapter 4: Reincarnation

My grandmother had not returned to her native Hanoi since 1954 when the country was split and she migrated south. On my first trip back to Vietnam in 1998, I accompanied her on her return trip to Hanoi, where she visited her sister and friends she hadn't seen in over forty years. At a friend's house, my grandmother asked me to join her in lighting incense at the altar. As my grandmother was slowly placing the incense into the burners, I took a moment to peruse the black-and-white photos of the ancestors on the altar [Fig. 4].

Almost every household here, rich or poor, has an altar with photos of ancestors for veneration [Fig. 4]. I wondered what people used on their altars before photography? Then I thought about the history of photography and how it paralleled French colonization here. How the timelines of each coincided. And how some of the first moving images in the world were shot here in Vietnam, by the Lumière brothers.

I took a moment to look at each photo on the altar. Some of the faces in the photos had been faded or disfigured by humidity and by time. My eyes then came to a photo of a group of men. A black-and-white image of seven men, black and brown men, posed together, wearing what seemed to be old military attire. An Asian man, holding a pipe, sat in the lower corner with his eyes gazing intently at the camera. This must be the woman's father or grandfather, I assumed.

That evening during dinner, I asked my grandmother's friend about the photo, and she told me this story:

A young woman in Indochine, prior to the defeat of the French in 1954, had joined the revolutionary army. Her vision was so sharp and her hand so steady that she enlisted to be a sniper. She was one of the first women to do so. On one of her missions, she had captured a French soldier. As she was interrogating him, the soldier, misunderstanding what she was saying, began to take off his clothes and while he was doing this, a photo fell out. The sniper picked up the photograph, and upon a closer look at the image, a black-and-white photo of seven prisoners of war, the woman immediately fell into a trance. And a moment later she began speaking in Wolof, the mostly widely spoken language of Senegal. The *tirailleur*—the colonial soldier of the French Army—fell into a state of complete and utter shock. The soldier was from Casamance, a coastal region in the southern part of Senegal. Although he was totally frozen and stunned to his core, he completely understood everything that the woman was saying.

One of the men in the photograph was his grandfather. When he was conscripted into the French military, his grandmother gave him the photo for good luck. The young woman, speaking in a deep and captivating voice, told the French soldier to care for the baobab tree she had planted behind her house, by the sea, years ago. Then she urged the young soldier to leave the army and find his way home as soon as he could. That he had to return to Senegal to care for his mother and grandmother. These were her last words before she fell unconscious. At which point, the young man grabbed his clothes and ran from the scene, leaving the photograph behind. When the young woman awoke, she found the photograph, then made her way home. Days later, she left the army and managed to survive the war. She kept the photograph on her altar next to the images of other ancestors

A tradition that her daughter, my grandmother's friend, had continued.

Chapter 5: Hollywood

In 2021, Rahul Kaushal, a third generation Indian American and a leading film producer in Hollywood, raised $150 million to make a film about World War I.

In the press conference, he states: "We all understand how Hollywosod has been complicit in writing an imbalanced history and memory of colonization and the roles that the colonized have played in the development of the West. It is now time that Hollywood begins to make stories that tell appropriate truths."

The epic film, titled 1918, tells the harrowing story of seven colonial soldiers who save a battalion of over eighteen thousand English and French soldiers during the last battles of World War I.

Kaushal invites filmmaker and visual artist Tuan Andrew Nguyen to bring his directorial vision to the film. This black-and-white image of seven colonial soldiers photographed in 1917, right before they are deployed for battle, is used as the official movie poster for the film—a marketing strategy noted by media critics, as well as art critics, as an industry breakthrough.

AS YOU GO. . .[1]

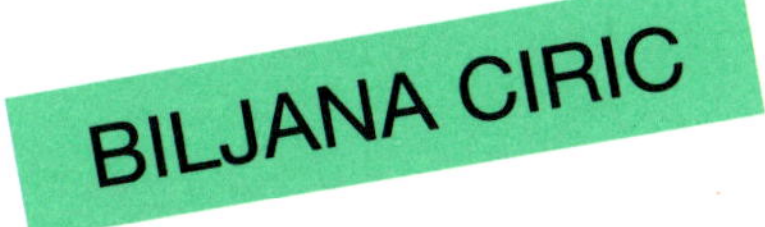

I hate taking photos. I rarely do. When I do, my images turn out to be blurry and fragmented. Whenever I am asked to take a photo for someone else, my hand when holding the camera becomes tense and starts to shake. My muscles refuse the stillness that secures a clear image. My body refuses this form of relation.

I am aware of the tension of capturing a moment and the power it could have and where this position comes from. I take it too seriously. But it is a physical reaction, more than it is an intellectual one.

Tina M. Campt asks how we might apprehend the practice of refusal in images. What kind of image can a precarious woman, defining herself as a "sub-human,"[2] produce? What kind of affective labor is necessary to produce images that propose different relationships?[3]

Close your eyes and focus on walking. Walking not as a way of getting somewhere but walking *with*; walking as sharing time and creating space for unevenness to co-exist. It is we but not we who are created of many I's. It is only we who exist in relational space with one another. Our walk is slow and long, most likely on foot, but it is not a run. It is a careful walk; we are trying to be conscious of the world under our feet, making each step lighter, acknowledging the world beneath. Our walk creates pathways that play between the invisible and visible, permanence and transience. They are built through walking *with* and thinking *with*; living marks of grass and flowers that grow back and make pathways invisible again.

We walk at different paces. Don't imagine us walking next to each other. Each of us has our own time and pace in relation to this walk, to the pandemic, to everyday struggles. Sometimes it feels that we don't walk—that we are still, and that nothing is happening. There is no sense of certainty in this walk...

It is different when only *he* walks.

While we walk, we teach each other to take only what we need. Never more than half. We twist loose knots in the grass to let the others behind us know we have been here, so "they know not to take any more."[4] If we use plants respectfully, they will flourish. If we ignore them, they will leave us.

The image you listen to[5] is fragmented because we are too close to each other. You cannot comprehend things in full; this image is cut in a rough way. It is full of gaps. It could even appear illogical to you at times. Occasionally, you might think it is a mistake.

Here the whole does not exist. It is a fiction.

We go in and out of focus. The image is constantly in the making. Many fragments. When you are close to one another, you can no longer look through the viewfinder. Fragments multiply our bodies and produce compositional views that reflect on the different textures of our skins.

It is reminiscent of cells inhabiting each other. Whenever the camera tries to capture the moment of penetration, white dots appear on the film. These white dots appear like stars, confusing our eyes, not allowing us to see what is behind them but acknowledging that something is happening.

Bruce Pascoe, an Aboriginal Australian writer and farmer, reminds us that when Indigenous Australians look at the sky, they do not look at the bright stars but rather at the dark space between them. This dark space is where Dark Emu emerges.[6]

Our eyes struggle to see it as we are so used to brightness.

At the beginning of 2020, Elon Musk's SpaceX launched 240 small satellites into space as part of its Starlink internet service; now there are around 1,300 with permission to launch a further 12,000.[7] Their brightness in the future will change how our night sky will look. Dark Emu might disappear forever.

In places like Chernobyl, radioactive energy can be captured by a camera. On photographs, this radioactivity appears as a form of light: white dots, shiny stars twinkling throughout the image.[8] We are constantly asked to step in front of light, and are exposed to different kinds: radioactivity, the flash of the camera, the light of our screens, of satellites.

The English term *opacity* comes from the French *opacité*, itself derived from Latin *opacus,* meaning darkened. Édouard Glissant reminds us that we may demand the right to opacity. That opacity is a condition for togetherness. It is a proposal to move away from the colonial relations that are embedded in us.[9] Opacity is a condition for intimacy.

Image-making comes from the touch of a finger, from pressing a button. Our bodies extend through our fingers into the world but now they browse via the splendid isolation of technology. If we extend all our fingers beyond our screens, allowing our hands to touch, we might encounter the imaginary. Such a position disrupts the hierarchy of image-making.

In a recent email conversation I had with Tala Hadid, she considered her process of filming in very close proximity to her filmed subject:

> An impossible proximity to imagine now, in our current situation. If it was always a relation of trust, then now that bond becomes even more stringent, in the sense of care and faith. I had a situation come up a few days ago, where I wanted to go with my camera to photograph something, people. And my first thought was [around] how to navigate proximity, apart from the evident introductions and then immersion into a group of people, with a camera, that would demand getting close. Is it safe for them? For me? How close can one get?[10]

You will hear the riverbed of Addis Ababa but also fish in the bathroom of a Chinese cook in the small town of Bor, in the eastern part of Serbia. You will hear the flow of water and feel a cold breeze. You will listen to the sounds of a teenage girl from Balkhash and her confusion between nationhood and community. You feel her youth spilling through her words.

You need to read the silence some of us use as a way to tell of the struggle.

You will need to hear different languages as a reminder that there are languages other than English that exist in the world.

Maybe you can see us from time to time but our connection cuts and there is a blackout.

Silence.

You will see Dark Emu and Blue Horse [*see page 108*] in that dark space.

Your freedom to imagine is regained.

Please nurture this space.

1. "As You Go. . . Roads under Your Feet, Towards the New Future" is long-term research inquiry looking at the Chinese Belt and Road Initiative and how it will alter everyday life. The inquiry is structured through partner cells situated in Addis Ababa, Almaty, Belgrade, Bor, Guangzhou, Ljubljana, and Shanghai. This writing is an experiment that attempts to im-agine inquiry through the process of image-making. I would like to thank Rasha Salti for this provocation to attempt to describe inquiry through image. I would like to acknowledge my peers, colleagues, and family members, with whom I spend time thinking through how to practice differently, including research cell participants Zdenka Badovinac, Nikita Choi, Sinkneh Eshetu, Larys Frogier, Algerim Kapar, Dragan Stojmenovic, and Robel Temesgen, as well as Fayen d'Evie, Teodor Hu, Hu Yun, and Tara McDowell.

2. Boaventura De Sousa Santos, "Future Begins Today" (lecture, Riga Biennial, 2020). https://www.rigabiennial.com/en/riboca-2/programme/event-ti-tle-boaventura-de-sousa-santos. De Sousa Santos discusses an "abyss line" that divides humanity between those who are fully dignified human beings of so-called metropolitan sociability, and sub-humans who belong to colonial sociability.

3. Tina M. Campt, *Listening to Images* (Durham: Duke University Press, 2017).

4. Robin Wall Kimmerer, *Braiding Sweetgrass: Indigenous Wisdom, Scientific Knowledge, and the Teachings of Plants* (New York: Penguin Books, 2020), 153.

5. Campt, *Listening to Images*, 8. Campt proposes listening to images as a methodology, offering an alternative to "watching" photos that manifests their transfigurations, albeit not in the form of statements of fact, nor as narratives of transit nor mobility. They are accessible instead at the haptic frequency of vibration, like the vibrato of a hum felt more in the throat than the ear.

6. To see Dark Emu in the southern hemisphere, first locate the Southern Cross. The darkness among the stars makes up the emu, which spans one of the most familiar features of the night sky: the Milky Way. Look closely at the Southern Cross to see the emu's head—a dark smudge near the bottom left of the constellation. Its neck passes between the two point-er stars, and its dark body stretches the length of our luminous galaxy. The best time to witness Dark Emu is in June. *Dark Emu: Black Seeds: Agriculture or Accident?* is also the title of a 2014 non-fiction book by Bruce Pascoe, which was republished in 2018 under a revised title: *Dark Emu: Aboriginal Australia and the Birth of Agriculture.*

7. Brian Resnick, "Astronomers Are Very Frustrated with Elon Musk's Satellites: Who Will Save the Night Sky?," *Vox*, April2021, 29, https://www.vox.com/science-and-health/22396388/space-x-elon-musk-starlink-too-bright-astronomy-stars-pollution.

8. See Alexander Kupny's photographs of Chernobyl.

9. Édouard Glissant, *Poetics of Relation* (Ann Arbor: Michigan University Press, 2010), 198.

10. Tala Hadid, in conversation with the author via email, September 2021.

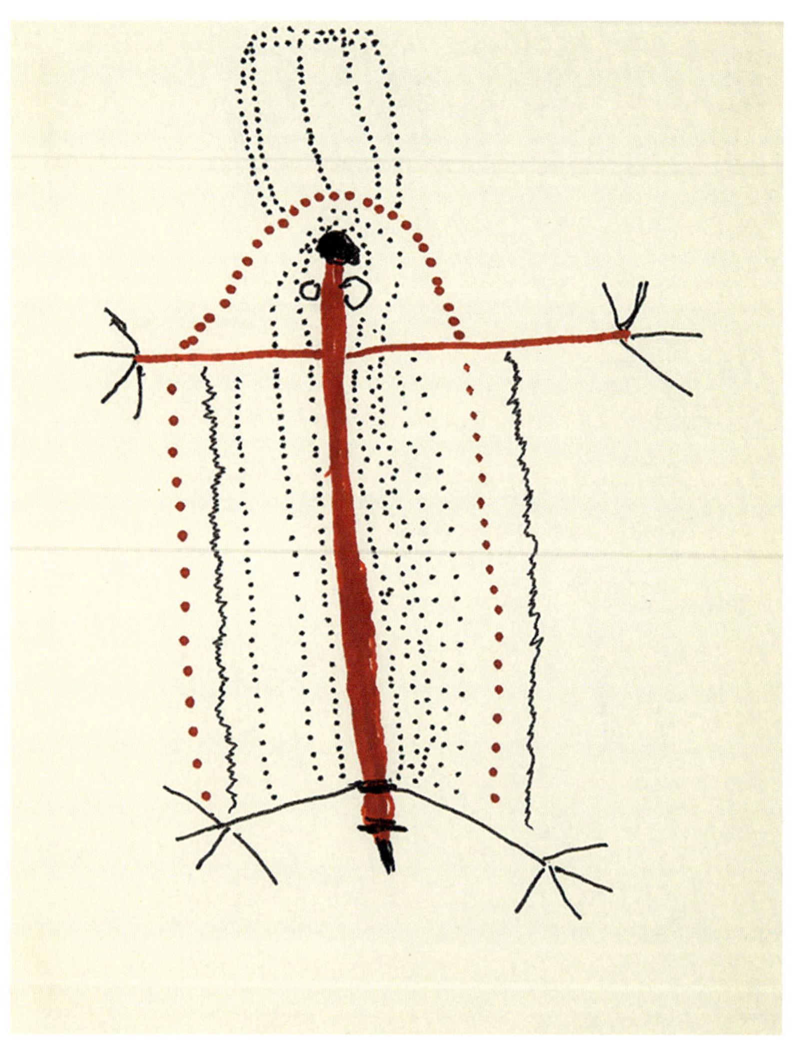

Desenho Yanomami [*Yanomami Drawing*], 1971–1975. By permission of Cortesia Galeria Vermelho and Instituto Moreira Salles [IMS].

THE CAMERA IS BROKEN

NATALIA BRIZUELA

The camera is broken. An aesthetic and political provocation to think photography otherwise. By this, I mean taking one of numerous instances when photography's foundational apparatus breaks, for in that breaking, interrogations arise immediately. Why did the camera break? When does it break? This is an interrogation of the medium, my asking which worlds cannot be delivered through it; which cannot be framed, individuated, isolated, captured, represented, reproduced, serialized; which forms of worlding and ways of understanding the human refuse photography—its camera, images, event, social encounter. One that wonders how people not subjected by the modern scopic regime see, and therefore considers what is seen when vision is decentered, when closing one's eyes is the preferred mode of experiencing, understanding, and making sense of the world to learn with it and be part of its ecology, when "images" are projections of the intermittently visible exterior reality.

The camera is broken is also a proposition, one that invites those of us who *have* been subjected by the scopic regime and its

numerous apparatuses to engage worlds and forms of life that assemble senses other than vision together with an understanding and practice of life in which photography makes little sense. When the camera is broken, we can escape the scopic regime and its construction of the modern Western episteme that places certain subjects at its center under the premise of universality, thereby justifying colonialism, racism, expansion, extraction, and accumulation.

The camera might break for multiple reasons. It malfunctions, is purposefully damaged, grows old, or is unwelcome. I am interested in the last of these possibilities because those places where the camera is not welcomed might be where the politics and history of the apparatus and the many things it does might be out of sync with the cosmologies and forms of worlding of the people who live there. For example, in a world in which techniques of listening are the core of being human; a world where the most important aspects of life are the entanglement of and relationships among visible and invisible entities; a world where the time and ability to dream is the most precious of activities because it is a way of

traveling to other realms and engaging in bodily mutation.

These broad strokes describe the Yanomami world. Of what use is photography in such a world? Can the camera ever work there? In the thick of the Amazon rainforest, does it make sense for a people whose way of being in the world and of understanding what the human *is* is "multi-perspectival,"[1] in the terminology of Brazilian anthropologists Tânia Stolze Lima and Eduardo Viveiros de Castro?

In a context like that of the Yanomami living in the rainforest, photography has historically been used in the service of ethnography and journalism as a tool to produce documents of truth and objectivity for information and study, to incorporate and assimilate Indigenous communities through faster or slower destruction. Yet the categories of objectivity and truth, anchored in the development of the modern project and linked to numerous technological developments, have neither place nor relevance in worlds like that of the Yanomami. I do not suggest the Yanomami people are incapable of using the photographic camera; indeed, they have made use of it (although they prefer the moving image), primarily to speak to non-Indigenous people in a register and a language with which they might be more willing to engage.

I am interested in thinking with the Yanomami technologies and preferred ways of visual depictions of the world to

263

engage with possibilities of "photography otherwise," of "writing with light" otherwise than through photography, and possibilities of "decolonizing thought." So, I have chosen a Yanomami drawing as the image for this errant photo album.

Claudia Andujar, a Swiss-born Romanian-Hungarian photographer who lived in Brazil starting in the mid-1950s, began spending time with the Yanomami in late 1971 when she visited their villages along the tributaries of the Catrimani River, which traverses southern Venezuela and northern Brazil. She had engaged in activist forms of photojournalism since the mid-1960s, placing images of Indigenous people in mainstream media during the early years of Brazil's military dictatorship, when large-scale projects were developed by the government to "conquer" and "tame" the Amazon rainforest so as to "include" it in Brazil's economic life via its "incorporation" through capitalist forms of productivity.

While Andujar spent time with the Yanomami, her photographs shifted—from registering and its static implications to exploring ways in which images could conjure the complex web of interconnected temporalities and forces that constitute Yanomami life. No nostalgic gaze, no insistence on Indigenous "extinction," past or present; rather, an attempt to present the forms of liveness and bonds that structure the Yanomami world. She arrived at this non-anthropological use of the camera through an accident that allowed her to complicate the human gaze in the ossifying and othering anthropological machine. A camera malfunction became an invitation to experiment with the boundaries of her instruments. Toying with low shutter speeds, wide-angle lenses, oil lamps, Vaseline on the lens, infrared film, and multiple exposures of a single frame, she complicated the long relationship of the apparatus to regulatory operations of power in which image capture and framing were tools employed in the surveillance, control, and study of bodies considered other to or outside the modern project.

In 1974, Andujar gave a group of Yanomami villagers paper and felt markers and invited them to draw scenes from their daily life, characters they deemed important, and, eventually, their cosmological universe. Over a period of three years, three hundred drawings were produced. This is one of those drawings [Fig. 1].

I could have chosen one of Andujar's photographs to interrogate the medium, since her camera broke down while she attempted to photograph the Yanomami. Why select a drawing for a discussion of photography? Because when invited to generate reflections of their world, the Yanomami produced images that are starkly different to those produced by photography—and not only because they are drawings and not photographs: the difference and distance is ontological, not medium-specific. The set of Yanomami drawings to which this one belongs shows humans, animals, and plants sharing similar shapes. They tend to present communities; when introduced, individuals are undergoing processes of transformation through time and space. The drawings offer movement and motion, which are central to the Yanomami people's world and are the basis of their cosmology. The drawings are projections of visible and invisible life, and are, as such, alive.

Like many Indigenous Peoples of the Americas, the Yanomami had a relationship to drawing and painting long before the arrival of Europeans and the violent imposition of the colonial system in the sixteenth and seventeenth centuries. Traditionally, drawing was not done on paper; rather, it was and is inscribed on bodies, vases, baskets, stones—lines and markings that speak of celebrations, belongings, alliances, and transformations. Drawings that hold the matter of the world.

Among such communities, the oral transmission of knowledge can be inscribed temporarily on physical surfaces—rocks, the ground, objects, human and non-human bodies—through drawing. Body drawings play a fundamental role in activating the interconnected relationality that is at the heart of their world paradigm. Surfaces are transformed by the lines drawn on them: like dreams, songs, and stories, the surfaces become transmitters of knowledge and times, and enable the passage or transfer of spirits and knowledge into and through the body. Among the Yanomami, drawings "jump" from one surface to another—from a human body to an object of daily use, to ritual objects.

Drawing extends further an encounter between what has been imprinted through ever-present oral and experiential transmission and the rest of the life forms of the world. For the Yanomami, drawing is indexical yet markedly different from the photographic index. It belongs to the fluid process of life and suggests a corporeal intimacy in which the drawer and that which is drawn are drawn toward each other. In drawings on the body, this is rendered literal: such markings do not freeze moments in time, do not register a body, space, or event but, rather, connect a collective interiority with an exteriority. Body and other surface drawings are not so much representations nor records as they are a road for encounters and transformations. Lines are an opening out, a way of connecting to and knowing the world. The act of drawing and its results are generative movement. Drawings, for the Yanomami, are alive; furthermore, they are precious because of their capacity to be temporary bridges. Drawings make sense because they contain ancestral knowledge and roadmaps for futurity, and because they vibrate with the vast temporal sonic universe that structures Yanomami cosmology.

I invoke sound because it, rather than vision, constitutes the mimetic impulse for the Yanomami people. As I have spent time with this image, I have been drawn to the inscription of the human's interior life as it travels to the edges of the sky through dots, as the body begins its transformation. I am also drawn to the accompanying text, which is Hiko's narration of it, without which non-Indigenous people might interpret it

otherwise. I listen to Hiko and his sharing of his knowledge through this small narrative as well as the drawing.

Is this narrative a caption? Yes? No. It points, among things, to sound, to listening practices.

Sound can be contained in part through recording but, ontologically speaking, it is unbound, unstable, traveling, mutating, and in fugue as it makes its way through space and time. Even when melodious and harmonic, sound contains the capacity for explosion, for rupture, for reorganizing the entire set of bodily relations it encounters. Sound is always a sort of disruption—of containment, of singularity, of isolation. Sounds complicate insides and outsides, reminding the listening ear that it is in relation to a vast soundscape. Sounds take the body from its apparent situatedness, pierce it, and take something of it, something invisible, elsewhere. For numerous Indigenous people in the Americas, sound cannot be possessed, accumulated or withheld, refuses individuation and constitutes what Ailton Krenak terms the collective-subject of Amerindian life.[2]

French anthropologist Bruce Albert, a longtime collaborator of the great Yanomami shaman Davi Kopenawa, links the Amazon rainforest's "sociodiversity" and "biodiversity" to show that the Yanomami people are in constant dialogue with the "multiplicity of forest voices" and that this sustained dialogue is the mark of

both forms of diversity.[3] The Yanomami acoustic knowledge is vast. Through "extreme acoustic concentration" and "permanent acoustic decodification" of the multiplicity of animal and plant sounds, the Yanomami people hunt, gather and tell the passing of time. Animal and plant sounds reveal "a complex associative web" that signals the presence of life-sustaining food, and indexes climatic and ecological events, building a sonic cartography that is both "rigid and constantly mutating." This sonic cartography is as much spatial as it is temporal, orienting and guiding bodies in time and space. The complex and rich soundscape, where the sound produced by any given body is in relation to other entities and energies, physical and natural, offers indexes of time. This vast knowledge is meant to allow for inter-species communication.

The Yanomami elders teach the younger generations to learn to recognize and mimic this dense and complex zoophonic and plantophonic ecosystem through a "quick sonic mimetism" they develop over years of study and by being in tune, *compassados* to the sonic vibrations of all that is visible and invisible. For the Yanomami people, the most sophisticated form of communication occurs when humans are able to communicate with the plants and animals they share life with in their ecosystem. The sonic cartography is drawn through two separate but related activities: on the one hand, sonic cartography is learned from the elders, who pass on the "polyglot" language system through their own learned imitation, which is reactivated and performed not only in stories shared but also in songs; on the other, the sounds made by plants, animals and insects are perceived and recognized in walks and journeys through the forest. Through this double approach, the Yanomami become cartographers, environmentalists, acoustic engineers, sound artists, and much more.

Acoustic simulation, or sonic becoming, is probably the most important education for an Indigenous person of the Yanomami region. When narrating the communications a member of a community might have had with a particular animal, they will make ample use of onomatopoeia and ideophones, the better to evoke inter-species communication. The verb *herii* is used to describe the animal and plant choruses as well as the collective singing of the Yanomami. Some members of the community become solo singers during the different feasts and celebrations because of their voices, mimicry, and repertoire of the vast forest soundscape, and they are referred to as *amoa hi*—"tree with songs." The highest communal recognition of sonic becoming is to have become a singing tree. Albert calls this the "mimetic vocation" of the Yanomami and observes that this becoming is one among other experiences that actualizes the time prior to speciation, that reactivates—or restores, to use Albert's term—the shared ontological condition of human and non-humans.[4] This onomatopoeic learning thus draws a cartography for "ontological regression," to the time before the "regrettable ontological separation" between humans and animals.[5]

Equilibrium is the result of attentive listening—*"ou voce houve a voz de todos os outros seres que habitam o planeta junto com voce, ou faz Guerra contra a vida na Terra"* [either you have the voices of all the other beings that inhabit the planet together with you, or you wage war against life on Earth].[6] Listening to rather than picturing—for which the broken camera delivers a prime opportunity—all the other beings that live alongside the human builds the connective tissue, the invisible vibratory link and connection that is a bond between a vast plurality of entities and life forms. Listening means being alive, staying alive, and keeping alive the ecosystems to which one belongs. Listening is caring. Not listening brings war—that is, a type of destructive encounter, forms of non-co-existence. Listening, through sonic mimetism and other practices, constitsutes the "ontological cosmopolitanism" whose polyglot nature is the texture of equilibrium.[7]

Attentive listening connects humans to their ecosystem and, in that connection, they are able to become guardians of the forest. Listening to all the voices of the forests, of the habitat, makes humans the "nervous terminal of what they [non-Indigenous people] call nature."[8] Living as nerve ending means the human is a hypersensitive point on the outer surface of the larger living organism called *Mapu, Pacha,* or *Gaia*—alerting the system to danger, passing on information, connecting with all the other life forms to send signals. In Indigenous cosmologies, humans are not the invaders and raiders of the planet but its defenders, they do not extract but protect, they are not the center of the universe but its outer edge, its delicate and sensitive perceptive motor. Most specifically, the human ear and its education to become acutely perceptive to its surroundings is one of the most important forms of participating in collective life and world-making practices. The human is not constituted as a subject of reason, as a body of and in sight, but as a quasi-silent noise sensor, pure eardrum.

1. See Tânia Stolze Lima, "O dois e seu múltiplo: reflexoes sobre o perspectivismo em uma cosmologia tupi," *Mana* 2, no. 2 (1996): 21–47; Eduardo Viveiros de Castro, "Os pronomes cosmológicos e o perspectivismo ameríndio," *Mana* 2, no. 2 (1996): 115–144; and "Exchanging Perspectives: The Transformation of Objects into Subjects in Amerindian Cosmologies," *Common Knowledge* 10, no. 3 (2004): 463–484.

2. Ailton Krenak, "A Potencia do Sujeito Coletivo," interview by Jailson de Souza e Silva, *Periferias* 1 (2018), https://revistaperiferias.org/materia/a-potencia-do-sujeito-coletivo-parte-i/.

3. Bruce Albert, "La forêt polyglotte," in *Le grand orchestre des animaux* (Paris: Fondation Cartier, 2016), 91–99.

4. Albert, "La forêt polyglotte," 97. *"Vocation mimétique"* in the original.

5. Albert, "La forêt polyglotte," 97.

6. Ailton Krenak, "A máquina de fazer coisas," in *A vida não é útil* (São Paulo: Companhia das Letras, 2020), e-book.

7. Albert, "La forêt polyglotte," 99.

8. Ailton Krenak, "Sonhos para adiar o fim do mundo," in *A vida não é útil.*

CONTRIBUTORS

Nancy Adajania is a Bombay-based cultural theorist and curator. She has curated a number of research-based exhibitions including the Nelly Sethna retrospective *The Unpaved, Crusty, Earthy Road*, Chatterjee & Lal with Cymroza Art Gallery, Bombay (2021); *Zigzag Afterlives: Film Experiments from the 1960s and 1970s in India*, Camden Art Centre, London (2020); the Sudhir Patwardhan retrospective *Walking Through Soul City*, NGMA, Bombay with the Guild Art Gallery (2019), and *Counter-Canon, Counter-Culture: Alternative Histories of Indian Art*, Serendipity Arts Festival, Goa (2019). Adajania has proposed several new theoretical models through her writing on subaltern art, media art, public art, transcultural art, and biennale culture from the Global South. She conceptualized and led the online curatorial workshop "Once Upon a Cultural Famine: A Curatorial Thought Experiment" for the Kochi Biennale Foundation (2021), and served as the juror for the Video/Film/New Media fellowship cycle of the Akademie Schloss Solitude between 2015 and 2017.

Akinbode Akinbiyi lives and works in Berlin. He has been a freelance photographer since 1977 and cofounded UMZANZSI, a cultural center in Clermont Township in Durban, South Africa, in 1993. Akinbiyi's primary focus is large and sprawling megacities, in which he wanders and meanders the highways and byways in an attempt to understand and deeply engage with the modern metropolis. His work has primarily concerned the African cities of Lagos, Cairo, Kinshasa, and Johannesburg, but also reflects the cities of Khartoum, Addis Ababa, Dakar, Bamako, São Paulo, and Chicago, among others. Recent exhibitions have been staged at documenta 14, in Athens and Kassel (2017), FotoFest Biennial, Houston (2020), steirischer herbst, Graz (2020), Martin-Gropius-Bau, Berlin (2020), and Västerås konstmuseum, Västerås (2020–21).

A theorist, film essayist, and curator, **Ariella Aïsha Azoulay** is Professor of Modern Culture and Media and Comparative Literature at Brown University. Her books include *Potential History—Unlearning Imperialism* (Verso, 2019), *Civil Imagination: The Political Ontology of Photography* (Verso, 2012), *The Civil Contract of Photography* (Zone Books, 2008), and *From Palestine to Israel: A Photographic Record of Destruction and State Formation, 1947–1950* (Pluto Press, 2011). She has made several films, including *Undocumented: Unlearning Imperial Plunder* (2019) and *Civil Alliances, Palestine, 47–48* (2012), and her exhibitions include *Errata* (Tapiès Foundation, 2019 and HKW, Berlin, 2020) and *Enough! The Natural Violence of New World Order*, (F/Stop photography festival, Leipzig, 2016).

Rizvana Bradley is Assistant Professor of Film and Media at the University of California Berkeley and was a Helena Rubinstein Critical Studies Fellow at the Whitney Museum of American Art in New York. Her monograph, *Anteaesthetics: Black Aesthesis and the Critique of Form*, a recipient of the Creative Capital and the Andy Warhol Foundation Arts Writers Grant, is forthcoming with Stanford University Press. Previously, she was Assistant Professor in the History of Art and African American Studies at Yale, Assistant Professor of Women's, Gender and Sexuality Studies at Emory University, and a Visiting

Research Fellow in the History of Art Department at University College London. Bradley has published articles in *Women and Performance: A Journal of Feminist Theory, TDR: The Drama Review, Discourse: Journal for Theoretical Studies in Media and Culture, Rhizomes: Cultural Studies in Emerging Knowledge, Black Camera: An International Film Journal*, and *Film Quarterly*, and has curated a number of academic arts symposia, including events at the British Film Institute, London, the Serpentine Gallery, London, and the Stedelijk Museum of Art, Amsterdam.

Natalia Brizuela is Class of 1930 Chair of the Center for Latin American Studies at the University of California Berkeley, where she is a Professor of Film & Media and Spanish & Portuguese. She specializes in modern and contemporary visual culture, art, film, media, literature, and critical theory from Latin America, with a particular focus on experimental practices that bridge aesthetics and politics. She is the author of *Fotografía e Imperio* (2012), *Depois da fotografia* (2014), *The Matter of Photography in the Americas* (2018), and *La cámara como método* (2021), among others. She has curated *No sé. (El templo del sol)* (2014), *Photography at its Limits* (2019), and is currently preparing *How to Change Everything* (2022). Together with Victoria Collis-Buthelezi and Leticia Sabsay, Brizuela co-edits *Critical South* at Polity and participates in other collective editorial practices in the Global South. She is currently completing a book on the refusal of time.

Antawan I. Byrd is a Weinberg Fellow in Art History at Northwestern University and an associate curator of Photography & Media at the Art Institute of Chicago, where he curated *Mimi Cherono Ng'ok: Closer to the Earth, Closer to My Own Body* (2021), and co-edited *The People Shall Govern! Medu Art Ensemble and the Anti-Apartheid Poster*, based on an exhibition he co-curated in 2019. Byrd co-curated the 2nd Lagos Biennial of Contemporary Art (2019) and *Kader Attia: Reflecting Memory* at Northwestern's Block Museum of Art (2017), and was an associate curator for the 10th Bamako Encounters, Biennale of African Photography (2015). From 2009 to 2011, he was a Fulbright fellow and curatorial assistant at the Centre for Contemporary Art, Lagos. His writing has appeared in *Sanlé Sory: Volta Photo* (2018) and *Recent Histories: Contemporary African Photography and Video Art* (2017), as well as recent issues of *Aperture* and *FOAM*.

Eduardo Cadava is Philip Mayhew Professor of English at Princeton University. He specializes in American literature and culture, comparative literature, media technologies, literary and political theory, and issues of citizenship and human rights. He has written extensively on literature, philosophy, photography, architecture, music, democracy, war, race, and slavery. He is the author of *Words of Light: Theses on the Photography of History* (Princeton University Press, 1998), *Emerson and the Climates of History* (Stanford University Press, 1997), and, with Fazal Sheikh, of *Fazal Sheikh: Portraits* (Steidl, 2010). His most recent book, *Paper Graveyards*, was published by MIT Press in 2021. He has also co-edited *Who Comes After the Subject?* (Routledge, 1991), *Cities Without Citizens* (The Slought Foundation and the Rosenbach Museum, 2004), a special issue of the *South Atlantic Quarterly* entitled *And Justice for All?: The Claims of Human Rights* (Duke University Press, 2004), and *The Itinerant Languages of Photography* (Princeton University Art Museum and Yale University Press, 2013).

Tina M. Campt is Owen F. Walker Professor of Humanities and Modern Culture and Media at Brown University, Providence, Rhode Island. Campt is a black feminist theorist of visual culture and contemporary art. She leads the Black Visualities Initiative at the Cogut Institute for Humanities and is the founding convenor of the Practicing Refusal Collective. She is the author of four books: *Other Germans: Black Germans and the Politics of Race, Gender and Memory in the Third Reich* (University of Michigan Press, 2004), *Image Matters: Archive, Photography and the African Diaspora in Europe* (Duke University Press,

2012), *Listening to Images* (Duke University Press, 2017), and, most recently, *A Black Gaze* (MIT Press, 2021).

Biljana Ciric is an interdependent curator. She was a co-curator of the 3rd Ural Industrial Biennale for Contemporary Art, Yekaterinburg, and curator in residency at the Kadist Art Foundation, Paris, in 2015; and a research fellow at Henie Onstad Kunstsenter, Høvikodden in 2016. Ciric was nominated for the ICI Independent Vision Curatorial Award in 2012. In 2018, she founded the educational platform What Could/ Should Curating Do and edited *From the History of Exhibitions Towards the Future of Exhibition Making: China and Southeast Asia* (2019). She is currently developing two projects: *Repetition as a Gesture Towards Deep Listening* for the first Trans-Southeast Asian Triennial in Guangzhou, and the long-term project *As you go . . . the roads under your feet*, which reflects on China's Silk Road Initiative while looking towards its future and changes to local living rituals, aesthetics, and connectivity. Ciric is also undertaking a practice-based PhD in Curatorial Practice at Monash University, Melbourne.

Robin Coste Lewis was the poet laureate of Los Angeles from 2017 to 2020. In 2015, her debut poetry collection, *Voyage of the Sable Venus* won the National Book Award in poetry—the first time a poetry debut by an African American had ever won the prize in the National Book Foundation's history, and the first time any debut had won the award since 1974. In 2018, the Museum of Modern Art commissioned Lewis and Kevin Young to write a series of poems to accompany Robert Rauschenberg's drawings in *Thirty-Four Illustrations of Dante's Inferno*. Lewis is currently at work on two new collections, *To the Realization of Perfect Helplessness and Prosthetic*, both of which are forthcoming from Knopf. Lewis's current research focuses on the intersecting production histories of early African American poetry and photography, for

which she also received the Anne Friedberg Memorial Grant from the University of Southern California's Visual Studies Research Institute.

Frieda Ekotto is Lorna Goodison Collegiate Professor of Afroamerican and African Studies, Comparative Literature and Francophone Studies at the University of Michigan, Ann Arbor. Her early work involves an interdisciplinary exploration of the interactions among philosophy, law, literature, and African cinema. She is the author of eleven books and numerous book chapters, as well as articles in various literary journals. She is currently working on LGBTQ+ issues, with an emphasis on West African cultures within Africa as well as in Europe and the Americas. She received the Nicolàs Guillèn Prize for Philosophical Literature in 2014, and in 2015 she was awarded the Benezet Award for excellence in her field. In 2016, she was awarded the John H. D'Arms Faculty for Distinguished Graduate Mentoring in the Humanities at the University of Michigan. In 2018, she was awarded an honorary degree from Colorado College.

Ariel Goldberg's publications include *The Estrangement Principle* (Nightboat Books, 2016) and *The Photographer* (Roof Books, 2015). They are a 2020 Andy Warhol Foundation Arts Writers Grant recipient for their book in progress *Just Captions: Ethics of Trans and Queer Image Cultures*. Goldberg's writing has most recently appeared in *Afterimage, e-flux, Artforum*, and *Art in America*. Their research and writing has been supported by the New York Public Library, the Franklin Furnace Fund, SOMA in Mexico City, and Smith College. Goldberg has been a curator at the Poetry Project and the Leslie-Lohman Museum of Art. They teach across multiple colleges and universities in the New York area.

Artists and filmmakers **Joana Hadjithomas and Khalil Joreige** investigate the fabrication of images and representations, the construction of imaginaries, and the writing of contemporary history. Their work builds thematic and formal links between photography, video, performance, installation, sculpture, and documentary and fiction film. Films such as *Memory Box* (2021), *The Lebanese Rocket Society* (2012), *Je veux voir* (2008), and *A Perfect Day* (2005) trace stories of the invisible and absent, from the missing people of the Lebanese Civil War to forgotten space projects and geological and archaeological cores. These works have been shown and awarded in major international festivals, and in 2017, they received the Marcel Duchamp Prize for their project *Unconformities*. Exhibitions of their work have been staged at the Centre Pompidou and Jeu de Paume, Paris; the Haus der Kunst, Munich; the Victoria and Albert Museum, the British Museum, and Whitechapel Gallery, London; the Hamburger Bahnhof, Berlin; the Sharjah Art Foundation; and Home Works Forum, Beirut, among others. Their numerous film retrospectives have been presented at the Flaherty Seminar, New York; the Mori Art Museum, Tokyo; the International Film Festival of Gijon; the Harvard Film Archive, Cambridge; the Lincoln Center, New York; the Locarno Festival; and the Museum of Modern Art, New York, among others.

Tala Hadid is a photographer and filmmaker. Her films have been screened at festivals around the world, including at the Berlin and Venice International Film Festivals, as well as at the Museum of Modern Art and the Lincoln Center, New York; the Walker Arts Center, Minneapolis; the Cinémathèque Française, Paris; and the Smithsonian Museum and the National Museum of Women in the Arts, Washington, DC. Her films have received numerous awards, including an Academy Award for her short film *Your Dark Hair Ihsan* (2005). Hadid's film, *House in the Fields* (2017), was an Official Selection of the 67th Berlinale and nominated for the Glashütte Documentary Award. Her work is part of the Ruben/Bentson Moving Image Collection at the Walker Art Center, and Hadid is a member of the Academy of Motion Picture Arts and Sciences.

Kapwani Kiwanga is a Franco-Canadian artist who lives and works in Paris. She studied Anthropology and Comparative Religion at McGill University in Montreal, and Art at the École des Beaux-Arts de Paris. In 2020, Kiwanga received the Prix Marcel Duchamp. She was also the winner of the Frieze Artist Award and the annual Sobey Art Award in 2018. She is represented by Galerie Jérôme Poggi, Paris; Goodman Gallery, Johannesburg, Cape Town, and London; and Galerie Tanja Wagner, Berlin. Kiwanga's work traces the pervasive impact of power asymmetries by placing historic narratives in dialogue with contemporary realities, the archive, and tomorrow's possibilities. Her work is research-driven, instigated by marginalized or forgotten histories, and articulated across a range of materials and mediums including sculpture, installation, photography, video, and performance. Kiwanga co-opts the canon; she turns systems of power back on themselves, in art and in parsing broader histories.

Léopold Lambert is the founder and editor-in-chief of *The Funambulist*, a bimestrial print and online magazine dedicated to the politics of space and bodies. He is the author of four books: *Weaponized Architecture: The Impossibility of Innocence* (dpr-barcelona, 2012), *Topie Impitoyable: The Corporeal Politics of the Cloth, the Wall, and the Street* (punctum books, 2015), *La politique du bulldozer: La ruine palestinienne comme projet israélien* [*Bulldozer Politics: The Palestinian Ruin as an Israeli Architectural Project*] (B2 Éditions, 2016), and *Etats d'urgence: Une histoire spatiale du continuum colonial français* [*States of Emergency: A Spatial History of the French Colonial Continuum*] (Premiers matins de novembre, 2021).

Miguel A. López is a Peruvian writer and researcher. His work investigates collaborative dynamics and transformations in the understanding of and engagement with Latin American politics, and feminist re-articulations of art and culture in recent decades. He has curated *Cecilia Vicuña, A Retrospective Exhibition*, Witte de With, Rotterdam (2019); *Social Energies/Vital Forces. Natalia Iguiñiz: Art, Activism, Feminism (1994–2018)*, ICPNA, Lima (2018); and *Teresa Burga: Structures of Air* (with Agustín Pérez Rubio), MALBA, Buenos Aires (2015), among others. His publications include *Ficciones disidentes en la tierra de la misoginia* [*Dissident Fictions in the Land of Misogyny*] (Pesopluma, 2019) and *The Words of Others: León Ferrari and Rhetoric in Times of War* (with Ruth Estévez and Agustín Diez Fischer, REDCAT and JRP-Ringier, 2017). He was the editor of *Giuseppe Campuzano. Saturday Night Thriller y otros escritos, 1998–2013*, a collection of writings by drag queen Giuseppe Campuzano, published by Estruendomudo in 2013. Until 2020, he was co-director and chief curator of TEOR/éTica, a center for exhibitions, research, and publications on Central American and Caribbean contemporary art in San José, Costa Rica.

Doreen Mende is a curator, theorist, and exhibition-maker, and is Head of the Research Department at the Staatliche Kunstsammlungen Dresden, prior to which she was Professor of the Curatorial/Politics seminar. She is Head of the CCC Research Master and PhD-Forum of the Visual Arts Department at HEAD–Genève, and Co-Director of the Harun Farocki Institut in Berlin. In her independent curatorial work, she has been conceptualizing the need for archival metabolism, geopolitics of exhibiting, navigational practices and vocabularies for decolonizing socialism through various collaborations, essayistic texts and peer-reviewed articles. Funded by the Swiss National Science Foundation, she initiated the research constellation entangledinternationalism.org (2019–2024) in collaboration with dasch.swiss, Exit Frame Collective, Vanabbe Museum, Haus der Kulturen der Welt (HKW), and Kunstverein Leipzig, among others. Recent texts

have been published with Sternberg Press, Archive Books, *e-flux journal*, Akademie der Künste Berlin, and the *Oxford Handbook of Visual Communist Cultures*.

Maaza Mengiste is the author of *The Shadow King* (2019), which was shortlisted for the 2020 Booker Prize, and a recipient of the American Academy of Arts & Letters Award in Literature, as well as an LA Times Books Prize finalist. It was named a Best Book of 2019 by the *New York Times*, NPR, *Time*, *Elle*, and other publications. *Beneath the Lion's Gaze* (2010), her debut work, was selected by *The Guardian* as one of the 10 Best Contemporary African Books.

Samaneh Moafi is Senior Researcher at Forensic Architecture (FA), a research agency at Goldsmiths, University of London, that investigates human rights violations with and on behalf of communities and individuals affected by police brutality, border regimes, and environmental violence. Moafi provides conceptual oversight across projects and, in particular, oversees the Centre for Contemporary Nature, where FA develops new evidentiary techniques for bringing accountability to environmental destructions. She earned her PhD from the Architectural Association School of Architecture with a thesis on the contemporary history of state-initiated mass housing in Iran and the gender roles and class identities it informed.

Bonaventure Soh Bejeng Ndikung is an independent curator, author, and biotechnologist. He is founder and Artistic Director of SAVVY Contemporary in Berlin, Artistic Director of sonsbeek20–24, and the 13th Bamako Encounters 2022. Ndikung was the curator-at-large for Adam Szymczyk's documenta 14 in Athens, Greece and Kassel in 2017; a guest curator of the Dak'Art biennale in Dakar, Senegal in 2018; and Artistic Director of the 12th Bamako Encounters in 2019. Together with the Miracle Workers Collective, he curated the Finland Pavilion at the Venice Biennale in 2019. He is currently a professor in the Spatial Strategies MA program at the Weissensee Academy of Art, Berlin. In 2023 he will take on the role of Director at Haus der Kulturen der Welt (HKW), Berlin.

Tuan Andrew Nguyen's practice explores strategies of political resistance enacted through counter-memory and post-memory. Extracting and reworking narratives via history and supernaturalisms is an essential part of Nguyen's video works and sculptures, in which fact and fiction are both held accountable. Nguyen co-founded the Propeller Group in 2006, a platform for collectivity that situates itself between an art collective and an advertising company. Accolades for the group include the grand prize at the 2015 Internationale Kurzfilmtage Winterthur and a Creative Capital award for their video project *Television Commercial for Communism*. Besides a major traveling retrospective that began at the MCA Chicago, the collective has participated in international exhibitions including *The Ungovernables*, New Museum Triennial, New York (2012), *Made in L.A.*, Los Angeles (2012), *Prospect.3*, New Orleans (2014), and the Venice Biennale (2015).

Uzma Z. Rizvi is Associate Professor of Anthropology and Urban Studies at the Pratt Institute, New York. Rizvi's work intentionally interweaves archaeology with cultural criticism, philosophy, critical theory, art, and design. She is the curator (with Murtaza Vali) of the National Pavilion for KSA for the Venice Architecture Biennale and has been a lead tutor (with Murtaza Vali) of Art Dubai's seminar program, Campus Art Dubai (CAD) since 2014. In 2016, she directed (with Amal Khalaf) Art Dubai's Global Art Forum (GAF 10), *The Future Was___*. In 2018, Rizvi was on the curatorial team as Head of the Department of Mapping Margins for the Fikra Graphic Design Biennial 01: Ministry of Graphic Design, Sharjah. With nearly two decades of work on decolonizing methodologies, intersectional and feminist strategies, and transdisciplinary approaches, Rizvi's work has intentionally pushed disciplinary limits, and demanded ethical decolonial praxis at all levels of engagement, from teaching to research.

Esther Ruelfs has been the Head of the Photography and New Media Department at the Museum für Kunst und Gewerbe Hamburg since 2012. She studied Art History and Philosophy, writing her doctoral thesis on the photographer Herbert List. She is interested in the connections between historical and cultural contexts and contemporary issues of social relevance. Recent publications and exhibition catalogues include *Amateur Photography: From Bauhaus to Instagram* (2019), *Machen Sie mich schön, Madame d'Ora* [*Make Me Beautiful, Madame d'Ora*] (2018), *When We Share More Than Ever* (2015), *Den Körper aktivieren. Mortifikation und Verlebendigung bei Herber List* [*Activate the Body: Mortification and Vitalization in Herbert List*] (2015), *ReVision: The Photography Collection at the Museum für Kunst und Gewerbe Hamburg* (2016), and *Fette Beute. Reichtum zeigen* [*Rich Pickings: Photography and Wealth*] (2014). She is currently at work on the project *Mining Photography: On the Ecological Footprint of Photography*.

Elias Sanbar is a writer. Born in Palestine, he studied in Lebanon and France before teaching at universities in Paris and at Princeton. He is the founder and moderator of the *Revue d'études palestiniennes* (Éditions de Minuit, 1981–2005) and a negotiator in the Israeli-Palestinian peace talks. Sanbar has also collaborated with several filmmakers, among them Simone Bitton and Jean-Luc Godard, and has published numerous works on the photographic image. He has translated the poetry of Mahmoud Darwish into French (*Actes Sud*). From 2005 to 2021, Sanbar served as the Ambassador of Palestine to UNESCO.

Andreas Schlaegel is a critic and artist based in Berlin. Since the late 1990s, he has written on contemporary art for international art magazines such as *Flash Art*

International, Frieze, and *Kunstkritikk*, as well as for publications for the UCLA Hammer Museum, Los Angeles; MUSAC, Leon; Aspen Museum, Colorado; Schirn Kunsthalle, Frankfurt/M; Kunsthalle Düsseldorf; TBA21, Vienna, and the Julia Stoschek Collection, Berlin/Düsseldorf. His artistic practice centers on the development of collaborative formats, which includes collaborations with artists such as Keren Cytter, John Bock, Gelitin, Paolo Chiasera, Nine Budde, and Melou Vanggaard. His ongoing musical projects include the Art Critics Orchestra with Raimar Stange and Micz Flor, and Die!Landschaft with Manfred Peckl. He teaches the History and Theory of Photography at HfG Offenbach.

Nicholas Tammens is Assistant Curator at the Kunstverein Hamburg. He is the founder of 1856, a curated program of exhibitions and events at a workers' union parliament in Melbourne, Australia, that focuses on conditions of labor and cultural production. He has produced exhibitions with artists such as Jef Geys (Yale Union, 2018), Patricia L. Boyd (1856, 2018), Fred Lonidier (1856, 2017), and B. Wurtz (2015), and presented talks at WIELS, Brussels (2019), and the Kunsthalle Zurich (2019). His writing has appeared in *Mousse Magazine* and the *May Revue*.

Françoise Vergès is a feminist theorist, educator, curator, and the cofounder of the collective Decolonize the Arts and of the free and open university Decolonizing the Arts. She has produced documentary films on Maryse Condé and Aimé Césaire, and served as a project advisor for the Triennale de Paris (2011) and documenta 11 (2002). Vergès's books include *The Wombs of Women* (2020) and *Monsters and Revolutionaries* (1999), among others.

BIBLIOGRAPHY

LITERATURE

Adajania, Nancy. "'Obey the Little Laws and Break the Big Ones': A Life in Feminism." In *Arc Silt Dive: The Works of Sheba Chhachhi*, edited by Kumkum Sangari. New Delhi: Tulika Books, 2016.

Alloa, Emmanuel, ed., *Penser l'image III. Comment lire les images?* Paris: Les presses du réel, 2017.

———. *Penser l'image*. Paris: Les presses du réel, 2010.

Appadurai, Arjun. ed., *The Social Life of Things: Commodities in Cultural Perspective*. Cambridge and New York: Cambridge University Press, 1986.

Arendt, Hannah. *Eichmann in Jerusalem: A Report on the Banality of Evil*. New York: The Viking Press, 1963.

———. *The Origins of Totalitarianism*. New York: Harcourt, Brace and Company, 1951.

Azoulay, Ariella. *Potential History: Unlearning Imperialism*. London and New York: Verso, 2019.

———. "Unlearning Decisive Moments in Photography." FotoMuseum Winterthur, 2018, https://www.fotomuseum.ch/en/explore/still-searching/series/155238_unlearning_decisive_moments_of_photography.

———. *Civil Imagination: A Political Ontology of Photography*. London and New York: Verso, 2012.

———. *From Palestine to Israel: A Photographic Record of Destruction and State Formation, 1947–1950*. London: Pluto Press, 2011.

———. "Photography." *Mafte'akh* 2e (Winter 2011): 65–80.

———. *The Civil Contract of Photography*. New York: Zone Books, 2008.

Al-Azzawi, Fadhil. "In Captivity." *PROMETEO: Latinoamerican Poetry Magazine* 84–85 (July 2008).Bailly, Jean-Christophe. *L'Imagement*. Paris: Fiction et Cie/Seuil, 2020.

Baker, George. "Photography's Expanded Field." *October* 114 (2005): 120–40.

Barthes, Roland. "The Reality Effect." In *The Rustle of Language*. New York: Hill and Wang, 1986.

———. "The Rhetoric of the Image." In *The Responsibility of Forms: Critical Essays on Music, Art, and Representation*. New York: Hill and Wang, 1985.

———. *Camera Lucida: Reflections on Photography*. New York: Hill and Wang/Noonday Press, 1981.

Batchen, Geoffrey. *Forget Me Not: Photography and Remembrance*. New York: Princeton Architectural Press, 2006.

Baudelaire, Charles. "The Salon of 1859," translated by P. E. Charvet. In *Selected Writings on Art and Literature*. London: Penguin Books, 1992, 285–324.

Beckwith, Naomi, ed., *The Propeller Group*. Chicago: Museum of Contemporary Art Chicago, 2016.

Benjamin, Walter. *The Arcades Project*, translated by Howard Eiland and Kevin McLaughlin. Cambridge: Belknap Press of Harvard University Press, 1999.

———. *Charles Baudelaire: A Lyric Poet in the Era of High Capitalism*, translated by Harry Zohn. London: New Left Books, 1973.

———. *Gesammelte Schriften*, edited by Rolf Tiedemann and Hermann Schweppenhäuser, 7 vols. Frankfurt am Main: Suhrkamp Verlag, 1974–1989.

———. *Illuminations: Essays and Reflections*, edited by Hannah Arendt, translated by Harry Zohn. New York: Harcourt, Brace and World, 1935 (1968).

———. "Central Park," translated by Lloyd Spencer. *New German Critique* 34 (winter 1985): 32–58.

———. *Origin of German Tragic Drama*, translated by John Osborne. London: New Left Books, 1977.

———. "The Author as Producer." In *Walter Benjamin: Selected Writings Vol 2, Part 2, 1931–1934*, edited by Michael W. Jennings, Howard Eiland, and Gary Smith, translated by Rodney Livingstone et al. Cambridge, MA: Harvard University Press, 2005, 768–782.

———. "A Short History of Photography." (1931), translated by Stanley Mitchell. *Screen* 13, no. 1 (1972): 5–26; originally published in *Die Literarische Welt*, September 18, September 25, and October 2, 1931.

Berger, John. *Photocopies: Encounters*. London: Bloomsbury, 1996.

———. *Understanding a Photograph*, edited by Geoff Dyer. New York: Aperture, 2013.

Blanchot, Maurice. *The Writing of the Disaster*, translated by Ann Smock. Lincoln: University of Nebraska Press, 1986.

Boyle, Ronald. "Language Contact in the United Arab Emirates." *World Englishes* 31, no. 3 (2012): 312–330.

Brizuela, Natalia. "Eleven Theses for Breaking Away." *Film Quarterly* 72, no. 3 (2019): 30–32.

———. *Fotografia e império: paisagens para um Brasil moderno*. São Paulo: Companhia das Letras, Instituto Moreira Salles, 2012.

Brizuela, Natalia and Jodi Roberts. *Photography at Its Limits*. Berkeley: OneEditionBooks, 2019.

Brown, Elspeth H. and Thy Phu, eds., *Feeling Photography*. Durham: Duke University Press, 2014.

Browne, Simone. *Dark Matters: On the Surveillance of Blackness*. Durham: Duke University Press, 2015.

Bruce, Albert. "La Forêt Polyglotte." In *Le Grand Orchestre des Animaux*. Paris: Fondation Cartier, 2016, 91–99.

Burbridge, Benedict. *Photography After Capitalism*. London: Goldsmiths Press, 2020.

Byrd, Antawan I. "Amplifications: Sanlé Sory's Great Movements Between Photography and Music." In *Volta Photo: Starring Sanlé Sory and the People of Bobo-Dioulasso in the Small but Musically Mighty Country of Burkina Faso*. Göttingen: Steidl, 2018, 145–157.

Cadava, Eduardo. ed., *The Itinerant Languages of Photography*. Princeton & New Haven, CT: Princeton University Art Museum & Yale University Press, 2013.

Campt, Tina M. *A Black Gaze: Artists Changing How We See*. Cambridge, MA: MIT Press, 2021.

———. "Black Visual Frequency: A Glossary." FotoMuseum Winterthur, June 5–July 31, 2018, https://www.fotomuseum.ch/en/explore/still-searching/articles/154907_frequency.

———. *Listening to Images*. Durham: Duke University Press, 2018.

———. *Image Matters: Archive, Photography, and the African Diaspora in Europe*. Durham: Duke University Press, 2012.

Castro, Eduardo Viveiros de. "Exchanging Perspectives: The Transformation of Objects into Subjects in Amerindian Cosmologies." *Common*

Knowledge 10, no. 3 (2004): 463–484.

———. "Os pronomes cosmológicos e o perspectivismo ameríndio." *Mana* 2, no. 2 (1996): 115–144.

Chang, Briankle G. "An interview with Marie-José Mondzain: what is an image?" *Inter-Asia Cultural Studies* 20, no. 3 (2019): 483–486.

Cole, Teju. "When the Camera was a Weapon of Imperialism. (And When It Still Is.)" *New York Times Magazine*. February 6, 2019, https://www.nytimes.com/2019/02/06/magazine/when-the-camera-was-a-weapon-of-imperialism-and-when-it-still-is.html.

———. "There's Less to Portraits Than Meets the Eye, and More." *New York Times Magazine*. August 23, 2018, https://www.nytimes.com/2018/08/23/magazine/theres-less-to-portraits-than-meets-the-eye-and-more.html.

———. *Known and Strange Things: Essays*. New York: Random House, 2016.

———. "The Digital Afterlife of Lost Family Photos." *New York Times Magazine*. April 26, 2016, https://www.nytimes.com/2016/05/01/magazine/the-digital-afterlife-of-lost-family-photos.html.

Coleman, Kevin and Daniel James, eds., *Capitalism and the Camera: Essays on Photography and Extraction*. London and New York: Verso, 2021.

Crawford, Anwen. *No Document*. Sydney: Giramondo Publishing Company, 2021.

Dafoe, Taylor. "The University of Pennsylvania Will Restitute a Group of Human Skulls Once Used to Propagate White Supremacist Theories." *Artnet*, April 13, 2021, https://news.artnet.com/art-world/penn-museum-morton-collection-1958672.

Davis, Adrienne and the BSE Collective, eds., *Black Sexual Economies: Race and Sex in a Culture of Capital*. Urbana: University of Illinois Press, 2019.

DeCavara, Roy and Langston Hughes. *The Sweet Flypaper of Life*. New York: First Print Press/David Zwirner Books, 2018.

Derrida, Jacques. *Archive Fever: A Freudian Impression*, translated by Eric Prenowitz. Chicago: University of Chicago Press, 1996.

———. *Memoirs of the Blind: The Self-Portrait and Other Ruins*, translated by Pascale-Anne Brault and Michael Naas. Chicago: University of Chicago Press, 1993.

———. "No Apocalypse, Not Now (Full Speed Ahead, Seven Missiles, Seven Missives." *Diacritics* 14, no. 2 (Summer 1984): 29–30.

———. *The Other Heading: Reflections on Today's Europe*, translated by Pascale-Anne Brault and Michael B. Naas. Bloomington: Indiana University Press, 1992.

Didi-Huberman, Georges. *Bark*, translated by Samuel E. Martin. Cambridge, MA: MIT Press, 2017.

Ekotto, Frieda. "Cinéates femmes d'Afrique, créatrices d'images poétique aux pluriels." In *Loin des yeux près du corps: entre théorie et création*.Montréal: Éditions du remue-ménage, 2012. 111–116.

———. *Race and Sex across the French Atlantic: The Color of Black in Literary, Philosophical, and Theater Discourse*. Minneapolis: Lexington Press, 2011.

Ekotto, Frieda and Adeline Koh, eds., *Rethinking Third Cinema: The Role of Anti-colonial Media and Aesthetics in Postmodernity*. Berlin: Lit Verlag, 2009.

Espinoza, Dionne, María Eugenia Cotera, and Maylei Blackwell, eds., *Chicana Movidas: New Narratives of Activism and Feminism in the Movement Era*. Austin: University of Texas Press, 2018.

Fleetwood, Nicole R. *Marking Time: Art in the Age of Mass Incarceration*. Cambridge, MA: Harvard University Press, 2020.

———. ed., *Prison Nation*. Aperture Magazine. New York, 2018.

———. *On Racial Icons: Blackness and the Public Imagination*. New Jersey: Rutgers University Press, 2015.

———. "Posing in Prison: Family Photographs, Emotional Labor, and Carceral Intimacy." *Public Culture* 27, no. 3 (2015): 487–511.

———. *Troubling Vision: Performance, Visuality, and Blackness*. Chicago: University of Chicago Press, 2011.

Flusser, Vilém. *Towards a Philosophy of Photography*. London: Reaktion, 2000.

Förster, Larissa. "Plea for a More Systematic, Comparative, International, and Long-Term Approach to Restitution, Provenance Research, and the Historiography of Collections." *Museumskunde* 81, no. 1 (2016): 49–54.

Foucault, Michel. "Of Other Spaces." *Diacritics* 16, no. 1 (Spring, 1986): 22–27. [Orig. "Des Espace Autres." Lecture by M. Foucault in 1967, translated by Jay Miskowiec and published in *Architecture/Mouvement/Continuité*, October 1984.

———. "Panopticism." In *Discipline and Punish: The Birth of the Prison*. New York: Pantheon Books, 1977.

Fox-Amato, Matthew. *Exposing Slavery: Photography, Human Bondage, and the Birth of Modern Visual Politics in America*. Oxford: Oxford University Press, 2019.

Franke, Anselm, ed., "Animism." *e-flux journal*. Issue #36, 2012.

Garanger, Marc. *Femmes Algériennes 1960*. Paris: Contrejour, 1989.

Gilroy, Paul. *The Black Atlantic: Modernity and Double Consciousness*. Cambridge, MA: Harvard University Press, 1993.

Glissant, Édouard. *Poetics of Relation*, translated by Betsy Wing. Ann Arbor: University of Michigan Press, 1997.

Goldberg, Ariel. "A Century: Reading and Conversation with Ariel Goldberg." Seattle: Henry Art Gallery, University of Washington, 2019, https://soundcloud.com/henry-art-gallery/a-century-reading-and-conversation-with-ariel-goldberg.

———. *The Estrangement Principle*. New York: Nightboat Books, 2016.

———. *The Photographer*. New York: Roof, 2015.

Goldberg, Ariel and Yazan Khalili. "We Stopped Taking Photos." *e-flux Journal* #115, February 2021, https://www.e-flux.com/journal/115/374500/we-stopped-taking-photos/.

Gombrich, E. H. "Standards of Truth: The Arrested Image and the Moving Eye." *Critical Inquiry* 7, no. 2 (1980): 237–273.

Hadjithomas, Joana, and Khalil Joreige, "Latency." In *Homeworks*. Beirut: Ashkal Alwan, 2002.

———. "A State of Latency." In *Iconoclash: Beyond the Image Wars in Science, Religion and Art*. Cambridge, MA: MIT Press, 2002.

Hamacher, Werner. "Des Contrées des temps." *Zeit-Zeichen: Aufschübe und Interferenzen zwischen Endzeit und Echtzeit*, edited by Georg Christoph Tholen and Michael O. Scholl. Weinheim: VCH, Acta Humaniora, 1990, 30–31.

———. "The Gesture in the Name: On Benjamin and Kafka." In *Premises: Essays on Philosophy and Literature from Kant to Celan*, translated by Peter Fenves. Cambridge: Harvard University Press, 1996

Haney, Erin, ed., *Priya Ramrakha*. Berlin: Kehrer Verlag, 2018.

Hartman, Saidiya. "An Unnamed Girl, A Speculative History." *New Yorker*, February 9, 2019, https://www.newyorker.com/culture/culture-desk/an-unnamed-girl-a-speculative-history.

———. *Wayward Lives, Beautiful Experiments: Intimate Histories of Riotous Black Girls, Troublesome Women and Queer Radicals*. New York: W. W. Norton, 2019.

———. *Lose Your Mother: A Journey Along the Atlantic Slave Route*. New York: Farrar, Straus and Giroux, 2007.

———. "Excisions of the Flesh." In *Lorna Simpson: For the Sake of the Viewer.* Chicago: Museum of Contemporary Art, 1992.

Haslett, Tobi. "The Other Susan Sontag." *New Yorker,* December 4, 2017, https://www.newyorker.com/magazine/2017/12/11/the-other-susan-sontag.

Hecken, Thomas. "Der deutsche Begriff "populäre Kultur"." *Archiv Für Begriffsgeschichte* 49 (2007): 195–204.

Hegel, Georg Friedrich Wilhelm. *Ästhetik,* 2 vols., edited by Friedrich Bassenge, Berlin/Weimar: Aufbau-Verlag: 1965.

Hlavajova, Maria, Simon Sheikh, and Jill Winder, eds., *On Horizons: A Critical Reader in Contemporary Art.* Utrecht and Rotterdam: BAK and Post Editions, 2011.

Hosoda, Naomi. "Kababayan Solidarity? Filipino Communities and Class Relations in United Arab Emirates Cities." *Journal of Arabian Studies* 3, no. 1 (June 2013): 18–35.

Iduma, Emmanuel and Akinbode Akinbiyi. "Down the Footpath." *Chimurenga Chronic,* November 6, 2017, https://chimurengachronic.co.za/down-the-footpath/.

Irani, Tara Fatehi. *Mishandled Archive.* London: Live Art Development Agency, 2020.

Jagori. *Living Feminisms. Jagori: A Journey of 20 Years.* New Delhi: Jagori, 2004.

Keenan, Thomas, and Eyal Weizman. *Mengele's Skull: The Advent of a Forensic Aesthetics.* Berlin: Sternberg and Portikus, 2012.

Khouri, Kristine, and Rasha Salti, eds., *Past Disquiet: Artists, International Solidarity and Museums in Exile.* Warsaw: Museum of Modern Art in Warsaw, 2018.

Kimmerer, Robin Wall. *Braiding Sweetgrass: Indigenous Wisdom, Scientific Knowledge, and the Teachings of Plants.* New York: Penguin Books, 2020.

Kioko, Ndinda. "The Image of Life and Death." *The Trans-African,* September 30, 2016, https://thetransafrican.com/the-image-of-life-and-death/.

———. "The City as a Photograph." *The Trans-African,* February 19, 2016, https://thetransafrican.com/the-city-as-a-photograph/.

Koerner, Michelle. "Line of Escape: Gilles Deleuze's Encounter with George Jackson." *Genre* 1, 44:2 (2011): 157–180.

Kopytoff, Igor. "The Cultural Biography of Things." In *The Social Life of Things.* Cambridge: Cambridge University Press, 1986, 64–91.

Krauss, Rosalind. "Notes on the Index." In *The Originality of the Avant-Garde and Other Modernist Myths.* Cambridge: MIT Press, 1985.

Krenak, Ailton. *A vida não é útil.* São Paulo: Companhia das Letras, 2020.

Krenak, Ailton, and Jailson de Souza e Silva. Ailton Krenak – A Potência do Sujeito Coletivo: Parte I." *Periferias* 1, [n.d.] 2018, https://revistaperiferias.org/materia/a-potencia-do-sujeito-coletivo-parte-i/.

Kumar, Radha. *The History of Doing: An Illustrated Account of Movements for Women's Rights and Feminism in India, 1800–1990.* New Delhi: Kali for Women, 1993.

Leonard, Karen. "South Asian Workers in the Gulf: Jockeying for Places." In *Globalization under Construction,* edited by Richard Warren Perry and Bill Maurer. Minneapolis: University of Minneapolis Press, 2003, 129–170.

Levi-Strauss, David. *Between the Eyes: Essays of Photography and Politics.* New York: Aperture, 2003.

Lewis, Robin Coste. *Voyage of the Sable Venus and Other Poems.* New York: Alfred A. Knopf, 2015.

López, Miguel A., and Agustín Pérez Rubio. *Teresa Burga. Estructuras de aire. Structures of Air.* Buenos Aires: MALBA, 2015.

———. *Giuseppe Campuzano. Saturday Night Thriller y otros escritos 1998–2013.* Lima: Estruendomudo, 2013.

Luban, David. "A Theory of Crimes Against Humanity." *Yale Journal of International Law* 29 (2004): 85–167.

Maclean, Ruth, and Alex Marshall. "In the West, the Looted Bronzes Are Museum Pieces. In Nigeria, 'They Are Our Ancestors.'" *New York Times,* June 23, 2021, https://www.nytimes.com/2021/06/23/world/africa/benin-bronzes-Nigeria-stolen.html

Mende, Doreen, "The Time Lag of Defa-Futurum: A Socialist Cine-Futurism from East Germany." In *The Oxford Handbook of Communist Visual Cultures,* edited by Aga Skrodzka, Xiaoning Lu, and Katarzyna Marciniak. Oxford: Oxford University Press, 2020.

———. "The Itinerant." PhD thesis. London: Goldsmiths, University of London, 2013.

Mende, Doreen, Estelle Blaschke, and Armin Linke, eds., *Double Bound Economies: On Reading an East German Photo Archive, 1967–1990.* Leipzig: Spector Books, 2013.

Mengiste, Maaza, and Zachary Rosen. "Confronting the Weapon of Photography." Interview, *Africa Is a Country,* May 22, 2020, https://africasacountry.com/2020/05/confronting-the-weapon-of-photography.

———. *The Shadow King.* New York: Norton, 2019.

Mitchell, W. J. T. *What Do Pictures Want?: The Lives and Loves of Images.* Chicago: University of Chicago Press, 2005.

Mofokeng, Santu. *The Black Photo Album: Look at Me: 1890–1950.* Göttingen/New York: Steidl/The Walter Collection, 2013.

Mondzain, Marie-José, *Confiscation; des mots, des images et du temps.* Paris: Éditions Les Liens Qui Libèrent, 2017.

———. *Le Commerce des regards.* Paris: L'ordre philosophique, 2003.

Ndikung, Bonaventure Soh Bejeng. *In a While or Two We Will Find the Tone. Essays and Proposals, Curatorial Concepts, and Critiques.* Berlin: Archive Books, 2020.

Ndikung, Bonaventure Soh Bejeng, Aziza Harmel, Kwasi Ohene-Ayeh, and Astrid Sokona Lepoultier, eds., *Streams of Consciousness: A Concatenation of Dividuals.* Berlin/Bamako: Archive Books/Editions Balani's, 2019.

Onley, James. Britain and the Gulf Shaikhdoms, 1820–1971: The Politics of Protection, CIRS Occasional Paper 4. Doha: Center for International and Regional Studies, Georgetown University School of Foreign Service in Qatar, 2009.

Parker, Lonnae O'Neal. "Monuments Men are having a moment, thanks in large part to Robert M. Edsel." *The Washington Post,* February 2, 2014, https://www.washingtonpost.com/entertainment/museums/monuments-men-are-having-a-moment-thanks-in-large-part-to-robert-m-edsel/2014/02/02/3f74eb26-89c1-11e3-a5bd-844629433ba3_story.html?tid=hpModule_1f58c93a-8a7a-11e2-98d9-3012c1cd8d1e.

Pascoe, Bruce. *Dark Emu: Aboriginal Australia and the Birth of Agriculture.* Broome, WA: Magabala Books, 2018.

Peirce, Charles Sanders. "Logic as Semiotic: The Theory of Signs." In *The Philosophy of Peirce: Selected Writings,* edited by Justus Buchler. New York: Harcourt, Brace & Company, 1950.

Phillips, Christopher, ed. *Photography in the Modern Era: European Documents and Critical Writings, 1913–1940.* New York: Metropolitan Museum of Art/Aperture, 1989.

Pinney, Christopher. *Camera Indica: The Social Life of Indian Photographs (Envisioning Asia Series)*. London: Reaktion Books, 2013.

Rancière, Jacques. "Hommage á Joana Hadjithomas & Khalil Joreige." In cat. Paris: Paris Cinéma, 2007.

Rankine, Claudia. *Citizen: An American Lyric*. Minneapolis: Graywolf Press, 2014.

Rastegar, Kamran. "Arab cinema through a narrow frame: a conversation with Tala Hadid." *Senses of Cinema* 82, March 2017, https://www.sensesofcinema.com/2017/movements-filmmaker-interviews/a-conversation-with-tala-hadid/.

Resnick, Brian. "Astronomers Are Very Frustrated with Elon Musk's Satellites: Who Will Save the Night Sky?" *Vox*, April 29, 2021, https://www.vox.com/science-and-health/22396388/space-x-elon-muskstarlink-too-bright-astronomy-stars-pollution.

Riskin-Kutz, Oliver L. "Massachusetts Court Dismisses Lawsuit Over Harvard's Possession of Slave Photos." *The Harvard Crimson*, March 4, 2021, https://www.thecrimson.com/article/2021/3/4/lanier-suit-dismissed/.

Rizvi, Uzma, Z. "Archaeological encounters: The role of the speculative in decolonial archaeology." *Journal of Contemporary Archaeology* 6, no. 1 (2019): 154–167.

———. "Critical Heritage and Participatory Discourse in the UAE." *Design and Culture* 10, no. 1 (2018): 55–70.

Roy, Arundhati. *The Algebra of Infinite Justice*. New Delhi and New York: Penguin Books, 2002.

Ruelfs, Esther and Sabine Schulze, eds., *ReVision: Photography at the Museum fur Kunst und Gewerbe Hamburg*. Göttingen: Steidl, 2017.

Samudzi, Zoé. "A Journey into the Heart of Whiteness." *Jewish Currents,* July 22, 2020, https://jewishcurrents.org/a-journey-into-the-heart-of-whiteness/.

Sanbar, Elias. *The Palestinians: Photographs of a Land and its People from 1839 to the Present Day*. Paris: Éditions Hazan, 2014.

———. *Les Palestiniens dans le siècle*. Paris: Découvertes Gallimard, 1994.

Santos, Boaventura De Sousa. "The Future Begins Today," [Lecture], Riga International Biennial of Contemporary Art, Riga, 2020.

Schivelbusch, Wolfgang. *Die Bibliothek von Löwen: Eine Episode aus der Zeit der Weltkriege*. Munich: Carl Hanser Verlag, 1988.

Sealy, Mark. *Decolonizing the Camera: Photography in Racial Time*. London: Autograph ABP, 2020.

Sekula, Allan. "The Body and the Archive." *October* 39 (1986): 3–64.

Shariatmadari, David. "'They're not property': the people who want their ancestors back from British museums." *Guardian*, April 23, 2019, https://www.theguardian.com/culture/2019/apr/23/theyre-not-property-the-people-who-want-their-ancestors-back-from-british-museums.

Silverman, Kaja. *The Miracle of Analogy or The History of Photography, Part 1*. Stanford: Stanford University Press, 2015.

Smith, Shawn Michelle. *At the Edge of Sight: Photography and the Unseen*. Durham: Duke University Press, 2020.

———. *Photographic Returns: Racial Justice and the Time of Photography*. Durham: Duke University Press, 2020.

Smith, Shawn Michelle, and Sharon Silwinski, eds., *Photography and the Optical Unconscious*. Durham: Duke University Press, 2017.

Sontag, Susan. *On Photography*. New York: Farrar, Straus and Giroux, 1977.

Spillers, Hortense J. "Shades of Intimacy: What the Eighteenth Century Teaches Us." Keynote Lecture. "The Flesh of the Matter: A Hortense Spillers Symposium," Cornell University, New York, 2016.

———. "Mama's Baby, Papa's Maybe: An American Grammar Book." *Diacritics* 17, no. 2 (1987): 65–81.

Spivak, Gayatri Chakravorty. "Can the Subaltern Speak?" In *Marxism and the Interpretation of Culture*, edited by Cary Nelson and Lawrence Grossberg. Urbana: University of Illinois Press, 1988, 279–313.

Sternweiler, Andreas. "Kunst und schwuler Alltag." In *Eldorado. Homosexuelle Frauen und Männer in Berlin 1850-1950, Geschichte, Alltag und Kultur*, exh. cat. Berlin: Berlin Museum, 1984.

Stiegler, Bernard. "L'image discréte." In *Èchographies: de la télévision*. Paris: Éditions Galilée, 1996.

Stolze Lima, Tnia. "O dois e seu múltiplo: reflexões sobre o perspectivismo em uma cosmologia tupi." *Mana* 2, no. 2 (1996): 21–47

Szendy, Peter. *Le Supermarché du visible*. Paris: Éditions de Minuit, 2017.

Toufic, Jalal. *Distracted*. Berkeley, CA: Tuumba Press, 2003.

———. *(Vampires): An Uneasy Essay on the Undead in Film*. Sausalito, CA: The Post-Apollo Press, 2003.

Trachtenberg, Alan. *Reading American Photographs: Images As History-Mathew Brady to Walker Evans*. New York: Farrar, Straus and Giroux, 1990.

Vergès, Françoise. *The Wombs of Women: Race, Capital, Feminism,* translated by Kamaia L. Glover. Durham: Duke University Press, 2020.

———. *A Decolonial Feminism*. London: Pluto Press, 2019.

Virilio, Paul. *The Information Bomb*, translated by Chris Turner. New York: Verso, 2000.

———. *War and Cinema: The Logistics of Perception*, translated by Patrick Camiller. New York: Verso, 1989.

Vora, Neha. *Impossible Citizens: Dubai's Indian Diaspora*. Durham: Duke University Press, 2013.

Weheliye, Alexander G. *Habeas Viscus: Racializing Assemblages, Biopolitics, and Black Feminist Theories of the Human*. Durham: Duke University Press, 2014.

Willis, Brian. "Black Bodies, White Science: Louis Agassiz's Slave Daguerreotypes." *American Art* 9, no. 2 (1995): 39–61.

Wolukau-Wanambwa, Stanley. *Dark Mirrors*. London: MACK Books, 2021.

———. "Lectures in Photography," Columbia College, Chicago, 2019 [video recording], https://vimeo.com/367880389.

———. *One Wall a Web*. Amsterdam: Roma Publications, 2018.

FILMS

Farocki, Harun, dir. *Images of the World and the Inscription of War*. 1988; 16 mm film transferred to video, black and white and color, sound. 75 min.

Hadjithomas, Joana, and Khalil Joreige, dirs. *I Want to See*. 2008; 35 mm, color, sound. 75 min.

———. *A Perfect Day*. 2005; Super 16, color, sound. 88 min.

Julien, Isaac and Mark Nash, dirs. *Frantz Fanon: Black Skin, White Mask*. 1996; 35 mm, color, sound. 70 min.

COLOPHON

This critical reader is published on the occasion of the 8th Triennial of Photography Hamburg, taking place May 20 to September 18, 2022, and curated by Koyo Kouoh (Artistic Director), Rasha Salti, Gabriella Beckhurst Feijoo, Oluremi C. Onabanjo, and Cale Garrido (Coordinating Curator). The Triennial of Photography Hamburg has taken place every three years since 1999 and is led by the Deichtorhallen Hamburg.

The texts in this volume are drawn from the Lucid Knowledge symposium, which took place from September 30 to October 2, 2021, and which gathered the perspectives of an international, interdisciplinary cohort of artists, critics, curators, filmmakers, poets, researchers, scholars, and theorists to reflect on the notion of currency today.

This volume is also available in a German-language edition, titled *Lucid Knowledge. Fotografie als Währung – zu Aktualität, Relevanz und Verbreitung von Bildern* and co-edited by Andreas Schlaegel.

www.phototriennale.de

Editors
Koyo Kouoh, Rasha Salti, Gabriella Beckhurst Feijoo, Oluremi C. Onabanjo

Managing Editor / Copy Editor
Nicholas Davies

Proofreader
Cecilia Tricker-Walsh

Transcriptions
Valerie Caesar

Translation
Jennifer Taylor
("Is Apollo Gay? Herbert List's Reinterpretation of Male Bodies")

Design Concept and Layout
Hatem Imam and Lynne Zakhour, Studio Safar

Production
Thomas Lemaître, Hatje Cantz

Reproductions
DruckConcept, Berlin

Printing and Binding
Livonia Print, Riga

Publisher
Hatje Cantz Verlag
Mommsenstraße 27
10629 Berlin
www.hatjecantz.com

A Ganske Publishing
Group Company

Printed in Latvia

ISBN: 978-3-7757-5310-4
(English)
ISBN: 978-3-7757-5309-9
(German)

Every effort has been made by the authors and editors to obtain permission to reproduce the images in this volume. Any omissions or errors are unintentional and details should be addressed to the publisher.

DEICHTORHALLEN HAMBURG

Management

General Director
Dirk Luckow

Commercial Director
Bert Antonius Kaufmann

TRIENNIAL OF PHOTOGRAPHY HAMBURG

Project Manager
Daniela Guhl

Project Assistant
Alicja Mazurkiewicz

Project Manager, Triennial Expanded
Sithara Pathirana

Press
PR-Netzwerk
Christine Gückel-Daxer and
Annette Schäfer

The international Lucid Knowledge symposium and this volume were funded by the German Federal Cultural Foundation, and by the Federal Government Commissioner for Culture and the Media.

Funded by the German Federal Cultural Foundation

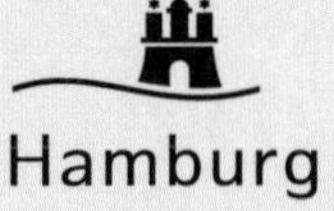

Funded by

Federal Government Commissioner for Culture and the Media

Main Supporter of the
8th Triennial of Photography Hamburg 2022

Hamburg | Ministry of Culture and Media

Partners of the 8th Triennial of Photography Hamburg 2022

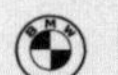
BMW Niederlassung Hamburg
www.bmw-hamburg.de

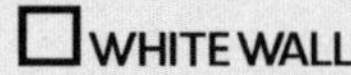

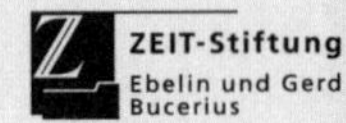
ZEIT-Stiftung
Ebelin und Gerd Bucerius